Developing a

Comprehensive

Faculty Evaluation System

Developing a Comprehensive Faculty Evaluation System

A Handbook for College Faculty and Administrators on Designing and Operating a Comprehensive Faculty Evaluation System

SECOND EDITION

Raoul A. Arreola
The University of Tennessee—Memphis

Anker Publishing Company, Inc.
Bolton, MA

DEVELOPING A COMPREHENSIVE FACULTY EVALUATION SYSTEM

A Handbook for College Faculty and Administrators on
Designing and Operating a Comprehensive Faculty Evaluation System

Second Edition

ISBN 1-882982-32-0

Composition by Lyn Rodger, Deerfoot Studios.
Cover design by Lyn Rodger, Deerfoot Studios.

Anker Publishing Company, Inc.
176 Ballville Road
P. O. Box 249
Bolton, MA 01740-0249

www.ankerpub.com

Dedicated to

Russell P. Kropp

Mentor, Colleague, Friend

About the Author

Raoul A. Arreola received his Ph.D. in educational psychology from Arizona State University in 1969, specializing in educational research and measurement. He has taught in the areas of statistics, educational psychology, personnel evaluation, and educational leadership, and has held a number of faculty and administrative positions involving planning, assessment, faculty evaluation, and faculty development. These positions include Director of the Office of Evaluation Services, Associate Director of the Learning Systems Institute, and Associate Professor of Educational Research and Measurement at Florida State University; Director of the Center for Instructional Services and Research and Professor of Educational Psychology at the University of Memphis; and Professor and Chair of the Department of Education, Assistant Dean for Assessment and Planning, and Director of Educational Technology at the University of Tennessee, Memphis. Dr. Arreola is currently Professor and Director of Institutional Research at the University of Tennessee, Memphis.

Dr. Arreola has worked and published in the field of faculty evaluation and development for 30 years and has served as a consultant nationally and internationally to over 200 colleges and universities in designing and operating faculty evaluation and development programs. He has also served as a consultant to the US Department of Labor and the Florida House of Representatives on designing and evaluating professional and occupational licensing examination procedures. He is president of his own consulting firm, the Center for Educational Development and Evaluation (CEDA), that annually conducts national workshops on faculty evaluation and assessing student learning. These workshops have been attended by thousands of faculty and administrators from more than 400 colleges and universities. Raoul Arreola is married to Dr. Mona J. Arreola, Administrative Director of the Hematology and Oncology Department of St. Jude Children's Research Hospital. They have four grown children and three grandchildren (so far).

Contents

<small>TABLES</small>

FIGURES

Acknowledgements

I want to acknowledge the special contributions made to this work by my good friend and colleague Dr. Lawrence M. Aleamoni, Professor and Chair of the Department of Special Education, School Psychology and Rehabilitation Sciences at the University of Arizona. I am indebted to Larry for allowing me to excerpt material from the Aleamoni Course/Instructor Evaluation Questionnaire (CIEQ), the CIEQ Optional Item Catalog, and several of his articles relating to peer evaluation and the development and use of student rating forms. I am especially grateful, however, for his continuous support and advice during the preparation of this second edition.

I also wish to acknowledge the contributions of Dr. Thomas F. Hawk of Frostburg State University and Dr. Margo Eden-Caman of Georgia Perimeter College in providing the new case study materials that describe their institutions' work in developing comprehensive faculty evaluation systems.

Finally, I wish to express my profound gratitude to Dr. Russell P. Kropp who, as director of the Division of Instructional Research and Service at Florida State University 30 years ago, told a fledgling "baby Ph.D." to "Get up to speed on faculty evaluation—it's the wave of the future." This book is dedicated to him.

Preface to the Second Edition

In the last decade of the 20th century, demands for accountability in higher education reached an all-time high. These demands were expressed not only in legislative mandates for evidence of the "value added" to society for its investment, but also as more rigorous standards for accreditation. High among the issues of interest resulting from such insistence on accountability was the performance of college and university faculty. The prestige and general high esteem in which faculty had traditionally been held, and which had tended to insulate them from normal societal standards of accountability, melted away in the bright light of the ubiquitous media and the Internet of the new information age. Market forces, responding to society's perception of the failure of traditional higher education, brought forth the rapid emergence and success of private online educational institutions, as well as corporate universities. Suddenly, rather than being the primary, if not sole, repository of information, knowledge, and educational opportunity, college faculty found themselves in competition not only with colleagues on remote campuses, but with commercial enterprises as well. The practice of tenure began to be questioned and calls for the evaluation, and possible dismissal, of tenured faculty began to be heard. All these factors led to a growing interest in the assessment and evaluation of faculty performance.

The result was an increasing demand throughout higher education for a systematic, practical procedure for building a faculty evaluation system based on sound administrative principles and research evidence. The first edition of this book, published in 1995, was in response to that demand. Its purpose—then and now—is to provide practical, proven models for developing and using a comprehensive faculty evaluation system. Based on 25 years of research and experience in building and operating large-scale faculty evaluation systems, as well as consulting experience with nearly 100 colleges and universities, the first edition presented a concise, step-by-step procedure for building and operating a comprehensive faculty evaluation system. Since the publication of the first edition

I have had the opportunity to serve as a consultant to thousands of administrators and faculty from hundreds of colleges, ranging from community colleges and technical schools to liberal arts colleges, to four-year colleges, to major research universities; from small private institutions to large public ones. This experience, along with new research, has contributed significantly to the preparation of this second edition.

THE EIGHT-STEP PROCESS FOR DESIGNING A SYSTEM

The heart of this new edition remains the same proven, reliable eight-step process. Following these eight steps will result in a customized faculty evaluation system that responds to the specific needs, concerns, and characteristics of faculty and administration of individual academic units. These eight steps are detailed in Chapters 1 through 8.

1) Determining the faculty role model

2) Determining faculty role model parameter values

3) Defining roles in the faculty role model

4) Determining role component weights

5) Determining appropriate sources of information

6) Determining information source weights

7) Determining how information should be gathered

8) Completing the system—selecting or designing forms, protocols, and rating scale

The explanation of each step in the process has been expanded and enhanced so as to provide more detailed guidance in building a faculty evaluation system. Much of the additional information provided is derived from the experiences of many institutions that followed the procedure as described in this book. Also, more definitions of the various roles to be evaluated are provided than in the first edition.

Chapters 9 through 16 focus on implementing and operating the faculty evaluation system. Chapters 9 and 10 present methods for generating an overall composite rating (OCR) and using it in promotion, tenure, merit pay, and post-tenure review decisions. Chapter 11 discusses peer review issues within the faculty evaluation system, and Chapters 12 through 15 present a wide range of information about and samples of student ratings forms, including legal issues, administration, interpretation of results, a catalog of items, and a checklist for identifying and selecting published forms with an abundant array of samples. Chapter 16 includes a detailed case study of Frostburg State University's design and operation of a faculty evaluation procedure and a complete description of Georgia Perimeter College's faculty evaluation system, with accompanying forms and measures. Both institutions designed their systems using the process presented in the first edition of Designing a Comprehensive Faculty Evaluation System.

CHANGES TO THE SECOND EDITION

In addition to expanding and updating the presentation of the eight steps, several other revisions characterize the second edition.

A new introductory section. The preliminary issues which need to be addressed prior to beginning the process of developing a comprehensive faculty evaluation system have all been gathered together in an introductory section. Many of these points were scattered throughout the book in the first edition. Here they have been brought together and expanded upon so as to provide a firm foundation of understanding and preparation for those undertaking the process of building or revising a faculty evaluation system.

New research. The research in the field has progressed to answer or clarify a number of issues related to student ratings. These findings are summarized and discussed in more detail than in the first edition.

More sample forms. The book provides more samples of commercially available student rating forms, along with their interpretive reports, than in the first edition. Detailed technical reviews of these forms, as well as information on whom to contact for further information, are provided.

A new section on legal issues. A new section on legal issues as they relate to the use of student ratings has been included in this edition. Although this book is not intended to serve as a guide on legal actions arising from the evaluation of faculty, several principles have emerged from case law which are of value in considering the design and operation of a faculty evaluation system.

A new section on post-tenure review. A new section on the issue of post-tenure review and how it relates to the evaluation of faculty performance has been included in this edition. Post-tenure review has emerged as a volatile issue, perhaps presaging the decline and eventual demise of tenure. The theoretical as well as practical issues surrounding the use of faculty evaluation data in post-tenure review systems are discussed.

Studies of two institutions. There is an entirely new chapter (16) which provides detailed case studies and the actual products of two different institutions that developed comprehensive faculty evaluation systems based on the process described in this book. One case study concerns the experience of Frostburg State University. The practical insights and solutions described are of value to any institution wishing to undertake such a project. Another section contains an excellent faculty evaluation system, including policies and forms, from Georgia Perimeter College, which built its system using the steps and principles described in the first edition.

Finally, since the first edition of this book came out in 1995, and as a result of working with thousands of administrators and faculty involved in developing large-scale faculty evaluation systems during that time, I have gained a heightened sense of awareness of the types of practical, political, psychological, sociological, and theoretical issues which confront those involved in this process. I have made every attempt to include the answers, recommendations, discussions, suggestions, and examples I have developed or encountered which address these issues. And I have included what I hope is a bit of wisdom in this edition—wisdom derived not only from the many successes experienced in applying the principles and practices described in this book, but from the difficulties and failures as well.

The task of either revising or building a faculty evaluation system from scratch is a difficult and time-consuming one. The steps described in this book, along with the many examples and forms, do not make the process quick and easy, but they do provide a guide which many institutions have followed to a successful result. If you are about to undertake the project of revising or building your institution's faculty evaluation system, I strongly recommend three things in addition to this book: patience, persistence, and good sense of humor.

Raoul A. Arreola

Introduction: Preliminary Issues in Planning for the Development of a Comprehensive Faculty Evaluation System

As we enter the new century the demand for account-ability in higher education is emerging as a major feature in the academic landscape. Increasingly, society is questioning the value it is receiving from its investment in institutions of higher learning. The use of part-time and nontenure-track faculty by colleges and universities is a growing phenomenon. In fact, the concept of tenure itself is being challenged and the practice of post-tenure review is beginning to be adopted by more and more institutions. Accrediting agencies are beginning to place greater emphasis on the evaluation components of their standards and criteria—especially on the evaluation of teaching effectiveness as evidenced by student learning outcomes and measures of faculty performance. We are also beginning to see movement toward performance-pay models in faculty reward systems where raises and rates of pay are being made contingent on evidence of satisfactory or exemplary performance (Healy, 1999; Leatherman, 1999).

The requirement of evidence of the quality of faculty performance has become a key expression of this demand for accountability. Accordingly, many governing boards and state legislatures are mandating the implementation of comprehensive faculty evaluation. Often these mandates leave little time for institutions to research, design, develop, and implement valid and reliable faculty evaluation programs. Thus, as institutions move to implement the increasingly important faculty evaluation systems, questions of fairness, validity, objectivity, and reliability of the evaluation systems inevitably arise. This book provides a practical, proven model for the development and use of a comprehensive faculty evaluation system that responds to these issues. However, before moving into the steps involved in building a comprehensive faculty evaluation system, several preliminary issues should be addressed in orienting ourselves to the scope of the task at hand.

FACULTY EVALUATION: FAST, FAIR, CHEAP (PICK ANY TWO)

The design and implementation of a successful faculty evaluation program is as much a political process as it is a technical or psychometric one. The development of a comprehensive faculty evaluation system is a challenging and time-consuming process. There is no shortcut that will lead to a valid, fair, and useful system. The process requires that the administration be committed to the project and be willing to provide the necessary support for the work that needs to be done. However, experience has shown that following the steps for developing a faculty evaluation system described in this book greatly facilitates the process. The faculty evaluation system, developed using the steps described herein, will have the greatest probability of acceptance and successful use by your faculty and administrators, because both constituencies will have had ample input to its design and construction.

SYSTEMATIC FACULTY INVOLVEMENT

The model for developing a faculty evaluation system described in this book assumes that there is no one best faculty evaluation system that could be successfully applied to any and all faculty groups. It is assumed that a necessary part of the process of developing a successful faculty evaluation system is the planned and systematic inclusion of the faculty. Experience has shown that the best approach to developing a faculty evaluation system is to appoint a committee, composed primarily of faculty, a few key administrators, and perhaps even a student or two, which is responsible for gathering the information and following the steps outlined in subsequent chapters. Thus, various steps in the process described in the following chapters will refer to the Faculty Evaluation Development Committee (FEDC) as the operational entity carrying out the process. If the process is carried out primarily or exclusively by administrative groups, the probability of a successful outcome is greatly reduced. This issue is examined more closely below in terms of the factors affecting faculty resistance. Thus, an essential component of the process described herein involves systematic faculty input. It is important that the faculty see their input being used as an integral part of the design and construction of the system.

FUNDAMENTAL DEFINITIONS AND ASSUMPTIONS

Before examining in detail the steps in developing a comprehensive faculty evaluation system, it is important to clarify several underlying definitions and assumptions on which the system will rest. Primary among these are the definitions of the terms "measurement" and "evaluation." Although these terms are common in higher education, it is essential to understand their true relationship in the faculty evaluation process.

Measurement

An essential element of any faculty evaluation system will be the measurement of some aspect of faculty performance. Therefore, it is good to begin by clarifying its definition.

Measurement is the process of systematically assigning numbers to the individual members of a set of objects or persons for the purpose of indicating differences among them in the degree to which they possess the characteristic being measured (Ebel, 1965, pp. 454-455).

Thus, by definition the result of any measurement is a number. It is important to deal with this issue early on. That is, since any faculty evaluation system will involve the measurement of some aspects of faculty performance, numbers will be unavoidable. There are those who have an aversion to the use of numbers in faculty evaluation. However, if our evaluation system is going to be based on measurements of some sort (i.e., student rating forms, peer observational checklists, etc.), we must accept the fact that numbers will be involved in the process and begin dealing with their appropriate use from the beginning.

Evaluation

The relationship between measurement and evaluation must also be clarified since confusion on this issue has been found to be a major source of difficulty in developing a faculty evaluation system.

Evaluation is the process of interpreting a measurement (or aggregate of measurements) by means of a specific value, or set of values, to determine the degree to which the measurement(s) represent a desirable condition.

Thus, the result of an evaluation is a judgment as to the degree to which the measurement or aggregate of measurements represents a desirable condition. Judgments may be expressed as either a word (i.e., "excellent," "good," "poor") or as a number where the number is used simply as a label equivalent to a word (e.g., excellent = 1, good = 2, poor = 3). This is not to be confused (as it often is) with the situation where an average rating is classified as representing "excellent," "good," or "poor" performance. For example, a faculty evaluation system may define an average rating between 1.0 and 1.5 as representing "excellent" performance, an average rating between 1.6 and 2.5 as "good" performance, and an average rating between 2.6 and 3.0 as "poor" performance.

It is useful at this point to take a closer look at the actual process of making an evaluation. Any evaluation rests upon a base of an implicitly assumed value or set of values. Basically, in conducting an evaluation, an observation is made of the performance of interest and then a judgment is made as to whether that performance conforms to the set of values held by those making the observations. If there is a good match between observed performance and values held, such performance is judged to be desirable and generally given a positive or "good" evaluation. If there is a discrepancy between what is observed and what is held to be of value, such performance is judged to be undesirable and is generally given a negative or "poor" evaluation.

For example, suppose one was asked to evaluate the following measurement:

Birth weight = 20 pounds

Would the evaluation be positive or "good" (indicative of a desirable condition)? Or would the evaluation be negative or "poor" (indicative of an undesirable condition)? The answer, of course, is "it depends." What the evaluation depends on is the value system or context within which the measurement is interpreted. If the measurement of 20 pounds is interpreted from the perspective of a *human female*, then the evaluation would likely be negative or "poor." Giving birth to a 20-pound infant is generally not a desirable situation for a human female.

However, if the measurement were interpreted from the perspective of a 250-pound female mountain goat, then the evaluation would likely be positive or "good." The important principle to note here is that the evaluation of the measurement (i.e., judgment as to whether the measurement represents a desirable or undesirable condition) depends on the context and the value system brought to the interpretation. Notice that the measurement "birth weight = 20 pounds" did not change, but the evaluation went from "poor" to "good" depending upon which value system was applied.

Clearly then, the evaluation process implies the existence and use of a contextual system or structure of values associated with the characteristic(s) being measured. Thus, before any evaluation system can be built, the values of those who intend to use it must be determined. In order to develop a faculty evaluation system that correctly reflects the values of the institution, we must not only determine those values and have them clearly in mind, but we must also express them in such a way that they may be applied consistently in our evaluation process. The model described in this book enables us to do just that.

Objectivity

Another major issue is that of the "objectivity" of the faculty evaluation system. Often, when embarking upon developing a faculty evaluation system, the goal of the institution's administration or Faculty Evaluation Development Committee (FEDC) is to devise an "objective" system. We must deal with this issue head-on and recognize that total objectivity in a faculty evaluation system is an illusion. The very definition of evaluation makes it clear that subjectivity is an integral component of the evaluative process. In fact, the term "objective evaluation" is an oxymoron. The measurements used in the faculty evaluation system (i.e., student rating forms, peer observational checklists, etc.) may and should achieve high levels of objectivity, but the evaluation process is, by definition, subjective.

The appeal of the ephemeral and oxymoronic objective faculty evaluation system is that it would produce the same evaluative outcome regardless of who evaluated the performance in question. Since objective evaluation is impossible, it is important to determine how to arrive at the goal of consistent evaluative outcomes of faculty performance using the necessarily subjective evaluative process.

Controlled Subjectivity

Objectivity in a faculty evaluation system can be found in the measurement of faculty performance. The tools used to measure faculty performance such as observation checklists and student and peer rating forms may produce objective data (measurements). However, as noted earlier, although measurements can and should be as objective as possible, the evaluation process is subjective by definition.

The value in objectivity is in the consistency of outcome it provides regardless of who is involved. If a truly objective faculty evaluation system were possible, any two individuals evaluating a faculty member would come to exactly the same judgment. However, since subjectivity in a faculty evaluation system is unavoidable, the goal should be to control its impact. The process for doing that may be called "controlled subjectivity."

For example, consider the earlier given objective measurement of birth weight = 20 pounds. If it were previously agreed that the measurement would be interpreted in terms of a mature female mountain goat, then everyone interpreting the measurement would most likely have judged it to be "good" or representative of a desirable condition. Subjectivity in an evaluation system is controlled when there is an a priori agreement as to what context and value system will be applied in the interpretation of the objective data. Thus, even though the evaluation process involves subjectivity, the consistency in judgment outcome that would derive from a hypothetical objective system is approximated. For our purposes, then, controlled subjectivity may be defined as

> the consistent application of a consensus-based set of values in the interpretation of measurement data.

A Comprehensive Faculty Evaluation System

The process of developing a faculty evaluation system involves attending to both the technical requirements of good measurement and the political process of gaining the confidence of the faculty. Thus, a well-designed comprehensive faculty evaluation program may be defined as one which involves the

> systematic observation (measurement) of relevant faculty performance to determine the degree to which that performance is consonant with the values and needs of the educational institution.

By design, any faculty evaluation system developed using the model described in this book interprets all measurement data by means of a consensus-based value system to produce consistent evaluative outcomes.

LINKING FACULTY EVALUATION AND FACULTY DEVELOPMENT

It should be noted that faculty evaluation and faculty development are really two sides of the same coin. Ideally, faculty evaluation programs and faculty development programs should work hand-in-hand. If some aspect of faculty performance is to be evaluated, then there should exist resources or opportunities that enable faculty to enhance or improve that performance. For maximal self-improvement effect, faculty evaluation systems must be linked to faculty development programs.

Faculty evaluation systems—no matter how well designed—which are implemented without reference to faculty development programs are inevitably viewed by faculty as being primarily punitive in intent. Such faculty evaluation systems tend to be interpreted as sending the message, "We're going to find out what you're doing wrong and get you for it!"

On the other hand, faculty development programs, which are implemented without clear reference to information generated by faculty evaluation systems, tend to be disappointing in their effect, no matter how well designed and funded. The reason for this is simple, if not always obvious. Without reference to a faculty evaluation system, faculty development programs tend to attract primarily those faculty who are already motivated to seek out resources and opportunities to improve their performance. In short, the "good" seek out ways to get better—which is what tends to make them good in the first place. However, those individuals who are not thus motivated and who, accordingly, are probably in greatest need of self-improvement opportunities, generally tend to be the last to seek them out. Only when the elements of a faculty evaluation program are carefully integrated into a faculty development program does the institution obtain the greatest benefit from both. Thus, if an instructor's skill in assessing student learning is going to be evaluated, somewhere there should be resources and training opportunities to become proficient in that skill. If a faculty member's ability to deliver a well-organized and exciting lecture is going to be evaluated, somewhere in the institution there should be resources available to learn and become proficient in that area. It should never be forgotten that most college and university faculty have had little or no formal training in the complex and highly technical skills involved in designing, delivering, and evaluating instruction. Most faculty tend to teach in the same way they were taught. Thus, if faculty performance is to be evaluated, especially performance in teaching, the institution should provide the resources to develop, support, and enhance that performance. The components of teaching performance are discussed in greater detail in Chapter 3.

A successful faculty evaluation system must provide 1) meaningful feedback information for faculty growth and development and 2) evaluative information on which to base personnel decisions. These two purposes can be well served by one system. The key to constructing a system that serves these differing purposes is in the policies determining the distribution of the information gathered. The general principle to be followed is that detailed information from questionnaires or other forms should be given exclusively to the faculty member for use in professional development and growth efforts. However, aggregate data that summarize and reflect the overall pattern of performance over time of an individual can and should be used for such personnel decisions as promotion, tenure, continuation, and merit raise determination. Later chapters in this book discuss in greater detail the design of the elements of the faculty evaluation system that relate to these two purposes as well as the relationship between them.

It is important to acknowledge that faculty evaluation data will be used both to provide faculty with diagnostic information to assist in their professional growth and to provide administrators with evidence for use in personnel decisions (promotion, tenure, pay raises, etc.). An institution may choose to emphasize one use over another, but it is a mistake to pretend that the faculty evaluation data will be used only for professional growth and development. Careful thought must be given to the appropriate design of the elements that may be used for personnel decisions even though the primary intent is to use the system for professional development. Interestingly, it is often the faculty themselves who begin using faculty evaluation data in support of their applications for promotion and tenure, even though the formal system may not require it. Accordingly, the steps of the process described herein consider both uses of faculty evaluation data.

OBSTACLES TO ESTABLISHING SUCCESSFUL PROGRAMS

A successful faculty evaluation program can be defined as one that provides information which faculty, administrators, and, where appropriate, students consider important and useful. Note that by this definition, no particular set of elements, forms, questionnaires, workshops, or procedures is being suggested.

Taking this same orientation to faculty development programs, a successful faculty development program is one perceived by the faculty as being a valuable resource or tool in assisting them to solve problems or achieve goals that both they and the administration consider to be important. From this perspective, the problem of establishing successful faculty evaluation and development programs does not lie so much in not knowing what procedures to follow in evaluating faculty or not knowing how to develop new skills or enhance old ones. The problem lies in getting faculty and administrators to change their behavior in important and fundamental ways.

The primary difficulty in establishing successful faculty evaluation and faculty development programs is not so much a technical one of developing the right questionnaires or procedures. Rather, the real problem lies in getting large numbers of intelligent, highly educated, and independent people to change their behavior. If we recognize this fact and deal with it openly from the beginning we have a much greater chance of establishing a successful program.

Faculty evaluation and development programs can fail for primarily two reasons: 1) the administration is not interested in whether it succeeds, and 2) the faculty are against it. The first reason will be referred to as administrator apathy and the second as faculty resistance. A close look at these two obstacles to establishing successful faculty evaluation and development programs can provide us with insights as to how to overcome them.

Administrator Apathy

Of the two threats to success, administrator apathy is the more deadly. If the administration is apathetic toward, or actively against, the whole program, it will not succeed. Anyone who has encountered a successful faculty evaluation and development program can point to one or two top administrators with a strong commitment to establishing and maintaining the program. Having a top administrator strongly committed to the program is a necessary but insufficient condition for success. The reasons for this will become obvious as we examine the issue.

One of the more common situations found in colleges and universities is where a second-level administrator, say a vice president or academic dean, is strongly committed to establishing a faculty evaluation and development program. The top-level administrator of the institution may be in favor of the program, apathetic toward it, or resistant to it. In the case of apathy, it is necessary to demonstrate to the top administrator the potential benefits of the program in terms of improved accountability evidence, as well as the improvement of faculty performance and student learning.

Resistance by the top-level administrator creates a different and more difficult problem to address. Such resistance tends to revolve around two issues: 1) fear of loss of control in the personnel decision-making process, and 2) concern about dealing with faculty resistance. The issue of dealing with faculty resistance is explored in some detail the next section. However, the fear of loss of control or threat to authority is serious, but several approaches have been found to be helpful.

Establishing the program on a purely experimental basis for a period of two years enables administrators to use the results of the program as they see fit. A consultant from another institution where a successful faculty evaluation and development program is already in place can present a more objective view to the administration as to how such a program can benefit the institution as a whole.

Another good strategy is to entice the resistant top administrator to attend one of the national conferences on faculty evaluation and development that are held annually. In this way he or she can interact with individuals from other institutions involved in the process and perhaps gain a better perspective on what is involved. In any case, it is helpful for administrators to see that their fears and concerns do not have to be realized. The key is to gain the support of at least a second-level administrator so that some resources can be allocated for an experimental trial of some part of the proposed program.

Administrator apathy diminishes the chances of implementing a successful faculty evaluation and development program, but outright resistance drops the chances of implementing a successful program practically to zero.

Faculty Resistance

Administrative commitment is a necessary but insufficient condition for establishing a successful faculty evaluation and development program. Faculty acceptance is also necessary. Faculty resistance to establishing faculty evaluation and development programs stems from numerous sources. Most of the resistance, however, reflects two or three major concerns.

In examining these concerns, let's begin, once again, by stating the obvious: No one enjoys being evaluated. Few people enjoy being told that they need to improve, or, worse, need to be developed—especially people who have spent six to eight years in college being evaluated and developed to the point where they have been awarded advanced degrees. Thus, the overall phenomenon of faculty resistance is composed of two reactions: resistance to being evaluated and apathy toward being developed. Faculty resistance to being evaluated appears to grow out of three basic concerns:

1. Resentment of the implied assumption that they may not be competent in their subject area

2. Suspicion that they will be evaluated by unqualified people

3. Anxiety that they will be held accountable for performance in an area in which they have little or no training or interest

This last anxiety is not unusual or unexpected, even though most faculty may attribute most of their concern to the second factor. Milton and Shoben (1968, p. xvii) point out the basis for this anxiety when they state that "college teaching is probably the only profession in the world for which no specific training is required. The profession of scholarship is rich in prerequisites for entry, but not that of instruction."

This statement holds the key to faculty resistance to establishing faculty evaluation and development programs. Faculty understandably resent being tacitly questioned on their competence in an area "rich in prerequisites" for which they have been well trained. They are, not surprisingly, apathetic toward the idea of receiving further training, although, ironically, professional seminars in one's content area are generally held in high esteem. Faculty also view with some concern and trepidation the prospect of being evaluated in an area in which they may have little or no training or interest—namely, the design, development, and delivery of instruction.

Several publications have addressed the issue of overcoming faculty resistance to evaluation programs (Grasha, 1977; O'Connell & Smartt, 1979; Seldin, 1980; Arreola, 1979). The underlying premise for developing a comprehensive faculty evaluation system described in this handbook is the careful and deliberate preclusion or reduction of faculty resistance. It is useful, therefore, to examine some of the common errors leading to faculty resistance that may not be immediately apparent.

COMMON ERRORS

Several errors are commonly made when establishing faculty evaluation and development programs. The first and most common error is committed when a faculty evaluation program is implemented without reference or clear relation to a faculty development program. As noted earlier, when this is done, the faculty tend to assume that its purpose is to gather evidence for disciplinary purposes.

However, by developing an integrated faculty evaluation and development program, it is easier for the faculty to see the relationship between the assessment of their strengths and weaknesses and programs to assist in their continued professional development. An integrated faculty evaluation and development program also serves to endorse the principle of continuous improvement within the institution.

Unfortunately, most often only a faculty evaluation program is implemented. Even then the form of its implementation almost guarantees faculty resistance. Generally, a faculty evaluation program begins by a committee constructing or adopting a questionnaire that is administered to students. These questionnaires usually contain questions that faculty perceive as boiling down to, "Was this instructor entertaining?" "Does this instructor know his or her stuff?" and "What grade would you give this instructor—A, B, C, D, or F?" The questionnaires are usually analyzed by computer and the results sent to the department head, college dean, or, in some instances, directly to the president. This action triggers all the concerns and anxieties that result in full-blown faculty resistance. Couple this, as occasionally happens, with a student publication that lists the best and worst teachers—perceived as job-threatening by the untenured—and hostile and negative reactions from the faculty are guaranteed.

On the other side of the coin, when faculty development programs are installed without reference to an evaluation system, apathy tends to run rampant among the faculty. This is not to say that the programs may not be innovative, creative, and effective for those who do participate. But what commonly occurs in the absence of a tie to an evaluation system is that only those faculty who are already committed to the concept of self-improvement will be the ones who seek out the program. Thus, the faculty who need the least improvement will tend to be the ones who use the program the most. Those faculty who don't have that commitment and who genuinely need assistance tend to avoid it. If a faculty development program is mandatory, based on the referral of the dean or department head, it is very easy for the program to take on the aura of being for losers only—a place where faculty are "sentenced" to several weeks of development when they are caught with a poor syllabus, bad student ratings, or declining enrollments.

How do we overcome these not inconsiderable obstacles? There is no easy answer to this question. However, the following suggestions, cautions, and strategies gleaned from the experiences of those establishing faculty evaluation and development programs may prove useful.

Guidelines for Overcoming Obstacles and Avoiding Errors

Seek Administrative Assistance. Identify and enlist the aid of a higher level administrator committed to establishing an integrated faculty evaluation and development program. The administrator must be prepared to overcome a year to 18 months of faculty resistance, some of which can become quite vocal.

Expect Faculty to Resist. Experience has shown that faculty resistance undergoes five predictable stages.

Stage 1: *Disdainful Denial.* During this stage, faculty generally take the attitude, "It'll never work" or, in the case of old-timers, "We tried something like that 10 years ago. It didn't work then, and it's not going to work this time either."

Stage 2: *Hostile Resistance.* During this stage, faculty begin to realize that the administration is going ahead with developing and implementing what they consider an overly complex and unwanted faculty evaluation system. Faculty senate meetings are hot and heavy. Special subcommittees are appointed. Complaints flow into the various levels of administration.

Stage 3: *Apparent Acquiescence.* Faculty seem to resign themselves to the fact that the new faculty evaluation system is going to be implemented despite their objections. Most faculty hope that if they ignore it the evaluation system will go away. A few voices of support are heard at this stage, however.

Stage 4: *Attempt to Scuttle.* At this stage, certain elements of the faculty and perhaps some department heads or deans greatly exaggerate the impact of the problems caused by the faculty evaluation system. Some isolated incidents of outright misuse may be perpetrated in an effort to get the system to collapse. Pressure on the sponsoring administrator to resign is intensified.

Stage 5: *Grudging Acceptance.* After 18 months to two years of operation, the faculty find that the system can actually be of some value. When all faculty are equally, but minimally, unhappy with the system, the faculty resistance barrier will have been successfully overcome. This is as good as it gets! There is no subsequent stage where faculty are happy with the system.

It should be apparent at this point why administrator commitment is so critical to the success of any faculty evaluation and development program. Only that commitment can get the institution through the first few stages of faculty resistance. If the administrator responsible for implementing the program is a second-level administrator and has to fight apathy or resistance from the top-level administrator, the probability of success is smaller and the probability of that administrator's departure from the institution is greater.

Be Prepared to Respond to Common Faculty Concerns. Some of those concerns and the responses that have been found helpful include:

"Students aren't competent to evaluate me!" It needs to be made clear that most well-designed faculty evaluation systems do not ask students to actually evaluate faculty in the sense that students make any final decisions. Opinions, perceptions, and reactions are solicited from students. This information is considered along with other information from other sources when the evaluation is carried out by the appropriate person or committee.

"Teaching is too complex an activity to be evaluated validly!" The best response to this concern is to point out that faculty are being evaluated in their teaching all the time by their colleagues and administrators. A formal system can make that evaluation fairer and more reliable and valid.

"You can't reduce something as complex as an evaluation of my performance to a number—some things just can't be measured!" In responding to this and similar concerns, it is best to point out that faculty are already being evaluated all the time. These evaluations, however determined, are translated into a number every time a list of applicants for promotion or tenure is placed in some priority order or a decision about merit raises is made. Comprehensive faculty evaluation systems attempt to improve on existing informal and perhaps unstructured procedures by developing a systematic and fair set of criteria using numerical values based on controlled subjectivity. It should also be noted that faculty consistently reduce the evaluation of complex student learning achievement to numbers (out to three decimal places), and, based on those numbers, colleges award credit and degrees. As a profession, we are not inexperienced in thé process of summarizing evaluations of complex human behaviors as numerical values.

Establish a Faculty Development and Evaluation Center or Office, Preferably not Located in the Office of the Vice President or Dean. One efficient and cost-effective way to do this is to combine the media center, test-scoring office, and any other instructional development and support office into one organizationally integrated unit. This unit should be directed by someone trained in evaluation and instructional development or educational psychology, and, most important, someone who has an affable, nonthreatening manner that inspires confidence. Remember that the objective is to facilitate the self-directed change in the behavior of faculty and administrators. The person in charge of the faculty development and evaluation facility should be able to grasp and deal with this concept in a positive manner.

Establish a Faculty Advisory Board. Although the faculty evaluation and development unit will ultimately report to a dean or vice president, it helps to have a faculty advisory board. The board can be elected by the faculty or faculty senate or appointed by an appropriate administrator. In any case, there should be some mechanism for faculty to have input into the policy development affecting the operation of the center and the program, even if that input is only advisory.

Consider Using a Consultant. An outside consultant can play an important role in the process of overcoming faculty and administrative resistance. The consultant serves as a valuable conduit between faculty and administration by communicating concerns, suspicions, and fears expressed by the faculty to the administration. The consultant can also assure administrators that other institutions have been able to implement successful programs. The function of serving as a conduit between faculty and administrators is often critical in the early stages of faculty resistance. The consultant can act as a lighting rod for all complaints, criticism, and confessions that might not ordinarily be expressed to a local colleague.

One of the most effective means of using a consultant for this purpose is to hold an open faulty meeting where, with the appropriate administrators present, the consultant presents an outline of the proposed faculty evaluation and development program and then responds to questions and comments. In this forum, the faculty can feel free to criticize the ideas presented by the consultant, or criticize the planned program, as if the consultant were solely responsible for the entire effort. What is really being communicated in this setting is a concern or an expression of opposition to the administration's proposals or practices without a direct confrontation with the administration. Breakthroughs in faculty resistance often occur in such forums. This approach also gives the administration the opportunity to present proposals that can receive perhaps a more honest appraisal by the faculty than they ordinarily might, with little risk being taken by either the faculty or the administration.

Integrate Faculty Evaluation and Faculty Development Programs. Make certain that for every element of the faculty evaluation program there is a corresponding and concomitant element in the faculty development program. For example, if an instructor's syllabus is going to be evaluated as part of the overall evaluation of teaching, make sure that workshops, seminars, or materials are available in the faculty development program to show an instructor how to construct a good syllabus. This approach ensures that faculty have institutionally supported recourse when the evaluation system detects a weakness in their performance.

Use a Variety of Sources in the Evaluation System. Make certain that the faculty evaluation system includes and uses input from such sources as peers, self, and administrators, as well as students. It is important to specify the impact each of these various sources of information has on the total evaluation. The following sections in this handbook describe in detail the process for doing this.

Make Every Effort to Ensure that the Faculty Evaluation Program Is Functionally Valid. The aspects of faculty performance being evaluated should be ones that both the faculty and the administration believe ought to be evaluated. In establishing the program's functional validity, it is important to remember that the process of evaluation requires that a set of data be weighed against a set of values. If the data show that the performance of an individual corresponds to the values being used or assumed by the evaluation system, that individual is evaluated favorably. If the faculty member's performance is at odds with the evaluation system's assumed values, an unfavorable evaluation results. The issue of the importance in determining values in the development of a faculty evaluation system is discussed in greater detail in Chapter 2.

To the extent that faculty are either unsure of, or disagree with, the assumed value structure of the faculty evaluation program, they will consider the program not to be valid and will thus resist it. Functional validity, or the extent to which the faculty believe in the fairness and utility of the faculty evaluation program is, in large measure, a function of the degree to which they are aware of, and agree with, the assumed values in the evaluation program. A number of specific and effective steps can be taken to establish the functional validity of a faculty evaluation program; these are described in detail in the following chapters.

Make Certain that Detailed Faculty Evaluation Information Is Provided Primarily and Exclusively to the Instructor. Policies may be established that call for mandatory periodic review of the evaluation information by an administrator. However, the issue of the initial control of the information must be resolved early so that the faculty evaluation and development unit does not come to be seen as a watchdog agency for the administration. If this occurs, the development or self-improvement function of the program is severely diminished. The faculty evaluation and development programs must be correctly seen as being confidential resources for faculty to use in improving and documenting the quality of their own performance.

Establish a Facilitative Reward Structure. Establish policies that treat documented faculty development efforts in a fashion similar to those of publication and research efforts. Successful faculty development and instructional improvement efforts should contribute meaningfully to promotion, tenure, and, where possible, merit pay decisions.

Tie Promotion, Tenure, and Merit Pay Decision-Making Procedures as Directly as Possible to the Faculty Evaluation and Development Program. This suggestion is critical if the program is to succeed. A primary objection often heard to the idea of linking promotion, tenure, and pay to the evaluation of performance is that tying performance to money or other nonintrinsic rewards cheapens the academic enterprise. It is argued that faculty should teach for the love of teaching and conduct research simply as an expression of their scholarly commitment to the discovery of truth.

There may be some faculty who teach for the sheer love of teaching and would do so even if they were not paid. There may be some faculty who have a passionate drive for discovering truth through research regardless of personal cost. There may be some faculty who are committed to a continual quest for self-improvement regardless of how they are viewed by others. However, the great majority of faculty are profoundly influenced in their professional performance by those aspects of job security, prestige, colleague respect, and monetary reward that their institution controls. If faculty perceive that decisions concerning their careers are still going to be carried out by an administrator who may or may not use faculty

evaluation and development data in a systematic, fair, and predictable manner, the program will ultimately fail. This is true no matter how benevolent the administration may be.

The faculty evaluation program will have a chance of success only when faculty see that 1) obtaining the rewards their profession and institution have to offer is a function of their performance and thus under their control, and 2) the faculty evaluation and development programs are valuable tools in helping them both identify and overcome the obstacles standing between them and these rewards.

PRACTICAL CONSIDERATIONS IN PLANNING THE DEVELOPMENT OF YOUR FACULTY EVALUATION SYSTEM

The literature in the field of faculty evaluation contains an abundance of research concerning the theoretical and psychometric underpinnings of a variety of forms, questionnaires, and procedures for use in a faculty evaluation system, especially student rating forms (see Chapters 12 and 13). However, less attention has been paid to the fundamental, practical, everyday issues and problems that face those responsible for actually operating a fully functioning faculty evaluation program.

Clarify the Purpose Your Faculty Evaluation System Is to Serve. From a practical standpoint, any faculty evaluation system must ultimately serve both a formative and a summative purpose. That is, the system must provide both the rich diagnostic information for improving or enhancing faculty performance, as well as for providing accurate, reliable, and relevant data on which to base personnel decisions. Faculty evaluation systems that start out ostensibly as formative (i.e., designed to provide feedback to facilitate professional growth and development) almost always end up serving a summative purpose as well. Sooner or later, a faculty member will submit evaluation data as part of the evidence in support of a promotion, tenure, or merit pay decision. Or, conversely, an administrator will ask for certain evaluative data to assist in making a difficult personnel decision concerning a faculty member.

In practice, a singular faculty evaluation system can be made to serve both formative and summative purposes. The key to developing and operating such a system is to carefully determine and prescribe the type of data to be gathered and what is to be done with it. The faculty evaluation system should be constructed in such a way that detailed frequently gathered data are provided in confidence only to the faculty member for diagnostic and feedback purposes. Specified formats for summarizing the detailed data should be developed. See the sample manual in Chapter 16 for several examples. These formats, which will be used for administrative purposes, should reflect only aggregated data that provide a clear picture of the faculty member's pattern of performance over time. In no case should any particular term's detailed evaluative information concerning a faculty member be used for administrative decision-making. The detailed data should provide the basis for self-improvement or faculty development efforts only. The principle to be followed in preparing summative data for administrative purposes is to make certain that the summative data convey a sense of a faculty member's overall performance across time as noted in Chapter 10 and not just a single term's performance, whether that performance was good or bad.

DATA STORAGE AND CONFIDENTIALITY

Virtually any faculty evaluation system will gather information from students, peers, and administrators, as well as various other sources, depending upon the specific design of the system. From a practical standpoint, a way must be developed for maintaining confidentiality while the data are stored. There are basically two approaches to this: the centralized department file and the individualized portfolio.

CENTRALIZED DEPARTMENTAL FILES

A number of institutions place the responsibility of gathering and storing faculty evaluation data on the department or division head. In this system, a centralized file location is specified, and the department head (or the department secretary) controls access to the files. This approach places the responsibility for security and confidentiality on a limited number of people, namely, the department head and the department secretary.

The advantage to this approach is that it is relatively unlikely that anyone will systematically violate the integrity of the information stored for a given individual faculty member. However, there are a number of disadvantages. First and foremost, it creates a great deal of work for the department head, especially if the department is relatively large. Second, if faculty perceive the central files as the primary evidence on which the administration will make decisions, there is a pronounced tendency for them to put voluminous amounts of material in their files, just

to be safe. Finally, faculty may feel that the confidentiality of the information has already been compromised because the department head, as an administrator, will have already seen it. However, if the department head is serving as the chief faculty development officer, as is sometimes the case, this approach can be very effective, especially in relatively small departments.

The Portfolio System

A system for accumulating and storing faculty evaluation information which has gathered some popularity is the so-called portfolio system. Under such a system, faculty members themselves are responsible for assembling and maintaining their own files in a specified style and format to create their faculty evaluation portfolio.

The faculty evaluation portfolio may take many forms. Institutions using the procedure described in this book to develop their faculty evaluation systems generally produce manuals containing clear, step-by-step instructions concerning gathering the faculty evaluation data into a portfolio type format. In some instances, the institution has special three-ring binders produced for the portfolio. Sometimes special file pockets are provided within which to store certain types of documentation, such as published articles, syllabi, and examples of tests. Various summary and data recording sheets are provided so that the faculty member may assemble, in a consistent standardized fashion, the aggregate statistical data which are to be used for personnel decisions. See Chapter 16 for a case study of one institution's work in developing a comprehensive faculty evaluation system using the steps described in this book. The case study includes a variation of the portfolio approach in assembling faculty evaluation data.

The advantage of the portfolio approach is that individual faculty members are responsible for assembling and maintaining their own evaluation data. No one person must assemble the data for all faculty, as is the case in the centralized filing system. However, this approach assumes a high level of trust between the faculty and the administration, because personnel decisions may rely heavily on the summary or aggregate data assembled in the portfolio. Peter Seldin (1991, 1993, 1997) has charted the growth of the portfolio approach to evaluating teaching and has developed a concise and highly effective procedure for assembling and using teaching portfolios to both improve faculty performance and provide data for personnel decisions.

USING THIS BOOK

If you have purchased this book expecting to find a fully developed faculty evaluation system with forms and policies all worked out and ready to be implemented in a couple of weeks, you will be disappointed. Although it would certainly be possible to prepare such a package, it would not work on your campus for the simple reason that each campus has unique needs and characteristics to which any faculty evaluation system must respond. No "canned" faculty evaluation system, no matter how technically correct or how well it works on some other campus, will automatically succeed on yours. What this book does provide is a systematic approach for developing a fair and consistent faculty evaluation system that responds to the unique values, needs, missions, traditions, and overall culture of your institution.

Many decision points in this book can lead to significantly different evaluation systems. However, any system developed by the process described herein will result in a faculty evaluation system that will have the maximum probability of being successfully implemented. The process has been used successfully by liberal arts colleges, community colleges, technical colleges, and universities to create customized faculty evaluation systems that worked best for them. No two institutions using this process may necessarily come up with the same system, although similarities will exist, of course, at least to the extent that the assumptions implicit in the process are accepted. Chapter 16 contains a case study and an example of a faculty evaluation system designed by one institution that used this model.

The following suggested schedule of key events is effective in using the model described herein for successfully developing a comprehensive faculty evaluation system. The events described generally take 18 to 24 months to complete. A more specific calendar for the steps in developing a comprehensive faculty evaluation system is found in Chapter 8.

Event 1: A Faculty Evaluation Development Committee (FEDC) is appointed to coordinate the development of the faculty evaluation system. The FEDC should include faculty members representing the various faculty constituencies, union representatives (if any), and one or two senior administrators. Student representatives may also be appointed to the committee, depending upon the culture and tradition of the institution.

Event 2: The FEDC becomes familiar with the steps in the process for developing a comprehensive faculty evaluation system described herein.

Event 3: A presentation is made to the administration concerning the approach to be taken. Administration becomes acquainted with the steps of the process.

Event 4: A presentation is made to the general faculty concerning the process to be followed in developing the faculty evaluation system. This event is critical. The faculty should be given the opportunity to become acquainted with the steps to be followed by the FEDC in developing the faculty evaluation system.

Event 5: The FEDC begins the process of gathering the information and data specified by the various steps in the process.

Event 6: A preliminary trial of the new faculty evaluation system is implemented.

Event 7: Any problems detected during the preliminary trial are corrected.

Event 8: The full system is implemented.

CHAPTER REFERENCES

Arreola, R. A. (1979, December). Strategy for developing a comprehensive faculty evaluation system. *Engineering Education*, 239-244.

Ebel, R. L. (1965). *Measuring educational achievement.* Upper Saddle River, NJ: Prentice Hall.

Grasha, A. F. (1977). *Assessing and developing faculty performance: Principles and models.* Cincinnati, OH: Communication and Education Associates.

Healy, P. (1999, March 26). Massachusetts governor seeks to free some colleges from tenure and most regulations. *The Chronicle of Higher Education*, p. A43.

Leatherman, C. (1999, April 9). Growth in positions off the tenure track is a trend that's here to stay, study finds. *The Chronicle of Higher Education*, p. A14.

Milton, O., & Shoben, E. J., Jr. (1968). *Learning and the professor.* Athens, OH: Ohio University Press.

O'Connell, W. R., & Smartt, S. H. (1979). *Improving faculty evaluation: A trial strategy, a report of the SREB faculty evaluation project.* Atlanta, GA: Southern Regional Education Board.

Seldin, P. (1980). *Successful faculty evaluation programs.* Cruger, NY: Coventry Press.

Seldin, P. (1991). *The teaching portfolio: A practical guide to improved performance and promotion/tenure decisions (1st edition).* Bolton, MA: Anker.

Seldin, P. (1993). *Successful use of teaching portfolios.* Bolton, MA: Anker.

Seldin, P. (1997). *The teaching portfolio: A practical guide to improved performance and promotion/tenure decisions (2nd edition).* Bolton, MA: Anker.

1

Step 1:
Determining the Faculty Role Model

The design and implementation of a successful faculty evaluation program is as much a political process as it is a technical or psychometric one. This is an important issue often overlooked by those involved in designing questionnaires, forms, or procedures for faculty evaluation systems. Much time and effort can be spent examining and discussing the reliability and validity of student ratings, peer evaluations, department chair evaluations, and the entire evaluation process. The literature abounds with research efforts to validate one form or another. However, even if the forms or procedures in a faculty evaluation system have been determined to be valid and reliable through appropriate research, if the faculty do not accept them for use they have no functional validity. If the faculty perceive the forms and procedures as measuring things they don't believe should be measured, or if they simply don't like the sound of some of the questions, then the forms and procedures will be of little positive use. Gaining faculty confidence in the design of the faculty evaluation system and all of its components is the key to establishing a successful faculty evaluation system.

Once the program's functional validity has been established (i.e., faculty "buy in" has been gained) and the system is operating, the issue of the psychometric validity of its various components can be tackled with accepted measurement and statistical techniques. If we take these steps in reverse order, as is often the case, we stand a very good chance of becoming bogged down by technical arguments that can defeat the complex political process of developing a faculty evaluation system in which the faculty have confidence.

In all that follows it is assumed that the FEDC (Faculty Evaluation Development Committee) has been appointed and is coordinating the process. We begin by involving the faculty, from the outset, in determining what should be evaluated in a faculty evaluation system. Depending upon the size of the institution, it has been found that working with faculty within their own first-line organizational structures (departments, divisions, etc.) greatly facilitates the process. However, some smaller institutions have successfully carried out this process in full faculty meetings.

In this first step faculty input is systematically gathered. That is, the faculty are asked to list the activities in which they individually engage as part of their professional responsibilities. Figure 1.1 shows an example of a worksheet that can be used by faculty in developing their list of activities. Note, also, that at the bottom of the worksheet the faculty are asked to group their activities into broad categories or roles, and to provide a preliminary name for the role. The list of activities should be developed without regard as to how they would be evaluated.

The broad categories in which the faculty activities fall define the operational faculty role model for the institution. Many institutions assume the traditional faculty role model of teaching, research, and service. However, faculty must engage in a wide variety of activities in response to their varied professional assignments. In addition to teaching, conducting research, and performing various service activities, faculty also advise students, publish articles and books, give presentations, serve on committees, administer programs, and perform many other essential duties (Table 1.1). Thus, a simple teaching, research, and service role model may be insufficient to adequately encompass the full range of legitimate faculty activities. Miller (1972) provides a more comprehensive treatment of activities that define possible roles in an academic institution. Other discussions concerning the description of faculty work can be found in Boyer (1990), Bowen and Schuster (1986), Rhodes (1990), and Rice (1991). By starting with the listing of activities in which faculty actually engage in pursuit of their professional assignments, the institution's true operational faculty role model may be determined.

The operational institutional faculty role model becomes the foundation on which the entire faculty evaluation system will be built. Constructing this foundation with the detailed input of the faculty begins the political process of gaining faculty acceptance and "buy in" to the design of the faculty evaluation process.

CHAPTER REFERENCES

Bowen, H. R., & Schuster, J. H. (1986). *American professors: A national resource imperiled.* New York, NY: Oxford University Press.

Boyer, E. L. (1990). *Scholarship reconsidered: Priorities of the professoriate.* Princeton, NJ: Carnegie Foundation for the Advancement of Teaching.

Miller, R. I. (1972). *Evaluating faculty performance.* San Francisco, CA: Jossey-Bass.

Rhodes, F. H. T. (1990). *The new American university.* Urbana, IL: David Dodds Henry Series, University of Illinois.

Rice, R. E. (1991). Toward a broader conception of scholarship: The American context. In I. T. G. Whitson & R. C. Geiger (Eds.), *Research and higher education: The United Kingdom and the United States.* Bristol, PA: Society for Research into Higher Education and Open University Press.

Table 1.1   Partial List of Possible Roles with Suggested Defining Faculty Activities

Teaching

Instruction
1. Teaching regular course offerings
2. Developing course materials
3. Developing replicable systems of instruction
4. Developing new courses/labs
5. Coordinating clinical teaching/independent study/tutorials

Advising
1. Advising students on programs of study
2. Sponsoring or advising student groups
3. Serving on master's or doctoral supervisory committees
4. Chairing master's or doctoral supervisory committees

Scholarly Research/Creative Endeavors

Publications
1. Books
2. Journal and magazine articles
3. Monographs, etc.
4. Presenting recitals and exhibitions
5. Staging, directing, or acting in musical, theatrical, and dance productions
6. Exhibiting paintings, sculptures, and other creative arts
7. Developing software/media
8. Reviews
9. Nonrefereed material
10. Citation counts
11. Invited/contributed presentations
12. Invited/contributed papers
13. Poster sessions

Ongoing Research
1. Basic scientific investigations, both theoretical and applied
2. Investigations of educationally relevant problems

Professional Recognition
1. Awards, honors, or invited presentations
2. Achieving advanced degrees, certification, etc.

Service

Faculty Service
1. Serving on departmental, college, or university committees
2. Serving on the faculty senate
3. Chairing any committee (student, faculty, etc.)
4. Serving as a sponsor for student activities/groups

Professional Service
1. Activity in professional organizations (holding office, serving on committees or boards)
2. Consulting to organizations or corporations
3. Consulting to universities/colleges, etc.

Public or Community Service
1. Participating in local, state, or national civic activities and organizations
2. Applying academic expertise in the local, state, or national community without pay or profit

Figure 1.1   Faculty Role Model Worksheet

Below list the various specific activities in which the faculty engage as part of their overall professional responsibilities at your institution.

1. _____
2. _____
3. _____
4. _____
5. _____
6. _____
7. _____
8. _____
9. _____
10. _____

(Use additional sheets if necessary to continue list of activities.)

Indicate the role categories into which the activities listed above may be grouped (e.g., teaching, scholarly research/creative endeavors, faculty service, public/community service, professional service).

Role 1: _____

Activities (numbers): _____

Role 2: _____

Activities (numbers): _____

Role 3: _____

Activities (numbers): _____

Role 4: _____

Activities (numbers): _____

Role 5: _____

Activities (numbers): _____

Arreola, R. A. (2000). *Developing a Comprehensive Faculty Evaluation System 2/e.* Bolton, MA: Anker Publishing Co., Inc.

2

Step 2:
Determining Faculty Role Model
Parameter Values

Once the decision has been made as to which faculty roles ought to be evaluated, the second step is to establish the relative importance of each role to the institution. That is, determine how much value or weight may be placed on each role in the faculty role model. Assume that teaching, research, and service are the three main roles of the faculty role model for a given institution. Which of these roles is valued the most? Which the least? What is the priority order of this set of roles for the institution? Generally, teaching is said to be the most valued role. However, in reality, when it comes time for promotion, tenure, and other personnel decisions, we may find that research is valued more than teaching—or at least more than was originally thought. Therefore, it is important to establish, in some more rigorous and specific fashion, the relative values of these different roles.

ESTABLISHING PARAMETER VALUES

Faculty role models can take one of two forms relative to their use in a faculty evaluation system: static or dynamic. Figure 2.1 is an example of a static faculty role model.

Figure 2.1   Sample Static Faculty Role Model

Teaching	40%
Research	40%
Service	20%

In a static faculty role model, faculty performance in each role carries the same specified proportion of weight or impact on the total evaluation for every faculty member. That is, in the example above, 40% of a faculty member's overall evaluation will be based on teaching performance, 40% on research performance, and 20% on service performance.

Traditionally, institutions have tended to use static models such as the one above. Static faculty role models have as their underlying premise that all faculty should be held accountable in the same degree for performance in all three faculty roles. This assumption would be valid if all faculty had precisely the same set of professional responsibilities, duties, and resources. Realistically, however, we know that some faculty will have professional responsibilities that concentrate almost exclusively on teaching, while others may have substantial assignments and commitments to various service activities. Still others may have substantial amounts of their time, energy, and resources tied up in research.

In addition, within any institution, a wide variety of opinions or positions concerning the relative value of the roles which faculty play will exist among the faculty. Some will hold teaching to be of primary importance, others will hold research to be of greatest importance, and others still will maintain that service is the most important faculty role.

Obviously, a static faculty role model cannot adequately represent the reality of the diversity of responsibilities and values of the faculty in a faculty evaluation system. The best approach is to define a dynamic faculty role model that establishes parameter values for each role. That is, determine the minimum and maximum weights that could be assigned to a role within the institution so as to adequately represent the variety of professional responsibilities and assignments.

Figure 2.2 shows an actual dynamic faculty role model developed by one institution using the process described here. Note that teaching values or weights range from a minimum of 50% to a maximum of 85%. This is to be interpreted to mean that teaching performance counts no less than 50% of the overall evaluation and no more than 85% in the final evaluation of a faculty member's overall performance. This does not mean that a faculty member may have a 50% to 85% teaching load. Rather, these numbers are an expression of how much impact or weight performance in the role of teaching can have on the faculty member's overall evaluation. The teacher may or may not have a full-time teaching load, but the value associated with teaching performance in this evaluation system would range from 50% to 85%.

This dynamic faculty role model clearly communicates that a faculty member's total evaluation will be based not only on teaching, but on some other factors as well. Thus, what is communicated to the faculty is that simply doing well in their teaching assignment is not enough. Obviously, between 15% and 50% of the evaluation will be based on something else. In our example (Figure 2.2), that something else includes scholarly research/creative endeavors (abbreviated to scholarly research), faculty service, and public/community service (abbreviated to community service). Here, scholarly research can count as little as 0% and as much as 35%. The 0% minimum weight communicates that activities that define scholarly research are not required. The 35% maximum weight communicates that such scholarly research activities cannot constitute the entire, or even the majority, of the activities on which a faculty member will be evaluated. The minimum and maximum weights for faculty service (10% to 25%) and community service (5% to 15%) communicate the

fact that these two activities or roles are expected of everyone to some degree. The smaller values also indicate that neither of these roles can constitute the primary or majority activity for a faculty member, at least insofar as the evaluation system is concerned.

Each department (or lowest organizational unit) should do the initial work of developing a dynamic faculty role model. Thus, it is possible that each department may develop a faculty role model that has somewhat different weights. Using the Weighted Faculty Role Model Worksheet (Figure 2.5), each department should list the roles identified in Step 1 and indicate its best estimate as to the minimum and maximum weights for each. The procedure for determining the final maximum and minimum weights is explained on the worksheet.

DETERMINING INSTITUTIONAL PARAMETER VALUES

In practice, determining the actual parameter values for the institutional faculty role model is a political process that involves consensus building between faculty and administration. The minimum and maximum weights should reflect both the values and priorities of the administration as well as the general sentiment of the faculty. This is best accomplished by taking the various departmental faculty role model values, as well as those developed by the administration, and combining them.

For example, assume that an institution had only two departments (designated as D1 and D2 in Figure 2.3). Each department would go through the process of determining the minimum and maximum weights for its faculty role model and the results would be displayed as follows:

In preparing the parameter values of a faculty role model care must be given to ensure that the combination of any maximum value and the remaining minimum values does not exceed 100%. Ideally, any combination of

Figure 2.2 Sample Dynamic Faculty Role Model

Minimum Weight (%)		Maximum Weight (%)
50	Teaching	85
0	Scholarly Research	35
10	Faculty Service	25
5	Community Service	15

Arreola, R. A. (2000). Developing *a Comprehensive Faculty Evaluation System 2/e.* Bolton, MA: Anker Publishing Co., Inc.

maximum and remaining minimum values should fall somewhere in the range of 85% to 100%. A range larger than that indicates consensus has not yet been achieved.

The preliminary institutional faculty role model would be composed of the lowest and highest values for each role as shown in bold in Figure 2.3. Figure 2.4 shows the resulting institutional faculty role model.

The institutional faculty role model resulting from the individual departmental faculty role models both represents the composite institutional value system and allows for diversity in values among departments. That is, although the institutional faculty role model may list the minimum value allowable for teaching is 50% and the maximum 85%, various departments could have different values as long as they fell within those limits. Department D2 as shown in Figure 2.3 would be one such department.

The following steps should be taken to gather and summarize these data:

1. Distribute questionnaires to faculty within each department and ask them to assign a maximum and minimum weight for each agreed upon faculty role. This questionnaire should include questions outlined in Step 3. Steps 2 and 3 should be carried out concurrently. (See Chapter 3 for a sample questionnaire.)

2. The department produces its faculty role model parameter values.

3. Assemble the separate departmental faculty role model parameter values into a single worksheet.

4. Determine the preliminary institutional faculty role model by using the absolute maximum and minimum values from the worksheet.

5. Ask the administration to determine an institutional faculty role model using their preferred parameter values.

6. Present the preliminary institutional faculty role model derived from the departmental input to the administration for review and approval.

7. Resolve any discrepancies between the administratively determined parameter values and those of the preliminary institutional faculty role model parameter values. Experience has shown that generally there is very little discrepancy between these two sets of values. If a large discrepancy does exist there may be a significant conflict between the values of the administration and those of the faculty. If such a conflict does exist it is not advisable to proceed with the project until the conflicts are resolved.

Figure 2.3 Departmental Faculty Role Models

| Weight | | | Weight | |
D1	D2		D1	D2
50%	55%	Teaching	**85%**	75%
0%	10%	Research	25%	**35%**
15%	5%	Faculty Service	25%	15%
5%	5%	Community Service	25%	15%

Figure 2.4 Institutional Faculty Role Model

Weight		Weight
50%	Teaching	85%
0%	Research	35%
5%	Faculty Service	25%
5%	Community Service	25%

Arreola, R. A. (2000). Developing *a Comprehensive Faculty Evaluation System 2/e*. Bolton, MA: Anker Publishing Co., Inc.

8. Once any discrepancies have been resolved the FEDC should publish a report to the faculty which delineates the adopted faculty role model for the institution. This report should include not only the minimum and maximum values but also the role definitions determined in Step 3.

Figure 2.5 Weighted Faculty Role Model Worksheet

WEIGHTED FACULTY ROLE MODEL FOR

_____

Name of Division/Department/College/Institution

Minimum %	Role	Maximum %
_____	_____	_____
_____	_____	_____
_____	_____	_____
_____	_____	_____
_____	_____	_____
_____	_____	_____
_____	_____	_____
_____	_____	_____

Setting Minimum and Maximum Weights

A. List the roles you have identified as being appropriate for your faculty evaluation system.

B. Indicate, by means of a minimum and maximum weight for each role, how much a faculty member's performance in that role should count in the overall faculty evaluation system.

C. Make sure the total of all your minimum weights does not exceed 100%. As a rule of thumb, the total of all your minimum weights should be some value between 40% and 70%.

D. Add the maximum weight of your first role to the minimum weights of the remaining roles. If the total is 100% or less, proceed to the next step. If the total exceeds 100%, you must reduce the value of one or more of the weights. Reduce either the maximum weight of the first role or one or more of the minimum weights in the remaining roles.

E. Repeat step D, above, using the maximum weight of each role in turn and the minimum weights of *all* the remaining roles.

Arreola, R. A. (2000). Developing *a Comprehensive Faculty Evaluation System 2/e.* Bolton, MA: Anker Publishing Co., Inc.

3

Step 3: Defining Roles in the Faculty Role Model

The definition of the specific roles within the faculty is the last step in the process of building the faculty role model upon which the evaluation system will be based. As noted earlier, it is assumed that a Faculty Evaluation Development Committee (FEDC) or similar committee coordinates the detail work associated with this project. Step 3 involves coming to a consensus as to how each of the roles identified is defined. For example, teaching as a role will readily be agreed upon. However, faculty from different disciplines or with different styles may mean different things when they use the word "teaching." Teaching a lecture course is different from teaching a lab course and different from teaching a vocational course in air conditioner servicing and repair. Teaching a graduate course is different from teaching an undergraduate course. Some faculty define meeting and counseling with students as part of teaching. Librarians consider the orientation seminars they give to students and new faculty as teaching. Thus, to say we are going to evaluate teaching doesn't necessarily mean the same thing to everyone—even though we may all agree that it is important to evaluate it.

The next several pages present the detailed development of a definition of the teaching role. Also provided are suggested definitions of the research, service, and other roles, although the detailed discussions concerning the conceptual underpinnings of these definitions are omitted. It is important to consider these definitions as simply examples rather than the correct definitions. Throughout the remainder of this book, the definition of teaching derived here will be used in all examples.

The key to the development of a successful faculty evaluation system is to engage faculty and administrators in discussions of the conceptual underpinnings of the definition of any role in the faculty role mode. It is important that both groups come to a consensus as to how each role should be defined for your system. Thus, you may not agree with the definition of teaching or any of the other roles developed below. The intent here is simply to show an example of the process involved and to provide a jumping-off point for your own campus discussions. In any case, a consistent definition for each role in your faculty role model must be developed as Step 3 of the process.

DEFINING THE TEACHING ROLE: PERSPECTIVES ON THE DEFINITION OF TEACHING

In the broadest sense, we can define teaching as involving an interaction between a teacher and a student such that learning occurs on the part of the student. Of course, the crux of the matter in defining teaching is to specify what kind of interaction occurs between teacher and student. Over the years, we seem to have evolved three different perspectives or philosophical positions on what does, or should, occur when a teacher interacts with a student to produce learning. These perspectives are founded on different assumptions that significantly affect how we approach the evaluation of teaching.

Teaching as Providing the Opportunity to Learn
Under this perspective teaching is conceptualized as an interaction between a teacher and a student conducted in such a way that the student is provided with the opportunity to learn.

Notice that this definition implies the assumption that a student has the responsibility for learning and that the primary responsibility of the teacher is to provide the student with the appropriate opportunity to learn.

If we accept this definition in which it is the teacher's responsibility to simply give the students the opportunity to learn (a very popular definition among college faculty), then the defining characteristic of a good teacher would simply be content expertise. Under this definition, the teacher's primary responsibility would be to maintain his or her content expertise, usually through research, and to share this expertise with students. The act of teaching would consist of sharing knowledge, insights, hypotheses, and professional experiences through lectures, seminars, presentations, and individual consultations. The primary role of the teacher would be that of scholar, knowledge generator, knowledge resource, role model, and, ideally, mentor.

Obviously, with this definition of teaching, student ratings or so-called student evaluations would be at best useless, and at worst insulting. Students, by definition, would not have the teacher's content expertise and would thus not be qualified to make any sort of evaluative statements or conclusions concerning the teacher's competence. The faculty criticism of student ratings which says, "If students were competent to evaluate me, they would be up here teaching the course!" would be entirely correct and justified under this assumed definition of teaching. If this definition is assumed, then peer evaluation or department head evaluation becomes the only really acceptable type of evaluation. It would be assumed that these individuals would be content experts and thus qualified to adequately assess the instructor's expertise.

Teaching as Enabling Learning

The second perspective conceptualizes teaching as an interaction between a teacher and a student conducted in such a way as to enable the student to learn.

This perspective of teaching still assumes that a student has the primary responsibility for learning. However, implied in this perspective is the assumption that a teacher has some responsibility for student learning, because now the teacher has the task of facilitating or enabling that learning.

If we choose this definition of teaching in which the teacher enables students to learn, then teaching becomes more complex. Under this definition, students still have the primary responsibility for learning, but the teacher has the responsibility for promoting or facilitating that learning. As with the first definition of

teaching, the teacher must still be the source of knowledge and must possess content expertise, but now must also be capable of creating an environment that is conducive to learning.

Implicit in this definition is the idea that the teacher must have the kind of social or human interactive skills which can engender interest in students and motivate them to learn. Teaching, under this definition, implies not only content expertise, but affective or personality traits not always under the direct conscious control of the teacher. People assuming this definition often say, "Good teachers are born and not made," or "Teaching is an art," or "You either have it or you don't." Such comments or beliefs reflect a heavy emphasis on the affective or personality component of this definition of teaching.

Peer or department head evaluations would still be considered to be most important. However, under this definition, student ratings could be viewed as having some use, because students can report how interested or motivated the teacher made them feel. Faculty subscribing to the first definition of teaching (i.e., providing the opportunity to learn) who encounter other faculty who subscribe to this second definition will often charge that student ratings are "just a popularity contest."

Teaching as Causing Learning

Finally, the third perspective conceptualizes teaching as an interaction between a teacher and a student conducted in such a way as to cause the student to learn.

This is the most severe definition of teaching insofar as teacher responsibility is concerned. This definition clearly implies that the teacher has the primary, if not the sole, responsibility for student learning.

If we assume a definition of teaching wherein the teacher has the primary responsibility for student learning, we are led to a somewhat different set of defining characteristics of a good teacher. This, of course, affects the ways in which we would set about evaluating teaching. Under this definition, the simplistic sine qua non of good teaching is student learning: A good teacher is one who produces the most learning in students.

In this case, if one wished to evaluate how good a teacher was, one would simply test the students. Those teachers whose students performed the highest on some prescribed test would be, ipso facto, the best teachers. The appeal of this definition, especially to the lay public and state legislators in particular, is so strong that we need to address it in more detail.

Because, in some measure, the entire faculty evaluation movement has grown out of the larger issue of accountability in education, it is apparent that, for the foreseeable future, teachers at all levels will be assumed to be responsible for student learning to one degree or another. This is not necessarily a bad thing.

DEFINING TEACHING: AN INTEGRATED DEFINITION

Virtually every educator's conception as to what constitutes good teaching involves one, or some combination, of these three conceptualizations of teaching. If we choose any one of these as the "right" one, we can easily demonstrate how these incomplete assumptions have led us astray in our efforts to develop a generally acceptable means for defining teaching for the purpose of evaluation. However, if we take our three partially right, partially wrong, definitions of teaching and try to integrate them into a coherent whole, we might get a more useful definition that will enable us to do a more effective job of evaluating teaching.

The total teaching act involves being able to interact with students in such a way as to 1) provide them an opportunity to learn, 2) create conditions that facilitate learning, and 3) use techniques and methods that, although not causing learning, at least create a high probability that learning will occur. Also, it is obvious that the teacher must have expertise in the content being taught. From this examination three broad interactive dimensions of teaching emerge:

1. Content expertise

2. Instructional delivery skills and characteristics

3. Instructional design skills

That is, teachers must know the subject matter being taught, must be able to present that subject matter in such a way that students are encouraged to learn, and must be able to design instructional experiences in such a way that there is some assurance that learning will occur when students engage the experience. Of course, teachers must also successfully deal with the myriad of bureaucratic tasks involved in managing a course. Drop/add slips must be turned in on time, as must final grades; field trips must be arranged; office hours must be posted and maintained; arrangements for guest lecturers must be made; laboratory supplies must be ordered; etc. Thus, a fourth dimension, course management skills, could reasonably be added to the overall definition of teaching. However, before specific definitions of each of these di-

mensions of teaching can be developed, we must carefully define what is meant by instruction and, even before that, what is meant by learning.

Defining Learning

Any text in educational psychology can provide us with a number of definitions of learning. However, because we want to develop definitions that will facilitate the ultimate objective of defining teaching in such a way as to make it more amenable to effective evaluation, we will define "learning" as a persistent, measurable, specified change in the behavior of the student resulting from an experience designed by the teacher. Such a definition, of course, has its limitations. A teacher who hits a student on the knee with a bat in such a way that the student walks, forevermore, with a limp, fits this definition of learning. So, for our purposes we will assume that the experience designed by the teacher is intended to promote the achievement of specified goals and objectives of a course or other approved instructional unit.

Defining Instruction

Next, instruction may be defined as presenting a set of experiences which induces student learning. With this definition, we take into account the responsibility of the teacher in causing learning to occur. Notice that by this definition, instruction has not occurred unless learning has occurred. With these two terms defined, we can go on to develop our definitions of the three broad dimensions of teaching.

Defining the Content Expertise Dimension

The content expertise dimension is defined as that body of skills, competencies, and knowledge in a specific subject area in which the faculty member has received advanced education, training, and/or experience.

From the point of view of evaluating this component, we can readily agree that, with the exception of advanced doctoral candidates or postdoctoral fellows, students are generally not competent to assess the degree to which a teacher is competent or knowledgeable in a field. In fact, rarely does a well-designed student rating form ask students to evaluate the content expertise of the teacher. However, students are competent to report the degree to which the faculty member appears to be knowledgeable in the subject matter being taught. Figure 3.1 relates the issues of real and apparent content expertise.

Ideally, we would like instructors to be both competent in the subject being taught and to appear competent to students. This type of teacher is Type A (Figure 3.1). Some research has suggested that, given two instructors who are equally competent in their content area, students tend to learn more from the one who appears most competent (Sullivan & Skanes, 1974; Leventhal, Perry, & Abrami, 1977; Ware & Williams, 1975; Williams & Ware, 1976). This stands to reason because, on the whole, students are likely to pay more attention to those whom they believe know what they are talking about than they would to someone whom they think does not.

Thus, from an evaluative point of view, faculty members who are competent in their content area but do not appear so to their students (Type B) could not be considered to be performing at the same level in their overall role as teachers. Type B teachers, however, are ideal candidates for faculty development programs. Already expert in their content field, all Type B teachers might need is some assistance in becoming more effective in their presentational or instructional delivery skills to move into the Type A category.

On the other hand, Type C teachers (i.e., faculty members who do not possess the desired level of content expertise) can, in certain instances, appear to be more competent than they really are. This phenomenon is generally referred to as the "Dr. Fox effect" (Perry, Abrami, & Leventhal, 1979; Meier & Feldhusen, 1979; Abrami, Leventhal, & Perry, 1982; Marsh & Ware, 1982). This type of faculty member may benefit from traditional faculty development efforts such as attending seminars or workshops in their content field, sabbaticals to study with another expert in the field, and so on.

Finally, logically, we have a category of instructors who are not competent in their content area and do not appear competent to their students. This type of instructor is labeled Type D. An effective faculty evaluation system can provide insights and mechanisms for ensuring that such individuals do not get hired in the first place. Candidates may be asked to conduct a class in their area as a guest lecturer and then be subject to the same student rating experience as a faculty member. Candidates may be asked to submit a syllabus for a course they would teach if hired and that syllabus could undergo the same scrutiny as that of regular faculty in their annual evaluations. Many institutions hire faculty on the basis of their research record and thus can reasonably be assured that they will not end up with Type D faculty. However, selecting candidates for the faculty solely on the basis of their content expertise may result in the appearance of many Type B instructors.

Insofar as the evaluation of content expertise is concerned, students should be able to provide information on the degree to which a faculty member appears competent in a given subject area. However, it should be kept in mind that this information may not necessarily reflect the true competence of an instructor as a content expert. Obviously, the true content expertise of an instructor, if it is to be evaluated at all, must be assessed in some other way, perhaps by peers. But to the degree that it is important to know how knowledgeable the instructor appears to the students, student rating forms, appropriately constructed, should be able to provide useful and reliable information.

Defining the Instructional Delivery Skills Dimension

The second dimension of teaching, instructional delivery skills, can be defined as those human interactive skills and characteristics which 1) make for clear communication of information, concepts, and attitudes, and 2) promote or

Figure 3.1   Categories of Teachers Based on Content Expertise Versus Instructional Delivery Skills

	Truly Competent	Not Competent
Appears Competent	**Type A**	**Type C** (Dr. Fox)
Does Not Appears Competent	**Type B**	**Type D**

Arreola, R. A. (2000). Developing *a Comprehensive Faculty Evaluation System 2/e*. Bolton, MA: Anker Publishing Co., Inc.

facilitate learning by creating an appropriate affective learning environment.

Such characteristics as clarity in exposition, demonstrated enthusiasm, the ability to motivate, the ability to capture and hold the interest and attention of students, and the ability to create an overall learning environment appropriate to the content being taught are included in this dimension. Interestingly, it is from this dimension that a great deal of the confusion and misconceptions concerning the validity and utility of student ratings originates.

We can readily agree that some teachers are better classroom performers than others. Someone with a clear and pleasant speaking style and an ability to set a class at ease when appropriate, who can motivate and capture the interest of students and who demonstrates an enthusiasm toward both the subject matter and student learning would be a highly prized teacher—if that person were also competent in the subject matter being taught and if the students taking the course actually learned the subject material. Certainly, such a person would be preferable to one who, though equally competent in the subject matter and whose students learned equally as much, was perceived by those students as uncaring or unenthusiastic and left the students feeling as if they had had an unpleasant experience in the course. It is interesting to note that if we define teaching as consisting of only instructional delivery skills, it becomes clear why we might see a lot of good teaching going on but very little learning occurring. Having good instructional delivery skills but poor content expertise is analogous to gunning the engine in your car but not putting it in gear. It sure sounds like you're racing along, but in reality you're not getting anywhere.

Student rating forms used in faculty evaluation systems almost always include items that ask students to provide information concerning the instructional delivery skills and characteristics of the instructor, although the forms may not label such items that way. From this fairly common practice has grown the often-heard charge that student ratings are "just a popularity contest." This charge generally comes from those faculty who tend to assume that the first dimension, content expertise, is the sole defining characteristic of teaching. However, taken in its proper perspective in an overall faculty evaluation program, the popularity of an instructor relative to the appropriate instructional delivery skills used in the classroom is important information to have if we are to obtain a comprehensive picture, and thus produce a fairer evaluation, of the instructor's total teaching performance.

There appears to be an underlying assumption in such charges that if an instructor is a good performer, he or she must not really be a good teacher (i.e., possess a high level of content expertise). Fortunately or unfortunately, depending on your perspective, such assumptions are not generally true. Teachers who are popular because they are good performers in the classroom are not necessarily poor in their content expertise, although we must watch out for the occasional Type C faculty member.

For the instructional delivery skills dimension, we can generally consider students competent to report their reactions to the performance characteristics of a faculty member relative to classroom presentations. Asking students to rate those human interactive skills and traits, which in and of themselves do not produce learning but rather create an environment or affective environment which promotes and facilitates it, is a valid endeavor. It should be noted that charges by faculty that student ratings can be raised by making classroom presentations more entertaining do have a basis in fact. To the extent that a faculty member becomes a better performer, those elements of student ratings which reflect instructional delivery skills will be affected, as they should be. The danger in this arises, however, when student rating forms are overloaded with items that measure only instructional delivery skills or when the tacit assumption is made by those reviewing the ratings that good instructional delivery skills are the predominate defining characteristic of good teaching. Of course, more sophisticated approaches besides student ratings can be taken in attempting to evaluate this dimension. Using television to videotape classroom presentations for later analysis by professionals, peers, and the instructor have been found to be highly effective. Classroom visitation by peers, on the other hand, has not necessarily proven itself to be the most efficient means of evaluating this dimension of teaching and is generally not recommended (Aleamoni, 1982; Centra, 1975, 1979, 1999; Cohen & McKeachie, 1980). Although many current researchers advise caution in using peer evaluation, especially for personnel decisions, a 1932 study by William R. Wilson, reprinted in 1999, eloquently expresses the underlying concern.

> It would unquestionably be a splendid thing if mature and experienced persons could be induced to visit classes and appraise and criticize them. The judgment of an outsider, however, is at best a second-hand impression of the effectiveness of a course. Presumably the mature visitor would appraise the course by better standards than students

possess. They would not, however, reveal the effect of the course upon the students who take it. If the students report that the course is interesting and the visitor reports that it is dull, the only conclusion that can be drawn is that the course is interesting to the students and dull to the mature visitor. If either set of appraisals is taken as a criterion, the other set is invalid. A distinguished scholar, dissatisfied with the ratings that he received from a large beginning class, complained that he was casting pearls before swine. The mature visitor doubtless would have agreed. But does the wise swineherd continue to lavish pearls upon his charges after he has found that the diet cannot be assimilated? (Wilson, 1999, p. 568).

Defining the Instructional Design Skills Dimension

The third dimension, instructional design skills, rounds out our definition of the overall act of teaching. This dimension is defined as those technical skills in 1) designing, sequencing, and presenting experiences which induce student learning, and 2) designing, developing, and implementing tools and procedures for assessing student learning outcomes.

The relationship between the definition of this dimension and the definitions of learning and instruction is direct and intentional. If instruction is defined as an activity that induces learning, and if learning is defined as a specified change in student behavior that must persist and be measurable, then the teacher must possess the skills to execute the necessary tasks involved. Such skills as designing tests; preparing learning objectives; developing syllabi, handouts, and other such supportive materials; properly using media and other forms of instructional technology; and organizing lectures and presentations for maximal instructional impact are included in this dimension.

Unfortunately, with the exception of those faculty whose area of content expertise encompasses educational psychology, instructional design, or teaching methodology, most college faculty have had little or no formal training in these areas. All too often faculty simply employ the teaching and testing strategies that were inflicted on them as students. It is ironic that most college faculty have never received even minimal formal exposure to two of the broad dimensions of teaching, namely instructional delivery skills and instructional design skills.

In evaluating instructional design skills, we find that several sources of information are available to us. Again,

although students would not generally be considered competent to evaluate the correctness of the instructional design of the course, they could report their observations, perceptions, and reactions to certain aspects of the design of the course. For example, if students report their opinion that the course examinations did not appear to be related to the course objectives, this reaction could serve as a flag for the instructor, department head, and/or peer review committee that there may be some problem with the instructional design of the course. Likewise, if the students report that the course appeared to be too difficult, this could serve as a flag that perhaps the material was inappropriate for the level of the course or that important connecting information between topics was missing or even that a curriculum problem existed such that students were not being adequately prepared prior to taking the course being evaluated. In any case, as a general principle, department heads and/or other instructional leaders and peers in the department would most likely be the best evaluators of this dimension. A more detailed and expert analysis could be conducted by these and other qualified people of the syllabus, tests, handouts, content, and general instructional design of the course, and they could make appropriate interpretations of the flags put up by the students' responses on the rating forms concerning this dimension.

Again, it is important to note that students, when they complete rating forms, are not evaluating the instructor in the sense that they are passing final judgment on the overall quality of the teaching in its entirety. Rather, student rating forms, if they are carefully designed and used, can solicit observations, opinions, reactions, and perceptions from students, which others, who are qualified, can examine and draw inferences from concerning the performance of the instructor.

Defining the Course Management Skills Dimension

As noted earlier, the activities surrounding the management of a course in and of themselves comprise an important dimension of teaching. For our purposes here, course management is defined as those bureaucratic skills in operating and managing a course including, but not limited to, timely grading of examinations, timely completion of drop/add and incomplete grade forms, maintaining published office hours, arranging for and coordinating guest lecturers, and generally making arrangements for facilities and resources required in the teaching of a course.

From this discussion, we can conclude that the total teaching act involves four broad, interactive dimensions:

1. Content expertise

2. Instructional delivery skills

3. Instructional design skills

4. Course management skills

By defining the total teaching act in terms of these four broad components or dimensions, it becomes clear that the evaluation of teaching cannot be accomplished by using simply one student rating form or another. Nor can it be done solely on the basis of the judgment of one individual administrator or peer committee based on a few classroom visits. No one person or group can have a sufficiently detailed and complete view of the entire process of teaching. A more accurate and valid perception of teaching performance would, of necessity, involve information from students on their opinions and reactions to the instructor's instructional delivery skills and characteristics; information from peers, and perhaps informed experts, on the instructor's instructional design skills; information from peers and department heads on the instructor's content expertise (if such information was required); and information from the department head, or perhaps even the department secretary, on the instructor's course management skills. Additionally, we would want information from students concerning the instructor's apparent content expertise as well as their reactions to several aspects of the course operation from which we could make inferences about the instructor's instructional design skills. Thus, the key to more effective evaluation of teaching is to carefully take all the parts of this mosaic and put them together in such a fashion that it accurately reflects the faculty member's overall teaching competence.

DEFINING OTHER ROLES

The following are brief definitions of other roles commonly found in faculty role models underpinning a comprehensive faculty evaluation system. They are offered here, with varying degrees of elaboration, primarily as a resource to provoke thought and discussion relative to developing your own definitions.

Scholarly and Creative Activities

Those activities in a faculty member's formally recognized area of expertise (i.e., content area in which the faculty member teaches) which do any of the following:

- contribute to the discovery of new knowledge

- the dissemination of knowledge in the professional community

- the development of personal professional skills and standing

Some possible scholarly and creative activities (representative, not exhaustive)

- research

- consulting

- grant writing

- funded research

- unfunded research

- review books

- review articles

- publish peer reviewed articles

- publish books

- publish monographs

- exhibits of professional/artistic products

- give presentations

- invited addresses

- professional/artistic performances

- keeping current in content field

- certification

- advanced degrees

- member or officer in professional organizations

Service

The general faculty role of service may have a number of different interpretations and definitions in a faculty evaluation system. The following classifications of service have been found to be useful in constructing comprehensive faculty evaluation systems.

Faculty Service (institutional or college service).

- serve on committees

- serve on institutionally determined projects

- mentor peers

- modify and develop curriculum

- maintain labs
- maintain budgets
- coordinate with outside agencies
- assist adjunct faculty
- role model for students
- administrative management
- teamwork
- chair committees
- attend meetings
- prepare class schedules
- program review
- evaluate new faculty
- handle complaints
- governance activities
- program review
- advise student organizations
- marketing and recruitment
- conduct faculty development workshop
- textbook selection
- participate in collective bargaining (unionized institution)

Community Service (personal and institutional). The role of community service as part of the overall issue of service in a faculty evaluation system needs to be viewed in two ways: personal and institutional.

Personal community service may be defined as the application of a faculty member's recognized area of expertise to the community without pay. In personal community service, the faculty member makes available his or her institutionally recognized area of expertise in the community. For example, a faculty member in the music department may direct the choir in his or her church (without pay) and thus be said to be performing a community service insofar as the faculty evaluation system is concerned. If, however, that same faculty member keeps the books (serves as an accountant) to the local boys club, this would not be considered community service for the purposes of faculty evaluation because the service would not

be in the area of the faculty member's recognized area of expertise. The reason for this is that good or poor performance on the part of the faculty member as an accountant would not necessarily reflect on the quality of the music program at the institution. On the other hand, good or poor performance in directing the church choir could. If the church choir performs poorly, an inference could be made as to the quality of the music program at the institution because the person conducting the choir is a music faculty member. No similar inference could be made to the quality of the accounting department if the music faculty member did a poor job of keeping the books for the local boys club. In order to be relevant to the faculty evaluation system, the definition of community service must be restricted to those activities that could reasonably reflect, positively or negatively, on the academic program in which the faculty member teaches.

There is often a temptation to include such activities as serving on the United Way board, or serving as a girl or boy scout leader, or participating in organizations that feed the homeless as being acceptable as evidence of community service. However, as soon as such an activity becomes an acceptable expression of community service in a faculty evaluation system, we cross over to the realm of good citizenship and thus come afoul of the issue of civil rights. Although we would certainly want all our faculty to be good citizens, it is unwise to include such activities as part of your faculty evaluation system. Doing so tends to open the doors to grievances and potential lawsuits. This may occur when a faculty member perceives themselves as being denied promotion or tenure simply because they chose to stay home on the weekends rather than coach a high school soccer team, volunteer to clean a city park, or raise money for the poor by baking goods for a church bake sale.

Institutional community service on the part of a faculty member may be defined as carrying out an institutional assignment as part of the institution's commitment to providing service to the community.

An example will illuminate this form of service and contrast it to personal community service. Suppose that a faculty member in nursing has for some time been voluntarily going to various shelters in the community to assist in the health care of the homeless individuals there. This faculty member is applying his or her recognized area of expertise in the community, without pay, and thus has been participating in individual community service.

However, suppose the institution decides to provide service to the community by reaching out with its various resources to assist segments of the citizens in the community. Part of this outreach program involves making available members of the nursing faculty to minister to the health care needs of various disadvantaged groups. Further suppose that the faculty member who has been voluntarily going to homeless shelters in the community is now given the assignment, under the institutional outreach program, to visit various shelters and provide assistance with the health care needs of the homeless individuals there. In this case, although the faculty member is providing exactly the same service to the same people as he or she was voluntarily doing before, this activity now becomes institutional community service. That is, the institution is serving the community by making available its resources to the community. The faculty member, on the other hand, is no longer engaged in individual community service, but, rather, is actually participating in faculty or college service. That is, the faculty member is carrying out an assignment that is part of the professional responsibilities that define his or her faculty position.

Service to the Profession. Service provided to one's profession may sometimes be found as part of the service role. Generally, the activities defining this type of service are identical to some of the activities in the scholarly and creative activities role. In fact, service to the profession is better placed as one of the menu items that define the scholarly and creative activities role and may include

- serving on committees or as an officer of a professional organization

- providing support services for the operation of a professional organization

- editing a journal or newsletter within the faculty member's recognized area of expertise

Consulting

Consulting is to be differentiated from moonlighting in which a faculty member may have another job (full- or part-time) in addition to his or her faculty position. For the purposes of developing a faculty evaluation system, consulting is best defined as the application of a faculty member's recognized area of expertise in the community for pay.

The important principle here is that the faculty member's performance be in his or her institutionally recognized area of expertise so that a reasonable inference may be drawn to the quality of the academic program in which he or she teaches. A faculty member whose skills and expertise in his or her content field are so valued that other institutions or organizations are willing to pay for his or

her consulting services is assumed to reflect well on their institution and thus enhance its prestige.

Advising (academic and counseling)

Advising is a generic term that may take on many meanings within a college or university. However, if advising is to be considered an activity which may be evaluated, the following definitions have been found to be useful:

- Academic advising may be defined as consulting with students on an individual basis for the purpose of providing guidance and advice concerning their academic endeavors.

- Counseling may be defined as consulting with students on an individual basis for the purpose of providing guidance and advice concerning their personal, emotional, and psychological concerns.

Collegiality

Collegiality is emerging as an issue of growing concern in the evaluation of faculty. Although no consistent body of literature yet exists on this issue, it is important to at least begin considering how we might define it. By including this brief consideration of collegiality, it should not be construed that the author is advocating its use as a role in a faculty role model. Rather, since the issue of collegiality in faculty evaluation systems comes up so often, it is appropriate to at least address the issue in a preliminary manner.

Discussion of the collegiality of an individual tends to focus on the negative. Such statements as "he doesn't fit in" or "she doesn't get along with anyone" may often be heard. However, in considering the issue of collegiality it is clear that simply not liking someone or saying they don't fit in is woefully insufficient in any sort of faculty evaluation system. Rather, the issue of the collegiality of an individual, at least insofar as a faculty evaluation system is concerned, must focus on the effect the individual has on the performance and productivity of colleagues. This is separate from the performance and productivity of the faculty member in question. The following definition encapsulates this concept:

The collegiality of an individual is a measure of the effect their interactions have on their colleagues' professional productivity.

Two examples may serve to clarify the principle underlying collegiality as a faculty evaluation issue.

First, suppose that there was a faculty member whom you did not like. Perhaps you objected to his or her lifestyle and sense of ethics or professionalism, or simply found him or her to be the kind of person you would prefer to not associate with socially. Further suppose that every time the two of you were on the same committee or were assigned to work on a project together, the intellectual interaction between you was stimulating and resulted in high-quality performance on your part. In this case, although you may not like the individual, your professional interactions served to enhance your own professional performance. In this case, the collegiality of the individual would be positive even though you did not like the person.

On the other hand, suppose there was another colleague whom you liked, or at least to whom you had no particular personal objection. Further suppose that every interaction with this individual, either personal or professional, inevitably ended up with his or her complaining about the lack of sufficient resources for teaching, or the poor quality of the support staff, or the inherent incompetence of the administration. After such interactions you invariably found yourself angry and frustrated with the situations the individual talked about and wondering if maybe you shouldn't try to find a job at a better institution. Suppose that after such interactions it was difficult to regain your enthusiasm to finish grading those exams, or write that report for the curriculum committee, or work on the manuscript for your book. In any case, suppose it took you several minutes or hours or perhaps days to regain your normal enthusiasm for your professional responsibilities. Such a person, regardless of his or her own individual professional productivity, would be said to have a negative collegiality effect.

Thus, if collegiality is to be considered as a role in a faculty evaluation system, care must be taken not to couch the discussion in terms of whether the person fits in to the existing group, or has a disagreeable personality, lifestyle, personal habits, or values. Rather, collegiality must be considered in terms of its effect on the professional productivity of colleagues. The legitimate valid and reliable measurement of such a role as collegiality would be extremely difficult and would most likely have to be based on principles articulated in the field of social psychology, sociology, and psychometrics.

Determining Role Definitions for Your Faculty Role Model

The purpose of Step 3, then, is to reach some agreement about defining the various roles that have been adopted as the formal faculty role model of the institution. To give your faculty evaluation system a measure of objectivity, or to at least control the effects of the unavoidable subjec-

tivity, it is important to define each of the roles in terms of observable or documentable achievements, products, or performances. This is obviously easier said than done. It is not reasonable to expect faculty to readily come up with concise definitions of the roles adopted in the faculty role model if they do not have the benefit of some prior thought on the matter. The discussion on the development of the definition of the teaching role demonstrates the kind of work the faculty evaluation development committee (FEDC) may wish to undertake in considering each role. Therefore, it is recommended that the FEDC, as one of its first efforts, develop preliminary definitions of the roles in the proposed faculty role model. In this way, when the questionnaire soliciting faculty values (Step 2) and their role definitions (Step 3) is distributed, it will contain some definitions to which the faculty can refer in expressing their own views.

Using the separate Role Definition Worksheet (Figure 3.2), develop some preliminary definitions of the roles you identified in Step 1. Give careful thought to your definitions and try to keep in mind the differing views that may be represented on your campus relative to each role. Remember that the ultimate objective is to arrive at a definition that will be generally acceptable to everyone who will be subject to the evaluation system. This may mean that you may have several subdefinitions. For example, you may have to define teaching differently for vocational education courses than you might for the traditional academic curriculum. You may have to define scholarly research/creative endeavors differently for faculty in the arts than you would for faculty in the sciences. There is no hard and fast rule, and no single definition will necessarily work for all institutions. The important issue here is the process of developing these definitions by consensus so that the evaluation system will be seen as functionally valid by the faculty. That is, it will be seen as measuring something that both the faculty and administration agree ought to be measured.

The following pages also include a sample questionnaire (Figure 3.3) that may be used to solicit role definitions and parameter values from the faculty. The questionnaire may be administered at the department, college, or institutional level. Ideally, such a questionnaire should be administered to departments separately and the data from the various departments in a college used to define the faculty role model for that college. Likewise, the faculty role models from the various colleges should be combined to form the institutional faculty role model. Accordingly, the sample questionnaire is constructed to be administered at the departmental level.

Figure 3.2   Role Definition Worksheet

Role	Definition
_____	_____
	_____
	_____
	_____
_____	_____
	_____
	_____
_____	_____
	_____
	_____
_____	_____
	_____
	_____
_____	_____
	_____
	_____
_____	_____
	_____
	_____
_____	_____
	_____
	_____

Arreola, R. A. (2000). Developing *a Comprehensive Faculty Evaluation System 2/e*. Bolton, MA: Anker Publishing Co., Inc.

Figure 3.3   Sample Questionnaire for Gathering Faculty Role Model Weights and Definitions

MEMORANDUM

TO: Faculty of the Department of _____

FROM: Faculty Evaluation Development Committee

RE: Faculty Evaluation System

The Faculty Evaluation Development Committee is charged with developing a faculty evaluation system which reflects the priorities and values of the faculty in each department. It is our view that, for a fair and valid faculty evaluation system to be developed, it must be based on information that permits us to address the following issues:

1. Which of the many roles faculty play do you think *ought* to be evaluated in your departmental evaluation system?

2. How should these roles be defined so that, when they *are* evaluated, the faculty are confident that the appropriate activities have been examined and/or observed in arriving at the evaluation?

3. For each role, what is the range of specific values or weights you believe to be appropriate for your department in reaching an overall evaluation of a faculty member?

As a first step, a preliminary set of roles and sample definitions has been developed by the committee. These roles and definitions are not final but are merely meant to serve as a reference as you consider your responses to the questions above. In Part 1, below, please list the roles which you think ought to be evaluated as part of our evaluation system. In Part 2, define the roles you identify in Part 1. The attachment to this memo includes a number of possible roles and some preliminary definitions to assist you in considering these issues. If you find any of the role categories and their definitions useful, please feel free to include them either as is or modify them in any way you see fit. If there are other roles you believe ought to be evaluated, please be sure to list them.

Also in Part 1, you are asked to indicate a minimum and maximum weight for each role. For example, considering the teaching role, should performance in teaching count at least 50% of the overall evaluation of a faculty member? Should it count at least 75%? In other words, what should be the minimum weight that teaching performance should count in the overall evaluation system? Likewise, what should be the maximum teaching should count? 85%? 95%? 100%? Should a faculty member's entire evaluation be allowed to be based only on teaching performance (e.g., 100% maximum)? Or should a faculty member be evaluated in some other activities besides teaching in arriving at an overall evaluation? The answers to all these questions reflect your values concerning the various roles to be evaluated. We need to have your values expressed so that the final evaluation system reflects the faculty as a whole.

Arreola, R. A. (2000). Developing *a Comprehensive Faculty Evaluation System 2/e*. Bolton, MA: Anker Publishing Co., Inc.

Figure 3.3 (continued)   Sample Questionnaire for Gathering Faculty Role Model Weights and Definitions

PART 1

Below, please write in the roles you think should be evaluated and the minimum and maximum weights each role should carry in the overall evaluation.

Minimum	Role	Maximum
_____	_____	_____
_____	_____	_____
_____	_____	_____
_____	_____	_____
_____	_____	_____
_____	_____	_____
_____	_____	_____
_____	_____	_____
_____	_____	_____

PART 2

Please list and define each of the roles indicated in Part 1. Your definition should be in terms of activities, products, or performances which can be readily observed for evaluative purposes.

_____

_____

_____

_____

_____

_____

_____

_____

_____

_____

_____

_____

_____

Thank you for your assistance with this important project.

Arreola, R. A. (2000). Developing *a Comprehensive Faculty Evaluation System 2/e*. Bolton, MA: Anker Publishing Co., Inc.

CHAPTER REFERENCES

Abrami, P. C., Leventhal, L., & Perry, R. P. (1982). Educational seduction. *Review of Educational Research, 52,* 446-64.

Aleamoni, L. M. (1982). Components of the instructional setting. *Instructional Evaluation, 7,* 11-16.

Centra, J. A. (1975). Colleagues as raters of classroom instruction. *Journal of Higher Education, 46,* 327-337.

Centra, J. A. (1979). *Determining faculty effectiveness.* San Francisco, CA: Jossey-Bass.

Centra, J. A. (1999). *Reflective faculty evaluation: Enhancing teaching and determining faculty effectiveness.* San Francisco, CA: Jossey-Bass.

Cohen, P. A., & McKeachie, W. J. (1980). The role of colleagues in the evaluation of college teaching. *Improving College and University Teaching, 28,* 147-154.

Leventhal, L., Perry, R. P., & Abrami, P. C. (1977). Effects of lecturer quality and student perception of lecturer's experience on teacher ratings and student achievement. *Journal of Educational Psychology, 69,* 360-374.

Marsh, H. W., & Ware, J. E. (1982). Effects of expressiveness, content coverage, and incentive on multidimensional student rating scales: New interpretations of the Dr. Fox effect. *Journal of Educational Psychology, 74*(1), 126-134.

Meier, R. S., & Feldhusen, J. F. (1979). Another look at Dr. Fox: Effect of stated purpose for evaluation, lecturer expressiveness, and density of lecture content on student ratings. *Journal of Educational Psychology, 71,* 339-345.

Perry, R. P., Abrami, P. C., & Leventhal, L. (1979). Educational seduction: The effect of instructor expressiveness and lecture content on students' ratings and achievement. *Journal of Educational Psychology, 71,* 107-116.

Sullivan, A. M., & Skanes, G. R. (1974). Validity of student evaluations of teaching and the characteristics of successful instructors. *Journal of Educational Psychology, 66,* 584-590.

Ware, J. E., & Williams, R. G. (1975). The Dr. Fox effect: A study of lecturer effectiveness and ratings of instruction. *Journal of Medical Education, 50,* 149-156.

Williams, R. G., & Ware, J. E. (1976). Validity of student ratings of instruction under different incentive conditions: A further study of the Dr. Fox effect. *Journal of Educational Psychology, 68,* 48-56.

Wilson, W. R. (1999, September/October). Student rating teachers. *Journal of Higher Education, 70*(5). Copyright 1932, 1999 by The Ohio State University.

4

Step 4: Determining Role Component Weights

At this point, you will have developed definitions for the various roles in your faculty role model. You will also have determined the relative impact or parameter values that the different roles can take in the overall evaluation of a faculty member. It now becomes important to consider how much weight or relative importance the various components of each role should have in the overall evaluation of that specific role. That is, we must express the proportion or weight that will be given to the performance of each component in the evaluation of the total role. In our example in Step 3, we defined teaching as involving four components: 1) instructional delivery skills, 2) instructional design skills, 3) content expertise, and 4) course management. The issue now is to determine how much relative importance each of these four defining components should have in the evaluation of the teaching role as a whole.

To aid in the process of determining the role component weights, we begin using one of several tools that will play an important part in the final design of our system. The first of these is the Source Impact Matrix, which provides the tool with which we can control the effect of the subjective data gathered as part of the overall evaluative process. Figure 4.1 shows an example of a

Figure 4.1   Component Weights of the Teaching Role

Source Impact Matrix for			TEACHING		

Arreola, R. A. (2000). Developing *a Comprehensive Faculty Evaluation System 2/e*. Bolton, MA: Anker Publishing Co., Inc.

partially completed Source Impact Matrix for the teaching role.

Note that the sources of information have not yet been determined and are left blank at this time. In this example, the instructional delivery skills component is weighted as 30%, the instructional design skills component as 40%, the content expertise component as 25%, and the course management component as 5%. These weights reflect the relative importance that the various defining components of the teaching role hold for the faculty in our hypothetical institution. Thus, whatever the rating or evaluation outcome is for the instructional delivery skills component for a given faculty member, that rating will count only 30% of the total evaluation of the teaching role. Likewise, the rating or evaluative outcome of the instructional design skills component will count 40%, and so on. The weights used in this example are entirely subjective. The weights you determine for your institution may vary considerably from these examples.

As you develop your various role definitions, it is possible that some roles may not have any separate defining components. In the event a role is defined in such a way that it stands as a complete singular statement, it is not necessary to develop separate role component weights. In some instances, however, you may develop "menu lists" of activities, any combination of which may define a role. The role of scholarly and creative activities is one such example (see the discussion of this role in Chapter 3). In this case a useful strategy is to assign percentage weights to each item on the list and give the faculty member the option of selecting any set of performance items as long as the total of the weights of the individual items equals 100%. Also, there may be some items on the list that are absolutely required and some that are optional. Again, an effective strategy is to assign component weights to each of the required items as well as the optional items. The faculty member would have the option of selecting any set of performance items, including the required items, as long as the total weight of all items equals 100%. For example:

Required

15% write and submit a grant proposal for federal funding

10% submit an article for publication in a peer reviewed journal

5% give a presentation at professional conference or meeting

Optional (Total of optional activities selected must equal 70%)

10% write and submit a grant proposal for state funding

5% write and submit a grant proposal for private foundation funding

50% obtain a federally funded research grant

10% conduct unfunded research

20% publish peer-reviewed article

2% review books

5% review articles

10% publish books

3% publish monographs

15% exhibits of professional/artistic products

10% give invited address to a professional organization or other institution

25% professional/artistic performances

2% keeping current in content field

5% acquire certification in your field

5% acquire an advanced degree

1% serve as a member of a professional organization

2% serve as a member or officer in professional organizations

5% serve as consultant

GATHERING THE ROLE COMPONENT WEIGHT INFORMATION

It is necessary at this point in our procedure to begin ascertaining the relative importance or weights your institution would hold for the different components for each role. On the following pages are master blank Source Impact Matrix (Figure 4.2) forms for making working copies. Begin one matrix for each role by first listing the role components down the left side and assigning role weights down the right side. Note that the total of all component weights for each role must equal 100%. When you have completed one matrix for each role for which you have developed defining components, place it aside. These matrices will be completed in Step 6. At this time, do not enter anything into the other cells in each matrix.

For those roles such as scholarly and creative activities, rather than complete a separate matrix simply develop the menu list of activities, assign relative weights, and identify required items.

Figure 4.2 Source Impact Matrix Worksheet Master

Source Impact Matrix for _____
(Role)

Role Components

Sources

Component Weight

(____ %)
(____ %)
(____ %)
(____ %)
(____ %)
(____ %)
(____ %)
(____ %)

= 100 %

Total Source Impact Weights

Arreola, R. A. (2000). *Developing a Comprehensive Faculty Evaluation System 2/e.* Bolton, MA: Anker Publishing Co., Inc.

5

Step 5: Determining Appropriate Sources of Information

In Steps 1 through 4, we focused on determining and defining the roles that should be evaluated, how much weight or value should be placed on the performance of each role in the overall evaluation, and how much weight the individual components of each role contribute in the evaluation of that role. The next step is to come to an agreement as to who should provide the information on which the evaluations will be based. Too frequently students are automatically selected as the sole or primary source of the information used in a faculty evaluation system. Students are certainly appropriate sources of information for certain kinds of activities, but they are by no means the best source of information for all the activities in which faculty engage and on which they may be evaluated. The most important principle in identifying and selecting sources of information is to make certain that the source identified has first-hand knowledge of the performance being evaluated. Too often peers or administrators are included in the evaluation of a faculty member's classroom performance when they have never, or rarely, seen that performance. However, peers and various administrators believe they have a good idea of the quality of such performance. The question is "where did these sources get their information?" The answer is almost always "from students." If you are ultimately going to depend upon students for information, go directly to the source—don't rely on second-hand information. Using second-hand information may give the random, or non-systematically obtained, input of a few students an inordinate effect on a faculty member's evaluation.

Here we will need to develop another tool, the Source Identification Matrix, for each of our roles. That is, we need to begin determining, by means of an analysis of the specific component activities that define each role, who are the most appropriate sources of information concerning each of those activities. Figure 5.1 shows an example of a completed Source Identification Matrix appropriate for the teaching role as defined earlier (see Figure 4.1).

As can be seen in Figure 5.1, teaching has previously been defined in terms of four components: 1) instructional design skills, 2) instructional delivery skills, 3) content expertise, and 4) course management. Depending on the definition developed for your institution for the teaching role, you may have three, four, five, or more defining components for teaching. These components are listed down the left side of the matrix. A number of possible sources of information are listed across the top of the matrix. In our example, we have listed only students, peers, and the department head. However, other sources such as self, alumni, parents, external consultants, and so on are also possible.

The Source Identification Matrix provides a tool for making important decisions concerning the design of the faculty evaluation system. In completing the matrix, "yes" or "no" decisions are made as to whether a particular source of information should be tapped for the role component in question. For example, in Figure 5.1, teaching is defined, in part, as consisting of instructional delivery skills. These skills include those human interaction and communication skills that the students experience every time they are in class. In examining the situation represented by the cell at the intersection of students as a source and instructional delivery as the teaching component, students would appear be a good source of information, so a "yes" is entered in that cell. However, note that a "no" has been entered in the cells representing the intersection of peers and department head as sources for instructional delivery skills. If, however, the decision were made to gather this information from these sources then classroom visitation issues must be discussed. In this case, unless the department is willing to undertake a peer visitation program or the department head is willing and able to regularly sit in on a faculty member's class, neither of those sources would really have first-hand information concerning instructional delivery skills and should probably thus not be included. However, in our example, teaching has been defined, in part, as also consisting of instructional design skills. These include those technical skills in designing the course, developing tests, selecting references, setting up laboratory experiences, and so on. For these kinds of skills, peers may be an excellent source of evaluative information; thus, a "yes" has been entered in the appropriate cell. Students, too, could provide certain kinds of information about these skills as they are exhibited in the course.

Proceeding in this way through each role's defining components, it is possible to make rational decisions and determinations as to what sources of information would be appropriate and acceptable to the faculty. Again, the important principle to follow in identifying sources is to always select the source which has the best opportunity to observe first-hand the performance to be evaluated.

The "yes" and "no" decisions represented in Figure 5.1 are merely examples and are not intended to represent the "right" decision in each case. The example merely serves to demonstrate the process of using the Source Identification Matrix tool in planning the design of a faculty evaluation system. The teaching components you develop and the sources you identify may be different from those shown in the example in Figure 5.1.

The process of developing the source identification matrices for each of the roles in the institution's faculty role model is best accomplished by the FEDC. Appropriate input from the faculty at large may be solicited and, in fact, the committee may wish to send out questionnaires asking faculty to indicate their preferred sources of information for each activity which defines a given role. However, this can become cumbersome and may delay the process considerably. Rather, the committee, through a series of discussions and meetings with faculty groups, can determine what source or sources would be most appropriate for each of the roles' defining activities.

On the following pages are blank Source Identification Matrix Worksheet Master forms (Figure 5.2) for making working copies. Using the definitions of the roles that you developed earlier, make a preliminary decision as to which sources of information would be appropriate and acceptable for each component of each role. Write the sources of information across the top of the matrix and enter the defining components along the left-hand side. As you consider each cell in the matrix, write either a "yes" or a "no" in that cell.

Figure 5.1   Source Identification Matrix for the Teaching Role

Source Identification Matrix for	TEACHING		
Role Components	Students	Peers	Dept. Head
Instructional Delivery Skills	Yes	No	No
Instructional Design Skills	Yes	Yes	No
Content Expertise	No	Yes	Yes
Course Management	No	No	Yes

Arreola, R. A. (2000). Developing *a Comprehensive Faculty Evaluation System 2/e*. Bolton, MA: Anker Publishing Co., Inc.

Figure 5.2 Source Identification Matrix Worksheet Master

Source Identification Matrix for _____
                                         (Role)

Sources

Role Components

Arreola, R. A. (2000). Developing a Comprehensive Faculty Evaluation System 2/e. Bolton, MA: Anker Publishing Co., Inc.

6

Step 6: Determining Information Source Weights

In any faculty evaluation system, judgments and evaluations will be based on information derived from a number of sources. This information will concern various elements or components of the roles being evaluated. The issue of the appropriateness of those sources was addressed in Step 5. Having determined where the information to be used in the evaluation system will come from, the issue of the credibility of those sources now needs to be addressed.

DETERMINING THE SOURCE WEIGHTS

As noted in the introduction of this book, the principle of controlled subjectivity requires that the values to be used in the interpretation of data must be specified and built into the evaluative process. At this point, we must consider the phenomenon of people assigning different value to information depending upon its source.

For example, suppose you are driving to work and see a new billboard that says, "Grand Opening! Mama Mia's. Serving the Best Tacos in Town!" Now, suppose later in the day you go to lunch with a friend who tells you, "We went to that new restaurant, Mama Mia's, last night. They serve the best tacos in town." In this situation you have received the same information (Mama Mia's serves the best tacos in town) from two sources: a billboard by the side of the road and a friend whom you trust. So here the simple question is, which source of that information do you trust more? In other words, which source of information will be more credible to you? Most likely you will believe your friend more than just words printed on a billboard. You might even be moved to go to the restaurant yourself because your friend liked it.

It must be recognized that simply obtaining information is not sufficient in our evaluation system. We must also consider where the information comes from because we may value that information differently depending upon the source. In many faculty evaluation systems, the most common sources of information are students, peers, and administrators at various levels. This is true whether data from these sources are systematically gathered or randomly acquired. Depending on the situation and the performance being evaluated, however, the credibility of the information coming from these sources varies. For example, students may be a credible source of information concerning classroom performance but not as credible for information concerning the faculty member's research activities. Likewise, peers may be a credible information source concerning the professional standing and publication record of an individual but not as credible for information concerning classroom teaching style. The credibility of any information source in a faculty evaluation system depends as much on the opportunity that source has to be a first-hand observer of the performance in question as it does on our willingness to accept and believe what that source has to say. Thus, our next step in developing a comprehensive faculty evaluation system is to arrive at some consensus as to the credibility of the various sources of information that have been previously identified. It is necessary to determine and define the impact the information from these sources will have on the overall evaluation of an individual. The tool used for this is another matrix, the Weighted Source by Role Component Matrix. Figure 6.1 shows an example of a completed Weighted Source by Role Matrix.

Note the values for each source for every defining role component in the example (Figure 6.1). In this example, after making the "yes" and "no" decisions in completing the Source Identification Matrix (Figure 5.1), the faculty have determined that whatever information students provide concerning instructional delivery skills will be all the information that will be considered in the evaluation of that component. This is because it was decided previously that neither peers nor the department head would be sources of information for this component. Thus, the total weight for student input on the instructional delivery skills component is 100%.

In completing your own Weighted Source by Role Component Matrix for each role (i.e., teaching, research, community service, etc.), make certain that the sum of the weights for any given role component equals 100%.

In Figure 6.1, because both students and peers have been determined to be appropriate sources of information for the instructional design skills component, the task is now to divide the 100% total weight across these two sources. This decision is a subjective one which is based, in large measure, on how these elements of teaching are defined and weighted (Steps 3 and 4) and how much credibility these two sources have with the faculty relative to the activities defining instructional design skills. If we can assume that instructional design skills speak more to the technicalities of course design (i.e., test construction, appropriateness of the readings, currency of content, etc.), then it might be considered appropriate to place the bulk of the weight (75%) on the input from faculty peers and 25% of the weight on input from students. In a similar fashion, appropriate weights must be determined for each cell in the matrix. However, as noted earlier, this is a subjective decision. The decision you make for your system may be quite different.

On the following page is a blank Weighted Source by Role Component Matrix Worksheet Master (Figure 6.2) for use in making working copies.

At this point, complete one form for each role by completing the following steps:

1. Write the name of the role at the top of the form.

2. Indicate the sources across at the top of the columns, leaving any extra columns blank.

3. List the defining components for the role down the left side.

4. Be sure to "zero out" those cells in the matrix for which you previously determined no information would be gathered. For example, previously we determined that no information would be gathered from students concerning the content expertise component of the teaching role. Therefore, enter a zero in the cell formed at the intersection of the student column and the content expertise row.

5. Once you have zeroed out the empty cells, indicate the weight or value for each source for every component. Note that the sum of all the source weights across a given component row must total 100%.

Figure 6.1   Source Weights for Teaching Role Components

Role Components	Sources			
	Students	Peers	Dept. Head	
Instructional Delivery Skills	100%	0%	0%	
Instructional Design Skills	25%	75%	0%	
Content Expertise	0%	80%	20%	
Course Management	0%	0%	100%	

Arreola, R. A. (2000). Developing *a Comprehensive Faculty Evaluation System 2/e.* Bolton, MA: Anker Publishing Co., Inc.

Figure 6.2   Weighted Source by Role Component Matrix Worksheet Master

Weighted Source by Role Component Matrix for _____
                                                            (Role)

Source Weights

Role Components					
					= 100%
					= 100%
					= 100%
					= 100%
					= 100%
					= 100%
					= 100%
					= 100%

Arreola, R. A. (2000). Developing *a Comprehensive Faculty Evaluation System 2/e.* Bolton, MA: Anker Publishing Co., Inc.

In actual practice, of course, these values would have to be determined by gathering overall faculty input and then combining this input to arrive at a consensus as to the specific values or weights for each defining component of each role. An example of the type of questionnaire that could be used in gathering this information is shown in Figure 6.4.

DETERMINING THE SOURCE IMPACT

To this point, we have reflected the credibility of various sources of information by completing the Weighted Source by Role Component Matrix. Further, in Step 4 we reflected the relative importance of each of the defining components for every role by determining the role component weights and recording them down the right side of a Source Impact Matrix for each role. The purpose of these exercises was to lead us to the point of determining (and thus permitting us to specify and control) the impact information from each source will have on the overall evaluation of a faculty member. We now return to the Source Impact Matrices and complete them to determine our source impact weights.

Figure 6.3 shows an example of a completed Source Impact Matrix for the teaching role. In this example, the information recorded on the Weighted Source by Role Component Matrix for teaching has been entered into the small boxes in the corresponding cells of the Source Impact Matrix for the teaching role. By multiplying the source weights for each cell by the row weight for that role component, it is possible to obtain a clear indication of the impact any one source of information will have on the overall evaluation of a role.

For example, in Figure 4.1, a value of 40% was assigned to the instructional design skills component of teaching. In Figure 6.1, it was determined that 75% of the information concerning instructional design skills would be provided by peers, so "75" has been entered in the small box of the upper left-hand corner of the peer X instructional design skills cell of the Source Impact Matrix. Now, as shown in Figure 6.3, by multiplying 40% by 75%, we get a source impact weight of 30% for peers, which is recorded in larger numbers in that cell. By adding all the source impact weights in each column, we compute the total impact weight for the information coming from each source. It is clear from the values shown in the Source Impact Matrix (Figure 6.3) that peer input will account for 50% of the overall evaluation of teaching, student input will account for 40%, and department head input will account for 10%. These values should be reported back to the faculty.

It is critical at this point in the process that a discussion take place as to appropriateness of the final source impact weights. In this case the result of all of the definitions, decisions, and weights determined in the previous steps has led us to point where the evaluation of teaching will be based 40% on student input, 50% on peer input, and 10% on department head input. If it were felt that the department head should have a greater impact on the evaluation of teaching, this would be the point to make the necessary adjustments.

Figure 6.3   Completed Source Impact Matrix for the Teaching Role

Role Components	Students		Peers		Dept. Head			Component Weight
Instructional Delivery Skills	100	**30**	0	**0**	0	**0**		(30 %)
Instructional Design Skills	25	**10**	75	**30**	0	**0**		(40 %)
Content Expertise	0	**0**	80	**20**	20	**5**		(25 %)
Course Management	0	**0**	0	**0**	100	**5**		(5 %)
Total Source Impact Weights	**40**		**50**		**10**			= 100 %

Arreola, R. A. (2000). Developing *a Comprehensive Faculty Evaluation System 2/e.* Bolton, MA: Anker Publishing Co., Inc.

For example, suppose it was determined at this step that a more appropriate mix of the weight on the three sources would be students 35%, peers 40%, and department head 25%. It would be necessary, then, to revisit the decisions that led to the original weights of 40% for students, 50% for peers, and 10% for department head. If it were determined that the department head's impact should be 25% rather than the original 10%, a decision would need to be made to either involve the department head in proving information on additional components of teaching, or give more weight to those components for which the department head already provides information. Likewise, since the impact weight of the students and peers would be reduced to 35% and 40%, respectively, decisions would need to be made to correspondingly reduce either the value of the components for which they are provide information or the number of components for which they serve as information sources.

If the values do not correspond to the expressed values of the institution, adjustments can now be made to bring the total final weights into agreement with the faculty's collective value structure. Note that the sums of both the component weights and source impact weights must each total 100%.

At this point, you should complete your Source Impact Matrix forms for each role by completing the following the steps:

1. For each role for which you have previously completed a Weighted Source by Role Component Matrix, copy the source weights from that matrix into the small boxes in the upper left-hand corner of the corresponding cells in the Source Impact Matrix.

2. At this point, your Source Impact Matrix should contain both component weights down the right side and source weights in the small boxes in the upper left-hand corner of each cell. Multiply the values in the small boxes in the upper left hand of each cell by the component weight for the row of that cell. Write the resulting product (source impact weight) in the larger portion of each cell.

3. Compute each of the column totals of the source impact weights and record them at the bottom of the matrix. These column totals are the total source impact weights for the given role. Note that the sum of the component weights and the sum of the source impact weights must each equal 100%.

GATHERING SOURCE AND SOURCE IMPACT VALUES FROM FACULTY

It should be remembered that the essence of a workable faculty evaluation system is that the value structure implicit in the system be clearly evident and agreed to by the majority of the faculty being evaluated. If this is not the case, the system, no matter how technically correct its structure, has little chance of long-term success. Thus, in determining the impact weights for the various sources that are to provide information for the components of each role, it is best to follow the same procedure described in earlier steps. That is, a simple questionnaire should be constructed and distributed to the faculty. At this point, building on the information gathered earlier, the questionnaire should list the various roles, their defining components, and the identified and agreed-upon sources. A suggested form for the questionnaire is shown in Figure 6.4.

It is not recommended that the faculty be asked to fill in the entire matrix as shown in Figure 6.3. Rather, the first part of the questionnaire simply asks faculty to indicate the credibility each source of information has for them for each of the roles as previously defined, and the second part asks them to indicate the relative value of the defining components of each role. Although it would be possible to ask them to complete the detailed matrix, experience has shown that this task is more cumbersome and complex than most faculty care to deal with on a questionnaire. Thus, in order to maximize the return and ensure that the system reflects the values of the greatest number of faculty, it is recommended that the questionnaire be kept in its simpler form, as shown.

COMPILING THE DATA

The task before the committee at this point is to aggregate and combine all the data to most appropriately reflect the expressed values of the faculty within a department. This is best done by making a rough distribution of the data for each cell and determining whether to use the mean, median, or modal value for the final institutional value. This determination is made, in part, by considering the range of the distribution. If the range is extremely wide or if the distribution is bimodal, these are signs that considerable disagreement exists among the faculty and must be resolved. However, if the greatest bulk of the faculty responses appear to cluster together, the mean or average may be used.

College-wide values should be determined by a similar consideration of the departmental values for that college. Ideally, the college-wide values should encompass and subsume each of the separate departmental value ranges. Thus, although individual departments may have different values associated with specific roles, reflective of their different emphases or cultures, the college value system as a whole should accommodate these differences. For example, the college-wide range for scholarly research may be 0% to 45%. However, a research-oriented department may have as its values for this role a range of 25% to 45%. Similarly, a nonresearch-oriented department may have the values of 0% to 15% for the same role. Both ranges are encompassed by the college-wide value range of 0% to 45% for scholarly research.

Once the FEDC has received all the questionnaire data and has arrived at college-wide figures for the various sources for each role, it is then appropriate to begin filling in the empty cells of the weighted role by source matrix. Referring once more to Figures 6.1 and 6.3, we can see that zeros (0%) have been entered into the cells for which it was determined in Step 5 that no data would be gathered from that source. Thus, 0% has been entered for

peers and department head in the instructional delivery skills portion of the teaching role. It was determined earlier that unless a structured peer or department head visitation procedure was to be put into place, neither of these would be an appropriate source of information concerning the instructional delivery skills. Likewise, zeros are placed in the content expertise and course management cells under students, because it was determined in Step 5 that students would not be an appropriate source of information for these elements of the teaching role.

Given the component and source weights derived from faculty input, the committee is left with the task of computing the relative impact of each role for the Source Impact Matrix (Figure 6.3). Use the Weighted Source by Role Component Matrix forms (Figure 6.2) to work through your best estimate of the source weights and role component values based on the definitions and determinations made in the earlier steps. Finally, complete the Source Impact Matrix for each role by transferring the cell values to the appropriate small boxes and then multiplying the values as described above.

Figure 6.4   Sample Questionnaire for Gathering Weighted Source by Role Information

MEMORANDUM

To: All Faculty

From: Faculty Evaluation Development Committee

Subject: Determining Weights for the Faculty Evaluation System

Previously, the faculty have indicated that our faculty evaluation system should address teaching, scholarly research, faculty service, and public/community service. Further, the faculty have provided specific definitions for these roles. The defining components of each role are shown on the next page. This questionnaire provides you with an opportunity to indicate (1) how much you wish each component of each role to count, and (2) what impact you want each of the sources of information to have in the final overall evaluation of each of the defined roles.

Part I: Determining Component Weights

To reflect the faculty's judgment about how much each element contributes to the overall impact of a given role, it is necessary to assign different weights to these elements or components. In the example shown below, teaching's four defining elements have been weighted as instructional delivery skills = 30%, instructional design skills = 40%, content expertise = 25%, and course management = 5%. Note the total of the individual weights of all defining components equals 100%.

Example (only): Component Weights for the Teaching Role

Components of Teaching:

Instructional Delivery Skills	=	30%
Instructional Design Skills	=	40%
Content Expertise	=	25%
Course Management	=	5%
		100%

On the reverse side, indicate how much weight you believe should be assigned to each defining component of each role. Please make sure that the sum of the component weights you assign for any role equals 100%.

Arreola, R. A. (2000). Developing *a Comprehensive Faculty Evaluation System 2/e*. Bolton, MA: Anker Publishing Co., Inc.

Name:_____   Department:_____

Part 1: Role Component Values

TEACHING:

Instructional Delivery Skills   [_____]

Instructional Design Skills   [_____]

Content Expertise   [_____]

Course Management   [_____]

_____   [_____]

                                                                              100%

SCHOLARLY RESEARCH/CREATIVE ENDEAVORS:

_____   [_____]

_____   [_____]

_____   [_____]

_____   [_____]

_____   [_____]

                                                                              100%

FACULTY SERVICE:

_____   [_____]

_____   [_____]

_____   [_____]

_____   [_____]

_____   [_____]

                                                                              100%

PUBLIC/COMMUNITY SERVICE:

_____   [_____]

_____   [_____]

_____   [_____]

_____   [_____]

_____   [_____]

                                                                              100%

Arreola, R. A. (2000). Developing *a Comprehensive Faculty Evaluation System 2/e*. Bolton, MA: Anker Publishing Co., Inc.

Part 2: Determining Source Weights

In analyzing the definitions shown on the first page of this questionnaire, you may find that different sources of information are appropriate for each of the defining components for each role. Completing the next step will enable us to determine how much weight the information from each of these sources should have in the overall evaluation of any role. The example below shows how to record the weights you believe should be given to evaluative information from the various sources for each defining component of the teaching role.

Example (only): Source Weights for the Teaching Role

Defining Elements/Sources	Students		Peers		Dept. Head	
Instructional Delivery Skills	100%	+	0%	+	0%	= 100%
Instructional Design Skills	25%	+	75%	+	0%	= 100%
Content Expertise	0%	+	80%	+	20%	= 100%
Course Management	0%	+	0%	+	100%	= 100%

In this example, students, peers, and the department head are, in general, appropriate sources of evaluative information concerning teaching. However, the figures shown indicate, in part, that the faculty would wish 100% of the information on instructional delivery skills to come from students, 80% of the information on content expertise to come from peers, and 100% of the information concerning course management to come from the department head.

For each of the roles shown on the reverse side, indicate the weight you feel is appropriate for each source of information for each role element identified. Please make sure that each row of cells adds to 100%. Leave blank any cell containing 0%, because it has been previously determined that no input is to be gathered from that source for that role component.

Arreola, R. A. (2000). Developing *a Comprehensive Faculty Evaluation System 2/e*. Bolton, MA: Anker Publishing Co., Inc.

Name:_____ Department:_____

Leave blank those cells with 0%.

TEACHING

	Students		Peers		Dept. Head	
Instructional Delivery	[_____]	+	[0%]	+	[0%]	= 100%
Instructional Design	[_____]	+	[_____]	+	[0%]	= 100%
Content Expertise	[0%]	+	[_____]	+	[_____]	= 100%
Course Management	[0%]	+	[_____]	+	[_____]	= 100%

SCHOLARLY RESEARCH/CREATIVE ENDEAVORS

	External		Peers		Dept. Head		Dean	
_____	[_____]	+	[_____]	+	[_____]	+	[_____]	= 100%
_____	[_____]	+	[_____]	+	[_____]	+	[_____]	= 100%

FACULTY SERVICE

	External		Peers		Dept. Head		Dean	
_____	[_____]	+	[_____]	+	[_____]	+	[_____]	= 100%

PUBLIC/COMMUNITY SERVICE

	Business		Peers		Dept. Head		Dean	
_____	[_____]	+	[_____]	+	[_____]	+	[_____]	= 100%

PLEASE RETURN THIS COMPLETED QUESTIONNAIRE BY [date] TO:

Arreola, R. A. (2000). Developing *a Comprehensive Faculty Evaluation System 2/e.* Bolton, MA: Anker Publishing Co., Inc.

7

Step 7: Determining How Information Should Be Gathered

Once the sources of the information for the evaluation system have been determined, we begin moving into the less political and more technical area of measurement. It is best at this point to enlist the aid of those people on your faculty whose area of expertise is tests and measurement. They will certainly be required in the next step, and it is generally a good idea to have this expertise represented on the Faculty Evaluation Development Committee (FEDC) in the first place.

In this step, we set about determining how the information we have specified in our role definitions is to be gathered from the sources we have identified and agreed are appropriate. This is a relatively simple process. However, it does require a careful review of the roles and the development of an operational plan for the final faculty evaluation system. In completing this step, we will make use of a new matrix worksheet, the Data Gathering Tool Specification Matrix. Figure 7.1 shows an example of a completed Data Gathering Tool Specification Matrix for the teaching role.

The matrix follows the example that has been used in previous chapters. Note that the cells that contained zeros (0%) in the previous Source Impact Matrix (Figure 6.3) completed in Step 6 are blanked out on this matrix. Since we will not be gathering data from those sources for these elements, we will not need to specify the tools or means for doing so. In the cells that are not vacant, however, we are faced with the task of determining how we will gather information from students, peers, and the department head. For example, if we wish to gather information from students concerning a faculty member's instructional delivery skills, there are several possible alternatives:

Figure 7.1   Data Gathering Tool Specification Matrix for the Teaching Role

Role	Sources		
Teaching	Students	Peers	Dept. Head
Instructional Delivery Skills	Questionnaire		
Instructional Design Skills	Questionnaire	Peer Review of Materials	
Content Expertise		Peer Analysis of Course	Interview
Course Management			Checklist/ Grade Report

Arreola, R. A. (2000). Developing *a Comprehensive Faculty Evaluation System 2/e*. Bolton, MA: Anker Publishing Co., Inc.

1. Interview each student.

2. Interview a random sample of students from each class.

3. Administer a questionnaire to a random sample of students from each class.

4. Administer a questionnaire to each student.

Unless the classes are unusually small and an appropriate team of individuals can be identified to serve as nonthreatening interviewers, interviewing students is generally not done. However, if that approach were desired, then an appropriate interview protocol would have to be developed. For example, in a music curriculum there may exist a number of courses that are individual tutorials. That is, each class has only one student in it. In such a case we might consider a structured exit interview as a means for gathering data.

Figure 7.1 shows a more common situation where a questionnaire has been identified as the way in which student information is to be gathered. This does not mean that a system that uses both questionnaires and a form of follow-up interview could not also be implemented. Only by discussing what is desired, what is acceptable, and what is feasible and affordable can an appropriate determination be made as to the best way the information for each role is to be gathered.

Referring to the example in Figure 7.1, note that peers have been identified as appropriate sources of information for both the instructional design skills and the content expertise components of the teaching role. For instructional design skills, peers will review the course materials. That is, the course syllabus, tests, handouts, text selected, and general design of the course will be assessed by a group of knowledgeable peers. This assessment may require a specific checklist and a set of standards by which the peers are to rate the course materials. Likewise, the peer source will provide information as to the content expertise of the faculty member. This may involve a careful analysis and review of the course in terms of the currency of the content, as well as the sequencing of the material. Note that gathering the information required for a given role or role component may require a form, a set of forms, a specified procedure or protocol, or some combination of forms and procedures.

On the following pages are two blank Data Gathering Tool Specification Matrix Worksheet Masters (Figure 7.2) for making copies. Using the information developed to this point, make a preliminary judgment as to what means will be used to gather the information from each source. Develop a brief explanation and rationale for the data gathering approach you identify for each cell.

Figure 7.2 Data Gathering Tool Specification Matrix Worksheet Master

Data Gathering Tool Specification Matrix for _____
(Role)

Sources

Role Components							

Arreola, R. A. (2000). Developing *a Comprehensive Faculty Evaluation System 2/e.* Bolton, MA: Anker Publishing Co., Inc.

8

Step 8: Completing the System—Selecting or Designing Forms, Protocols, and Rating Scale

We now arrive at the last step in developing a comprehensive faculty evaluation system—designing the questionnaires and other forms. It should be apparent at this point that designing forms without first having clearly identified what is to be measured (Steps 1 and 4), and deciding from whom the information will be gathered (Step 5), could lead to the development of inappropriate and perhaps invalid forms. Unfortunately, many institutions make designing a questionnaire, usually a student rating form, their first step in the process of developing a faculty evaluation system. This is a serious error that can stymie the entire process. Committees charged with such tasks can argue interminably over specific questions to be included on the form and the faculty almost always universally criticize the resultant product.

However, because we have clearly defined what it is we wish to measure, from whom we wish to get the information, and how we are going to gather the information, the design of the forms and procedures becomes a relatively straightforward technical matter. There is no specific recipe for accomplishing the development of your forms and procedures. Rather, what is provided here is simply a word of caution and some resources.

The word of caution is, "Don't reinvent the wheel." Many questionnaires have already been developed and are used in faculty evaluation systems around the country. In addition, there are a number of commercially available forms and systems available. Chapter 14 contains a complete description and critical review of several of the better known commercially available student rating forms. In addition Chapter 15 provides guidelines for constructing a customized student rating form and includes a catalog of 520 sample items. An example of a faculty evaluation manual from one institution that developed its faculty evaluation system using the approach in this book is provided in the Chapter 16.

It is recommended that a small team of faculty expert in psychometrics design and develop a final set of forms rather than assigning the task to the full committee. The full committee has determined all the specifications as to what is to be measured and who is to be tapped for the information. This specification provides sufficient directions for the technical team to follow in developing the questionnaires, protocols, and so on. Experience has shown that if the full committee takes on this task, previous agreements can unravel once the item-by-item determination of the forms and questionnaires gets under way. Faculty unfamiliar with the principles of psychological measurement are likely to overlook the fact that well-designed questionnaires may include questions that, when taken in isolation, may be appear inappropriate, but when taken in the aggregate provide valid and reliable measures of the characteristic or role component in question. Anyone who has taken such instruments as the Minnesota Multiphasic Personality Inventory or the Myers Briggs Type Indicator can appreciate the fact that questions, which individually may not seem to be related, can in the aggregate provide accurate, valid, and reliable measures of human characteristics.

COMMON NUMERICAL RATING SCALE

It is necessary to clarify one assumption before we move to actually constructing the forms, questionnaires, protocols, and so on. We must assume that all information gathered from each source will be reported on a common scale. That is, regardless of whether we use a questionnaire, an interview schedule, or some other technique in gathering evaluative information from the various sources identified, those data will be reported on the same scale. For example, we may agree to assume that all information will use a scale of 1 to 4 where 1 is a low rating and 4 is a high one. That is, student ratings of instructional delivery skills would be reported on a scale from 1 to 4. Likewise, peer ratings of instructional design skills would be reported on a scale from 1 to 4, and so on. Thus, the faculty evaluation committee would need to specify the scale *before* the various questionnaires, forms, and protocols were developed.

The first step in accomplishing the development of a consistent rating scale requires the development and definition of an overall system scale. That is, we need to establish a scale that will be used to communicate the final evaluative outcome for each individual evaluated. Figure 8.1 shows a recommended four-point overall scale, with scale point definitions. Note that the scale requires that an institutional set of standards of professional performance be developed. An example of the types of standards statements is shown in the following section.

Figure 8.1 Standards Based Faculty Evaluation Scale

STANDARDS BASED FACULTY EVALUATION SCALE

EX = Exemplary Performance
This rating is given to those individuals who, during the rating period, consistently exceeded the institution's standards of professional performance. Individuals receiving this rating stand as exemplars of the highest levels of professional academic performance within the institution making significant contributions to their department, college, academic field, and society.

PL = Professional Level Performance
This rating is given to those individuals who, during the rating period, consistently met the institution's standards of professional performance. The individuals receiving this rating constitute those good and valued professionals on whom the continued successful achievement of the institution's mission, goals, and objectives depends.

IR = Improvement Required
This rating is given to those individuals who, during the rating period, did not consistently meet the institution's standards of professional performance. This rating must be given with 1) specific feedback as to which standards of professional performance were not met, 2) suggestions for improvement, and 3) a written commitment to assist the individual in accessing resources required for improvement. Improvement in performance is required within the next evaluation period.

UN = Unprofessional (Unacceptable)
This rating is given to those individuals who, during the rating period, did not meet the institution's standards of professional performance. This rating represents performance that is not acceptable and/or is inconsistent with the conditions for continued employment with the institution. Failure to meet these standards in any one of the three following ways will result in a rating of "Unprofessional":

1. Received an "IR" rating the previous rating period but did not make the improvements required

2. Consistently violated one or more of the institution's standards of professional performance

3. Violated one or more of the standards of conduct as specified in the faculty handbook

---

Arreola, R. A. (2000). Developing *a Comprehensive Faculty Evaluation System 2/e*. Bolton, MA: Anker Publishing Co., Inc.

For computational purposes, the following numerical equivalencies of the rating scale in Figure 8.1 may be made.

EX = Exemplary Performance = 4
PL = Professional Level = 3
IR = Improvement Required = 2
UN = Unprofessional Performance = 1

However, any forms designed to rate performance must use the alphabetic abbreviations and not the numerical values as response definitions.

DEVELOPING INSTITUTIONAL STANDARDS OF PROFESSIONAL PERFORMANCE

In order to use the scale shown in Figure 8.1 it is necessary for the institution to draw up a specific statement of professional standards. These standards must be institutional in nature, although additional departmental, divisional, or other organizational sub-unit standards may be added for faculty within the sub-unit. These standards may include specific policy statements regarding such issues as office hours, advising responsibilities, absences from class, development of syllabi, service on committees, and so on.

The following are examples of the type of statements that may be found in a more complete statement of the standards for professional performance within an institution. The statements below apply primarily to the teaching role. Similar statements would need to be developed for the other roles in the institution's faculty role model.

Standards for Professional Performance in Teaching

Each faculty member is expected to:

- Be present for all class periods for courses which he or she is teaching, or arrange for either a substitute or a means for students to make up the work lost resulting from the absence of the instructor

- Have a syllabus on file in the departmental office for every course he or she is teaching. Each syllabus must be constructed in accordance with departmental guidelines and specifications

- Advise at least 20 students per semester

- Post and keep regular office hours

- Teach without a sexist, racist, or ethnic bias

Often the institution's faculty handbook, or if unionized, the union contract, will contain the core criteria and standards for professional performance.

FACULTY EVALUATION TOOLS AND PROCEDURES

Since different forms in our system will ask different questions, thus requiring different response options, care must be exercised in choosing a scale for the form. The scale selected must both fit the type of questions being asked and contain the same number of response categories as the institutional scale (such as the one shown in Figure 8.1). Figure 8.2 shows several examples of different response scales, all using a four-point format, which would be appropriate for different types of questions.

The following is a summary of a number of tools and procedures that have been used in evaluating faculty performance. Each summary contains a brief overview of the strengths, weaknesses, and characteristics of the particular tool or procedure. This listing is by no means exhaustive but, rather, simply summarizes a number of more commonly used tools and procedures in faculty evaluation systems.

Figure 8.2 Sample Rating Form Response Formats Using a Common Numerical Scale

AS	=	Agree Strongly	=	4
A	=	Agree	=	3
D	=	Disagree	=	2
DS	=	Disagree Strongly	=	1
VG	=	Very Good	=	4
G	=	Good	=	3
P	=	Poor	=	2
VP	=	Very Poor	=	1
HS	=	Highly Satisfactory	=	4
S	=	Satisfactory	=	3
LS	=	Less Than Satisfactory	=	2
HU	=	Highly Unsatisfactory	=	1

Arreola, R. A. (2000). Developing *a Comprehensive Faculty Evaluation System 2/e*. Bolton, MA: Anker Publishing Co., Inc.

Student Ratings

Students rate an instructor's performance through a structured or unstructured questionnaire or interview.

Strengths of This Approach. Can produce extremely reliable and valid information concerning faculty classroom performance, because students observe the teacher every day. Instructors are often motivated to change as a result of student feedback. Results show high correlation with other peer and supervisor ratings if a professionally designed student rating form is used. Assessments are reliable and not affected by grades if a well-designed form is used.

Weaknesses. Unless a professionally developed student rating form is used, factors other than teacher performance (e.g., class size, time of day) may inappropriately contribute to student ratings. Students may tend to be generous in their ratings.

Conditions for Effective Use. Need student anonymity. Need teacher willingness to accept student feedback. Instruments must be carefully developed by appropriate reliability and validity studies.

Nature of Evidence Produced. Student perceptions of what they have learned, how they have changed. Student opinions of how various teaching acts affected them. Student reaction to instructor actions. Student perceptions of what they like and dislike about an instructor.

Purposes for Which This Approach Is Most Appropriate. Help instructors improve. Identify faculty for merit recognition. Make personnel decisions.

Tests of Student Performance

Measures of what students have learned or how they have changed over a period of time in working with the instructor.

Strengths of This Approach. Student attainment of objectives is a legitimate source of data on faculty performances. Measures impact of instructor on students over a period of time.

Weaknesses. Difficulty of designing appropriate tests. Gains on standardized tests often an inadequate measure of performance. Other factors may considerably affect performance (e.g., student intelligence, family background, previous schooling).

Conditions for Effective Use. Must have systematic and comprehensive data collection plan. Need personnel skilled in collecting performance data.

Nature of Evidence Produced. Student work samples. Test results (standardized and others). Attitude measures.

Purposes for Which This Approach Is Most Appropriate. Improve student learning. Identify teachers for merit recognition.

Simulated Teaching

Brief unit taught to a special selected group of students on content normally not taught by the instructor with pre- and posttest measures of student gains in the content.

Strengths of This Approach. Evaluates instructor skills in terms of student learning. Provides short-term feedback. Increases control over nonteacher variables assumed to influence student.

Weaknesses. Does not allow for assessing student growth over time. Expensive to conduct. Not a normal classroom situation.

Conditions for Effective Use. Need personnel trained in design of controlled situation evaluations and in student performance testing. Requires extra teacher preparation time.

Nature of Evidence Produced. Evidence on student learning under controlled conditions.

Purposes for Which This Approach Is Most Appropriate. Improve student learning. Make personnel decisions.

Self-Evaluation

Instructor uses various means to gather information to assess performance relative to own needs, goals, and objectives.

Strengths of This Approach. May be used as part of a program of continuous assessment. Faculty are more likely to act on data which they collect themselves. The data collected are more clearly related to a faculty member's own goals and needs.

Weaknesses. Results not consistent with other raters. May be unwilling to collect and/or consider data relative to own performance. Tend to rate themselves higher than students do.

Conditions for Effective Use. Instructor must have self-confidence and security. Need skills in identifying goals and collecting appropriate data. Must not be weighted highly in the determination of personnel decisions (promotion, tenure, merit pay, etc.).

Nature of Evidence Produced. Information on progress toward one's own goals.

Purposes for Which This Approach Is Most Appropriate. Help instructors improve. Determine best assignments.

Supervisor or Department Head Observation

Administrators evaluate an instructor's performance through classroom observation, review of student learning data, feedback from students.

Strengths of This Approach. Supervisor is familiar with college and community goals, priorities, and values and may often have additional information about faculty performance. Can compare instructors within the college, school, division, or department. Requires minimal resources for observation, feedback, follow-up. Have legal responsibility for evaluation and related decision-making.

Weaknesses. Bias due to previous data, personal relationships, reason for observation, own values, and favored teaching methods. Situation being observed is, by definition, not normal because the observer is present.

Conditions for Effective Use. Supervisor needs adequate time and observational and review skills. Observation must focus on characteristics of teaching that research has established relates to desired student outcomes.

Nature of Evidence Produced. Comments on relations between instructor acts and student behaviors. Information on how instructors compare on certain factors. Comparisons with methods supervisors consider to be good. Directions on changes to be made.

Purposes for Which This Approach Is Most Appropriate. Guide professional growth and development. Information produced should not be used for personnel decisions unless supervisor is a part of a team of observers who use a standardized observation tool and who have been trained and have made sufficiently frequent observations to produce interrater reliability of the data.

Peer Evaluation

Other faculty evaluate an instructor's performance through classroom observation, review of instructional materials, course design.

Strengths of This Approach. Familiar with college (departmental, divisional) goals, priorities, values, and problems faculty face. Encourages professional behavior (e.g., motivation to help upgrade own profession). Can be chosen from instructor's subject area and thus may be able to give specific suggestions.

Weaknesses. Bias due to previous data, personal relationships, or peer pressure to influence evaluation. Relationships among peers may suffer. Possible bias due to evaluator's preference for his/her own teaching method.

Conditions for Effective Use. Requires high degree of professional ethics and objectivity. Requires training in observational and analysis skills. Need time for multiple reviews.

Nature of Evidence Produced. Comments on relations between instructor acts and student behaviors. Comparisons with methods peers consider to be good. Suggestions for instructors on methods, etc., to use.

Purposes for Which This Approach Is Most Appropriate. Guide professional growth and development. Information produced should not be used for personnel decisions unless peer is a part of a team of observers who use a stan-

dardized observation tool and who have been trained and have made sufficiently frequent observations to produce interrater reliability of the data. See Chapter 12 for a more detailed discussion of the characteristics of peer evaluation.

Visiting Team of Experts

People external to the system recognized as qualified in faculty (teacher) evaluation procedures observe faculty performance and/or review student learning data.

Strengths of This Approach. Can select evaluators with special skills. External to politics, problems, and biases of the college (school). Provides reliable data through pooling of independent ratings.

Weaknesses. Bias of evaluators due to own values, preferences, etc. Evaluators not accountable to the academic unit (college, school, division, department, etc.).

Conditions for Effective Use. Experts must be properly selected, oriented, and trained. Need time for multiple observations and reviews. Must use a standardized observer rating form on which team has been trained.

Nature of Evidence Produced. Comments on relations between instructor acts and student behaviors. Comparisons with methods experts consider to be good. Suggestions for teachers on methods, etc., to use.

Purposes for Which This Approach Is Most Appropriate. Guide professional growth and development. Aid in making personnel decisions. If data are to be used for personnel decisions, the team of experts must have been trained and have made sufficiently frequent observations to produce interrater reliability of the data.

TIMETABLE FOR DEVELOPING A COMPREHENSIVE FACULTY EVALUATION SYSTEM

Once the questionnaires, protocols, checklists, and other forms have been designed, the system is ready to be implemented. This assumes, however, that the appropriate support systems have been developed and put in place as noted in the introduction of this book.

The following timetable has been found to be typical in the successful development of a comprehensive faculty evaluation system:

Month 1   Appoint Faculty Evaluation Development Committee (FEDC). Familiarize committee with system development procedure. Hold general faculty meeting, sponsored by the committee, where procedure is presented and explained.

Month 2–6   FEDC distributes questionnaires to faculty to develop the faculty role model, weights for the roles, definitions of roles, sources of information, and weights for each source.

Month 7   FEDC reports to the general faculty the total value structure and role definitions as determined by faculty input.

Month 7–12   System forms and protocols are designed, selected, and developed. Policy decisions concerning confidentiality and the use of the information in promotion, tenure, and merit pay decisions finalized.

Month 12–24   Pilot run of the system. Debug system and make adjustments. One common strategy is to use for volunteers among the faculty for the pilot run. At the end of the trial the FEDC and the volunteers may present the results of the using the system to the general faculty. This is a time of stress, however, because decisions concerning promotion, tenure, and merit pay will still have to be based on the old system that is to be modified or phased out.

Month 25   Full implementation of system.

9

Generating an Overall Composite Rating (OCR)

In developing your comprehensive faculty evaluation system as specified in Steps 1 through 8, you have made the following determinations:

- Which faculty roles should be evaluated.

- What the defining activities or components are for each role

- How much weight each component contributes to overall role definition

- How much the evaluation of any one role may impact the total evaluation of an individual

- Where information concerning each role is to be gathered and how much that information will impact or influence the total evaluative outcome

- The methods and forms by which the information specified will be gathered from the sources agreed upon

At this point you are ready to begin using the system. The task now is to combine all the data resulting from the system into a usable form. Previously, it was determined that all information gathered from each source would be reported on a common scale. In our examples we have used a common 1 to 4 scale where 4 is the highest rating and 1 is the lowest. That is, regardless of whether a questionnaire, an interview schedule, or some other technique has been used in gathering evaluative information from the various sources identified, those data will be reported on the same 1 to 4 scale. Thus, student ratings, peer ratings, and department head ratings will all be reported on

a scale of 1 to 4. This is not to suggest that 5-point or other point scales may not be used in a comprehensive system, merely that whatever scale is used must be consistent throughout the system.

COMPUTING THE COMPOSITE ROLE RATING

Having determined and specified the weights to be assigned to various activities and sources in the overall faculty evaluation system, it is now possible to compute an overall rating for each role that reflects the collective values of the faculty. This rating will be referred to as the Composite Role Rating (CRR) because it will be derived from various sources, with each source providing information concerning various components of each role and with the information from each source and component weighted in ways which reflect the consensus value structure of the institution. That is, the overall rating will be determined using the principle of controlled subjectivity discussed in the introduction of this book. The following is an example of how the composite role rating for teaching would be computed.

In Figure 6.3, we determined that the information students provided concerning the faculty member's instructional delivery skills would impact the overall rating of the teaching role by 30%. Likewise, student information concerning the instructional design skills component would count 10%, and peer information would count 30%. We also determined that peer input on content expertise would count 20%, and department head input would count 5%. Finally, it was determined that department head input concerning course management would count 5% of the overall rating on teaching.

Figure 9.1 shows these weights along with the rating each source has given each role component. Note that all ratings, shown in brackets, use the common scale of 1 to 4. Here the students rated the instructor 4 in instructional delivery skills. Because it was determined in Figure 6.3 that whatever data the students provided concerning the instructional delivery skills component would count as 30% of the overall evaluation of the teaching role, we simply multiply the rating of 4 by 30% to arrive at a weighted rating of 1.2. In a similar fashion, the ratings provided by the various sources on the different components of the teaching role are multiplied by their impact weights. Finally, all weighted ratings are added together to form a CRR of 3.45. For ease of computation, the ratings in Figure 9.1 are shown as whole numbers. In practice, the ratings may be averages and may thus include decimal values.

Note that the CRR of 3.45 was not determined by any one student, peer, or administrator. Rather, this value represents a composite of the information concerning activities the faculty agreed should be evaluated, collected from sources that were agreed to be appropriate, and weighted to reflect both the credibility of the sources and the relative importance of each component of the entire role. Although the CRR does not represent an objective measure, the subjectivity involved in computing it has been carefully controlled and prescribed by the values assigned to the sources and role components. A similar procedure would be followed in determining the composite role ratings for the other roles (i.e., research, faculty service, community service, etc.).

INDIVIDUALIZING THE EVALUATIONS: THE OVERALL COMPOSITE RATING (OCR)

As a first step in developing a comprehensive faculty evaluation system, a faculty role model was developed with minimum and maximum parameter values, reflecting the

Figure 9.1   Composite Role Rating for Teaching

TEACHING	Students	Peers	Dept. Head	Weighted Rating
Instructional Delivery	30% × [4]			1.20
Instructional Design	10% × [3]	30% × [3]		1.20
Content Expertise		20% × [4]	5% × [3]	.95
Course Management			5% × [2]	.10
COMPOSITE ROLE RATING				CRR = 3.45

Figure 9.2   Composite Role Ratings for Professor Drake

Role	Composite Role Ratings
Teaching	3.45
Research	3.20
Faculty Service	3.60
Community Service	2.60

Arreola, R. A. (2000). Developing *a Comprehensive Faculty Evaluation System 2/e*. Bolton, MA: Anker Publishing Co., Inc.

collective values of the faculty and the institution, assigned to each role. These minimum and maximum values were expressions of the variability that may appropriately occur in faculty assignments. Using the matrices and values developed to this point, it is now possible to begin individualizing the evaluations of different faculty.

Assume that Professor Drake has received the composite role ratings shown in Figure 9.2.

The individual composite role ratings shown for Professor Drake were computed as shown in Figure 9.1. That is, each composite role rating is the result of gathering specific information from specified sources, weighted in ways that reflect the value system of the faculty and the institution. Of course, it is possible to stop at this point and use the various CRRs separately. However, using them in isolation does not permit us to reflect the specific nature of Professor Drake's assignment.

Assume that Professor Drake has an assignment as reflected in Figure 9.3. Recall that the faculty role model for our hypothetical institution (Figure 2.2) allowed a minimum of 50% weight on teaching and a maximum of 85%. Likewise, the minimum and maximum weights were 0% and 35% for scholarly research, 10% and 25% for faculty service, and 5% and 15% for community service.

In Figure 9.3, the 50% weighting for teaching for Professor Drake does not necessarily imply a 50% teaching load. Rather, it simply reflects the fact that, given the particular roles the faculty member is engaged in, it has been agreed that whatever rating Professor Drake receives for the teaching role will count 50% of the comprehensive overall rating.

To combine Professor Drake's several separate CRRs into an Overall Composite Rating (OCR), we simply multiply each composite role rating by the assignment weights shown in Figure 9.3 and compute the total. These computations are shown in Figure 9.4.

Note that Professor Drake's OCR of 3.34 was not determined by any single individual or group. Rather, the

Figure 9.3   Assigned Role Weights for Professor Drake

Teaching	50%
Research	35%
Faculty Service	10%
Community Service	5%
TOTAL	100%

Figure 9.4   Computation of Professor Drake's Overall Composite Rating (OCR)

Role	Assigned Weight	×	Composite Role Rating	=	Weighted Composite Rating
Teaching	50%	×	3.45	=	1.73
Research	35%	×	3.20	=	1.12
Faculty Service	10%	×	3.60	=	0.36
Community Service	5%	×	2.60	=	0.13
OVERALL COMPOSITE RATING			OCR	=	3.34

Arreola, R. A. (2000). Developing *a Comprehensive Faculty Evaluation System 2/e*. Bolton, MA: Anker Publishing Co., Inc.

OCR may be thought of as a singular "index of success," because it was assembled by gathering information from various sources, weighted in ways that reflect the credibility of those sources, and further weighted by the assignment emphasis for this faculty member. That is, given the particular assignment Professor Drake had this year, the various appropriate sources provided a mosaic of information that is expressed in the OCR. This approach permits us to more fairly compare the ratings of two faculty who may have considerably different assignments. For example, look at the OCR for a different faculty member, Professor Lamb (Figure 9.5).

The assigned role weights for Professor Lamb differ considerably from those of Professor Drake. Professor Lamb did not engage in any scholarly research, as indicated by the absence of that role. In contrast, however, Professor Lamb placed the maximum weight (85%) on the teaching role. Yet, if we consider the OCR to be an index of success, it can readily be seen that both Professor Drake and Professor Lamb, with OCRs of 3.34 and 3.35, respectively, were rated as essentially equally successful in accomplishing their assignments. Again, it should be noted that no one individual assigned these rating values to Professors Drake and Lamb. Rather, their overall composite ratings (OCR) were the results of information gathered from a number of appropriate sources, weighted in such ways as to reflect the value structure of the institution as well as the individual faculty.

RESPONDING TO CONCERNS IN USING A SINGLE NUMERICAL INDEX (OCR)

The development of the OCR as a single numerical index representing a summary of a faculty member's professional performance provides the academic decision-maker with the kind of numerical index that student rating averages are often used as, but never really are. That is, a singular value has been determined which represents a complex set of behaviors and performances and which takes into account the interaction between the values of both the institution and the person being evaluated. Although the assignment of a singular numerical index to represent complex human performance may be criticized, it is a practice used throughout society and in education especially. Colleges and universities routinely make critical decisions and award scholarships, certificates, and degrees on the basis of summary singular numerical indices of complex human behavior (i.e., student GPAs). As a profession, we are not unfamiliar or unskilled in this practice.

Criticisms may also be made that using a singular numerical index such as the OCR can fool us into making significant decisions on the basis of insignificant differences, such as in the examples of Professors Drake and Lamb whose ratings differed by only 0.01. This is an important issue that must be considered.

The criticism that small numerical differences in faculty evaluation results cannot be used to make significant decisions would be well founded if the OCR were a singular measure. It is important to recognize that an OCR value represents an aggregate measurement. The forms used in gathering the data constitute the individual measurements in the system. The OCR is a numerical expression based on the weighting of measurements. An OCR is the sum of measurement data weighted by subjective values. These subjective values are embedded in the definition of each role and the specification of the role weights, role component weights, identified sources,

Figure 9.5 Computation of Professor Lamb's Overall Composite Rating (OCR)

Role	Assigned Weight	×	Composite Role Rating	=	Weighted Composite Rating
Teaching	85%	×	3.53	=	3.00
Faculty Service	10%	×	2.00	=	.20
Community Service	5%	×	2.90	=	.15
OVERALL COMPOSITE RATING				=	3.35

Arreola, R. A. (2000). Developing *a Comprehensive Faculty Evaluation System 2/e*. Bolton, MA: Anker Publishing Co., Inc.

source weights, and individual assignment weights that have been previously determined.

Of course, appropriate care must be taken in the development and use of the forms used to measure faculty performance to ensure that they are reliable and that they produce accurate and valid measures. In considering this issue it is important to ask what alternative may be used to making significant decisions on the basis of what some may consider insignificant differences in the numerical ratings of individuals.

- One alternative often mentioned is to round the OCR values from the nearest hundredth to the nearest tenth. However, this provides no real solution because the same objection can still be made in the difference between tenths of a point as it was between hundredths of a point.

- Another alternative often suggested is to take other factors into account besides the OCR in making decisions. The flaw in this alternative, however, is that if the faculty evaluation system were developed as specified in Steps 1 through 8, all relevant performances and evidence would have already been taken into account. Thus, to consider any other factor at the time of making a significant decision would be, by definition, to consider irrelevant data.

- Another alternative that is sometimes suggested is that faculty be placed within groups representing a range of rating values and that everyone within the group is treated the same in terms of any personnel decisions. Although this approach can find some use in the distribution of merit pay (see Chapter 10), the flaw in this alternative is that someone may still miss being put into a particular grouping by a hundredth or tenth of a point and we are left with the same problem.

The only practical response to this situation is to make sure that the all definitions, criteria, and standards within the faculty evaluation system have been clearly specified and that they relate to observable or documentable products, performances, or achievements. Further, ensure that all forms used in the system have been constructed using accepted professional psychometric techniques and that all forms are as valid, reliable, objective, and accurate as possible. However, regardless of the accuracy of the measures, they are not going to be perfect. No matter where the cutoff for a decision point is set there is always the possibility that someone will just miss it. Since mathematical and psychometric accuracy can take us just so far, we must be prepared to take a policy stance and stick to it. Nothing is worse than an inconsistent evaluation process.

Finally, make certain that those performances considered important (significant) and those considered less important (not significant) are given the appropriate values or weights in the faculty evaluation system. If this is done then the final aggregate measures, even though they may differ by only a tenth or hundredth of a point, will reflect issues and performances that the faculty consider to be important. It is preferable to make significant decisions on the basis of small differences along relevant and appropriate dimensions than to make significant decisions on the basis of larger differences along irrelevant and inappropriate dimensions.

With the computation of an individualized OCR, which can be correctly characterized as an index of perceived success, we now possess an aggregate measure that may appropriately be used in decisions concerning promotion, tenure, continuation, and merit pay. The OCR also provides important information for post-tenure review considerations.

10

Using the OCR in Promotion, Tenure, Merit Pay, and Post-Tenure Review Decisions

Computing an Overall Composite Rating (OCR) in the manner described to this point greatly simplifies the use of faculty evaluation information in making several personnel decisions including

- Promotion

- Continuation of contract

- Tenure

- Post-tenure review

- Merit pay raises

Decisions regarding the determination and distribution of merit raises are fundamentally different from those concerning other personnel decisions. It is important to recognize this difference in the establishment of the policies that will guide these decisions.

Promotion, tenure (or continuation), and post-tenure review decisions are based essentially on a prediction concerning the faculty member's future performance. That is, when we promote someone from the rank of assistant professor to that of associate professor, the underlying prediction is that the faculty member will continue to perform at a level that is appropriate to an associate professor. If we decide to tenure or award a continuing contract to someone, we are making a prediction that they will continue to perform in a manner that will be of value to the institution. If a post-tenure evaluation determines that a tenured professor is consistently performing below minimally acceptable standards despite opportunities to improve, the prediction is that the faculty member will

persist in that poor performance and thus the institution may initiate termination procedures.

Merit pay decisions, on the other hand, are based on recognition of meritorious performance during the evaluation period. The intent is to reward that meritorious performance and encourage continued meritorious performance. Thus, promotion, tenure, continuation, and post-tenure review decisions require data on which to base a prediction of future performance, and merit pay decisions require data on which to base the reward of past performance.

The best data we can use on which to base a prediction concerning a person's future performance is his or her pattern of past performance. Personnel decisions should be based on information that clearly demonstrates the pattern of performance of a faculty member over a length of time, preferably several years. The particular student ratings for one class, the peer critiques of a single article, or similar such specific data are rarely appropriate for making decisions of this sort. Thus, for a faculty evaluation system to be truly effective for personnel decisions, it must gather an aggregate of relevant performance data and demonstrate a pattern of performance over some specified length of time. Generally, positive personnel decisions are based on a body of evidence that says, in essence, "no matter what the professional responsibilities assigned, this faculty member achieves a certain level of success time after time." The system you will have developed up to this point using the model in this book can provide the academic decision-maker with relevant information concerning the pattern of performance and level of success of a faculty member over time.

PROMOTION DECISIONS

Making decisions on whether to promote a faculty member is significantly simplified using the OCR. It is assumed, of course, that the institution has policies concerning the length of time faculty members must be in a given rank or level before they are eligible for promotion to the next rank or level. One such policy, using the overall composite rating, could read as follows:

Promotion Policy Statement (example).
Promotions from one rank to the next are based on achieving a specified minimum overall composite rating for a specified number of years. Ratings are based on a 4-point scale where 4 is the highest rating.

To be promoted from assistant professor to associate professor, the applicant must have served as an assistant professor, or the equivalent, for at least four years and must have achieved a minimum overall composite rating (OCR) of 2.75 for the three consecutive years prior to consideration for promotion.

Note this policy statement specifies that the applicant must have served a minimum of four years as an assistant professor and must have achieved a minimum overall composite rating of 2.75 or higher. The minimum number of years in rank in this example is arbitrary, as is the value of 2.75. Different institutions may have varying requirements concerning length of time in rank. However, the point is that such a policy statement makes it clear that the applicant must achieve and sustain a certain level of "success" for the three years prior to applying for promotion from assistant to associate professor. An effective way to display the information required in making personnel decisions is to simply maintain a graph (Figure 10.1) of the yearly OCR values of the a faculty member. The following graph shows a faculty member's pattern of performance over seven consecutive years. The graph is prepared by plotting the OCR value resulting from the annual faculty evaluation process for each year the instructor has been on the faculty.

In Figure 10.1 we can see that, although the faculty member got off to a slow start, over the years the pattern of performance shows continuous growth. Not only does the faculty member meet the technical requirements for promotion from assistant to associate professor (OCR greater than 2.75 for the last three consecutive years), but the overall pattern of performance gives us confidence in predicting that the faculty member will continue to perform at a high level.

Figure 10.1 Graph of Faculty Member's OCR Values from 1993 to 1999

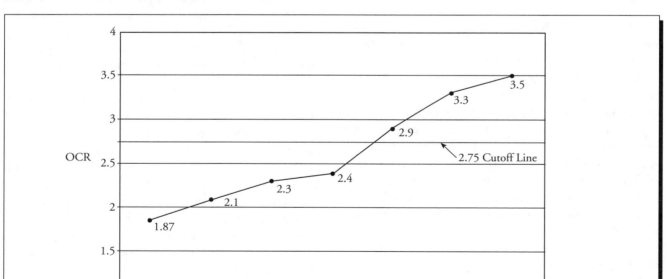

Arreola, R. A. (2000). Developing *a Comprehensive Faculty Evaluation System 2/e*. Bolton, MA: Anker Publishing Co., Inc.

Note that it is the pattern of performance over time that is important. Also, by specifying a minimum overall composite rating (in this case 2.75), one can ensure that, regardless of the assignment given, this faculty member is able to consistently achieve a level of success that is comparable to faculty already at the associate professor level. One suggested approach to determining what should be the value of the cutoff for the overall composite rating for promotion from assistant to associate professor is to determine the average overall composite rating for associate professors and set the minimum entry level at one-half a standard deviation below that average. Similar policy statements with different times in rank and different (higher) cutoff values could be developed for promotion from associate to full professor.

TENURE DECISIONS

Even more than decisions concerning promotion, the decision on whether to tenure or grant a continuing contract needs to be based on the complete performance history. Again, the concern is what prediction concerning future performance can be made from the faculty evaluation data. As noted in the example above, promotion decisions may be based on an individual's achieving and sustaining a specified level of performance in the three years prior to application for promotion. Tenure decisions, however, should be based on the individual's pattern of performance over the entire span of time the faculty member has been employed at the institution. The following is an example of the type of policy statement that applies the OCR to tenure decisions:

Policy for Awarding Tenure (example).
The awarding of tenure is determined, in part, on achieving of an average overall composite rating (OCR) of 2.5 for the entire length of time the faculty member has been employed by the college. Tenure may not be granted to anyone who has had more than two consecutive years of declining OCR values below 2.5 even if they meet the 2.5 average OCR value criterion. No faculty member may be awarded tenure before the completion of five years of continuous employment with the institution. However, credit may be given for previous employment as specified in the initial appointment letter. It is noted that the number of applicants for tenure in any given year may exceed the number of available tenure positions as determined by the Board of Regents. Thus achieving the required OCR in the fifth year of employment does not

Figure 10.2 Pattern of Performance Indicating Growth

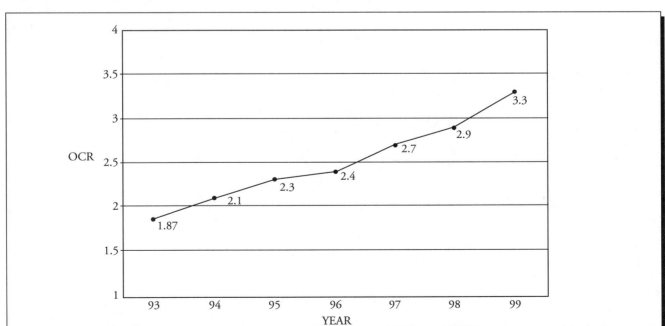

Arreola, R. A. (2000). Developing *a Comprehensive Faculty Evaluation System 2/e.* Bolton, MA: Anker Publishing Co., Inc.

automatically ensure the granting of tenure in the subsequent academic year.

This policy statement specifies a level of success as indicated by the average overall composite rating for the entire length of time the faculty member has worked at the institution. Again, it is the pattern of performance over time that is being used to make the decision. This policy implies that, regardless of the mix of professional responsibilities or the normal ups and downs that affect most careers, on the average the faculty member is able to perform at such a level that the college is willing to make a long-term commitment for continued employment. The policy also specifies that a prolonged decline in performance (more than two years) below the cutoff value of 2.5 disqualifies the applicant for tenure regardless of their average OCR value over the length of their employment. By using the complete OCR pattern, one or two bad years do not automatically disqualify the person from applying for and being awarded tenure, although prolonged decline does. The following examples provide three general possibilities.

Figure 10.2 shows the performance pattern over time of one faculty member being considered for tenure. Note the pattern of performance, as indicated by the OCR values, shows a consistent growth in performance level from year to year. This graph takes on special significance when we realize that the OCR values are expressions of the success the faculty member achieved in a given year's assignment of professional duties. Thus, even if a faculty member's mix of professional duties changes from year to year, the OCR graph gives us a powerful tool in making decisions. In this first example, not only does the faculty member qualify technically (i.e., the average OCR value across the length of time of employment is 2.5 or greater), the pattern of performance over time strongly suggests a high probability of continued high levels of performance.

The growth in performance documented in this graph might be the function of simple maturation on the part of a new doctoral graduate in his or her first academic position, the result of a concerted faculty development program offered by the institution, or both.

Figure 10.3 shows a somewhat different pattern of performance over time. As with the previous example, the faculty member technically qualifies for tenure because the average OCR value is greater than 2.5. However, this pattern demonstrates another benefit of maintaining OCR graphs. The obvious dip that occurs in the middle of the graph in this example is indicative of a sudden change in the performance level. The cause for such a change in performance could be due to many factors,

Figure 10.3 Pattern of Performance Indicating Sudden Change

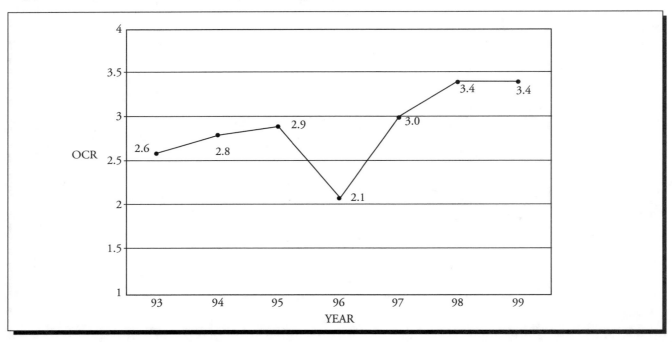

Arreola, R. A. (2000). Developing *a Comprehensive Faculty Evaluation System 2/e.* Bolton, MA: Anker Publishing Co., Inc.

such as a death in the family, a divorce, a stroke, an accident, or a departmental change in the required texts of several courses. Or, it could have been the result of a new experimental teaching technique that required some adjustment but ultimately resulted in even better performance after the adjustment was completed. Noting sudden declines in performance at the time they occur provides a powerful tool for identifying faculty who may require support and thus provides a link to possible faculty development efforts. The OCR graphs also provide a useful tool as part of departmental, college, or institutional program evaluations in providing evidence of faculty performance without the necessity of identifying individuals. OCR graphs may also be used to monitor the effect of administrative changes in policy or the restructuring of resources.

Figure 10.4 shows an OCR graph of a faculty member whose performance started out well upon hiring but has progressively deteriorated over time. This might be called the "flash-in-the-pan" faculty performance pattern. Here, the faculty member achieves an average OCR value greater than 2.5 for the entire length of employment. However, the pattern of performance indicates several years of continuous decline below the 2.5 level. This pattern strongly supports a prediction that the faculty member's performance may continue to deteriorate in the future. Accordingly, the policy requirement that no one may be tenured if they have a decline of more than two years below the 2.5 cutoff value disqualifies this person from being granted tenure.

Second, the OCR graph in Figure 10.4 provides decision-makers with a means of taking appropriate action on declining performance at the time it occurs. In the case of the faculty member whose graph is shown in Figure 10.4, some sort of professional development intervention would be well advised at the time of the third consecutive year of decline before it falls below the established cutoff of value of 2.5.

In reality, the pattern of performance shown in Figure 10.4 should never be allowed to occur. Such patterns on the part of one or more faculty within an academic unit may serve as indicators of the performance of the administrator responsible for monitoring faculty performance and assisting in their continued growth and development.

POST-TENURE REVIEW

In response to intense societal demands for accountability, there is a growing movement in the direction of a tenure-free academic environment among colleges and universities. The increased use of adjunct and nontenure

Figure 10.4 Declining Pattern of Performance

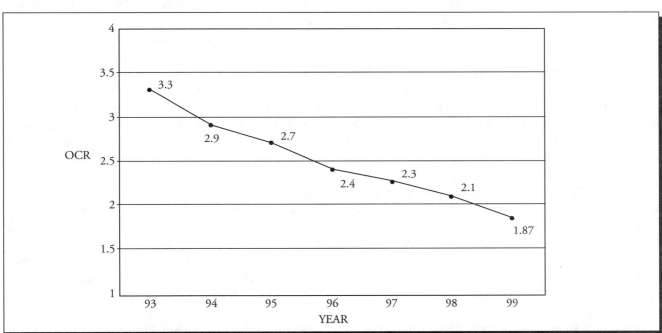

Arreola, R. A. (2000). Developing *a Comprehensive Faculty Evaluation System 2/e*. Bolton, MA: Anker Publishing Co., Inc.

track faculty is partial evidence of this movement. The other is the adoption and implementation of a post-tenure review process.

The primary purpose of the post-tenure review process is to provide a mechanism for systematically gathering data on which to base the termination of tenured faculty whose performance no longer meets accepted professional standards. Although virtually every post-tenure review policy speaks to the intent to promote continuous professional growth and development and thus facilitate and promote excellence, the heart of each policy statement is to provide a mechanism for the termination of tenured faculty.

Although proponents of post-tenure review speak to its value in promoting professional development, opponents see it as a threat to the entire concept of academic freedom (AAUP, 1998). In truth, post-tenure review is the academic community's response to society's demand to get rid of the "dead wood" among the faculty (i.e., those tenured faculty who have ceased to perform at an acceptable professional level but remain employed simply by virtue of being tenured).

The relationship between tenure, post-tenure review, and faculty evaluation in general is best understood in terms of the shifting of responsibilities. Prior to the granting of tenure, it is the responsibility of the faculty member to provide evidence to the institution in support of continued employment. That is, prior to tenure, a faculty member may be terminated without great effort. His or her faculty appointment simply does not have to be renewed the following year. Of course, institutions have different policies as to how and when and under what conditions a nontenured faculty member may be terminated. Fundamentally, however, it is the responsibility of the faculty member to provide evidence in support of the continuation of his or her faculty appointment.

After the granting of tenure, the responsibility shifts. Whereas before tenure it is the responsibility of the faculty member to show why he or she should continue to be employed, after tenure it becomes the institution's responsibility to provide evidence as to why the faculty member should not continue to be employed. This constitutes a subtle but significant shift in responsibility with great ramifications. There have always been policies in place to terminate tenured faculty, which have generally revolved around egregiously offensive and/or illegal behavior on the part of the faculty member. The post-tenure review process, however, adds the element of nonsatisfactory professional performance to this mix.

This shift in responsibility is based on a new assumption. That is, prior to post-tenure review, the underlying assumption has been that tenured faculty would continue to perform at a satisfactory professional level and that no further evaluation was necessary. However, the underlying assumption of post-tenure review policies is that the professional performance of tenured faculty may fall to unacceptable levels and remain there. The previous assumption speaks to an earlier, golden age when college professors were held in high regard by society, often on par with physicians and clergy. The latter assumption speaks to the practical reality of today's "Information Age" society. Under post-tenure review, it becomes the responsibility of the tenured faculty member to periodically provide evidence that his or her professional performance has not fallen to an unacceptable level.

Interestingly, this subtle but significant shift in responsibility does little to change the landscape in terms of faculty evaluation. Prior to tenure faculty evaluation, data are generally gathered systematically every year. It is in the faculty member's best interest to participate in the faculty evaluation system and systematically gather evidence in support of his or her continued employment. In addition, as discussed elsewhere in this book, gathering evidence that conveys an accurate picture of the faculty member's pattern of professional performance over time can provide substantial support for promotion and tenure applications.

Tenured faculty traditionally have not had to be overly concerned with faculty evaluation. Historically, colleges and universities have tended to make participation in the faculty evaluation process optional for tenured faculty. Some universities have even adopted polices which specify that tenured faculty are never to be evaluated again. Most post-tenure review policies, however, specify that the evaluation of a tenured faculty member take place once every five or seven years. This evaluation often takes a form similar, if not identical to, the evaluation procedure used for awarding tenure in the first place. Heavy peer evaluation is often a component, with special emphasis placed on research. Student ratings may also be seen as a component in providing evidence of the quality of teaching performance. If substandard performance, or performance that would be inconsistent with the granting of tenure in the first place, is detected, a process of focused improvement efforts is initiated. If performance does not improve, termination procedures are initiated (Banks, 1997).

Although continuous participation by tenured faculty in the faculty evaluation may be recommended, generally most post-tenure review policies do not mandate it.

However, since a significant responsibility has been shifted back to the faculty member (i.e., to provide evidence that his or her professional performance has not fallen to unacceptable levels), it continues to be in his or her best self-interest to participate continuously in a systematic faculty evaluation process. In the absence of the data provided by continuous participation in the faculty evaluation process, the tenured faculty member may have to assemble evidence for a post-tenure review committee in a fashion similar to when he or she first applied for tenure.

Suppose, for example, that the post-tenure review process requires an evaluation once every five years. Further, suppose that a tenured faculty member's performance has been at acceptably high levels for four of those years but on the fifth year he or she experiences problems. Perhaps a death in the family, a divorce, or an accident affects professional performance. The post-tenure review finds an unacceptable level of professional performance in that fifth year and triggers the entire focused development and round of subsequent evaluations pursuant to the possibility of termination. The faculty member is now in the position of trying to reconstruct his or her positive performance for the previous four years. If, however, the tenured faculty member had participated continuously in the faculty evaluation process, he or she would have considerable evidence as to the pattern of performance over time similar to that shown in Figure 10.3. Thus, the poor performance in the fifth year may be more accurately seen as an aberration rather than an indication that the faculty member's performance has sunk to an unacceptably low level. If, however, the pattern of performance over time of the tenured faculty member shows a significant and consistent decline in professional performance similar to that in Figure 10.4, appropriate termination procedures may be initiated on this firm evidence. More importantly, however, continuous participation in the faculty evaluation process provides an early indication to the tenured faculty member that he or she may need to engage in faculty development before performance sinks to an unacceptable level.

In short, from a faculty evaluation system perspective, it is recommended that all faculty, tenured and non-tenured, participate in the annual evaluation process. The data for nontenured faculty may be used for promotion, tenure, and merit pay decisions as specified earlier. The data for tenured faculty should be maintained by the faculty member to monitor his or her own performance and provide an early warning system for a potential serious decline in performance. These data may be made available for presentation at five- or seven-year intervals to provide evidence that the level of professional performance has not declined to an unacceptable level. In addition, continuous participation in the faculty evaluation process would provide normative data on the performance level of tenured faculty for use in program evaluations, legislative or board inquiries, and/or accreditation reviews.

In summary, the use of both OCR graphing techniques and appropriate promotion, tenure (continuation), and post-tenure review decision policies moves us further in the direction of consistency in the faculty evaluation process. Using this approach, no single person makes the tenure decision. Here the decision-making rationale of the administration has been codified in terms of policy statements and it is clear what conditions must be met before tenure may be granted. The same holds true for the promotion decisions described previously. Post-tenure review becomes a matter of periodically checking the pattern of performance over time records of tenured faculty as part of the enhanced evaluation procedure often prescribed by post-tenure review policies. It must be emphasized that these procedures do not restrict, or in any way limit, the decision-making authority of the administration. The values and decision-making rules used are simply built into the procedure for using the faculty evaluation data rather than being left to the subjective interpretation of the individual administrator or review committee.

PAY RAISE CALCULATIONS

General Concerns. This section does not address cost-of-living pay raises or raises associated with market or equity adjustments. Rather, the focus is on merit raises and the growing practice of performance-based pay raises. A merit pay raise is defined here as a raise in base pay given solely on the basis of, and in proportion to, evidence of meritorious performance. A merit raise, to be a true merit raise, must be given in addition to, rather than in place of, a cost-of-living raise.

In contrast to a merit pay raise, a performance-based pay raise is a raise granted upon the demonstration that the faculty member has achieved a certain level of performance and is thus eligible to receive the pay scale associated with that level. In certain respects, standard pay raises given for promotion in rank, in addition to cost of living or merit raises, are a form of performance-based pay raises. In performance pay models, the levels of performance are usually defined in terms of specific accomplishments or the demonstration of certain skills and competencies.

The development of a comprehensive faculty evaluation system that results in an annual Overall Composite Rating (OCR) for every faculty member significantly simplifies the process of determining both merit and performance-based pay raises. However, before proceeding with a discussion of the use of the OCR in determining merit pay raises, it is useful to consider the purpose of merit pay and the practices used in its distribution.

True merit pay raises are intended to perform essentially two functions: reward past meritorious performance and encourage future meritorious performance. In actual practice, merit pay raises rarely successfully serve either of these two purposes. Sufficient funds are rarely available to provide substantial enough raises that would make the recipients feel truly rewarded solely on the basis of money. Also, since the merit pay raise is usually simply added to the monthly paycheck, the effect is diluted even further. As a complicating factor, merit raises are often given as a percentage of existing salary. This means the rich get richer and the merit raise becomes a lifetime-compounding reward for a one-time performance. These factors contribute to a generally negative feeling about the use of merit raises. Therefore, in the absence of significant amounts of money available for merit raises, we must concern ourselves with more effective strategies for the distribution of the money that is available in order to meet these desired purposes.

First, in order to meet the purpose of encouraging future meritorious performance, merit raises should be given as a one-time bonus rather than as a permanent addition to base pay. These bonuses should be specific dollar amounts rather than a percentage of existing salary. Systems that compute pay raises on the basis of existing salary are almost always seen as unfair by younger and/or lower paid faculty who may be performing as well or better than senior, better paid faculty. They can also be seen as unfair by senior faculty when, owing to market conditions, new entering faculty start out with salaries the same or greater than the senior faculty.

Second, the merit pay raise bonus should be distributed in a lump sum, preferably as part of some celebratory function. A pay raise of $1,200 spread over 12 months, when adjusted by taxes and other deductions, may amount to an increase of $70 in take-home pay each month—not much to celebrate about. But a check for $850 (taxes and other deductions prepaid) given as part of an awards dinner along with a plaque and a round of applause from peers has a greater chance of achieving the purpose of giving the faculty member a sense of appreciation and reward.

Merit Pay Raises. The examples that follow assume that the amount of merit money available in the merit raise pool has been determined in the customary fashion for a given institution. State-supported institutions may have their pay raise pool determined by state legislators, while private institutions may have their pay raise pool determined by their board of governors. In any case, it is assumed that a pay raise pool of funds is available for distribution on the basis of demonstrated merit.

In computing the merit pay raise for a faculty member based on evidence provided by the faculty evaluation system, it is important to make the merit raise a direct function of the faculty member's OCR. The first step in this process is to compute what can be called the Merit Unit Amount (MUA). The MUA will then serve as the basis for the final determination of a merit raise. Computation of the MUA assumes that:

1. The academic unit within which all meritorious faculty will receive a merit raise has been determined. The academic unit may be a department, division, college, or an entire university.

2. A pool of merit raise money has been made available by whatever process is customary at the institution.

3. A specified OCR value has been set which defines the eligibility of faculty for merit raises.

4. A specific decision regarding the model of merit raise money distribution has been established. Merit pay distribution models include the following:

   • *Large Distribution Range:* There should be a large range in merit pay raises among faculty in proportion to their OCR values. Faculty who attain the highest meritorious levels are to be rewarded to a significantly greater degree than those who just make it into the meritorious category.

   • *Moderate Distribution Range:* There should be moderate range in merit pay raises among faculty in proportion to their OCR values with a moderate difference between faculty who attain the highest meritorious level and those who just make it into the meritorious category.

   • *Intact Group Distribution:* Meritorious levels are established based on different OCR ranges and everyone within a given level receives the same merit raise. Under this approach faculty are placed in groups defined by a preset range of OCR values and all faculty within the same group receive the same merit raise.

The following examples demonstrate the use of the OCR in computing the merit raise amounts to be distributed to eligible faculty under the different distribution models described in above. In each case, it is also assumed that the faculty evaluation system has used the same common 1 to 4 rating scale that has been used in the examples throughout this book.

Large Distribution Range

Under this approach, the merit unit amount would be computed as follows:

$$MUA = \frac{\text{Total funds available in merit raise pool*}}{\text{Grand total of the excess OCRs of eligible faculty}}$$

* The academic unit may be a department, division, or entire college.

Example: Assume that a policy has been established which states that only faculty members who achieve an OCR greater than 3.00 on our 4-point scale are eligible for a merit raise. With our definition of merit raises, such raises are given in addition to any cost-of-living or across-the-board raises. Further, assume that our academic unit is a department with 10 faculty members and $10,000 has been made available for its merit raise pool. The faculty in this department, with their various different assignments, have achieved the following OCRs for the year just completed:

Name	OCR	Name	OCR
Prof. Cole	4.00	Prof. Lamb	3.35
Prof. Drake	3.34	Prof. Phillips	3.96
Prof. Fox	2.45	Prof. Smith	2.99
Prof. Greer	2.89	Prof. Thomas	3.77
Prof. Jones	3.01	Prof. Woods	3.63

As can be seen, Professors Fox, Greer, and Smith do not qualify for merit raises this year, because their OCRs are less than 3.00. The first step under this option is to compute how much the seven remaining eligible faculty members exceeded the minimum OCR cutoff for merit raise eligibility. This is computed by simply subtracting the OCR cutoff value of 3.0 from each faculty member's individual OCR:

Name	OCR		Cutoff		OCR Excess
Prof. Cole	4.00	–	3.00	=	1.00
Prof. Drake	3.34	–	3.00	=	.34
Prof. Jones	3.01	–	3.00	=	.01
Prof. Lamb	3.35	–	3.00	=	.35
Prof. Phillips	3.96	–	3.00	=	.96
Prof. Thomas	3.77	–	3.00	=	.77
Prof. Woods	3.63	–	3.00	=	.63
Total OCRs in excess of			3.00	=	4.06

The merit unit amount for this department is then computed as

$$MUA = \frac{\$10,000}{4.06} = \$2,463$$

The merit raise for each faculty member is then computed by multiplying the OCR excess by the MUA as follows:

Name	OCR Excess		MUA		Merit Raise
Prof. Cole	1.00	×	$2,463.00	=	$2,463.00
Prof. Drake	.34	×	$2,463.00	=	$837.42
Prof. Jones	.01	×	$2,463.00	=	$24.63
Prof. Lamb	.35	×	$2,463.00	=	$862.05
Prof. Phillips	.96	×	$2,463.00	=	$2,364.48
Prof. Thomas	.77	×	$2,463.00	=	$1,896.51
Prof. Woods	.63	×	$2,463.00	=	$1,551.69

Note the large difference between the merit raises of Professor Jones, who barely makes it into the meritorious category, and of Professor Cole, who is at the top of the meritorious category.

Moderate Distribution Range

This approach takes the position that those who barely make it into the meritorious range are still meritorious and should receive more than token merit raises. With this approach, the merit unit amount is computed as follows:

$$MUA = \frac{\text{Total funds available in merit raise pool*}}{\text{Grand total of OCRs of eligible faculty}}$$

* The academic unit may be a department, division, or entire college.

Example: In this situation, as before, assume that only faculty who achieve an OCR greater than 3.00 on our 4-point scale are eligible for a merit raise. Further, assume that our academic unit is a department which has been given $10,000 for its merit raise pool.

Once again the faculty in this department, with their various different assignments, have achieved the following OCRs for the year just completed:

Name	OCR	Name	OCR
Prof. Cole	4.00	Prof. Lamb	3.35
Prof. Drake	3.34	Prof. Phillips	3.96
Prof. Fox	2.45	Prof. Smith	2.99
Prof. Greer	2.89	Prof. Thomas	3.77
Prof. Jones	3.01	Prof. Woods	3.63

As before, Professors Fox, Greer, and Smith do not qualify for merit raises this year because their OCRs are equal to or less than 3.00. Under this option, we simply add up all the OCRs for the eligible faculty and divide that total into the raise pool to compute our MUA:

Name	OCR
Prof. Cole	4.00
Prof. Drake	3.34
Prof. Jones	3.01
Prof. Lamb	3.35
Prof. Phillips	3.96
Prof. Thomas	3.77
Prof. Woods	3.63
Total OCR	25.06

Under this option, the MUA is computed as:

$$\text{MUA} = \frac{\$10,000}{25.06} = \$399.04$$

Computing the individual merit raises then becomes a simple matter of multiplying each faculty member's OCR by the MUA for the department. The resulting merit pay raises, which are now computed as a direct function of the faculty member's OCR, are

Name	OCR		MUA		Merit Raise
Prof. Cole	4.00	×	$399.04	=	$1,596.16
Prof. Drake	3.34	×	$399.04	=	$1,332.79
Prof. Jones	3.01	×	$399.04	=	$1,201.11
Prof. Lamb	3.35	×	$399.04	=	$1,336.78
Prof. Phillips	3.96	×	$399.04	=	$1,580.20
Prof. Thomas	3.77	×	$399.04	=	$1,504.38
Prof. Woods	3.63	×	$399.04	=	$1,448.52

Under this option, there is less variability among raises. Professor Jones receives a merit raise of $1,201.11 for an OCR of 3.01, whereas in the large distribution range option the computed merit raise was only $24.63. Which approach you choose depends upon the particular value system of your institution.

Intact Group Distribution

Another approach is to place the eligible faculty into intact groups based on specific OCR ranges and give the same raise to everyone within the group. Although this approach sounds simple, it is mathematically a little more complex than the previous distribution models. The following are the steps for computing the merit raise amount for blocks or groups of meritorious faculty:

- Decide how many meritorious levels or groups you wish to have.

- Decide the values of the OCR cutoffs for each meritorious level.

- Divide your meritorious faculty into groups based on the cutoffs established and count the number of people in each group. Label the lowest group (the baseline group) as Group 1, the next higher group as Group 2, and so on up to the highest group.

- Using the lowest group as the baseline group, decide how much more (on a percentage basis) the faculty in Group 2 will receive over those in Group 1 (the baseline group); decide how much more (on a percentage basis) Group 3 will receive over those in the baseline group, and so on.

- Use the following general formula to compute the MUA:

$$MUA = \frac{\text{Total Money Available in Merit Raise Pool}}{[G_1 + G_2(1+P_1) + \cdots + G_i(1 + P_{i-1}) + G_N(1+P_{i-N})]}$$

Where: N = the total number of groups

i = 1, 2, 3, ... , N

G_i = the number of faculty in a given group

P_{i-1} = the percentage increase over the first group a given group is to receive. This value must be expressed in its decimal equivalent.

P_0 = 0.0. By definition.

- Compute the merit raises for the faculty in each group. The general formula for computing the merit raise amount (MRA) for a given group is:

MRA for Group i = MUA $(1.00 + P_{i-1})$

Where: i = 1 to N and P_0 is defined as being equal to zero (0.0).

Example: Let's assume once again that we have $10,000 in our merit raise pool and that we have divided our faculty into three groups with the cutoffs for Group 1 being OCR values ranging from 3.01 to 3.50 and the cutoffs for Group 2 are 3.51 to 3.80. All faculty with OCR values higher than 3.80 fall into Group 3. The cutoff points may be subjectively determined using the natural breaks method often used to set cutoff points for different grades or by setting fixed ranges independent of the distribution of OCR values received.

Prof. Jones	3.01	
Prof. Drake	3.34	Group 1
Prof. Lamb	3.35	
Prof. Woods	3.63	Group 2
Prof. Thomas	3.77	
Prof. Phillips	3.96	Group 3
Prof. Cole	4.00	

Group 1 (the baseline group) contains three faculty, Group 2 contains two, and Group 3 contains two. Further assume that we have decided that faculty in Group 2 will receive 50% more than those in the baseline group (Group 1), and faculty in Group 3 will receive 75% more than those in the baseline group (Group 1). As with the cutoff points for the groups, these percentage increases are subjectively determined.

Thus, in terms of our formula for the MUA

N = 3 (number of groups)

G_1 = 3 (number of faculty in Group 1)

G_2 = 2 (number of faculty in Group 2)

G_3 = 2 (number of faculty in Group 3)

P_0 = 0.0 (by definition)

P_1 = 0.50 (faculty in Group 2 will get 50% more)

P_2 = 0.75 (faculty in Group 3 will get 75% more)

Then, computing

$$MUA = \frac{\text{Total Money Available in Merit Raise Pool}}{[G_1 + G_2(1 + P_1) + \cdots + G_i(1+P_{i-1}) + G_N(1+P_{i-N})]}$$

$$MUA = \frac{\$10,000}{[3 + 2(1.50) + 2(1.75)]}$$

MUA = $1,052.63

Using the formula MRA = MUA $\times$ $(1 + P_{i-1})$, we compute the merit raises for each group as follows:

Group 1: MRA = $1,052.63 $\times$ $(1 + 0.0) = $1,052.63

Group 2: MRA = $1,052.63 $\times$ $(1 + .50) = $1,578.95

Group 3: MRA = $1,052.63 $\times$ $(1 + .75) = $1,842.10

Thus, the three faculty in Group 1 would each receive a merit raise of $1,053.63, the two in Group 2 would each receive $1,578.95, and the two in Group 3 would each receive $1,842, for a grand total of $9,999.99 or $10,000.

			Merit Raise
Prof. Jones	3.01		$1,052.63
Prof. Drake	3.34	Group 1	$1,052.63
Prof. Lamb	3.35		$1,052.63
Prof. Woods	3.63	Group 2	$1,578.95
Prof. Thomas	3.77		$1,578.95
Prof. Phillips	3.96	Group 3	$1,842.10
Prof. Cole	4.00		$1,842.10
TOTAL			$9,999.99

Performance Based Pay Raises. Institutions may determine any number of performance levels, although they generally they tend to range from three to nine levels, with a different pay increment associated with the achievement of each level. To be faithful to the principle behind performance-based pay, faculty should be able to move up or down the levels in accordance to their performance with appropriate adjustments in pay. In other words placement in a level is not permanent but, rather, contingent upon the continued demonstration of the required level of performance.

By policy, different levels of performance could be established on the basis of the average OCR range for a specific length of time. Below, the performance-based pay levels are defined both in terms of the average OCR achieved by the faculty member and the length of time employed.

Level 1 = Average OCR 2.0–4.0
(during first three years of employment)

Level 2 = Average OCR range of 2.5–2.9
(after at least 3 years of employment)

Level 3 = Average OCR range of 3.0–3.5
(after at least 4 years of employment)

Level 4 = Average OCR range of 3.6–4.0
(after at least 5 years of employment)

Thus, faculty in their first three years of employment may only be placed in Level 1, assuming they are performing in such a way to achieve an average OCR of 2.0 or greater on a 4-point scale. Faculty may achieve Level 2 after they have been employed three or more years, Level 3 after four or more years, and Level 4 after five or more years assuming their average OCR falls within the specified range.

The base pay level should be established as a specific dollar amount. For example,

Level 1 = $35,000 per year

Level 2 = $40,000 per year

Level 3 = $47,500 per year

Level 4 = $55,000 per year

Thus, someone moving from Level 2 to Level 3 would receive an increase of $7,500. Conversely, someone moving from Level 4 back to Level 3 would return to Level 3 base pay. Of course, the OCR average ranges and the length of employment requirements used in this example are arbitrary and are only meant to demonstrate the application.

SUMMARY

Note that in each of the examples given in this chapter, no single administrator or decision-maker determined, in isolation, whether to promote, tenure, or grant a specific merit raise to any given individual. Each decision was arrived at by the application of policies based on the performance of the individual as reflected by the OCR. To be sure, the use of the OCR in making personnel decisions does not eliminate the ability of an administrator or administration to be arbitrary. Arbitrary decisions such as setting of cutoff values, determining the merit raise pool amounts to be given to any particular department, and similar decisions may a still need to be made. What the OCR and its application does constrain is capriciousness—that is, the inconsistent application of agreed-upon criteria, standards, and procedures in making personnel decisions. In this way, the faculty may have greater confidence in the fairness of the personnel decision-making mechanism. Conversely, although the use of the OCR in making personnel decisions does not eliminate faculty complaints and grievances, it does tend to protect the administration from unwarranted charges of prejudice, bias, and unfairness in making personnel decisions.

CHAPTER REFERENCES

AAUP. (1998). *Post-tenure review: An AAUP response.* Washington, DC: American Association of University Professors.

Banks, R. F. (1997). *Post-tenure review: A summary of other comparable university policies.* East Lansing, MI: Michigan State University.

11

Operating the Faculty Evaluation System: Peer Review Issues

In many faculty evaluation systems, peer review or peer evaluation plays an important political, if not psychometric, role. Although the idea of peer review is appealing to many faculty, peer review systems are touchy and complicated at the very least. In actual practice, peer review components of faculty evaluation systems provide one of the biggest sources of problems and confusion.

The first step in developing a peer evaluation system should always be the careful review and consideration of the purpose of the system, proposed methods of implementing the system, and the expected outcomes. Distinctions should be made especially between the use of peer evaluation for formative (improvement) versus summative (judgmental) purposes. Although a system may be adequate for formative development of faculty, it may not fulfill administrative needs or legal requirements for summative purposes. Ideally, this first step is tempered by the study of reports of existing systems and the research literature on peer evaluation. Systems that are developed hastily are seldom adequate or effective.

What Should Peers Evaluate?

The first consideration in developing a peer evaluation system should involve the definition of what should be evaluated by peers. Typically, three broad components of faculty activity are defined: teaching, research, and service. Within each of these components, however, numerous activities of the faculty member are potentially available for inclusion in the evaluation process. It is especially important to realize that the ultimate validity of a peer system rests directly on what faculty activities are chosen for re-

view by peers. That is, peers may be excellent judges of certain activities but very poor judges of other activities. Therefore, the development of a good peer evaluation system requires that careful consideration be given to those activities or elements that are to be judged by peers, by students, and so on. For example, most experts agree (Aleamoni, 1982; Centra, 1979, 1999; Cohen & McKeachie, 1980) that peer observation data should not be used or at least should not weigh very heavily in a faculty evaluation system. A more cost-efficient and reliable use of peer judgments of teaching effectiveness would be in reviewing written documentation (e.g., instructional plans, course materials and examinations, instructional methods). Therefore, an important initial step in developing a peer evaluation system is the complete specification of the faculty activities to be reviewed by peers. This specification process is not unlike creating instructional objectives for teaching a course or the specification process that occurs in designing and reporting an experiment. For the purposes of reliability, and to conform with various legal decisions, this specification process should result in an explicit, written protocol that defines exactly what activities are to be reviewed by peers and what weights are assigned to each activity reviewed (i.e., some faculty activities may be deemed more important than others).

How Should Peer Input Be Gathered?

A second consideration involves how peer judgments are to be elicited, categorized, and summarized. Several methods of peer evaluation have been used, including surveys and questionnaires, rating and ranking systems, and open-ended written questions and comments. In designing methods for a peer evaluation system, the developer should be concerned primarily with the objectivity and reliability of the method chosen. That is, the particular method chosen is much less important than the development of procedures that will ensure impartial, less subjective, and reliable peer judgments. This process is facilitated to the extent that written documentation is submitted for peer review. For example, peer review of written course materials (e.g., course syllabus, course outline, texts and reading assignments, handouts, homework) is more likely to result in less subjective and more reliable peer judgments of teaching effectiveness than peer responses to a general attitude or opinion survey.

The research literature is quite consistent in reporting a strong positive bias in any peer evaluation system. The peer system must, therefore, be designed to ensure the reliable differentiation of different levels of faculty performance. This process is aided by explicitly defining criteria for evaluation and by establishing minimum standards for each criterion. For example, peer review of the adequacy of an instructor's course materials might focus on several criteria for judgment: comprehensiveness, organization, relation to course and learning objectives, currency, and so on. Ideally, each criterion must be defined explicitly and accompanied by a minimum standard of performance. For example, the currency of course materials might be accompanied by a standard requiring that at least 20% of course content is based on recent developments (last five years, perhaps) in the field. See Chism (1999) for examples of structured peer review procedures as well as suggested tools or instruments.

Figure 11.1 Examples from Two Peer Review Documents That Do Not Allow for Consistent and Accurate Judgments

Example 1

1. Course Materials	Comments	Overall Rating
A. Clarity		
B. Consistency		
C. Coverage		Low 1 2 3 4 5 High
D. Currency		
E. Depth		

Example 2

1. What is the quality of materials used in teaching?

SUGGESTED FOCUS IN EXAMINING COURSE INFORMATION

Are the materials current? Do they represent the best work in the field? Are they adequate and appropriate to course goals? Do they represent superficial or thorough coverage of course content?

Peer Reviewer's Rating   Low___/___/___/___/___/___/___ Very High

Arreola, R. A. (2000). Developing *a Comprehensive Faculty Evaluation System 2/e*. Bolton, MA: Anker Publishing Co., Inc.

Care must also be exercised in designing peer evaluation systems to ensure that peer judgments are not influenced or confounded by irrelevant factors. A common difficulty in many instruments used for peer evaluation is the inadequacy of the response or rating scales. To reduce these difficulties, descriptions used to label points on a response scale should be relevant for the item and should define each point on the scale. Such scales should always be accompanied by explicit instructions and, whenever possible, the minimum standard for each scale point.

Two examples of peer review documents that are unlikely to produce consistent and accurate judgments are presented in Figure 11.1.

Several difficulties may arise with an instrument like that presented as Example 1. First, no standards are provided to allow the reviewers to judge the degrees of, for example, clarity and consistency relative to departmental requirements. Additionally, without explicit definitions of these criteria, reviewers may not agree in their interpretation of the criteria. The overall rating scale is also not well defined. The labels are only marginally relevant to several of the criteria. Furthermore, the interior points of the scale are not labeled. This allows the possibility of divergent definitions of these points by different respondents.

The potential for difficulties in Example 2 as shown in Figure 11.1 is similar to that in Example 1. In both of these examples, it is left to the whim of the reviewer to determine what standards to use in making a qualitative judgment. Such poorly developed systems may therefore result in judgments that are based on questionable or irrelevant information. For example, Centra (1979) reports a study in which peer ratings of teaching effectiveness were related to office location! Such approaches to peer evaluation may result in little more than popularity ratings.

WHO ARE PEERS?

A third major consideration in developing peer evaluation systems involves those included in the peer judgment process. Some peer evaluation systems include all members of a department in the judgment process. In such a system, each faculty member would evaluate all other departmental faculty. This approach is very expensive in time expended. Furthermore, such approaches are often less reliable and less effective than alternative approaches. For example, Centra (1975) reported an average correlation of only +0.26 among ratings of faculty by all peers in a department. Additionally, many peer evaluation systems attempt to guard against several potential problems of peer review by selecting smaller numbers of peer judges. For example, several systems attempt to avoid problems arising from direct competition for promotion and tenure by using only tenured faculty in the peer review process. For the purposes of obtaining reliable measurement, a minimum of three peers is necessary. It also appears from the research literature that the use of more than six peer evaluators does not improve the quality of evaluation and may, in some cases, be a detriment to valid and reliable measurement.

A second issue in considering who conducts the evaluation relates to whether reviewers should be anonymous. As with student ratings of faculty, anonymity is more likely to produce candid and meaningful peer evaluation. In fact, if peer evaluation is not anonymous, the positive bias of peers may result in undifferentiated, high evaluations of faculty.

Many different methods have been used to select peer evaluators. Several systems have used departmental standing committees for peer evaluation and others have formed committees by general departmental election. Neither approach safeguards against problems of committee composition (positive or negative bias, etc.). Several systems that do provide some safeguards for composition include procedures for the selection of peers by the faculty member and also by the dean or department head.

PEER REVIEW AND EVALUATION COMMITTEES

Generally, peer review components of faculty evaluation systems involve a committee, sometimes made up of all the tenured faculty, all the senior faculty, or some like combination. The function of such a peer committee is to review all the evidence (e.g., student rating form printouts, letters of recommendation, other peer or colleague comments, and articles published) and make a decision or recommendation to the administration. When there are a number of faculty submitting their materials for review at the same time, the task can be daunting. In addition, such committees can often bring subjective impressions, friendships, and hostilities into the decision-making process. Such an approach also has the unfortunate side effect of giving second-hand information or hearsay evidence much greater impact than should be the case. Committee members may bring to the deliberations positive or negative opinions concerning the faculty member's teaching performance based on random or limited student comments. This approach may be considered as a traditional hierarchical peer review model (Figure 11.2).

Figure 11.2 Traditional Hierarchical Peer Review Model

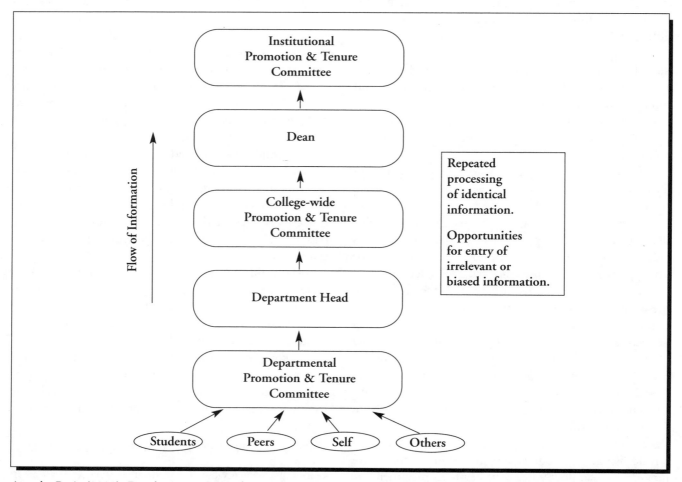

Arreola, R. A. (2000). Developing *a Comprehensive Faculty Evaluation System 2/e.* Bolton, MA: Anker Publishing Co., Inc.

Note that in the traditional hierarchical peer review model, there is repeated processing of the same material. That is, the peer committees, the department head, and the dean all have the opportunity to examine all of the information available in the faculty member's file. This information may include student ratings; peer or colleague reports concerning research, teaching, or college service; self-reports; and reports of others such as alumni, employers of graduating students, and so on. With the traditional hierarchical peer review model, opportunities exist at each level for the entry of new or anecdotal information that may or may not be relevant to the decision being made. Such information may have the effect of biasing the recommendations made at each level. In these situations, it is possible for a faculty member to be recommended positively at each level for promotion, tenure, or some other personnel action, yet be turned down at the highest level. The converse is also possible, although less frequent. This result is possible in the traditional hierarchical peer review model because different value systems may be applied to the evaluation of the data provided. What a peer review committee or administrator at one level finds good and valuable performance, a peer review committee or an administrator at another level may find to be of little or no value.

If the value structure of the institution has been determined and carefully integrated into the construction of the faculty evaluation system as specified in earlier chapters, peer review can assume a much more consistent and valuable role. In a faculty evaluation system where 1) the values assigned to teaching, research, and service by the department, college, and university have been determined and specified; 2) the value or weight to be placed on the information provided by the sources has been agreed to;

Figure 11.3 Lateral Peer Review Model

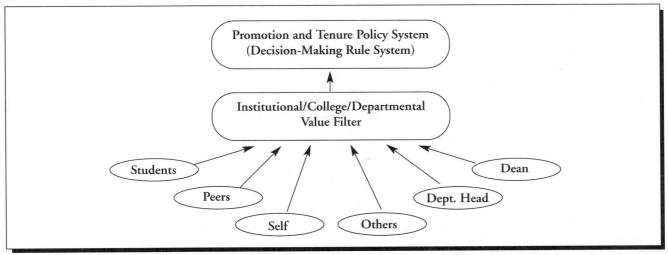

Arreola, R. A. (2000). Developing *a Comprehensive Faculty Evaluation System 2/e.* Bolton, MA: Anker Publishing Co., Inc.

and 3) the performance levels which qualify for promotion, tenure, continuation, or merit pay have all been determined and placed into policy statements, an alternate and potentially much fairer peer review model becomes possible (Figure 11.3).

In this model, the peer review committee that examines all the information for all faculty and then forwards it to the next level administrator is replaced by what may be called the institutional/college/departmental value filter. That is, as noted in earlier chapters, all constituencies to the faculty evaluation system—students, peers, self, department head, dean, and others—have been identified and the appropriate information gathered from each. That information has been weighted in accordance with the consensus value structure of the institution and combined with all other information to form the overall evaluation. This process of gathering, weighting, and combining information can be thought of as the application of the value filters for the department, college, and entire institution. The outcome of such a process may then be interpreted through the previously determined set of policies governing promotion, tenure, and so on. These policies form the decision-making rule system for the institution. Notice that with this approach the power and authority of the administration is neither diminished nor diluted. Rather, the decision-making rule system followed by the administration is simply codified in advance so everyone knows what it is. This approach does not keep administrators from being arbitrary. However, it does constrain them from being capricious. The administra-

tion may still arbitrarily determine procedures, criteria, and standards by which faculty performance will be judged. However, this approach constrains the administration to apply these procedures, criteria, and standards consistently to all faculty because the decision-making rule system is codified and built into the evaluation system. In this model, the peers are represented by a peer review committee or several peer review committees using the triad peer review committee structure described later.

Earlier in this handbook, we noted that faculty evaluation requires the careful combination of both political and psychometric requirements. Therefore, it should be recognized that, for political reasons, it may be necessary to have a peer review oversight committee somewhere in the faculty evaluation system. Figure 11.4 shows an alternate lateral peer review model which accommodates this requirement.

In this variation, it is recommended that the peer review oversight committee limit its work to simply ensuring that due process has been followed in gathering and assembling the information from the various sources and that the appropriate value filter has been correctly applied to the data. If the oversight peer review committee concerns itself with reevaluating all the data provided by the various sources, we are once again faced with the possibility of the entry of irrelevant or biasing information into the decision-making process. However, this possibility is somewhat less than in the traditional hierarchical peer review model (Figure 11.2). If a strong need is felt to have an oversight peer review committee, two questions must be

Figure 11.4 Alternate Lateral Peer Review Model

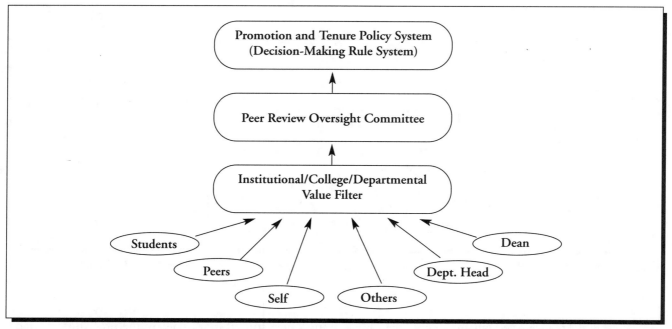

Arreola, R. A. (2000). Developing *a Comprehensive Faculty Evaluation System 2/e.* Bolton, MA: Anker Publishing Co., Inc.

asked: What information is the committee going to consider that has not been considered earlier by someone closer to the source of information? What criteria for judging the information is the oversight peer review committee going to apply that have not been applied to the data earlier? If some new criteria, values, or information need to be considered by the oversight peer review committee, then those criteria, values, and information requirements should be built into the system at an earlier level.

The primary need for an oversight peer review committee generally grows out of the situation where the values and criteria for evaluating faculty performance at the departmental or college level differ markedly from that at the institutional or university-wide level. If the process for developing a comprehensive faculty evaluation system described in earlier chapters has been followed, such differences should have already been resolved and the need for an oversight peer review committee obviated.

PEER REVIEW: THE BEST SOURCE PRINCIPLE

In practice, peer input should be provided as simply one of several sources of information in a comprehensive faculty evaluation system. A peer review component of a faculty evaluation system should limit itself to using colleagues or peers to provide information which requires a professional perspective or for which peers are the primary, best source of information. If peer input is to be gathered concerning a faculty member's classroom teaching performance, then the faculty evaluation system should specify a classroom visitation policy or procedure. Guidelines must be developed which clearly specify what behavior or performance is to be observed and rated. Ideally, a training program should be set up to prepare faculty peers to be accurate and reliable observers.

Practical experience leads one to suggest that faculty peer evaluation restricts itself to those areas of professional performance requiring knowledge of the content field of the faculty member: for example, assessing the correctness and completeness of the content in a given course or judging the contribution a given article makes to the literature in the faculty member's content field. In any case, the principle recommended concerning peer evaluation is to gather only that information from faculty peers for which they are the primary or best source. Peer evaluation systems which ask a peer committee to review the ratings of students or other such evaluative information and come forth with another, singular evaluation based on their deliberations tend to create more problems than they solve.

Figure 11.5 Triad Peer Review Committee Model

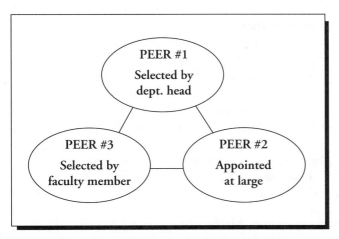

Arreola, R. A. (2000). Developing *a Comprehensive Faculty Evaluation System 2/e*. Bolton, MA: Anker Publishing Co., Inc.

Peer Review: The Triad Model

If separate peer review committees are required and tasked with making such summary judgments, a good form to follow is the three-member, or triad, peer committee structure (Figure 11.5). In the triad peer review committee model, a three-person committee is appointed for every faculty member. One member of the committee is selected by the department head, one member is selected from a group of peers recommended by the faculty member being evaluated, and one member is appointed from the faculty at large, perhaps by the dean. In this way, no one faculty member will have to sit on more than three peer review committees, and each committee will concern itself with only one faculty member.

Under this triad approach, the third member appointed from the faculty at large does not necessarily have to be from the same content field as the person being evaluated. The primary function of the at-large third member is to ensure that proper deliberative process, prescribed by the faculty evaluation system, is followed. It is assumed that the other two members will adequately represent the perspective of professionals from the content field. Also, because the faculty member being evaluated will have one person on the committee that he or she nominated, it is unlikely that any negative biases on the part of the other two members will unduly affect the outcome of the committee's deliberations. Likewise, any unwarranted positive biases by the two content peers will be offset by the assumed neutrality of the at-large member.

Because the triad peer review committee concerns itself with only one faculty member, it is much easier to assign it more detailed and evaluatively relevant tasks. Such tasks may include in-depth assessment of course design, course materials, examinations, published articles, professional development, or any of a host of other activities and roles which only peers may be best qualified to judge. Separate triad peer review committees may be assigned to provide evaluative information on different aspects of a faculty member's performance. For example, one triad committee may provide information concerning the instructional design of the courses being taught. Another committee may provide information concerning the faculty member's research performance, and yet another on the college or community service provided by the faculty member. In any case, the operational principles to be followed here are that 1) each triad committee considers the performance of only one individual, and 2) the triad committee members be selected on the basis of the best source principle noted earlier.

Peer Observation of Classroom Performance

For a variety of political reasons peer observation of classroom teaching performance is becoming a more frequent part of the faculty evaluation landscape. From a measurement perspective, valid and reliable peer observation data are costly to obtain. As noted earlier, researchers in the field of faculty evaluation generally do not recommend that peer observation data be used in summative faculty evaluation (Aleamoni, 1982; Centra, 1979; Cohen & McKeachie, 1980). Further, Centra (1999, p. 117), notes that it would be a mistake to design peer evaluation procedures to rely heavily on classroom observations. Although peer observation of classroom performance may provide useful data for self-improvement purposes, such data should play little or no part in a summative faculty evaluation on which personnel decisions (promotion, tenure, etc.) may be based.

However, since many institutions require peer observation data as part of the information provided by a faculty evaluation system, it is important to at least consider the basics. If classroom observations of teaching performance are to be undertaken, we must consider them to be simply another measure of teaching and thus be concerned with the reliability and validity of the data being produced.

One of the issues of the measurement of complex behavior is that of sampling. That is, how can we be sure that the "slice" of teaching that has been observed is truly representative? Another issue revolves around the old scientific principle that one cannot measure a phenomenon without affecting the phenomenon itself. Thus we must be concerned with what effect the actual observation has on the performance being observed.

The following suggestions address the issues cited above as well as other practical matters related to observing classroom performance for the purpose of gathering data that may impact personnel decisions.

Develop or Adopt a Valid, Reliable Observational Checklist

Any two people observing a performance may not see the same thing if their attention is not focused on the specific performance elements of interest. Therefore, it is necessary to design and construct an observational checklist based on agreed-upon performances to be observed. The checklist should undergo standard reliability and validity studies to ensure that the resulting data are valid and reliable. One of the more popular processes for coding teacher behaviors is the Flanders Interaction Analysis System. Another is the Cognitive Interaction Analysis System, which is described in Chism (1999) with appropriate forms.

Assemble Peer Observer Team

In order to obtain inter-rater reliabilities and thus ensure the overall reliability of the data from classroom observations, it is necessary to have at least three, and preferably four, members on a peer review team. The team may not necessarily be composed of content peers if the behaviors to be observed are content-independent.

Train Peer Observer Team

To further ensure the reliability of the peer observation data, the observers must be trained in the use of the observational checklist. Training the observers increases the probability that their observations will be valid and consistent.

Schedule Multiple Visits

As noted earlier, we must make certain of a sufficient sampling of the behavior or performances in question. To do this it is important to schedule at least 8 to 10 visits to the class by the peer observation team. It is recommended that the entire team not attend class at the same time.

Prepare the Students

Since having a team of peer observers in the classroom is likely to significantly alter the learning environment, it is important to prepare and desensitize the students to the presence of the observation team. The class should be prepared for the visitations by having the instructor explain the purpose of the team's visits. Each member of the team should be introduced to the class and students should be allowed to ask questions of the team members. It is important that each team member visit the class two or three times before undertaking the actual observations so that the students become accustomed to having him or her in the room. In this way, once the real observations begin to take place, the performance being observed and the students' reactions to it will have a greater probability of being representative of the instructor's teaching performance.

Prepare the Instructor

Millis (1992) recommends a pre-visit conference between the observers and the instructor. During a pre-visit conference, the two parties should review the instrument the observers will use so as to familiarize the instructor with the issues of importance. The instructor should communicate to the observers any teaching strategies or issues he or she considers important. In addition, an agreement should be reached with the observers as to what role student input will play in the observation.

It is generally not recommended that members of the observation team ask questions or otherwise participate in the classroom activities, even if the instructor invites them to do so. Any activity by the visitors other than observing further serves to affect the learning environment, thus increasing the likelihood that the performance being observed is not truly representative of normal classroom activity.

Schedule a Post-Observation Conference

Once all the observation visits have been completed it is recommended that a conference be held with the instructor to review the overall conclusions of the team. It is recommended that the feedback be honest, accurate, focused, concrete, positively phrased, and action-oriented so as to facilitate individual faculty self-improvement (Millis, 1992; Chism, 1999).

CONCLUSION

Peer input can and should play a significant role in a comprehensive faculty evaluation system. The steps for building such a faculty evaluation system, as described in this book, provide many opportunities for specifying peer input. In certain roles, such as scholarly and creative activities, peers may be the single most important source of information. Care should be taken, however, not to insert peers as a source of information into those areas where others may be better sources of that information. Chief among these are the gathering of data from peers concerning classroom performance. It is strongly recommended that peer observation of classroom performance not be part of a summative faculty evaluation system. The cost, in terms of time and effort, of gathering valid and reliable peer observation data which may legitimately be used to support personnel decisions (promotion, tenure, etc.) is generally prohibitive. However, if peer observation of classroom performance is required for policy or political reasons, the data gathered from such observations should be provided, in confidence, to the faculty member for his or her personal use in self-improvement. Finally, if the peer observation data are required to be used as part of the personnel decision-making process, such data should be weighted as low as possible.

CHAPTER REFERENCES

Aleamoni, L. M. (1982). Components of the instructional setting. *Instructional Evaluation, 7,* 11-16.

Centra, J. A. (1975). Colleagues as raters of classroom instruction. *Journal of Higher Education, 46,* 327-337.

Centra, J. A. (1979). *Determining faculty effectiveness.* San Francisco, CA: Jossey-Bass.

Centra, J. A. (1999). *Reflective faculty evaluation.* San Francisco, CA: Jossey-Bass.

Chism, N. (1999). *Peer review of teaching: A sourcebook.* Bolton, MA: Anker.

Cohen, P. A., & McKeachie, W. J. (1980). The role of colleagues in the evaluation of college teaching. *Improving College and University Teaching, 28,* 147-154.

Millis, B. J., (1992). Conducting effective peer classroom observations. In D. Wulff & J. Nyquist (Eds.), *To improve the academy, 11,* 189-201, Stillwater, OK: New Forums Press.

Portions of this chapter appeared earlier in the following publication. Used by permission.

Aleamoni, L. M. (1984, October). Peer evaluation. *Note to the Faculty, 15.* Tucson, AZ: The University of Arizona.

12

Student Ratings: Common Questions, Concerns, and Beliefs

Student ratings are one of the most common features of faculty evaluation systems. More than 85% of all faculty evaluation systems make regular and routine use of student ratings (Seldin, 1993). Despite the continued recommendations in the literature that faculty evaluation systems use multiple sources of data, many working faculty evaluation systems continue to use student ratings of instructor and instruction as their only component. It is not surprising, therefore, that student ratings have tended to become synonymous with faculty evaluation. And, because the evaluation of faculty performance, especially for the purpose of making personnel decisions, is not always the most popular and well received of administrative activities, faculty and administrators continue to ask questions concerning the factors that may, or may not, influence student ratings of instructors and instruction.

The great body of research on student ratings has taken place in the last 25 years, although research on student ratings goes back more that 75 years (Guthrie, 1954, cites a study on student ratings dating back to 1924). Even today the design, development, use, and interpretation of student ratings continues to be one of the most heavily researched topics in the general area of faculty evaluation. The results of all this research have led to some fairly firm conclusions. At this point, it is helpful to review some of the more common questions about student ratings and examine what the research tells us.

COMMON QUESTIONS CONCERNING STUDENT RATINGS

In examining the research findings relative to the most common questions concerning student ratings, it is important to note that the conclusions drawn are based on the assumed use of professionally developed, valid, and reliable student rating forms. What the literature demonstrates to be a reliable finding concerning how student ratings work may, in fact, not be true for student rating forms that have been "home-made" by either student, faculty, or administrative groups. Such forms have generally not undergone the rigorous psychometric and statistical procedures required to construct a valid and reliable rating. Most of the answers provided to the following common questions concerning student ratings are derived primarily from Lawrence M. Aleamoni's excellent review of the literature on student rating research (Aleamoni, 1999). The questions addressed are:

- *Aren't student ratings just a popularity contest?*

- *Aren't student rating forms just plain unreliable and invalid?*

- *Aren't students too immature, inexperienced, and capricious to make any consistent judgments about the instructor and instruction?*

- *Isn't it true that I can "buy" good student ratings just by giving easy grades?*

- *Isn't it generally easier to get good ratings in higher level courses?*

- *Isn't it true that students who are required to take a course tend to rate the course more harshly than those taking it as an elective?*

- *Isn't there a gender bias in student ratings? Don't female faculty tend to get lower ratings than male faculty?*

- *Isn't it more difficult for math and science faculty to get good ratings?*

- *Isn't it true that the only faculty who are really qualified to teach or evaluate their peers' teaching are those who are actively involved in conducting research in their field?*

- *Don't students have to be away from the course, and possibly the college, for several years before they are able to make accurate judgments about the instructor and instruction?*

- *Isn't it true that the size of the class affects student ratings?*

- *Does the time of the day the course is taught affect student ratings?*

- *Do majors in a course rate it differently than nonmajors?*

- *Does the rank of the instructor (instructor, assistant professor, associate professor, or professor) affect student ratings?*

- *Why bother with 20 or 30 questions on a student rating form? Can't we just use single general items as accurate measures of instructional effectiveness?*

- *What good are student ratings in efforts to improve instruction?*

Aren't Student Ratings Just a Popularity Contest? The answer to this first most vexing of questions is "no"—if you are using a student rating form that has been constructed using professional psychometric procedures and has demonstrated reliability and validity. Student rating forms that have not been constructed according to professional psychometric standards, however, may be unreliable and thus able to be influenced by such factors as "popularity" or temperature of the classroom, instructor gender, or anything else. Unfortunately, many institutions use "home-made" student rating forms which have not been constructed and validated using professional psychometric standards. Without rigorous reliability and validity data on such forms, it is impossible to tell for certain what influences the final student rating.

Well-designed student rating forms (i.e., those designed according to professional psychometric standards), on the other hand, carefully measure many different aspects of faculty performance including the approachability or friendliness of a faculty member which might be interpreted as a "popularity" issue. However, well-designed forms also measure a number of other factors that are unrelated to the "popularity" issue. Thus, the complete student rating is not simply a measure of "popularity" but a measure of various instructional design and delivery skills and characteristics. Many studies show that, given a well-designed form, students can be reliable judges of instructional effectiveness.

Studies conducted by Aleamoni and Spencer (1973), while developing and using the Illinois Course Evaluation Questionnaire (CEQ) subscales, indicated that no single subscale (e.g., Method of Instruction) completely overlapped the other subscales. This result meant that an instructor who received a high rating on the Instructor subscale (made up of items such as "The instructor seemed to be interested in students as persons") would not be guaranteed high ratings on the other four subscales (General Course Attitude, Method of Instruction, Course Content, and Interest and Attention). In reviewing both written and objective student comments, Aleamoni (1976) found that students frankly praised instructors for their warm, friendly, humorous manner in the classroom, but if their courses were not well organized or their methods of stimulating students to learn were poor, the students equally frankly criticized them in those areas. In fact, Feldman (1989) and Tang (1997) pointed out that students were using preparation and organization, stimulation of interest, motivation, answering questions, and treating students courteously as the basis for their ratings. See also Aleamoni and Spencer (1973), Aleamoni (1976), Arreola (1983), Beatty and Zahn (1990), Benz and Blatt (1995), Costin et al. (1971), Dukes and Victoria (1989), Frey (1978), Grush and Costin (1975), Johannessen and Associates (1997), Krehbiel and Associates (1997), Macdonald (1987), Marlin (1987), Marsh and Bailey (1993), Perry, Abrami, and Leventhal (1979), Rodabaugh and Kravitz (1994), Shepherd and Trank (1989), Tollefson and Associates (1989), Ware and Williams (1977), and Waters and Associates (1988).

Aren't Student Rating Forms Just Plain Unreliable and Invalid? The answer to this question is, surprisingly, "yes and no." Most student rating forms in use today suffer from unreliability and invalidity problems. This derives from the fact that most student rating forms used by colleges and universities are "home-made." That is, they have been developed by committees made up of students, faculty, and/or administrative groups who have not followed the rigorous psychometric and statistical procedures required to produce a professional, well-developed student rating form. Well-developed instruments have been shown to be both reliable and valid. Arubayi (1987), Costin et al. (1971), and Marsh (1984) reported reliabilities for such forms to be about 0.90. Aleamoni (1978a) reported reliabilities ranging from 0.81 to 0.94 for items and from 0.88 to 0.98 for subscales of the CIEQ. It should be noted, however, that wherever student rating forms are not carefully constructed with the aid of professionals, as in the case of most student- and faculty-generated forms (Everly & Aleamoni, 1972), the reliabilities may be so low as to negate completely the evaluation effect and its results.

Validity is much more difficult to assess than reliability. Most student rating forms have been validated by the judgment of experts that the items and subscales measure important aspects of instructor (Costin et al., 1971). These subjectively determined dimensions of instructional setting and process have also been validated using statistical tools, such as factor analysis (Aleamoni & Hexner, 1980; Burdsal & Bardo, 1986; Ellett et al., 1997; Marsh, 1984). Further evidence of validity comes from studies in which student ratings are correlated with other indicators of teacher competence, such as peer (colleague) ratings, expert judges' ratings, graduating seniors' and alumni ratings, self ratings, and student learning (Abrami & associates, 1990; Baird, 1987; Cohen, 1989; Dickinson, 1990; Drews & associates, 1987; Gigliotti & Buchtel, 1990; Harrison & associates, 1996; Koon & Murray, 1995; Nimmer & Stone, 1991; O'-Connell & Dickinson, 1993; Prave & Barill, 1993; Prosser & Trigwell, 1990; Ryan & Harrison, 1995; Shmanske, 1988; Stroh, 1991; Teven & McCroskey, 1997; Vu et al., 1997). The 14 studies cited by Aleamoni and Hexner (1980) in which student ratings were compared to 1) colleague ratings, 2) expert judges' ratings, 3) graduating seniors' and alumni ratings, and 4) student learning measures all indicated the existence of moderate to high positive correlations, which can be considered as providing additional evidence of validity. This is in contrast to two studies (Bendig, 1953; Rodin & Rodin, 1972) that found a negative relationship between student achievement and instructor rating. The latter study, however, has been soundly criticized for its methodology by several researchers (Centra, 1973b; Frey, 1973; Gessner, 1973; Menges, 1973).

Aren't Students Too Immature, Inexperienced, and Capricious to Make any Consistent Judgments About the Instructor and Instruction? The answer to this question is "no." Evidence dating back to 1924, according to Guthrie (1954), as well as more recent literature by Albanese (1991), Hativa (1996), and Palchik and associates (1988), indicates just the opposite. The stability of student ratings from one year to the next results in substantial correlations in the range of 0.87 to 0.89. Other literature on the subject, cited by Costin, Greenough, and Menges (1971), and studies by Gillmore (1973) and Hogan (1973) indicated that the correlation between student ratings of the same instructors and courses ranged from 0.70 to 0.87.

Isn't It True That I Can "Buy" Good Student Ratings Just By Giving Easy Grades? The answer to this question is "no—if you are using a valid and reliable student rating form." Considerable controversy has centered around the relationship between student ratings and their actual or expected course grades, the general feeling being that students tend to rate courses and instructors more highly when they expect or receive good grades. Correlational studies have reported widely inconsistent grade-rating relationships. Some 24 studies have reported zero relationships (Aleamoni & Hexner, 1980; Baird, 1987; Gigliotti & Buchtel, 1990). Another 37 studies have reported significant positive relationships (Aleamoni & Hexner, 1980; Blunt, 1991; Cohen, 1989; Goldberg & Callahan, 1991; Nimmer & Stone, 1991; Rodabaugh & Kravitz, 1994; Sailor, Worthen, & Shin, 1997; Scherr & Scherr, 1990; Trick & associates, 1993; Wilson, 1998). One study by Sailor, Wonthen, & Shin (1997) reported a negative relationship in graduated courses. In most instances however, these relationships were relatively weak, as indicated by the fact that the median correlation was approximately 0.14, with the mean and standard deviation being 0.18 and 0.16 respectively.

A widely publicized, but methodologically flawed, study by Rodin and Rodin (1972) reported a high negative relationship between student performance on examinations and their ratings of graduate teaching assistants. This study has proven to be a wart on the literature in faculty evaluation and is often cited, especially in the popular press, by those with a political agenda of eliminating student ratings from a faculty evaluation system. The Rodin and Rodin (1972) study been contested on methodological grounds by Rodin, Frey, and Gessner (1975). Subsequent replications of the study using regular faculty rather than teaching assistants and using more sophisticated rating forms have resulted in a positive rather than a negative relationship (Frey, 1973; Gessner, 1973; Sullivan & Skanes, 1974).

Generally the studies on this issue indicate that the relationship between grades and ratings is, at best, extremely weak, with the average correlation across all studies being 0.0. Clearly, the idea that student ratings are highly correlated with grades is not supported by the literature.

Again, however, it must be noted that we can't be sure what will influence the ratings of individual "homemade" student rating forms that have not been designed in accordance with professional psychometric standards.

Isn't It Generally Easier to Get Good Ratings in Higher Level Courses? The answer to this question is "yes." Actually, freshmen tend to rate a course more harshly than sophomores, sophomores more harshly than juniors, juniors more harshly than seniors, and seniors more harshly than graduate students. The majority of studies on this issue tend to support this belief. Aleamoni and Hexner (1980) cited 18 investigators who reported that graduate students and/or upper division students tend to rate instructors more favorably than did lower division students. They also cited eight investigators who reported no significant relationship between student status (freshman, sophomore, etc.) and ratings assigned to instructors. More recent studies by Donaldson and Associates (1993), Conran and associates (1991), Goldberg and Callahan (1991), and Moritsch and Suter (1988) confirm the differences in ratings by the level of the course/student.

Isn't It True That Students Who Are Required to Take a Course Tend to Rate the Course More Harshly Than Those Taking It as an Elective? Interestingly, the answer to this question is "yes." The bulk of the literature tends to support this conclusion. Several investigators have found that students who are required to take a course tend to rate it lower than students who elect to take it (Cohen & Humphreys, 1960; Divoky & Rathermel, 1988; Gillmore & Brandenburg, 1974; Pohlmann, 1975). This finding is supported by Gage (1961), Lovell and Haner (1955), Petchers and Chow (1988), and Scherr and Scherr (1990), who found that instructors of elective courses were rated significantly higher than instructors of required courses. In contrast, Heilman and Armentrout (1936) and Hildebrand, Wilson, and Dienst (1971) reported no differences between students' ratings of required courses and elective courses.

Isn't There a Gender Bias in Student Ratings? Don't Female Faculty Tend to Get Lower Ratings Than Male Faculty? The literature on this question is not as plentiful as it is on other issues in student rating research but the research

that has been done appears to be fairly consistent in answering the question as "no." Earlier research provided conflicting results relating the gender of the student to student evaluations of instruction. Aleamoni and Thomas (1980), Amin (1994), Doyle and Whitely (1974), Dukes and Victoria (1989), Feldman (1993), Fernandez and Mateo (1997), Freeman (1994), Goodhartz (1948), Goodwin and Stevens (1993), Hancock and Associates (1992), Isaacson and Associates (1964), Ludwig and Meacham (1997), O'Reilly (1987), Petchers and Chow (1988), Wheeless and Potorti (1989), and Winocur and associates (1989) all reported no differences between faculty ratings made by male and female students. In addition, Costin et al. (1971) cited seven studies that reported no differences in overall ratings of instructors made by male and female students or in the ratings received by male and female instructors. Conversely, Bendig (1952) found female students to be more critical of male instructors than their male counterparts. Basow and Silberg (1987) and Summers and associates (1996) reported that male and female students both rate female instructors lower than male instructors. Kierstead and associates (1988) and Tatro (1995) reported that female instructors are rated higher than males. Walker (1969) found that female students rated female instructors significantly higher than they rated male instructors, whereas Atamian and Ganguli (1993), Goldberg and Callahan (1991), and Luek and associates (1993) reported male students rate male instructors higher. In addition, Aleamoni and Hexner (1980) cited five studies which reported female students rate instructors higher on some subscales of instructor evaluation forms than do male students.

Several recent studies on the question of gender bias in faculty evaluation have found no consistent evidence of its existence. See Basow and Howe (1987), Feldman (1992 & 1993), Ferber and Huber (1975), Goodwin and Stevens (1993), and Kaschak (1978). However, the appearance of gender bias in student ratings may occur if a greater percentage of females are assigned to teach the lower level required courses. In such a case the bias would not lie in the student ratings but in the assignment of disproportionate numbers of female faculty to teach lower level, required courses that tend to get lower ratings regardless of the gender of the instructor.

Isn't It More Difficult for Math and Science Faculty to Get Good Ratings? Surprisingly the answer to this question is "yes." Studies by Andrew and associates (1993), Cashin (1990), Goldman (1993), Goodwin and Stevens (1993), and Zahn and Schramm (1992) indicate that there are disciplinary differences in student ratings. Ratings tend to be higher for the humanities and social science disciplines as compared to the physical science and engineering disciplines. This does not necessarily mean that all math and science faculty are poor teachers. Although no definitive reason for this tendency has yet been determined we do know that different disciplines produce different rating norms. That is, student ratings can be affected by the discipline being taught. It is important, therefore, in interpreting student rating results that we do so by using the appropriate norm group.

Isn't It True That the Only Faculty Who Are Really Qualified to Teach or Evaluate Their Peers' Teaching Are Those Who Are Actively Involved in Conducting Research in Their Field? The answer to this question is "no." There is a widely held belief (Borgatta, 1970; Deming, 1972) that good instruction and good research are so closely allied that it is unnecessary to evaluate them independently. However, the research is divided on this point. To be sure, weak positive correlations between research productivity and teaching effectiveness have been found by Maslow and Zimmerman (1956), McDaniel and Feldhusen (1970), McGrath (1962), Riley, Ryan, and Lipschitz (1950), and Stallings and Singhal (1968). On the other hand, Aleamoni and Yimer (1973), Guthrie (1949, 1954), Hayes (1971), Linsky and Straus (1975), and Voeks (1962) found no significant relationship between instructors' research productivity and students' ratings of their teaching effectiveness. One study (Aleamoni & Yimer, 1973) also reported no significant relationship between instructors' research productivity and colleagues' ratings of their teaching effectiveness. Thus, no clear and consistent evidence has emerged in the literature to substantiate the belief that only good researchers can be good teachers and are the only people qualified to evaluate teaching, so the belief must be held to be essentially untrue. It is ironic that those individuals who persist in believing this myth, and who claim to value research highly, apparently do not read the literature on this issue.

Don't Students Have to Be Away from the Course, and Possibly the College, for Several Years Before They Are Able to Make Accurate Judgments About the Instructor and Instruction? The qualified answer to this question is "no." This very popular belief is continuously bolstered by anecdotes passed from teacher to teacher. However, conducting research on this belief has proven to pose certain problems. For example, it is very difficult to obtain a comparative and representative sample in longitudinal follow-up studies. The sampling problem is further compounded by the fact that almost all student attitudinal data relating to a course or instructor are gathered anony-

mously. Most studies in this area, therefore, have relied on surveys of alumni and/or graduating seniors. Early studies by Drucker and Remers (1951) showed that alumni who have been out of school five to ten years rated instructors much the same as students currently enrolled. More recent evidence by Aleamoni and Yimer (1974), Marsh (1977), Marsh and Overall (1979), and McKeachie, Lin, and Mendelson (1978) further substantiated the earlier findings. Thus, the literature up to this point leads to the conclusion that this popularly held belief is generally not true.

Isn't It True That the Size of the Class Affects Student Ratings? The answer to this question is "no—there is no consistent relationship between class size and student ratings." However, the belief that class size affects student ratings is one of the oldest and most popular myths in education. Faculty members frequently suggest that instructors of large classes may receive lower ratings because students generally prefer small classes, which permit more student-instructor interaction. Although this belief is supported to some extent by the results of eight studies cited by Aleamoni and Hexner (1980), and two studies by Mateo and Fernandez (1996) and Watkins (1990), other investigations do not support it. For example, Aleamoni and Hexner (1980) cited seven other studies that found no relationship between class size and student ratings. Also, studies cited by Lin (1992) and Van Arsdale and Hammons (1995) as well as one conducted by Shapiro (1990) indicate no relationship between class size and student ratings. Some investigations have also reported curvilinear relationships between class size and student ratings (Gage, 1961; Kohlan, 1973; Lovell & Haner, 1955; Marsh, Overall, & Kesler, 1979; Pohlmann, 1975; Wood, Linsky, & Straus, 1974). The research literature does not support the belief that a consistent relationship between class size and student ratings of any sort exists. It is interesting to note, however, that most large, required courses tend to be offered early in the curriculum of a college. Thus, most of the large required courses may be offered in the freshman and sophomore years, just the time when students tend to rate their teachers most harshly. It would be easy to conclude from personal experience with such courses that the problem lies with the size of the course when, in fact, the research indicates it is the level (freshman, sophomore, etc.) and the fact that the course is required that are the factors which contribute to generally lower student ratings.

Does the Time of the Day the Course Is Taught Affect Student Ratings? The answer to this question is "we don't think so." There hasn't been much research on this question, but the limited amount of research in this area (Feldman, 1978; Guthrie, 1954; Yongkittikul, Gillmore, & Brandenburg, 1974) indicates that the time of day the course is offered does not influence student ratings.

Do Majors in a Course Rate It Differently Than Non-majors? The answer to this question is "no." Although there is only a limited amount of research in this area (Aleamoni & Thomas, 1980; Cohen & Humphreys, 1960; Divkoy & Rothermel, 1988; Null & Nicholson, 1972; Rayder, 1968), all studies indicate that there are no significant differences and no significant relationships between student ratings and whether they were majors or nonmajors.

Does the Rank of the Instructor (Instructor, Assistant Professor, Associate Professor, or Professor) Affect Student Ratings? The answer to this question "not really." The literature on this issue, in general, does not support the idea that faculty of higher professorial rank get higher student ratings because no consistent relationship between faculty rank and student ratings has been found. Some investigators reported that instructors of higher rank receive higher student ratings (Clark & Keller, 1954; Downie, 1952; Gage, 1961; Guthrie, 1954; Walker, 1969), whereas Schuckman (1990) reported that teaching assistants were rated higher than the ranked faculty; however, others reported no significant relationship between instructor rank and student ratings (Aleamoni & Graham, 1974; Aleamoni & Thomas, 1980; Aleamoni & Yimer, 1973; Linsky & Straus, 1975; Petchers & Chow, 1988; Singhal, 1968). Conflicting results have also been found when comparing teaching experience to student ratings. Rayder (1968) reported a negative relationship, whereas Heilman and Armentrout (1936) found no significant relationship.

Why Bother with 20 or 30 Questions on a Student Rating Form? Can't We Just Use Single General Items as Accurate Measures of Instructional Effectiveness? The use of single general items on student rating forms has been popular for some time. These items can be very reliable but do not provide information that is as useful as that produced by the multiple-item student rating form. The limited amount of research in this area (Aleamoni & Thomas, 1980; Burdsal & Bardo, 1986; Cashin & Downey, 1992; McBean, 1991; McBean & Lennox, 1987) indicates that there is a low relationship between single general items and specific items and that the single general items had a much higher relationship to descriptive variables (gender, status, required–elective, etc.) than did the specific items. These findings suggest that the use of single general items should be avoided, especially for tenure, promotion,

or salary considerations. In any case, single general items provide little useful diagnostic information for use in faculty development efforts compared to multiple items that measure specific components of teaching performance.

What Good Are Student Ratings in Efforts to Improve Instruction? The answer to this question is that "under the right conditions, student ratings can be very helpful in assisting faculty to improve their instruction." Studies by Braunstein, Klein, and Pachla (1973), Centra (1973a), and Miller (1971) were inconclusive with respect to the effect of feedback at midterm to instructors whose instruction was again evaluated at the end of the term. However, L'Hommedieu and associates (1990), Marsh and Roche (1993), Marsh, Fleiner, and Thomas (1975), Overall and Marsh (1979), and Sherman (1978) reported more favorable ratings from and improved learning by students by the end of the term. In order to determine if a combination of a printed report of the results and personal consultations would be superior to providing only a printed report of results, Aleamoni (1978b), Arubayi (1987), Cohen (1991), McKeachie (1979), Schmelkin and Spencer (1997), Schum and Vindra (1996), and Stevens and Aleamoni (1985) found that instructors significantly improved their ratings when personal consultations were provided. The key finding that emerges here is that student ratings can be used to improve instruction if used as part of a personal consultation between the faculty member and a faculty development resource person.

SUMMARY

Given the use of a well-designed, valid, and reliable student rating form, the literature suggests that:

- *Faculty cannot "buy" good ratings by giving easy grades.*

- *Teaching a small class does not automatically guarantee high student ratings, nor does teaching a large class automatically guarantee low ratings.*

- *Lower level students (freshmen, sophomores) do tend to rate more harshly than upper level students (seniors, graduate students).*

- *Students in required courses tend to rate their instructors more harshly than students in elective courses.*

- *Math and science courses tend to be rated more harshly than courses in the humanities.*

- *There is no gender bias in student ratings.*

- *Students do not generally rate faculty lower in classes*

taught early in the morning or right after lunch.

- *Student ratings can be quite helpful in instructional improvement efforts when used as part of a faculty development program that includes personal consultations.*

Obviously the proper interpretation of student ratings must take a variety of issues into account. The important conclusion to be drawn here is the necessity to systematically incorporate research findings into the interpretation of student ratings in a comprehensive faculty evaluation system. See Chapter 14, especially the section on the Course Instructor Evaluation Questionnaire (CIEQ), for ways professionally developed, commercially available student rating form services address these issues.

CHAPTER REFERENCES

Abrami, P. C., & Associates. (1990). Validity of student ratings of instruction: What we know and what we do not know. *Journal of Educational Psychology, 82(2),* 219-231.

Albanese, M. A. (1991). The validity of lecturer ratings by students and trained observers. *Academic Medicine, 66(1),* 26-28.

Aleamoni, L. M. (1976). Typical faculty concerns about student evaluation of instruction. *National Association of Colleges and Teachers of Agriculture Journal, 20(1),* 16-21.

Aleamoni, L. M. (1978a). Development and factorial validation of the Arizona course/instructor evaluation questionnaire. *Educational and Psychological Measurement, 38,* 1063-1067.

Aleamoni, L. M. (1978b). The usefulness of student evaluations in improving college teaching. *Instructional Science, 7,* 95-105.

Aleamoni, L. M. (1999). Student rating myths versus research facts: An update. *Journal of Personnel Evaluation, 13(2),* 153-166.

Aleamoni, L. M., & Graham, M. H. (1974). The relationship between CEQ ratings and instructor's rank, class size, and course level. *Journal of Educational Measurement, 11,* 189-202.

Aleamoni, L. M., & Spencer, R. E. (1973). The Illinois course evaluation questionnaire: A description of its development and a report of some of its results. *Educational and Psychological Measurement, 33,* 669-684.

Aleamoni, L. M., & Hexner, P. Z. (1980). A review of the research on student evaluation and a report on the effect of different sets of instructions on student course and instructor evaluation. *Instructional Science, 9,* 67-84.

Aleamoni, L. M., & Thomas, G. S. (1980). Differential relationships of student, instructor, and course characteristics to general and specific items on a course questionnaire. *Teaching of Psychology, 7(4),* 233-235.

Aleamoni, L. M., & Yimer, M. (1973). An investigation of the relationship between colleague rating, student rating, research productivity, and academic rank in rating instructional effectiveness. *Journal of Educational Psychology, 64,* 274-277.

Aleamoni, L. M., & Yimer, M. (1974). *Graduating senior ratings relationship to colleague rating, student rating, research productivity, and academic rank in rating instructional effectiveness (Research Report No. 352).* Urbana, IL: University of Illinois, Office of Instructional Resources, Measurement and Research Division.

Amin, M. E. (1994). Gender as a discriminating factor in the evaluation of teaching. *Assessment and Evaluation in Higher Education, 19(2),* 135-143.

Andrew, M. D., & Associates. (1993). Comparing student perceptions of instruction in teacher education and on education courses. *Journal of Personnel Evaluation in Education, 6(4),* 359-366.

Arreola, R. A. (1983). Students can distinguish between personality and content/organization in rating teachers. *Phi Delta Kappan, 65(3),* 222-223.

Arubayi, E. A. (1987). Improvement of instruction and teacher effectiveness: Are student ratings reliable and valid? *Higher Education, 16(3),* 26-278.

Atamian, R., & Ganguli G. (1993). Teacher popularity and teaching effectiveness: Viewpoint of accounting students. *Journal of Education for Business, 68(3),* 163-169.

Baird, J. S., Jr. (1987). Perceived learning in relation to student evaluation to university instruction. *Journal of Educational Psychology, 79(1),* 90-91.

Basow, S. A., & Howe, K. G. (1987). Evaluations of college professors: Effects of professors' sex-type and sex and students' sex. *Psychological Reports, 60,* 671-78.

Basow, S. A., & Silberg, N. T. (1987). Student evaluations of college professors: Are female and male professors rated differently? *Journal of Educational Psychology, 3,* 308-314.

Beatty, M. J., & Zahn, C. J. (1990). Are student ratings of communication instructors due to "easy" grading practices? An analysis of teacher credibility and student-reported performance levels. *Communication Education, 39(4),* 275-282.

Bendig, A. W. (1952). A preliminary study of the effect of academic level, sex, and course variables on student rating of psychology instructors. *Journal of Psychology, 34,* 2-126.

Bendig, A. W. (1953). Relation of level of course achievement of students, instructor, and course ratings in introductory psychology. *Educational and Psychological Measurement, 13,* 437-488.

Benz, C., & Blatt, S. J. (1995). Factors underlying effective college teaching: What students tell us. *Mid-Western Educational Researcher, 8(1),* 27-31.

Blunt, A. (1991). The effects of anonymity and manipulated grades on student ratings of instructors. *Community College Review, 18(4),* 48-54.

Borgatta, E. F. (1970). Student ratings of faculty. *American Association of University Professors, Bulletin, 56,* 6-7.

Braunstein, D. N., Klein, G. A., & Pachla, M. (1973). Feedback, expectancy, and shifts in student ratings of college faculty. *Journal of Applied Psychology, 58,* 254-258.

Burdsal, C. A., & Bardo, J. W. (1986). Measuring students' perceptions of teaching: Dimensions of evaluation. *Educational and Psychological Measurement, 46,* 63-79.

Cashin, W. E. (1990). Students do rate academic fields differently (pp. 113-121). In M. Theall & J. Franklin (Eds.), *Student ratings of instruction: Issues for improving practice.* New Directions for Teaching and Learning, No. 43. San Francisco, CA: Jossey-Bass.

Cashin, W. E., & Downey, R. G. (1992). Using global student rating items for summative evaluation. *Journal of Educational Psychology, 54(4),* 563-572.

Centra, J. A. (1973a). Effectiveness of student feedback in modifying college instruction. *Journal of Educational Psychology, 65,* 395-401.

Centra, J. A. (1973b). The student as godfather? The impact of student ratings on academia. In A. L. Sockloff (Ed.), *Proceedings of the First Invitational Conference on Faculty Effectiveness as Evaluated by Students.* Philadelphia, PA: Temple University, Measurement and Research Center.

Centra, J. A. (1998). *The development of the student instructional report II.* Princeton, NJ: Educational Testing Service.

Centra, J. A., & Gaubatz, N. B. (1999). *Is there gender bias in student evaluations of teaching?* Princeton, NJ: Educational Testing Service.

Clark, K. E., & Keller, R. J. (1954). Student ratings of college teaching. In R. A. Eckert (Ed.), *A university looks at its program.* Minneapolis, MN: University of Minnesota Press.

Cohen, J., & Humphreys, L. G. (1960). Memorandum to faculty (unpublished manuscript). University of Illinois, Department of Psychology.

Cohen, P. A. (1989). Do grades influence students evaluations of clinical courses? *Journal of Dental Education, 53(4),* 238-240.

Cohen, P. A. (1991). Effectiveness of student rating feedback and consultation for improving instruction in dental schools. *Journal of Dental Education, 55(2),* 145-150.

Conran, P. B., & Associates. (1991). High school student evaluation of student teachers: How do they compare with professionals? *Illinois School Research and Development, 27(2),* 81-92.

Costin, F., Greenough, W. T., & Menges, R. J. (1971). Student ratings of college teaching: Reliability, validity, and usefulness. *Review of Educational Research, 41,* 511-535.

Deming, W. E. (1972). Memorandum on teaching. *The American Statistician, 26,* 47.

Dickinson, D. J. (1990). The relationship between ratings of teacher performance and student learning. *Contemporary Educational Psychology, 15(2),* 142-151.

Divoky, J. J., & Rathermel, M. A. (1988). Student perceptions of the relative importance of dimensions of teaching performance across type of class. *Educational Research Quarterly, 12(3),* 40-45.

Donaldson, J. F., & Associates. (1993). A triangulated study comparing adult college students' perceptions of effective teaching with those of traditional students. *Continuing Higher Education Review, 57(3),* 147-165.

Downie, N. W. (1952). Student evaluation of faculty. *Journal of Higher Education, 23,* 495-496, 503.

Doyle, K. O., & Whitely, S. E. (1974). Student ratings as criteria for effective teaching. *American Educational Research Journal, 11,* 259-274.

Drews, D. R., & Associates. (1987). Teacher self-ratings as a validity criterion for student evaluations. *Teaching of Psychology, 14(1),* 23-25.

Drucker, A. J., & Remers, H. H. (1951). Do alumni and students differ in their attitudes toward instructors? *Journal of Educational Psychology, 42,* 129-143.

Dukes, R. L. & Victoria, G. (1989). The effects of gender, status, and effective teaching on the evaluation of college instruction. *Teaching Sociology, 17(4),* 447-457.

Ellett, C. D., Loup, K. S., & Culross, R. R. (1997). Assessing enhancement of learning, personal learning environment, and student efficacy: Alternative to traditional faculty evaluation in higher education. *Journal of Personnel Evaluation in Education, 11(2),* 167-192.

Everly, J. C., & Aleamoni, L. M. (1972). The rise and fall of the advisor . . . students attempt to evaluate their instructors. *Journal of the National Association of Colleges and Teachers of Agriculture, 16(2),* 43-45.

Feldman, K. A. (1978). Course characteristics and college students' ratings of their teachers: What we know and what we don't. *Research in Higher Education, 9,* 199-242.

Feldman, K. A. (1989). The association between student ratings of specific instructional dimensions and student achievement: Refining and extending the synthesis of data from multisection validity studies. *Research in Higher Education, 30(6),* 583-645.

Feldman, K. A. (1992). College students' views of male and female college teachers: Part I, Evidence from the social laboratory and experiments. *Research in Higher Education, 33,* 317-375.

Feldman, K. A. (1993). College students' views of male and female college teachers: Part II, Evidence from students' evaluations of their classroom teachers. *Research in Higher Education, 34(2),* 151-211.

Ferber, M. A., & Huber, J. A. (1975). Sex of student and instructor: A study of student bias. *American Journal of Sociology, 80,* 949-963.

Fernandez, J., & Mateo, M. A. (1997). Student and faculty gender in rating of university teaching quality. *Sex Roles: A Journal of Research, 37* (11-12), 997-1003.

Freeman, H. R. (1994). Student evaluations of college instructors: Effects of type of course taught, instructor gender and gender role, and student gender. *Journal of Educational Psychology, 86(4),* 627-630.

Frey, P. W. (1973). Student ratings of teaching: Validity of several rating factors. *Science, 182,* 83-85.

Frey, P. W. (1978). A two-dimensional analysis of student ratings of instruction. *Research in Higher Education, 9,* 69-91.

Gage, N. L. (1961). The appraisal of college teaching. *Journal of Higher Education, 32,* 17-22.

Gessner, P. K. (1973). Evaluation of instruction. *Science, 180,* 566-569.

Gigliotti, R. J., & Buchtel, F. S. (1990). Attributional bias and course evaluations. *Journal of Educational Psychology, 82(2),* 341-351.

Gillmore, G. M. (1973). *Estimates of reliability coefficients for items and subscales of the Illinois course evaluation questionnaire (Research Report No. 341)*. Urbana, IL: University of Illinois, Office of Instructional Resources, Measurement and Research Division.

Gillmore, G. M., & Brandenburg, D. C. (1974). *Would the proportion of students taking a class as a requirement affect the student rating of the course? (Research Report No. 347)*. Urbana, IL: University of Illinois, Office of Instructional Resources, Measurement and Research Division.

Goldberg, G., & Callahan, J. (1991). Objectivity of student evaluations of instructors. *Journal of Education for Business, 66(6),* 377-378.

Goldman, L. (1993). On the erosion of education and the eroding foundation of teacher education (or why we should not take student evaluation of faculty seriously). *Teacher Education Quarterly, 20(2),* 57-64.

Goodhartz, A. S. (1948). Student attitudes and opinions relating to teaching at Brooklyn College. *School and Society, 68,* 345-349.

Goodwin, L. D., & Stevens, E. A. (1993). The influence of gender on university faculty members' perceptions of "good" teaching. *Journal of Higher Education, 64(2),*166-185.

Grush, J. E., & Costin, F. (1975). The student as consumer of the teaching process. *American Educational Research Journal, 12,* 55-66.

Guthrie, E. R. (1949). The evaluation of teaching. *Educational Record, 30,* 109-115.

Guthrie, E. R. (1954). *The evaluation of teaching: A progress report*. Seattle, WA: University of Washington.

Hancock, G. R., & Associates. (1992). Student and teacher gender ratings of university faculty: Results from five colleges of study. *Journal of Personnel Evaluation in Education, 6(4),* 359-366.

Harrison, P. D., & Associates. (1996). College students' self-insight and common implicit theories in ratings of teaching effectiveness. *Journal of Educational Psychology, 88(4),* 775-782.

Hativa, N. (1996). University instructors' rating profiles: Stability over time, and disciplinary differences. *Research in Higher Education, 37(3),* 341-365.

Hayes, J. R. (1971). Research, teaching, and faculty fate. *Science, 172,* 227-230.

Heilman, J. D., & Armentrout, W. D. (1936). The rating of college teachers on ten traits by their students. *Journal of Educational Psychology, 27,* 197-216.

Hildebrand, M., Wilson, R. C., & Dienst, E. R. (1971). *Evaluating university teaching*. Berkeley, CA: University of California, Center for Research and Development in Higher Education.

Hogan, T. P. (1973). Similarity of student ratings across instructors, courses and time. *Research in Higher Education, I,* 149-154.

Isaacson, R. L., McKeachie, W. J., Milholland, J. E., Lin, Y. G., Hofeller, M., Baerwaldt, J. W., & Zinn, K. L. (1964). Dimensions of student evaluations of teaching. *Journal of Educational Psychology, 55,* 344-351.

Johannessen, T. A., & Associates. (1997). What is important to students? Exploring dimensions in their evaluations of teachers. *Scandinavian Journal of Educational Research, 41(2),* 165-177.

Kaschak, E. (1978). Sex bias in student evaluations of college professors. *Psychology of Women Quarterly, 2,* 235-243.

Kierstead, D., & Associates. (1988). Sex role stereotyping of college professors: Bias in students' ratings of instructors. *Journal of Educational Psychology, 80(3),* 342-344.

Kohlan, R. G. (1973). A comparison of faculty evaluations early and late in the course. *Journal of Higher Education, 44,* 587-597.

Koon, J., & Murray, H. G. Using multiple outcomes to validate student ratings of overall teacher effectiveness. *Journal of Higher Education, 66(1),* 61–81.

Krehbiel, T. C., & Associates. (1997). Using student disconfirmation as a measure of classroom effectiveness. *Journal of Education for Business, 72(4),* 224-229.

L'Hommedieu, R., & Associates. (1990). Methodological explanations for modest effects of feedback from student ratings. *Journal of Educational Psychology, 82(2),* 232-241.

Lin, W. Y. (1992). Is class size a bias to student ratings of university faculty? A review. *Chinese University of Education Journal, 20(1),* 49-53.

Linsky, A. S., & Straus, M. A. (1975). Student evaluations, research productivity, and eminence of college faculty. *Journal of Higher Education, 46,* 89-102.

Lovell, G. D., & Haner, C. F. (1955). Forced-choice applied to college faculty rating. *Educational and Psychological Measurement, 15,* 291-304.

Ludwig, J. M., & Meacham, J. A. (1997). Teaching controversial courses: Student evaluations of instructor and content. *Educational Research Quarterly, 21(1),* 27-38.

Luek, T. L., & Associates. (1993). The interaction effects of gender on teaching evaluations. *Journalism Educator, 48(3),* 235-248.

Macdonald, A. (1987). Student views on excellent courses. *Agricultural Education Magazine, 60(3),* 19-22.

Marlin, J. W., Jr. (1987). Student perceptions of end-of-course evaluation. *Journal of Higher Education, 58(6),* 704-716.

Marsh, H. W. (1977). The validity of students' evaluations: Classroom evaluations of instructors independently nominated as best and worst teachers by graduating seniors. *American Educational Research Journal, 14,* 441-447.

Marsh, H. W. (1984). Students' evaluations of university teaching: Dimensionality, reliability, validity, potential biases, and utility. *Journal of Educational Psychology, 76,* 707-754.

Marsh, H. W. (1987). Students' evaluations of university teaching: Research findings, methodological issues, and directions for future research. *International Journal of Educational Research, 11(3),* 253-388.

Marsh, H. W., & Bailey, M. (1993). Multidimensional students' evaluation of teaching effectiveness. *Journal of Higher Education, 64(1),* 1-18.

Marsh, H. W., Fleiner, H., & Thomas, C. S. (1975). Validity and usefulness of student evaluations of instructional quality. *Journal of Educational Psychology, 67,* 883-889.

Marsh, H. W., & Overall, J. U. (1979). Long-term stability of students' evaluations: A note on Feldman's consistency and variability among college students in rating their teachers and courses. *Research in Higher Education, 10,* 139-147.

Marsh, H. W., Overall, J. U., & Kesler, S. P. (1979). Class size, students' evaluations, and instructional effectiveness. *American Educational Research Journal, 16,* 57-69.

Marsh, H. W. & Roche, L. (1993). The use of students' evaluations and an individually structured intervention to enhance university teaching effectiveness. *American Educational Research Journal, 30(1),* 217-251.

Maslow, A. H., & Zimmerman, W. (1956). College teaching ability, scholarly activity, and personality. *Journal of Educational Psychology, 47,* 185-189.

Mateo, M. A., & Fernandez, J. (1996). Incidence of class size on the evaluation of university teaching quality. *Educational and Psychological Measurement, 56(5),* 771-778.

McBean, E. A. (1991). Analyses of teaching and course questionnaires: A case study. *Engineering Education, 81(4),* 439-441.

McBean, E. A., & Lennox, W. C. (1987). Measurement of quality of teaching and course by a single question versus a weighted set. *European Journal of Engineering, 12(4),* 329-335.

McDaniel, E. D., & Feldhusen, J. F. (1970). Relationships between faculty ratings and indexes of service and scholarship. *Proceedings of the 78th Annual Convention of the American Psychological Association, 5,* 619-620.

McGrath, E. J. (1962). Characteristics of outstanding college teachers. *Journal of Higher Education, 33,* 148.

McKeachie, W. J. (1979). Student ratings of faculty: A reprise. *Academe, 65,* 384-397.

McKeachie, W. J., Lin, Y. G., & Mendelson, C. N. (1978). A small study assessing teacher effectiveness: Does learning last? *Contemporary Educational Psychology, 3,* 352-357.

Melland, H. I. (1996). Great researcher . . . good teacher? *Journal of Professional Nursing, 12(1),* 31-38.

Menges, R. J. (1973). The new reporters: Students rate instruction instruction (pp. 59-75). In C. R. Pace (Ed.), *Evaluating learning and teaching.* New Directions in Higher Education. San Francisco, CA: Jossey-Bass.

Miller, M. T. (1971). Instructor attitudes toward, and their use of, student ratings of teachers. *Journal of Educational Psychology, 62,* 235-239.

Moritsch, B. G., & Suter, W. N. (1988) Correlates of halo error in teacher evaluation. *Educational Research Quarterly, 12(3),* 29-34.

Nimmer, J. G., & Stone, E. F. (1991). Effects of grading practices and time of rating on student ratings of faculty performance and student learning. *Research in Higher Education, 32(2),* 195-215.

Null, E. J., & Nicholson, E. W. (1972). Personal variables of students and their perception of university instructors. *College Student Journal, 6,* 6-9.

O'Connell, D. Q., & Dickenson, D. J. (1993). Student ratings of instruction as a function of testing conditions and perceptions of amount learned. *Journal of Research and Development in Education, 27(1),* 18-23.

O'Reilly, M. T. (1987). Relationship of physical attractiveness to students ratings of teaching effectiveness. *Journal of Dental Education, 51(10),* 600-602.

Overall, J. U., & Marsh, H. W. (1979). Midterm feedback from students. Its relationship to instructional improvement and students' cognitive and affective outcomes. *Journal of Educational Psychology, 71,* 856-865.

Palchik, N. S., & Associates. (1988). Student assessment of teaching effectiveness in a multi-instructor course for multidisciplinary health professional students. *Evaluation and the Health Professions, 11(1),* 55-73.

Perry, R. P., Abrami, P. C., & Leventhal, L. (1979). Educational seduction: The effect of instructor expressiveness and lecture content on student ratings and achievement. *Journal of Educational Psychology, 71,* 107-116.

Petchers, M. K., & Chow, J. C. (1988). Sources of variation in students' evaluations of instruction in a graduate social work program. *Journal of Social Work Education, 24(1),* 35-42.

Pohlmann, J. T. (1975). A multivariate analysis of selected class characteristics and student ratings of instruction. *Multivariate Behavioral Research, 10(1),* 81-91.

Prave, R. S., & Barill, G. L. (1993). Instructor ratings: Controlling for bias from initial student interest. *Journal of Education for Business, 68(6),* 362-366.

Prosser, M., & Trigwell, K. (1990). Student evaluations of teaching and courses: Student study strategies as a criterion of validity. *Higher Education, 20(2),* 135-142.

Rayder, N. F. (1968). College student ratings of instructors. *Journal of Experimental Education, 37,* 76-81.

Riley, J. W., Ryan, B. F., & Lipschitz, M. (1950). *The student looks at his teacher.* New Brunswick, NJ: Rutgers University Press.

Rodabaugh, R. C., & Kravitz, D. A. (1994). Effects of procedural fairness on student judgments of professors. *Journal on Excellence in College Teaching, 5(2).*

Rodin, M., Frey, P. W., & Gessner, P. K. (1975). Student evaluation. *Science, 187,* 555-559.

Rodin, M., & Rodin, B. (1972). Student evaluation of teachers. *Science, 177,* 1164-1166.

Ryan, J. M., & Harrison, P. D. (1995). The relationship between individual instructional characteristics and the overall assessment of teaching effectiveness across different instructional contexts. *Research and Development in Education, 36(5),* 577-594.

Sailor, P., Worthen, B. R. & Shin, E. H. (1997). Class level as a possible mediator of the relationship between grades and student ratings of teaching. *Assessment and Evaluation in Higher Education, 22(3),* 261-269.

Scherr, F. C., & Scherr S. S. (1990) Bias in student evaluation of teacher effectiveness. *Journal of Education for Business, 65(8),* 356-358.

Schmelkin, L. P., & Spencer, K. J. (1997). Faculty perspectives on course and teacher evaluations. *Research in Higher Education, 38(5),* 75-92.

Schuckman, H. (1990). Students' perception of faculty and graduate students as classroom teachers. *Teaching of Psychology, 17(3),* 162-165.

Schum, T. R., & Vindra, K. J. (1996). Relationship between systematic feedback to faculty and ratings of clinical teaching. *Academic Medicine, 71(10),* 1100-1102.

Seldin, P. (1993, October). How colleges evaluate professors 1983 v. 1993. *AAHE Bulletin,* 6-12.

Shapiro, E. G. (1990). Effect of instructor and class characteristics on students' class evaluations. *Research in Higher Education, 3(2),* 135-148.

Shepherd, G. J., & Trank, D. M. (1989). Individual differences in consistency of evaluation: Student perceptions of teacher effectiveness. *Journal of Research and Development in Education, 22(3),* 45-52.

Sherman, T. M. (1978). The effects of student formative evaluation of instruction on teacher behavior. *Journal of Educational Technology Systems, 6,* 209-217.

Shmanske, S. (1988). On the measurement of teacher effectiveness. *Journal of Economic Education, 19(4),* 307-314.

Singhal, S. (1968). *Illinois course evaluation questionnaire items by rank of instructor, sex of the instructor, and sex of the student (Research Report No. 282).* Urbana, IL: University of Illinois, Office of Instructional Resources, Measurement, and Research Division.

Stallings, W. M., & Singhal, S. (1968). *Some observations on the relationships between productivity and student evaluations of courses and teaching (Research Report No. 274).* Urbana, IL: University of Illinois, Office of Instructional Resources, Measurement and Research Division.

Stevens, J. J., & Aleamoni, L. M. (1985). The use of evaluative feedback for instructional improvement: A longitudinal perspective. *Instructional Science, 13,* 285-304.

Stroh, L. (1991). High school student evaluation of student teachers: How do they compare with professionals? *Illinois School Research and Development, 27(2),* 81-92.

Sullivan, A. M., & Skanes, G. R. (1974). Validity of student evaluation of teaching and the characteristics of successful instructors. *Journal of Educational Psychology, 66,* 584-590.

Summers, M. A., & Associates. (1996). The camera adds more than pounds: Gender differences in course satisfaction for campus and distance learning students. *Journal of Research and Development in Education, 29(4),* 212-219.

Tang, T. L. (1997). Teaching evaluation at a public institution of higher education: Factors related to the overall teaching effectiveness. *Public Personnel Management, 26(3),* 379-389.

Tatro, C. N. (1995). Gender effects on student evaluations of faculty. *Journal of Research and Development in Education, 28(3),* 169-173.

Teven, J. J., & McCroskey, J. C. (1997). The relationship of perceived teacher caring with student learning and teacher evaluation. *Communications Education, 46(1),* 1-9.

Tollefson, N., & Associates. (1989). The relationship of students' attitudes about effective teaching to students' ratings of effective teaching. *Educational and Psychological Measurement, 49(3),* 529-536.

Trick, L. R., & Associates. (1993). Do grades affect faculty teaching evaluations? *Journal of Optometric Education, 18(3),* 88-92.

Van Arsdale, S. K., & Hammons, J. O. (1995). Myths and misconceptions about student ratings of college faculty: Separating fact and fiction. *Nursing Outlook, 43(1),* 33-66.

Voeks, V. W. (1962). Publications and teaching effectiveness. *Journal of Higher Education, 33,* 212.

Vu, T. R., Marriott, D. J., Skeff, K. M., Stratos, G. A., & Litzelman, D. K. (1997). Prioritizing areas for faculty development of clinical teachers by using student evaluations for evidence-based decisions. *Academic Medicine, 72(10),* 57-59.

Walker, B. D. (1969). An investigation of selected variables relative to the manner in which a population of junior college students evaluate their teachers. *Dissertation Abstracts, 29(9-B),* 3474.

Ware, J. E., & Williams, R. G. (1977). Discriminate analysis of student ratings as a means of identifying lecturers who differ in enthusiasm or information giving. *Educational and Psychological Measurement, 37,* 627-639.

Waters, M., & Associates. (1988). High and low faculty evaluations: Descriptions by students. *Teaching of Psychology, 15(4),* 203-204.

Watkins, D. (1990). Student ratings of tertiary courses for "alternative calendar" purposes. *Assessment and Evaluation in Higher Education, 15(1),* 12-21.

Wheeless, V. E., & Potorti, P. F. (1989). Student assessment of teacher masculinity and femininity: A test of the sex role congruency hypothesis on student attitudes toward learning. *Journal of Educational Psychology, 81(2),* 259-262.

Wilson, R. (1998). New research casts doubt on value of comparing adult college students perceptions of effective teaching with those of traditional students. *Chronicle of Higher Education, 44(19),* Al 2-Al 4.

Winocur, S., & Associates. (1989). Perceptions of male and female academics within a teaching context. *Research in Higher Education, 30(3),* 317-329.

Wood, K., Linsky, A. S., & Straus, M. A. (1974). Class size and student evaluation of faculty. *Journal of Higher Education, 45,* 524-534.

Yongkittikul, C., Gillmore, G. M., & Brandenburg, D. C. (1974). *Does the time of course meeting affect course ratings by students? (Research Report No. 346).* Urbana, IL: University of Illinois, Office of Instructional Resources, Measurement and Research Division.

Zahn, D. K., & Schramm, R. M. (1992). Student perception of teacher effectiveness based on teacher employment and course skill level. *Business Education Forum, 46(3),* 16-18.

———————————

Portions of this chapter appeared in the following article. Used by permission.

Aleamoni, L. M. (1999). Student rating myths versus research facts from 1924 to 1998. *Journal of Personnel Evaluation in Education, 13(2),* 153-166.

13

Operating the Faculty Evaluation System: Designing and Using Student Rating Forms

LEGAL ISSUES

Easily the largest and most visible component of a faculty evaluation system is the student rating form and its computerized output. Over the years, for good or ill, student ratings have come to be the single most important component of faculty evaluation systems. In response, many institutions have developed their own student rating forms, generally designed by faculty, students, administrators, or a committee made up of some combination of these. The use of these forms may pose a legal liability for the institution.

In the general area of faculty evaluation the courts have tended to accept faculty-determined criteria and standards of professional performance, focusing instead on the consistent application of contractual conditions or procedures (Kaplan, 1978). Centra (1999) points out that, from a legal perspective, institutions must take care to comply with faculty evaluation procedures specified in the contract or faculty handbook. In addition, an institution may not use criteria or processes that create a discriminatory assessment based on ethnic background, race, or gender (Braskamp & Ory, 1999). Thus, the issues of what to measure and how to measure it have tended to be left to faculty to determine. Primarily, institutions must have a procedure in place that does not violate basic civil rights and, in the event of an audit, must be able to provide evidence that their procedure has been applied correctly and consistently. The legal ramifications surrounding the design and use of student rating forms in a faculty evaluation system must be considered within the context of these principles.

Carr and Padgett (1992) reviewed the legal liability in all 50 states concerning the design and use of student rating forms. They concluded that the primary legal issue revolves around statistical validity and reliability of such forms. Legal liability is posed when unreliable and invalid student rating forms are used in support of personnel decisions. The legal liability of the institution includes discrimination, defamation, and violations of individual privacy and academic freedom.

State laws provide an additional environmental element creating possible legal liability. Of particular concern are the open records laws. Unless exceptions are made, these laws provide that employment records such as salary and performance evaluations of public employees are public information. Some colleges and universities publish the results of student ratings of faculty. Some do not. Under open records laws, ratings would have to be made public for a single faculty member or for all faculty members if an individual or group requested this information. In this litigious society liability for publishing student evaluations of faculty members based on forms of dubious statistical validity seems rather apparent (Carr & Padgett, 1992, p. 69).

The following were found to have no exceptions to the state statutes pertaining to the release of faculty personnel records:

Alaska	North Carolina
Arizona	North Dakota
Arkansas	Ohio
Georgia	Tennessee
Massachusetts	Texas
Maine	Utah
Minnesota	Virginia
Missouri	Wisconsin
Montana	

The following states were found to have only general exceptions to public records laws pertaining to the release of faculty personnel records:

Washington, DC	Pennsylvania
Kentucky	Washington
Louisiana	West Virginia
Nevada	

Finally, the following states were found to specifically exclude faculty records from open records laws:

Alabama	Michigan
California	Mississippi
Colorado	Nebraska
Connecticut	New Hampshire
Delaware	New Jersey
Hawaii	New York
Iowa	Oklahoma
Idaho	Rhode Island
Illinois	South Dakota
Indiana	Vermont
Kansas	Wyoming
Maryland	

Thus, institutions in states that have no, or only general, exceptions to public records laws may find themselves at greater risk for possible legal action revolving around the publication of faculty records that include

data from unreliable and invalid student rating forms. In those states where public disclosure of faculty records is less likely owing to specific exceptions, the risk of legal liability still exists if faculty personnel decisions are challenged in court.

In terms of the design, or the adoption, of student rating forms, the key issue is to establish their reliability and validity of prior to their use in a faculty evaluation system. The adoption of commercially available student rating forms such as those reviewed in Chapter 15 ensures that the forms are reliable and valid since they have undergone rigorous psychometric procedures in their development. It is generally recommended that an institution consider the adoption of a commercially available student rating form prior to embarking on the task of building one from "scratch." However, if the institution determines to design and use its own student rating form, the administration must be willing to commit to the year-long rigorous psychometric process involved in producing a reliable and valid instrument. To fail to do so places the institution at unnecessary legal risk.

Civil rights legislation has provided a legal environment in which employment tests and performance evaluations must in most cases be statistically reliable and valid. That is, there must be statistical documentation that they are reliable measures, are job related and predict job performance. Otherwise, the employer's legal defense is likely to be inadequate in cases of discrimination (Carr & Padgett, 1992, p. 68).

DESIGNING A STUDENT RATING FORM

The design and development of a valid, reliable form intended to measure the teaching performance of an instructor and/or the perceived effectiveness of a course is a technical task requiring professional expertise in statistics and psychological measurement. It is a common fallacy among educators that all that is required to develop a questionnaire is to sit down and write a set of questions. It should be noted that what is being constructed is a measurement instrument. The fact that the measurement instrument is being designed to measure psychological phenomena (i.e., perceptions, opinions, reactions, etc.) does not excuse it from being held to the same standards of accuracy, reliability, and validity as any other measurement tool or instrument. To assume that all one has to do to construct a psychometric instrument is to write a set of questions is analogous to assuming that all one has to do to construct an automobile is to get a motor and attach some wheels to it. Both tasks are easier said than done. And both tasks require not only precision and skill but also an understanding of the underlying principles and science involved.

As was noted earlier, student rating instruments are frequently developed by faculty, students, administrators, and/or committees who lack questionnaire design and scaling expertise. Such instruments typically are not subjected to reliability and validity studies and, therefore, may be easily influenced by extraneous variables in the classroom such as time of day, class size, and the instructor's personality.

In order for student evaluation ratings to be considered an integral part of a comprehensive instructional evaluation system, they must be both reliable and valid. As a practical matter, certain steps must be followed when designing and/or selecting a student rating instrument.

Determine Purpose of the Form

The first step is to determine the purpose for which the instrument is to be used. One primary purpose is to provide formative evaluation information to the faculty member for use in improving instruction. Another is to provide summative evaluation information to colleagues, administrators, and students for use in promotion, tenure, merit, and course selection decisions. In practice, most faculty evaluation systems use student rating data for both formative and summative purposes.

Specify Evaluative Elements

The second step is to specify the elements to be addressed in the instrument. If the instructional design of the course is to be judged, then there must be questions or statements addressing organization, structure, objectives, difficulty, pace, relevance, content, usefulness, and so on. If, on the other hand, the instructional techniques are to be judged, then there must be questions or statements addressing method of presentation, student interaction, pacing, level of difficulty, and so on. If the instructor's presentation skills are to be judged, then there must be questions or statements addressing personal characteristics, skill, rapport, preparation, interest, commitment, and so on. If the impact on student learning is to be judged, then there must be questions or statements addressing level of student satisfaction, student perceived competency, student desire to continue study in the field, and so on.

Determine the Types of Items

The third step in constructing a student rating form is to determine the types of items the instrument should con-

tain. The accuracy of the students' responses and the meaningfulness of the ratings to the instructor depend upon the appropriateness of the item and response formats.

Low Inference–High Inference Items. If the purpose of gathering student ratings is to produce measures that require considerable inference from what is seen or heard in the classroom to the labeling of the behavior, then higher inference measures are needed. These measures are obtained as ratings of the instructor on scales such as partial–fair, autocratic–democratic, or dull–stimulating. Such measures are appropriate when making summative (final and global) decisions about the instructor and/or the instruction. If, on the other hand, the purpose is to produce measures that require the student to classify teaching behaviors according to relatively objective categories, then low-inference measures are needed. These measures are obtained as frequency ratings of the instructor on scales such as gesturing, variation in voice, asking questions, or praise and encouragement. Such measures are appropriate when making formative decisions about the instructor and instruction, because it is easier to translate them into specific behaviors that can be used in instructional improvement programs.

Open-Ended and Closed-Ended Items. Open-ended (free-response) items such as "What part of the course did you like the best?" are often found on the back side of student rating forms. These types of questions usually produce a colorful array of responses in the students' own words but provide very little representative (consensus) information for the instructor to use in formative evaluation. However, instructors like such items because they enjoy reading comments to which they can attach their own interpretations.

The use of closed-ended (limited-response) items such as generally found on the front of student rating forms, on the other hand, can provide accurate counts on the types of responses to each item. The most acceptable and frequently used approach is to use a combination of closed-ended and open-ended items.

The type of closed-ended responses one should use is largely determined by the type of question or statement being asked or made. When care is not taken to match the appropriate responses to each question or statement, incongruous and unreliable responses will result. For example, an item stated as, "Was the instructor's grading fair?" dictates a Yes or No response; if it is stated as, "The instructor's grading was fair," a response along an Agree Strongly to Disagree Strongly continuum is dictated. Neutral or Don't Know responses should generally not be used unless they represent truly necessary options; otherwise they will be used by those students who do have an opinion but are somewhat reluctant to indicate it.

If a continuum response format is used with only the end points anchored such as

Excellent_1_2_3_4_5_6_Poor

the item tends to produce unreliable responses. It is necessary that each response point along the continuum be identified and, furthermore, that the numbers be replaced with acronyms or abbreviations so that the students will know what they are responding to. In general, the Agree Strongly to Disagree Strongly continuum is appropriate whenever an item is stated either positively or negatively. Another type of closed-ended response scale that can be used is one that requires elaborate behavioral descriptions along the continuum. Such scales are called behaviorally anchored rating scales (Aleamoni, 1981).

Prepare or Select Items

The fourth step is to prepare or select the items. If one is preparing the items then it is important to prepare the appropriate item types along the lines indicated in the third step above, and have the items independently edited and reviewed by other colleagues competent in the field of psychometrics. If, on the other hand, one is selecting items or instruments in their entirety, then a careful content analysis of the instrument and items must occur to see if the issues described in the first three steps, above, have been satisfied.

Organize the Items

The fifth and final step in the design of a student rating form or in the selection of items is the organization of the items within the instrument. One has to decide how the items are to be grouped and labeled, how they should be organized for easy reading and answering, and how and where the responses should be recorded. If there is a logical or chronological flow to the items, then their organization on the form should reflect that. If there are only a few negative items, then one or two should appear very early in the instrument to avoid positive response set mistakes (i.e., before students get in the habit of thinking the response to the extreme right is always the most positive). It is advisable to have a few negatively stated items in the instrument, but only if they can be stated negatively in a logical manner.

Most questionnaire items can be grouped into subscales. If the original grouping was done on a logical basis, then an empirical analysis using a statistical technique such as factor analysis should be used to ensure that the grouped items do, in fact, represent a common scale.

Determine Form Reliability and Validity

Once an instrument has been constructed, it is important to determine its reliability and validity through experimental administration. Reliability may be defined in two ways. The first describes the instrument's capability of producing stable student responses from one time to another in a given course. The second describes the consistency (or degree of agreement) among the responders. Because most student rating instruments ask students to respond to different aspects of the instructional setting (e.g., instructor, instruction, textbook, homework), the reliability of the items and the subscales should be the major concern. If one cannot demonstrate that the items and subscales of a particular instrument can yield stable student responses, then the data and resulting evaluations may be meaningless.

If the instrument contains highly reliable items and subscales (e.g., .70 and higher), then one needs to determine how accurate the student responses are. Once the reliability problem has been resolved, attention should be focused on the validity of student ratings. Logical validation is concerned with the question, "What does the instrument measure?" and empirical validation is concerned with the question, "To what extent does the instrument measure what it is intended to measure?" A logical validation requires judgment on the content validity of the instrument. This is usually accomplished by carefully constructing the instrument so that it contains items and subscales that will yield measures in the areas that are considered appropriate by an individual or group of experts in the field under consideration. Empirical validation procedures require the use of criterion measures against which student ratings may be compared. Validity studies normally report the magnitude of the correlation between criterion measures and student ratings. The rule of thumb here is the higher the correlation, the better the validity.

In constructing a valid and reliable student rating form it is necessary to conduct various studies and analyses of the functioning of the items. It is essential that an institution embarking upon the construction of its own form become familiar with the process involved. A good example of such a study is *Differential Relationship of Student, Instructor, and Course Characteristics to General and Specific Items on the Course Evaluation Questionnaire* (Aleamoni & Thomas, 1980).

TYPES OF STUDENT RATING SYSTEMS

Keeping in mind the steps for designing a student rating instrument and the necessity of conducting reliability and validity studies on the resulting instrument, several different student rating systems that may be considered.

Instructor-Constructed

The least defensible type of system is the one made up by a particular instructor for a particular course. Such a situation really does not constitute a rating system but rather is generally the result of an attempt to do something about responding to pressure to have a student rating system—without really doing anything.

Instructor-Selected

A more defensible type of system is one where the instructor may select from a finite pool of items made available by the institution for use in evaluating teaching. The students respond to these items on a standardized rating form that includes a common set of general items used by all instructors. One of the earliest examples of such a pool is the Purdue Cafeteria System, which provides a 200-item catalog. Instructors select their items, which are then computer-printed on an optically scanned answer sheet along with five standard general items. Normative data are provided only for the five general items. Derry (1977) reported that the average reliability of a cafeteria rating form was 0.88. Other similar examples of this type are the Instructor and Course Evaluation System (ICES) of the University of Illinois at Urbana-Champaign, the Instructor Designed Questionnaire (IDQ) of the University of Michigan, and the Student Perceptions of Teaching (SPOT) of the University of Iowa (Abrami & Murphy, 1980).

Standard Form—Optional Items

The most defensible type of student rating system is one that has a standard section of items applicable to almost all courses and instructors with additional optional item sections that allow the instructor to select supplementary (or more diagnostic) items from a catalog. One of the earliest and continuing examples is the Course/Instructor Evaluation Questionnaire (CIEQ) system which provides a standard section of 21 items on which normative data are provided by item and five subscales and two optional 21-item response sections that allow instructors to select up to 42 additional items from a 373-item catalog. Aleamoni and Stevens (1986) reported test-retest reliabilities for the 21 standard items from 0.81 to 0.94 and for the subscales and total from 0.92 to 0.98. Other examples of this type are the

Instructional Development and Effectiveness Assessment System (IDEA) of Kansas State University, the Student Instructional Report (SIR) of Educational Testing Service, and the Student Instructional Rating System (SIRS) of Michigan State University (Abrami & Murphy, 1980).

Multiple Standard Forms

Another type of system is one that consists of multiple standard forms. The instructor's only choice here is the type of form, not the items. The University of Washington Instructional Assessment System (IAS) provides six forms to faculty, one for small lecture/discussion courses, one for large lecture courses, one for seminar courses, one for problem-solving courses, one for skills-oriented or practicum courses, and one for quiz sections. Reliabilities from 0.15 to 0.34 for single raters to 0.88 and above for classes of 40 students have been reported (Abrami & Murphy, 1980).

ADMINISTRATION OF STUDENT RATING SYSTEMS

After an appropriate instrument has been developed or selected, administration procedures need to be established. As noted earlier, if possible the responsibility for managing and directing a campus-wide program of administering student ratings should be placed in the hands of instructional development, evaluation, or testing personnel. One should avoid placing such responsibility either in the hands of students or faculty in individual departments or colleges, because its application would be restricted and the possibility of a lasting program would be reduced. As a last option, the responsibility may be assumed by the office of the chief academic officer of the institution. However, the danger of having the program perceived as a watchdog program of the administration is increased in such cases.

In keeping with the concept of designing and operating the faculty evaluation system in such a way as to serve both formative and summative purposes, several guidelines related to student rating systems may be stated. First, it must be recognized that the value of any student rating system relies on the confidence the students have that their input will 1) cause them no harm, and 2) have some effect on the instructor (Arreola, 1987). In actual practice, operating a student rating system requires a careful balancing of the needs and concerns of the students, faculty, and administration. These needs and concerns are sometimes antithetical to one another. This can often place the person in charge of the office or agency running the student rating system in a very difficult and tricky situation.

On the one hand, faculty may be fearful and distrustful of the administration. Faculty go through a predictable set of stages in resisting or attempting to escape from a faculty evaluation system as noted earlier. On the other hand, students are fearful of retribution by the faculty if they give negative ratings and don't believe the faculty or the administration will pay any attention to what they say anyway. Finally, the administration may desperately want any kind of quantitative or hard data on which to base difficult personnel decisions. Long experience with these circumstances leads to the following practical guidelines pertaining to running a student rating system.

1. If at all possible, do not locate a student rating coordination or processing agency in the office of a dean, vice president, or other major administrator. Such placement only reinforces the idea that the student rating system and the faculty evaluation office are simply watchdog agencies of the administration.

2. Try to locate the student rating form processing office in a test-scoring center, computer center, media center, or, ideally, in a faculty development center.

3. Arrange the processing schedule so that the completed analyses of the student rating forms are not available until after final grades have been reported.

4. Maintain student credibility. Conduct a program to maintain the credibility of the students in the student rating system. Include regular contacts with student government, appoint student representative(s) to the faculty evaluation development committee, and include stories concerning use of student ratings in student newspapers at least once each term. A constant communication campaign with the students must be maintained which informs them that the faculty member will not see the student rating results until after grades have been reported and that the student ratings are taken seriously by the faculty and the administration (Arreola, 1983). Without such a campaign, the student rating system will experience serious problems, including refusal of the students to complete forms, completing forms by simply marking the same response for all items, and covering the forms with various types of graffiti. The GIGO (garbage in, garbage out) principle applies here.

5. Make it clear that the student rating form-processing office is a service to the faculty and not the administration or the student government. Do not automatically send results of the ratings to the administration

or the student newspaper, even though written permission has been given by the instructor. Such actions will forever taint the credibility of the processing office. Require anyone wanting information concerning the student ratings of a faculty member to get them from that faculty member.

6. Make certain that the issue of the distribution of copies of faculty evaluation printouts is a matter between the administration and the faculty or between the students and the faculty. Provide the faculty member with multiple copies of the student rating form analyses or other results; do not keep copies in the processing office. Make it physically difficult to recover or reconstitute a given faculty member's computer analysis. The best approach is to maintain only raw data files on disk or tape. Then, if a request is received by the processing office to provide copies of a particular faculty member's evaluation results, it can truthfully be said that the processing office has no copies but that the faculty member has several.

The issue of the confidentiality and distribution of student rating or faculty evaluation results should be a matter between the faculty member and the administration and not between the processing office and the administration. The processing office must not be perceived as an arm of a "big brother" administration.

The method of administering and gathering student responses can determine the quality of the resulting data. It is advisable to administer the instrument in a formalized manner in the classroom by providing a standard set of instructions and enough time to complete all the items. If the instrument is administered in an informal manner, without a standard set of instructions and a designated time to fill it out, the students tend not to take it seriously and possibly do not bother to turn it in. Furthermore, if the students are permitted to take the instruments home to fill them out and return them at the next class meeting, very few instruments will be returned.

The following practical procedures have been successfully used in managing large student rating systems. These procedures assume that the faculty member will not be the primary person administering the rating forms in class to the students.

1. Set up a log system for maintaining control of student rating form distribution and collection. This log should contain the name of the faculty member, the number of the course, and the enrollment. Such information is generally available from the registrar's office.

2. Prepare student rating packets with at least five more sheets than the official number enrolled in the course. Log in the actual number of sheets sent to the instructor.

3. In addition to the student rating forms, the packet should contain a standardized script to be read when administering the forms and a Proctor Identification Form (PIF). Upon receipt of the packet, the faculty member should remove the PIF and indicate the name of the student in the class who has been selected to administer the rating forms. The faculty member must sign the PIF and return it separately to the processing office. The processing office should log in the date of the receipt of the form and the name of the student proctor.

4. After removing the PIF, the faculty member should give the student rating form package to the chosen student proctor. The student proctor removes and distributes the student rating forms and removes and reads a special form identified as the proctor administration form. It contains the standardized script for administering the student rating form. In addition to the standard information concerning the use of a #2 pencil to record student responses, the script should note that

   a. The faculty member is not in the room.

   b. The results of the rating will not be returned to the instructor until after final grades have been turned in.

   c. The students' responses will be an important part of the information considered in improving the course or making promotion, tenure, retention, and merit pay decisions.

5. The proctor must sign the proctor administration form, certifying that the student rating forms were administered in accordance to the instructions, that the script was read as part of the administration, and that the faculty member was not in the room.

6. Finally, cross-checking items should be included on the student rating forms that ask such questions as, "Was the instructor in the room when this form was administered?" "Did the proctor read the administration directions out loud to the class?" and, "Do you have confidence that your responses will make a difference?"

7. After the forms are completed and returned to the proctor, they should all be placed in the envelope along with the signed proctor administration form, and dropped in the campus mail to the processing office.

8. Upon receipt of the packet, the date of receipt should be logged in; the name on the proctor administration form should be checked against the name reported by the instructor on the proctor identification form. A count is made of the incoming completed student rating forms to make sure that the number does not exceed the official enrollment figure for the class. This latter step is designed to discourage stuffing of completed student rating packets by either students or, in certain instances, the faculty themselves.

9. Before machine processing, the student rating forms must be visually scanned for stray marks. Often the students doodle in the margins or simply cross out an incorrect response rather than erase it. These types of marks must be erased before the sheets can be processed. Experience has shown that the student rating processing office would be well advised to buy electric erasers rather than using the eraser end of a pencil. The time and staff size required to carry out this necessary step is often much larger than would first be anticipated. This is especially true if the system is new and the students are not yet familiar with the rating forms.

10. Finally, log the date when the completed computer analysis and student rating forms were returned to the faculty member.

OPTIONS FOR ADMINISTERING RATING FORMS IN CLASS

The steps above assume that a student proctor, selected from the class itself, administers the rating form. Other options, some less desirable than others, are possible.

Self-Administered

In systems where instructors administer their own questionnaires, they also should read the standard set of instructions after the forms have been distributed and then remain in the front of the room until all forms have been completed. The instructor may then select a student from the class to gather the completed forms and deposit them in the campus mail. As before, the statement read should specify that the instructor will not see the results until after the term grades have been turned into the admissions and records office. The exception to this procedure is when the instructor has informed the students that their responses will be used in a formative way to improve the current course.

Student Government Administered

Another option is to have representatives of the student government association administer the instruments if the faculty and department or college administrators are willing or request them to do it. The students administering the instruments should also read a similar standard set of instructions and request that the instructor leave during the administration. The student organization could use the campus newspaper to announce when the instruments are going to be used and how they will be administered as a final cross-checking procedure.

Staff Administered

If an administrator decides to designate a staff member to administer the instrument, then the same procedures should be followed as suggested above. This option should be avoided, however, unless there is no other way to ensure a common administration of the instruments. As noted earlier, faculty and students tend to feel threatened if they know that an administrator is controlling and directing the administration or processing of the instruments.

When the rating instrument is administered, the students should have all necessary materials. Students should generally fill out the forms in their regular classroom near the beginning of a particular class session. Above all, the students must be left with the impression that their frank and honest comments are desired and not that this is their chance to get back at the instructor. If the students get the impression that the instructor is not really interested in their responses, they will not respond seriously. If the students feel the instructor is going to see their responses before final grades are in, they will respond more positively and write very few comments. This is especially true if the students are asked to identify themselves on the instrument. If the instrument is administered immediately before, during, or after the final examination (or any other meaningful examination), the students tend to respond in an inconsistent manner. If students are allowed to discuss the course and instructor while filling out the forms, then biases will enter into their ratings.

REPORTING STUDENT RATING RESULTS

One of the most important aspects of any program is the method of reporting the results. If the results are not reported in an appropriate, accurate, and timely manner,

the usefulness of the instrument and the system as a whole will be seriously compromised. When tabulating and summarizing item responses, the following procedures should be considered.

1. The item responses should be given numerical values in order to calculate descriptive statistics, and the descriptive statistics should be reported. However, the response positions on the form should be labeled only with abbreviations and not the numerical values used in later computations.

2. The results should be reported by item and subscale, if appropriate.

3. The results should be summarized by class section, department, college, and so on.

Directionality of Numerical Scale

When items are presented with defined response scales, such as Agree Strongly, Agree, Disagree, and Disagree Strongly, they should be weighted to reflect direction and ideal response when the results are tabulated and summarized. For example, if the above response scale were weighted 4, 3, 2, 1, respectively, it would indicate that the item was positively stated with the ideal response being Agree Strongly. With such a weighting, it is possible to calculate a mean and standard deviation for each item for a given class of students. The mean value indicates their average rating and the standard deviation indicates how similar or dissimilar their responses were. With such a weighting scheme and the resulting means and standard deviations, the results can then be reported for both items and subscales. The results can also be summarized and reported by class section, course, selected courses, courses within a department, courses within a college, and courses within the university. Such complete reporting schemes permit meaningful comparisons when necessary.

Distributing Rating Result—Voluntary Systems

An important aspect of any system of reporting student evaluation rating results is who will or should actually see the results. If the administration of the instruments is completely voluntary, then only the faculty members themselves should receive the results. As noted earlier, the processing office is ill-advised to enter into an arrangement that places it between the faculty and the administration.

Distributing Results—Mandatory Systems

If the administration of the student rating form is mandatory, as is the case in many systems, then every effort should be made by the processing office to remove itself from the responsibility of distributing rating results directly. However, if the processing office has no choice and the system must be designed to provide faculty with the option of releasing copies of their results to other interested parties, great effort must be taken to ensure that the instructor feels no pressure to release the results. In such a circumstance, a procedure must be implemented that requires a formal written release by the instructor. The processing office in such a situation would be well-advised to consult with the college or university attorney in developing the wording of such a release. Every effort must be made to make faculty members aware of who is to receive copies of their results and how frequently. Under no circumstances, however, should students' written comments be reported to administrators or student organizations, because those comments tend to be susceptible to widely discrepant subjective interpretations by the reader.

Publishing Rating Results

If the faculty or administration has entered into an agreement with the campus student organization to publish the results of the student ratings, every effort should be made to ensure fair and accurate reporting of the results. Such results are usually reported in a book divided by discipline or content area. Student-published books are usually promoted as course and instructor guides for prospective student enrollees as well as vehicles to encourage instructional improvement. Unfortunately, due to the zealousness of some student editors and the vendettas of others, such publications have tended to simply generate antagonistic relationships between the rated faculty and student editors.

One vehicle to disseminate student ratings of faculty to a wider segment of the student body is the student newspaper. The most effective way to present such results is to do so in a positive manner. For example, only the names or course numbers of the most highly rated are reported; the others are not mentioned. Whoever is responsible for publishing student ratings for mass consumption should remember that accentuating the positive, rather than focusing on the negative, results in better acceptance, continued participation, and potential instructional improvement on the part of the participating faculty members. Any attempt to be cute or to "get" an instructor usually results in short-lived systems with serious negative repercussions.

Recently, the Internet has become an outlet for student rating results. Student organizations may publish student ratings on a web site and, in a few instances, invite comments to be made via email. These anonymous email comments are then posted to the site. This approach to distributing faculty rating data poses new challenges, not the least of which is the issue of confidentiality. It is one thing to publish student rating data in a local student newspaper; it is quite another to post the data on a web site available to the world. In a setting where it is illegal for faculty to publicly post student grades with identifying names and social security number, it is likely that the emerging practice of posting faculty ratings on the Internet will generate legal challenges in the future.

FORMAT OF THE STUDENT RATING FORM COMPUTERIZED ANALYSIS OUTPUT

It has been assumed that virtually every operational student rating form system produces some form of computerized analysis output. This output may range from a simple frequency count for each response to each item up to a very sophisticated printout showing normative data of various sorts. Experience has shown that most faculty react to a sophisticated printout that contains page after page of indices, norms, graphs, and tables with something less than total enthusiasm. Although professional standards demand that the analysis of student rating data be accurate and statistically sound, it must be remembered that most faculty are not well versed in the intricacies of item analysis, measurement theory, or statistical analysis. Moreover, most faculty have no real desire to become well versed in these areas. Thus, for the computerized analysis of student rating results to have the desired effect of providing useful information that may be acted upon by the faculty member for self-improvement, an effort must be made to make these computerized analyses user friendly. One way of doing this is to provide a verbal summary sheet that translates the statistical information into general statements.

For example, if the student rating form has four response choices per item, it is clear that a standard deviation exceeding 1.00 would indicate wide disparity of responses to the item. In such a case, the mean value of the item would have little value other than to represent the numerical average of the responses. The computer program can be written to produce a statement such as the following:

On item _6_, the standard deviation was _1.3_. This can be interpreted to mean that there was CONSIDERABLE DISAGREEMENT among the students on this item and thus the Average Response value should **NOT** be interpreted as representing a consensus rating by the class.

Or, the program could present a statement such as

On item __18__ , the average response was __3.1__ and the standard deviation was __0.4__ . This can be interpreted to mean that the students rated you as being MODERATELY HIGH on this item and there was a HIGH degree of consensus among the students in this rating.

Ideally, such statements should be printed as either the first or the last page in a computer analysis so they are easily found. Obviously, the program must be written to make the proper interpretations of various combinations of data relative to the appropriate norms. The point, though, is that even though the processing office may produce reports which are statistically sophisticated and correct, one must never lose sight of the fact that for the analyses to be useful they must be understood and used by the faculty. Again, as a practical guideline, providing computerized, written interpretations of the statistical information listed in the printout is highly effective in helping to promote the effectiveness of the student rating information.

INTERPRETING AND USING STUDENT RATING RESULTS

Although we may wish our analyses to be user friendly, they must still present data of sufficient clarity and detail to permit sophisticated interpretations. How accurately and meaningfully the results of student ratings are interpreted and used depends on the type of information provided to the participating faculty member and other interested parties. The research on student ratings has revealed a definite positive response bias, which needs to be addressed when interpreting and using the results. That is, if students are asked to respond to positively stated items using a 4-point scale of Agree Strongly, Agree, Disagree, and Disagree Strongly, the responses tend to be distributed as shown in Figure 13.1.

To someone not familiar with statistics, the midpoint of the 4-point scale (2.5) could easily be interpreted as average, and any rating higher than 2.5 could be interpreted as a positive rating. But, as Figure 13.1 shows, the easy interpretation that any rating of 2.5 or higher is good can be seen as being substantially in error. In fact, because the distribution of student ratings is skewed, the average or mean rating tends to fall closer to 3.0 than 2.5.

One effective way of reporting student rating data is to present decile information based on the appropriate

Figure 13.1 Skewed Student Rating Response Curve

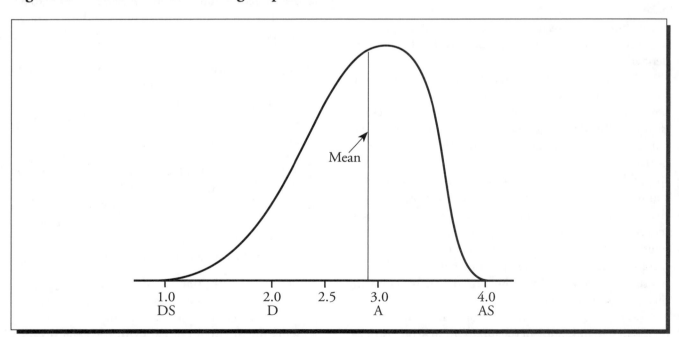

Arreola, R. A. (2000). Developing *a Comprehensive Faculty Evaluation System 2/e*. Bolton, MA: Anker Publishing Co., Inc.

Developing a Comprehensive Faculty Evaluation System

norm base. In this way, the bias of the student rating distribution can be taken into account. Figure 13.2 shows one way of representing student rating data in deciles.

The use of comparative (normative) data, such as the deciles shown in Figure 13.2, when reporting results can serve to counteract the positive response bias and result in a more accurate and meaningful interpretation of the ratings. For example, comparative data gathered on freshmen level courses in the anthropology department allow the instructors to determine how they and their courses are perceived in relation to the rest of the courses in the department. When such comparative data are not available, the instructor will be interpreting and using results in a void with very little substantiation for the resulting conclusions and actions taken.

Qualitative judgments can also be provided to the instructor by identifying course mean intervals in the comparative data, which can be defined as representing levels of excellence or needed improvement. For example, the comparative data for the freshmen courses in the anthropology department consisting of course means on student rating questionnaires could be divided into 10 equal portions. Each portion could be defined as representing a 10% interval of rated courses with a defined minimum and maximum course mean. These 10 intervals could then be defined as follows:

UN = Unacceptable
Any course mean falling in the lowest 10%, 20%, or 30% interval is defined as being of unacceptably low quality.

IR = Improvement Required
Any course mean falling in the 40% or 50% interval is defined as being of low quality and indicates that improvement is required.

PL = Professional Level
Any course mean falling in the 60% or 70% interval is defined as being of professional level quality and, although improvement is always desirable, no improvement is required.

EX = Exemplary
Any course mean falling in the upper 80%, 90%, or 100% interval is defined as being of extremely high quality surpassing standard professional performance.

Figure 13.2 Decile Interpretation of Student Ratings

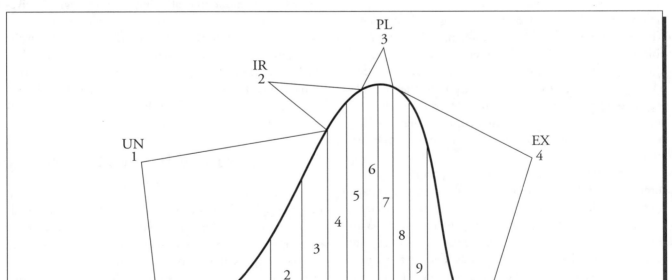

Arreola, R. A. (2000). Developing *a Comprehensive Faculty Evaluation System 2/e*. Bolton, MA: Anker Publishing Co., Inc.

This information could be provided to each participating instructor in a computerized format along with the appropriate interpretive materials. Or, as noted earlier, these values could be built into the computer program to produce appropriate written interpretive statements.

Further, the numerical values of 1, 2, 3, and 4 have been assigned to the labels UN, IR, PL, and EX, respectively. Thus, a raw student rating average of 3.2 may translate into either a decile of 8, a category rating of exemplary, or provide an appropriately norm-referenced summary qualitatively determined value of 4 since EX = 4.

Once established on a representative number of courses, the normative database should not change appreciably from year to year. Additional courses can be added to the normative database without significantly changing the distribution and comparative judgments. For some of the sources of invalidity identified as nontrivial by research studies, such as class level and required–elective status, comparative data stratified by course level and required–elective status will provide meaningful interpretations of the results. Aleamoni and Stevens (1986) include particular examples.

Once faculty members are provided with both comparative data and interpretive materials, they are then ready to interpret their results. The comparative interpretations result from the normative data provided, and the subjective interpretations result from reflections on what had taken place in the classroom that could be related to the comparative interpretations. Using this procedure, in addition to a careful reading of the students' written comments (if available), each instructor should be able to generate diagnostic interpretations of instructional strengths and weaknesses in the course. If an instructor has results on two or more similar sections, then the ratings of one section may be compared to those of another section to determine what instructional behaviors may have led to the higher comparative ratings in one section.

If the faculty are not able to generate any diagnostic interpretations, they may need to talk with the department head, dean, or instructional development specialist about the results. This assumes, of course, that these individuals know how to interpret the results. Finding that this approach still does not adequately identify the source of instructional difficulty, the instructor may want to consider other procedures (such as the use of additional diagnostic optional items, classroom visitation, videotaping, etc.) in future evaluations.

After identifying their instructional strengths and weaknesses, instructors can use the information to plan an improvement strategy. In some instances, the strategy may simply require minor modifications in the course or teaching method. In other instances, the strategy may require a substantial commitment of time and resources on the part of both the faculty member and the department. It has been through a process such as this that instructors have been able to use student evaluation ratings to identify instructional problems and then rectify them. Obviously, the success or failure of such a venture rests solely with the instructors and their willingness to both gather and use the data provided.

If faculty members decide to submit copies of their student rating results to their department head or dean for rank, pay, and tenure considerations, then all of the appropriate interpretive materials should also be provided. Ideally, the student rating results should be interpreted by someone with expertise in the field of measurement and instructional development. Deans and department heads should be made aware of the necessity of using the comparative data to interpret the results rather than relying on the more subjective and highly unreliable written and oral comments of students. Interpretations of student rating results may also be carried out by peer review triads using several other assessments of instructional effectiveness such as self-evaluation, quality of student learning, and peer evaluation of content (Aleamoni, 1987).

Student course/instructor evaluation data should never be used alone in evaluating instructional effectiveness for rank, pay, and tenure decisions, because such data are not completely diagnostic of all elements in the instructional domain. How such student rating data should be used in a comprehensive system of instructional evaluation and how much weight they should carry is something that should be determined at the departmental level.

FACULTY EVALUATION AND FACULTY DEVELOPMENT

Experience has shown, time and again, that a faculty evaluation system implemented without reference or connection to a faculty development program will generate greater amounts of anxiety and resistance among the faculty than if it is part of a larger faculty development/instructional improvement effort. Likewise, experience has also shown that faculty development programs, operated in isolation or without reference to a faculty evaluation program, tend to attract mainly those faculty who need their services the least.

Ideally, a faculty evaluation system should be an integral part of a larger faculty evaluation/faculty development program. To achieve maximal benefit from these two programs, each element of the faculty evaluation system should have a corresponding and concomitant element in the faculty development program. Thus, if the faculty evaluation system is going to evaluate how well faculty teach courses or how frequently they publish scientific articles, there should be seminars, workshops, and instructional materials available to assist them in learning how to teach better or how to write manuscripts that are more likely to be accepted for publication. In short, the faculty evaluation system should provide diagnostic information on the strengths and weaknesses a faculty member possesses and then follow up with programs or materials to aid the faculty member in enhancing strengths or overcoming weaknesses.

Again, as a practical matter, the computerized report derived from student ratings should include written comments that not only highlight the major areas of concern but also provide information on where to seek assistance. For example, a computer printout could include a statement such as the following:

> On the TESTING AND GRADING section of the student rating form, the majority of the students (87%) indicated that your tests did not seem to relate well to the course objectives. The Office of Assessment and Professional Enrichment offers a seminar for faculty on Test Construction that may be of some interest. Call 555-1234 for information about the next seminar.

Thus, to be truly effective, a faculty evaluation program must be linked to, and work in concert with, a faculty development program. Only in this way will both programs stand a reasonable chance of achieving the common goals of improving instruction and enhancing faculty performance.

CHAPTER REFERENCES

Abrami, P. C., & Murphy, V. (1980). *A catalogue of systems for student evaluation of instruction.* Montreal, Canada: McGill University, Centre for Teaching and Learning.

Aleamoni, L. M. (1981). Student ratings of instructor and instruction. In J. Millman (Ed.), *Handbook on teacher evaluation.* Beverly Hills, CA: Sage.

Aleamoni, L. M. (1987). Evaluating instructional effectiveness can be a rewarding experience. *Journal of Plant Disease, 71(4),* 377-379.

Aleamoni, L. M., & Stevens, J. J. (1986). *Arizona course/instructor evaluation questionnaire (CIEQ): Results interpretation manual.* Tucson, AZ: University of Arizona, Office of Instructional Research and Development.

Aleamoni, L. M., & Thomas, G. S. (1980). Differential relationships of student, instruction, and course characteristics to general and specific items on a course evaluation questionnaire. *Teaching of Psychology, 7(4),* 233-235.

Arreola, R. A. (1983, March). Establishing successful faculty evaluation and development programs (pp. 83-90). In A. Smith (Ed.), *Evaluating faculty and staff.* New Directions for Community Colleges, No. 41. San Francisco, CA: Jossey-Bass.

Arreola, R. A. (1987, Fall). The role of student government in faculty Evaluation (pp. 39-46). In L. M. Aleamoni (Ed.), *Techniques for evaluating and improving instruction.* New Directions for Teaching and Learning, No. 31. San Francisco, CA: Jossey-Bass.

Braskamp, L. A., & Ory, J. C. (1999). *Assessing faculty work.* San Francisco, CA: Jossey-Bass.

Carr, J. W., & Padgett, T. C. (1992). Legal liability when designing or adopting student rating forms. In R. A. Arreola (Ed.), *Proceedings of the first annual CEDA conference on practical issues in faculty evaluation* (pp. 68-76). Memphis, TN: Center for Educational Development and Assessment.

Centra, J. A. (1999). *Reflective faculty evaluation: Enhancing teaching and determining faculty effectiveness.* San Francisco, CA: Jossey-Bass.

Derry, J. O. (1977). *The cafeteria system: A new approach to course and instructor evaluation.* West Lafayette, IN: Purdue University.

Kaplan, W. A. (1978). *The law of higher education: A comprehensive guide to legal implications of administrative decision making.* San Francisco, CA: Jossey-Bass.

14

Catalog of
Student Rating Form Items

The following is a lengthy, but by no means exhaustive, collection of possible course and instructor rating items. Many of the items are from the CIEQ Optional Item Catalog (Aleamoni & Carynnk, 1977). These items are offered only as a beginning resource to aid in the construction of a student rating form. The items have been divided into 24 categories on the basis of their apparent content. The category headings for the items should not be considered as definitive identifiers since they were chosen primarily as an aid in finding items that appear to be related. No inference should be drawn that the items presented here have sufficient statistical support (i.e., factor loadings) to define the category in which they are listed.

All items are written so as to be responded to in either one of the two Agree Strongly to Disagree Strongly formats shown below.

5-point scale
AS	Agree Strongly
A	Agree
N	Neither Agree nor Disagree
D	Disagree
DS	Disagree Strongly

4-point scale
AS	Agree Strongly
A	Agree
D	Disagree
DS	Disagree Strongly

Other similar response scales may be used, but the items are written in such a way as to make best use of either one of the scales shown above. Also note that some of the items are stated in a negative fashion. In developing a student rating form it is a good idea to include a few negative items which measure the same dimension or category as a check on whether students have fallen into a response set. A response set is the habit students may fall into of marking all the choices down the middle or one side of the rating scale. When using negatively stated items, care must be taken to ensure that the computer analysis program correctly weights the responses to reflect the reversed scale.

In categories A, B, E, F, G, H, I, J, L, M, N, O, P, Q, R, S, T, and U, the subject in each sentence can be changed depending upon how the instructor wants to state the item. If this catalog is used to develop a customized student rating form, it will be necessary to conduct a factor analysis of the final set of items in order to determine if the items cluster in appropriate categories. At least four items should be picked as a measure of each category to be represented in the final form of the questionnaire.

A. Contributions by the Instructor and Teaching Assistants (in the lecture, laboratory, discussion)

1. The instructor gave clear explanations to clarify concepts.

2. The instructor's lectures broadened my knowledge of the area beyond the information presented in the readings.

3. The instructor demonstrated how the course was related to practical situations.

4. The instructor demonstrated that the course material was worthwhile.

5. The instructor related the course material to my previous learning experiences.

6. The instructor incorporated current material into the course.

7. The instructor made me aware of the current problems in this field.

8. The instructor's use of examples helped to get points across in class.

9. The instructor stresses important points in lectures/discussions.

10. The instructor was enthusiastic about the course material.

11. The instructor seemed to enjoy teaching.

12. The instructor's use of personal experiences helped to get points across in class.

13. The instructor clarified complex sections of the text.

14. The instructor gave useful writing assignments.

15. The instructor adapted the course to a reasonable level of comprehension.

16. The instructor exposed students to diverse approaches to problem solutions.

17. The instructor accepted other viewpoints that could possibly be valid.

18. The instructor provided information that supplemented assigned material.

19. The instructor provided essential material that was not in the text.

20. The instructor puts material across in an interesting way.

21. The instructor used his/her knowledge of other fields to help my understanding of the field being studied.

22. The instructor's explanations were clear.

23. The instructor encouraged independent thought.

24. The instructor's methods of evaluating me were fair.

25. The instructor guided the preparation of student reports.

26. The instructor gave useful writing assignments.

27. The instructor stressed important points in lectures.

28. The instructor taught near the class level.

29. The instructor provided opportunities for self-directed learning.

30. The instructor did NOT appear receptive to new ideas.

31. The instructor did NOT provide a sufficient variety of topics.

32. The instructor required that students employ concepts to demonstrate comprehension.

33. The instructor provided discussion material that supplemented lecture content.

34. The instructor did NOT provide for students' self-evaluation of their learning.

35. The instructor was an excellent resource person.

36. The instructor's evaluation of students' performances was constructive.

37. The instructor did NOT invite questions.

38. The instructor presented contrasting points of view.

39. The instructor related topics to other areas of knowledge.

40. The instructor did NOT combine theory and practical application.

41. The instructor did NOT encourage discussion of a topic.

42. The instructor answered all questions to the best of his/her ability.

43. The instructor carefully answered questions raised by students.

44. The instructor stimulated class discussion.

45. The instructor did NOT cover the reading assignments in sufficient depth in class.

46. The instructor was too involved with lecturing to be aware of the class.

47. The instructor provided very helpful critiques of student papers.

48. The instructor adequately prepared me for the material covered in his/her section.

49. The instructor clarified lecture material.

50. The instructor appeared to have a thorough knowledge of the subject.

51. The instructor seemed knowledgeable in many areas.

52. The instructor provided adequate individual remedial attention.

53. The instructor stressed important points in discussion.

54. The instructor overemphasized minor points.

55. The instructor showed mastery of the subject matter.

56. The instructor gave me a great deal which I would not get by independent study.

57. The instructor's lack of facility with the English language was a hindrance to the communication of ideas.

58. The instructor seems to keep current with developments in the field.

59. The instructor's teaching methods are effective.

60. The instructor uses novel teaching methods to help students learn.

61. The instructor uses teaching methods to help students learn.

62. The instructor allows students to proceed at their own pace.

63. The instructor provides extra discussion sessions for interested students.

64. The instructor adequately helped me prepare for exams.

65. The instructor is careful and precise when answering questions.

66. The instructor is available during office hours.

67. The instructor's quizzes stress important points.

68. The instructor helps me apply theory for solving homework problems.

69. The instructor demonstrated formal knowledge of the topic.

70. The instructor accepts suggestions from students.

71. The instructor shows enthusiasm when teaching.

72. The instructor offers specific suggestions for improving my weaknesses.

73. The instructor returns assignments quickly enough to benefit me.

B. Attitude Toward Students

74. The instructor was receptive to the expression of student views.

75. The instructor was concerned with whether or not the students learned the material.

76. The instructor intimidated the students.

77. The instructor embarrassed the students.

78. The instructor developed a good rapport with me.

79. A warm atmosphere was maintained in this class.

80. The instructor recognized individual differences in students' abilities.

81. The instructor seemed to dislike students.

82. The instructor often made me feel as if I was wasting his/her time.

83. The instructor treated students as inferiors.

84. The instructor seemed genuinely interested in me as a person.

85. The instructor maintained an atmosphere of good feeling in the class.

86. The instructor treated students with respect.

87. The instructor encouraged class discussion.

88. Students in this course were free to disagree.

89. The instructor was friendly.

90. The instructor could be relied upon for support in stressful situations.

91. The instructor criticized students in the presence of others.

92. The instructor treated students fairly.

93. The instructor promoted a feeling of self-worth in students.

94. Students were encouraged to express their own opinions.

95. The instructor helped students to feel free to ask questions.

96. The instructor treated students with respect.

97. The instructor was skillful in observing student reactions.

98. The instructor was permissive.

99. The instructor was friendly.

100. The instructor gave individual attention to students in this course.

101. The instructor demonstrated sensitivity to students' needs.

102. The instructor was aloof rather than sociable.

103. The instructor was flexible in dealing with students.

104. The instructor encourages students to talk about their problems.

105. The instructor meets informally with students out of class.

106. The instructor stimulates my thinking.

107. The instructor deals fairly and impartially with students.

108. The instructor makes me feel I am an important member of this class.

109. The instructor relates to students as individuals.

110. The instructor tells students when they have done particularly well.

111. The instructor motivates me to do my best work.

112. The instructor provided me with an effective range of challenges.

113. The instructor stimulates intellectual curiosity.

114. The instructor offers specific suggestions for improving my weaknesses.

115. The instructor helps me realize my full ability.

116. The instructor provides me with incentives for learning.

117. The instructor rewards success.

C. Student Outcomes

118. I now feel able to communicate course material to others.

119. This course has increased my capacity for analytic thinking.

120. This course was helpful in developing new skills.

121. I learned more in this course than in similar courses.

122. I understood the material presented in this course.

123. This course challenged me intellectually.

124. I have become more competent in this area because of this course.

125. My opinions about some of the course topics changed because of taking this course.

126. I learned more in this course than I expected to learn.

127. Some of the ideas discussed really made me think.

128. I am a better person because of taking this course.

129. The course helped me to become a more critical thinker.

130. The course helped me become a more creative thinker.

131. The course was intellectually exciting.

132. I learned a great deal of factual material in this course.

133. I developed the ability to communicate clearly about the subject.

134. I developed creative ability in this field.

135. I developed the ability to solve real problems in this field.

136. I learned how to identify formal characteristics of works of art.

137. I learned how to identify main points and central issues in this field.

138. I developed the ability to carry out original research in this field.

139. I developed an ability to evaluate new work in this field.

140. I was stimulated to discuss related topics outside of class.

141. I participated actively in class discussion.

142. I developed leadership skills in this class.

143. I developed greater awareness of societal problems.

144. I became interested in community projects related to the course.

145. I learned to value new viewpoints.

146. I gained a better understanding of myself through this course.

147. I gained an understanding of some of my personal problems.

148. I developed a greater sense of personal responsibility.

149. I increased my awareness of my own interests.

150. I increased my awareness of my own talents.

151. I feel that I performed up to my potential.

152. I read independently beyond the required readings in this course.

153. The course significantly changed my outlook on personal issues.

154. I felt free to ask for extra help from the instructor.

D. Relevance of Course

155. This course material will be useful in future courses.

156. The course provided me with a general background in the area.

157. The course material was of personal interest to me aside from its professional application.

158. I have learned the basic concepts from this course that I will be able to relate to other situations.

159. This course has stimulated me to take additional courses in this field.

160. The material covered in this course will be directly relevant to my future occupation.

161. The course gave me skills that will be directly applicable to my career.

162. The concepts in this course were pertinent to my major field.

163. The course was valuable only to majors in this field.

164. This course should be required for a major in this area.

165. The course was related to my personal goals.

166. The course did NOT prepare me to reach my personal goals.

167. The course had NO relevance outside of a grade and credit hours.

168. I was interested in the subject before I took this course.

169. The course stimulated me to read further in the area.

170. The course content was valuable.

171. I gained an excellent understanding of concepts in this field.

172. I learned to apply principles from this course to other situations.

173. I deepened my interest in the subject matter of this course.

174. I developed enthusiasm about the course material.

175. I developed skills needed by professionals in this field.

176. I learned about career opportunities.

177. I developed a clearer sense of professional identity.

178. I would take this course if it were not required.

179. This course has changed my behavior (instructor should specify a behavior here).

180. The class demonstrations were effective in helping me learn.

181. The course content was up-to-date.

182. The catalog description of this course gave an accurate description of its content.

183. The course content included information from related fields.

E. Use of Class Time

184. The instructor should do more to restrain students who monopolize class time.

185. I participated more in class discussions in this course than in similar courses.

186. The instructor should spend less time in class discussions.

187. The instructor should encourage students to participate more actively in class discussions.

188. The class discussions broadened by knowledge of the area beyond what I learned from the readings.

189. More opportunity should be allowed for answering questions in class.

190. Students had an opportunity to ask questions.

191. The amount of time allotted for this class should be reduced.

192. The instructor used student questions as a source of discovering points of confusion.

193. The instructor overemphasized minor points.

194. The instructor was NOT willing to deviate from his/her course plans to meet the needs of the students.

195. Regular class attendance was necessary for understanding course material.

196. The instructor used class time well.

197. The instructor provided time for discussion.

198. The instructor encourages students to ask questions.

199. The instructor encourages class participation.

200. The instructor encourages contributions concerning the conduct of this class.

201. The instructor makes me feel free to ask questions.

F. Organization and Preparation

202. The instructor followed his/her stated course outline.

203. The instructor's class presentations were designed for easy note taking.

204. The instructor presented material in a clear manner.

205. The course was well organized.

206. The course material appeared to be presented in logical content units.

207. There was continuity from one class to the next.

208. The instructor presented a systematic approach to the course material.

209. Instructor presentations were well organized.

210. Course concepts were related in a systematic manner.

211. The instructor was well prepared for each class.

212. The instructor was well prepared for lectures.

213. The instructor frequently digressed too far from the subject matter of the course.

214. The instructor rarely digressed from a given topic to the detriment of the course.

215. Lectures often seemed disjointed and fragmented.

216. Class discussions were well organized.

217. The instructor was prepared for topics brought up during impromptu class discussions.

218. The instructor provided a good mixture of lecture and discussion.

219. The instructor wrote legibly on the blackboard, papers, etc.

G. Clarity of Presentation

220. The instructor's voice was audible.

221. The instructor's voice was understandable.

222. The instructor's vocabulary made understanding of the material difficult.

223. At times it was difficult to hear what the instructor was saying.

224. The instructor expressed ideas clearly.

225. The instructor could communicate his/her subject matter to the students.

226. The instructor should define the words he/she uses.

227. The instructor's tendency to stammer or stutter was annoying.

228. The instructor often mumbled.

229. The instructor often talked with his/her back to the students.

230. The instructor recognizes when some students fail to comprehend course material.

231. The instructor emphasizes conceptual understanding of course material.

232. The instructor lectures at a pace suitable for students' comprehension.

H. Instructor Characteristics

233. The instructor should improve his/her personal appearance.

234. The instructor flustered easily.

235. The instructor seemed to be interested in teaching.

236. The instructor was enthusiastic when presenting course material.

237. The instructor was relaxed in front of class.

238. At times, the instructor displayed only a shallow knowledge of course materials.

239. The instructor seemed genuinely interested in what he/she was teaching.

240. At times the instructor seemed tense.

241. The instructor exhibited self-confidence.

242. The instructor displayed a know-it-all attitude.

243. The instructor was too cynical or sarcastic.

244. The instructor often appeared arrogant.

245. The instructor was very entertaining.

246. The instructor's jokes sometimes interfered with learning.

247. The instructor demonstrated role model qualities that were of use to me.

248. The instructor demonstrated an appropriate sense of humor.

249. The instructor seemed to enjoy teaching.

250. The instructor was confused by unexpected questions.

251. The instructor encouraged constructive criticism.

252. The instructor has an interesting style of presentation.

253. When lecturing, the instructor holds the attention of class.

254. The instructor senses when students are bored.

255. The instructor is a dynamic and energetic person.

256. The instructor seems to have a well-rounded education.

257. The instructor appears to grasp quickly what a student is saying.

258. The instructor knows about developments in other fields.

259. The instructor shows enthusiasm when teaching.

260. The instructor exhibited distracting mannerisms.

261. The instructor's accent prevented me from understanding what was being said.

I. Interest of Presentation

262. The instructor should reduce the monotony of his/her speech.

263. The instructor made the subject matter interesting.

264. The instructor was boring.

265. The instructor's presentations were thought provoking.

266. The instructor's classroom sessions stimulated my interest in the subject.

267. It was easy to remain attentive in class.

268. The instructor was quite lifeless.

269. Remaining attentive in class was often quite difficult.

270. The course was quite interesting.

271. The instructor was an effective speaker.

272. The class presentations were too formal.

J. Expectations and Objectives

273. The course assignments were clearly specified.

274. I was informed of the direction the course was to take.

275. The objectives of the course were well explained.

276. The objectives of this course should be modified.

277. The content of this course was appropriate to the aims and objectives of the course.

278. Student responsibilities in this course were defined.

279. The instructor should rewrite the description of the course in the catalog.

280. It was not clear why I was being taught some things.

281. The instructor's expectations were NOT clearly defined.

282. The instructor informed students of their progress.

283. The instructor defined realistic objectives for the students.

284. I have made careful preparations for this course.

285. I really had to think about some of the ideas discussed.

286. Objectives were stated for each unit in the course.

287. The course objectives were clear.

288. I understood what was expected of me in this course.

289. The course objectives allowed me to know when I was making progress.

290. In general, too little work was required in this class.

291. In general, too much work was required in this class.

292. I have made careful preparations for this course.

293. I really had to think about some of the ideas discussed.

K. Behavioral Indications of Course Attitude

294. The time spent in this course was worthwhile.

295. My attendance in this course was better than for most other courses.

296. I usually delayed studying for this course as long as possible.

297. I spent more time than usual complaining about this course to others.

298. I would take this course again even if it were not required.

299. I would recommend this course to a fellow student.

300. I looked forward to this class.

301. I cut this class more frequently than I cut other classes.

302. This was a good course.

303. Students frequently volunteered their own opinions.

304. One real strength of this course was the classroom discussion.

305. I had a strong desire to take this course.

306. I enjoyed going to class.

307. In this course I used my study time effectively.

308. I spent more time studying for this course than for other courses with the same amount of credit.

L. General Attitude Toward Instructor

309. I would rather NOT take another course from this instructor.

310. In comparison to all the other instructors I have had, he/she was one of the best.

311. I would recommend this instructor to a fellow student.

312. I would avoid courses taught by this instructor.

313. The instructor was excellent.

314. The instructor was inadequate.

M. Speed and Depth of Coverage

315. Too much material was covered in this course.

316. Prerequisites in addition to those stated in the catalog are necessary for understanding the material in this course.

317. Within the time limitations, the instructor covered the course content in sufficient depth.

318. For the time allotted, topic coverage was exhaustive enough.

319. The course material was presented at a satisfactory level of difficulty.

320. The instructor attempted to cover too much material.

321. The instructor presented the material too rapidly.

322. The instructor should present the material more slowly.

323. The instructor moved to new topics before students understood the previous topic.

324. The course seemed to drag at times.

325. The course was too easy for me.

326. The course was too difficult for me.

327. The amount of material covered in the course was reasonable.

328. The instructor used appropriate amounts of information to teach new concepts.

N. Out of Class

329. Assistance from the instructor outside of class was readily available.

330. Talking to the instructor in his/her office was helpful.

331. I was able to get personal help in this course if I needed it.

332. The office hours were scheduled at times that were convenient for me to attend.

333. The instructor was readily available for consultation with students.

334. The instructor encouraged out-of-class consultations.

335. The instructor made it clear that he/she did not want to be bothered by students at times other than when the class met.

O. Examinations

336. The types of test questions used were good.

337. The instructor should give more examinations.

338. Emphasis on memorizing for examinations should be reduced.

339. The instructor should cover the course material more adequately in the examinations.

340. The exams were worded clearly.

341. Examinations were given often enough to give the instructor a comprehensive picture of my understanding of the course material.

342. The exams covered the reading assignments well.

343. The exams concentrated on factual material.

344. The exams concentrated on reasoning ability.

345. The exams concentrated on important aspects of the course.

346. The exams and quizzes were given too frequently.

347. The exams were fair.

348. The instructor took reasonable precautions to prevent cheating.

349. Course objectives were reflected in the exams.

350. Exams adequately covered the text material.

351. Exams were mainly composed of material presented in class.

352. The answers to exam questions were adequately explained after the exam was given.

353. Enough time was provided to complete the examinations.

354. Too much emphasis was placed on the final exam.

355. Examinations were not too difficult.

356. The exams did not challenge me enough.

357. The instructor should use essay examinations rather than multiple-choice.

358. The instructor should use multiple-choice examinations rather than essay.

359. Examinations should contain a better mixture of multiple-choice and essay questions.

360. The exams covered the lecture material well.

361. The exams were creative.

362. The exams required original thought.

363. The exams concentrated on the important aspects of the course.

364. The exams were too long.

365. The exams were returned promptly.

366. The exams were graded carefully.

367. The exams were graded fairly.

368. The exams were used to improve instruction as well as to assign grades.

369. The exams were used to help students find their strengths and weaknesses.

370. The exams were of instructional value.

371. The exams stressed the important points of the lectures.

372. The exams required conceptual understanding of the material in order to be able to get a high score.

373. Feedback on the exams indicated my relative standing within the class.

374. Exams emphasized understanding rather than memorization.

P. Visual Aids

375. The instructor should use more audiovisual aids (charts, movies, models, etc.).

376. The audiovisual aids were a valuable part of this course.

377. The audiovisual aids confused me more than they aided my learning.

378. Some of the audiovisual aids did not seem relevant.

379. Audiovisual aids were used too much in this class.

380. Audiovisual aids used in this course were stimulating.

381. The audiovisual aids generally contained material different from the instructor's material.

382. The instructor generally used the audiovisual aids effectively.

383. The audiovisual aids presented material or situations which could not normally be seen in real life.

384. The audiovisual aids were generally effective.

385. Certain ideas were presented effectively through the use of audiovisual aids than otherwise could have been presented.

386. The audiovisual aids (charts, movies, slides, etc.) used were effective in helping me learn.

Q. Grading

387. Relative to other courses, the grading in this course was harder.

388. I expected to get a higher grade in this course than I received.

389. My fieldwork was given appropriate weight in the formulation of the final grade.

390. My grades accurately reflected my performance in the course.

391. I knew my relative standing in the course.

392. The instructor adequately explained the grading system.

393. The instructor adequately assessed how well students mastered the material.

394. The procedure for grading was fair.

395. I do not feel that my grades reflected how much I have learned.

396. The method of assigning grades seemed very arbitrary.

397. It was easy to get a good grade in this class.

398. The instructor had a realistic definition of good performance.

399. My papers had adequate comments on them.

400. The grades reflected an accurate assessment of my knowledge.

401. The exam accurately reflected my performance on the tests.

R. Assignments (homework, reading, written, textbook, laboratory, etc.)

402. The assignments were challenging.

403. The nontext assignments were helpful in acquiring a better understanding of course materials.

404. I found the coverage of topics in the assigned readings too difficult.

405. The course required a reasonable amount of outside reading.

406. The instructor should have required more outside reading.

407. The text used in this course was helpful.

408. The instructor helped the students avoid duplication of content in selecting topics.

409. The instructor supplemented student summaries with additional material when necessary.

410. The amount of work was appropriate for the credit received.

411. The textbook was easy to understand.

412. The textbook presented various sides of issues.

413. The _____ assignments were relevant to what was presented in class.

414. The _____ assignments provided background for the lectures.

415. The _____ assignments were too time consuming relative to their contribution to my understanding of the course material.

416. The _____ assignments were interesting.

417. The _____ assignments appeared to be chosen carefully.

418. The _____ assignments were stimulating.

419. The _____ assignments made students think.

420. More _____ should have been assigned.

421. There was too much _____ required for this course.

422. Directions for _____ assignments were clear.

423. Directions for _____ assignments were specific.

424. _____ assignments were helpful in understanding the course.

425. _____ assignments covered both sides of issues.

426. _____ assignments required a reasonable amount of effort.

427. _____ assignments were graded fairly.

428. _____ assignments were returned promptly.

429. The instructor did not cover reading assignments in sufficient depth in class.

430. The instructor should have given additional sources where supplementary information might be found.

431. The course assignments required too much time.

432. The assignments were related to the goals of the course.

433. The assignments were of definite instructional value.

434. Homework assignments were given too frequently.

435. The assigned readings were well integrated into the course.

S. Laboratory and Discussion

436. I found the laboratory/discussion section interesting.

437. The laboratory/discussion instructor adequately prepared me for the material covered in his/her section.

438. The laboratory/discussion instructor clarified lecture material.

439. The laboratory/discussion instructor carried on meaningful dialogue with the students.

440. The laboratory/discussion instructor provided adequate individual remedial attention.

441. The laboratory/discussion instructor knew my name.

442. The laboratory/discussion instructor discovered my trouble areas.

443. The laboratory/discussion instructor helped me find supplemental references.

444. The laboratory/discussion instructor was available during office hours.

445. The questions on the laboratory/discussion quizzes were a good sample of what I was expected to know.

446. The laboratory increased my competence in manipulating laboratory materials.

447. The laboratory equipment was, on most occasions, effectively set up.

448. The laboratory/discussion instructor presented materials supplemental to the lecture material.

449. The laboratory/discussion instructor has the potential for being a competent teacher.

450. The laboratory/discussion instructor graded my papers (exams, homework, etc.) fairly.

451. The laboratory/discussion instructor extended the coverage of topics presented in lecture.

452. The laboratory/discussion section appeared well integrated with the lecture.

453. My laboratory/discussion work was beneficial in terms of the goals of this course.

454. My laboratory/discussion work was beneficial in terms of my personal goals.

455. My laboratory/discussion work was given appropriate weight in the formulation of final grades.

456. The use of laboratory equipment was satisfactorily explained.

457. The laboratory/discussion section was a valuable part of this course.

458. The laboratory/discussion section was a great help in learning.

459. There was ample opportunity to ask questions in the laboratory/discussion section.

460. The laboratory/discussion section clarified lecture material.

461. Students received individual attention in the laboratory/discussion section.

462. The instructor gave every student a chance to practice.

463. The laboratories covered too much material to be absorbed in only one period.

464. The material in the laboratories was too easy.

465. I generally found the laboratory (recitations, clinical) sessions valuable.

466. The laboratory (recitations, clinical) instructor related lecture material to real life situations.

467. The laboratory/discussion instructor explained experiments and/or assignments.

468. The laboratory/discussion instructor adequately helps me prepare for examinations.

469. The laboratory/discussion instructor is precise when answering questions.

470. The laboratory/discussion instructor deals fairly with students.

471. The laboratory/discussion instructor is available through the lab/discussion period.

472. The laboratory/discussion instructor's quizzes stress important points.

473. The laboratory/discussion instructor helps me apply theory for solving problems.

474. The laboratory/discussion instructor demonstrates formal knowledge of the topic.

475. The laboratory/discussion instructor makes me feel I am an important member of the class.

476. The laboratory/discussion instructor accepts criticism from students well.

477. The laboratory/discussion instructor accepts suggestions from students well.

478. The laboratory/discussion instructor shows enthusiasm when teaching.

479. The laboratory/discussion instructor offers specific suggestions for improving my weaknesses.

480. The laboratory/discussion instructor evaluates my work quickly enough to benefit me.

481. The laboratory/discussion instructor plans the lab/discussion time effectively.

482. The laboratory/discussion instructor thoroughly understands the experiments and assignments.

483. The course would be improved by adding a laboratory/discussion section.

484. The lab had adequate facilities.

485. There was opportunity to do imaginative work in the labs.

486. Generally, the equipment used in the lab was adequate and reliable.

487. Most of the lab work was simply routine.

488. The course should require more time in the lab.

T. Clinical

489. The teaching done in clinical settings increased my learning.

490. The instructor provided relevant clinical experiences.

491. The instructor was NOT helpful when students had questions concerning patient care.

492. The instructor's questions in clinical discussions were thought provoking.

493. The instructor observed students' techniques of interviewing.

494. The instructor helped me develop good clinical techniques.

495. The instructor observed students' techniques of physical examination.

U. Student-Instructor Interaction

496. Questions were answered satisfactorily by the instructor.

497. The instructor had a tight rein on the conduct of the class.

498. I participated more in class discussion in this course than in similar courses.

499. I had an opportunity to participate in discussions with the instructor.

500. I was hesitant to ask questions in this course.

501. The instructor knew the names of the students.

502. The instructor encouraged constructive criticism.

V. Seminars

503. The seminar approach was effectively implemented in the course.

504. The seminar method met my needs.

505. The seminar provided me with diverse insights into the course materials.

506. The seminar leader effectively included everyone's views into the discussion.

507. The seminar allowed me to learn from other students.

W. Team Teaching

508. The team teaching method provided me with a valuable learning experience.

509. Instruction was well coordinated among the team members.

510. The team teaching approach was effectively implemented in this course.

511. The team teaching approach met my needs.

512. Team teaching provided me with diverse insights into course materials.

513. Team teaching provided insights that a single instructor could not.

X. Field Trips

514. The field trips were of instructional value.

515. The field trips were well planned.

516. The course should include a field trip.

517. The field trips were useful learning experiences.

518. The field trips fit in with the course objectives.

519. The timing of the field trips was well planned relative to the progress of the course.

520. The field trips offered insights that the lectures and/or readings could not provide.

CHAPTER REFERENCE

Aleamoni, L. M., & Carynnk, D. B. (1977). Optional item catalog (revised), *Information Memorandum No. 6.* Tucson, AZ: University of Arizona, Office of Instructional Research and Development.

15

Commercially Available Student Rating Forms

Student rating forms constitute a critical element of virtually every faculty evaluation system. Because the data generated by student rating forms can play a major role in the evaluation of faculty performance, it is important that the forms used be both reliable and valid and provide meaningful information that can be used for improvement purposes as well as personnel decision-making purposes. As has been noted earlier, the development of a valid and reliable student rating form is a process that requires the application of a host of professional measurement and statistical skills.

Because numerous student rating forms have been developed locally and may not possess the necessary psychometric qualities of reliability and validity, it is generally a good idea to consider adopting or adapting a professionally developed form rather than developing one from scratch. This chapter provides guidelines for selecting from among a number of available student rating forms. Included here is a checklist for selecting forms and technical reviews of a several well-known and commercially available forms including the Aleamoni Course/Instructor Evaluation Questionnaire (CIEQ) system, Kansas State University's IDEA forms, and the Educational Testing Service's Student Instructor Rating (SIR II) form. Information on whom to contact for information or sample kits, as well as web site addresses, are also provided.

CHECKLIST FOR IDENTIFYING AND SELECTING PUBLISHED FORMS

In examining the field of published student rating forms for possible adoption or adaptation by your institution, it is best to follow a specific set of steps that give you the best possibility of identifying the better forms to consider. The following checklist is suggested as a guide for finding and testing such forms.

___ 1. Use the *Mental Measurement Yearbook (MMY)* and *Tests in Print* to learn what forms are available. The *MMY* and the *Tests in Print* should be available in your library and provide critical reviews by experts concerning each form.

___ 2. Write to the publishers, universities, or private corporations identified in the *MMY* as producing or reviewing such forms. Request any manuals and announcements for references to forms, services, and technical data from the publishers.

___ 3. Review the literature on student ratings of instruction. Professional publications such as the American Educational Research Association's *Instructional Evaluation* or the National Council on Measurement in Education's *Measurement News* or *Journal of Educational Measurement* often contain announcements and/or reviews of new forms as well as general articles on the use and analysis of student rating forms. The bibliography at the end of this handbook provides an excellent starting point for reviewing the literature.

____ 4. Send for a specimen set of the form or forms selected for consideration. Publishers will often provide such sets to institutions wishing to consider their purchase or use. Examine the specimen set to analyze in depth the questions used and material covered.

____ 5. Try out the form. It is a good idea to simply try out the questionnaire or rating form in its original form. Check with the form's publisher to determine policies concerning trial administrations.

____ 6. After trying out a number of possible forms, have the individuals responsible for the courses or course sections in which such forms might be used critically review their appropriateness.

____ 7. As part of the process in selecting a form for possible adoption or adaptation, determine whether the form publisher provides any of the following services and how much these services cost:

    a. Form scanning and processing

    b. Rapid turn-around in providing computer analyses of form results

    c. Comparative norms for appropriate groupings of faculty and courses

    d. Willing to sell the system to your institution including debugged computer software and the rights to print modified forms

In many instances, it may be more cost effective to buy the entire processing system. Buying a complete service or adapting an existing operating student rating system saves a good bit of time and effort in the overall development of your faculty evaluation system.

REVIEW OF SELECTED PUBLISHED OR COMMERCIALLY AVAILABLE STUDENT RATING FORMS

The following are reviews of several selected systems for student rating of instruction in higher education. The systems included here are representative of the field and do not present an exhaustive listing of all commercially available student rating forms and systems. Rather, the information provided is intended to be used as a starting point for faculty and administrators who are may be interested in adopting a commercially available student rating system. The information contained in the reviews

may also be helpful as an aid to those designing local systems to meet unique needs. However, you are urged to familiarize yourself with the relevant original reports and descriptions of a system and to obtain the most recent technical descriptions of products and services from the contact person listed.

It is generally not recommended that an institution develop its own student rating form unless it is willing to conduct the appropriate psychometric studies required to do it correctly. However, if none of the commercially available forms meet the needs of your institution and you wish to design and develop your own student rating form, please refer to Chapters 13 and 14.

For each of the student rating systems described below, the person to be contacted as well as a technical review is presented. In addition, sample forms and interpretation manuals are shown. In some cases where there are a number of forms for a system, a web site address (URL) is provided at which they may be viewed.

Aleamoni Course/Instructor Evaluation Questionnaire (CIEQ)

Contact: Lawrence M. Aleamoni, Director
                Comprehensive Data Evaluation Services, Inc.
                6730 N. Camino Padre Isidoro
                Tucson, AZ 85718
                PH: (520) 621-7832
                FAX: (520) 297-9427

Format. The CIEQ rating form is available on a computer scorable answer sheet that is divided into five sections. The first section elicits student background information including student level, whether the student is taking the course as pass–fail, an elective, student gender, expected grade, the proportion of students taking the course as a part of their major, and the semester in which the evaluation takes place. The second section consists of three general items that elicit student responses to the course content, the instructor, and the course in general. Ratings in this section are made on a 6-point scale ranging from excellent to very poor. Section three includes 21 statements which represent five subscales or factors labeled General Course, Attitude, Method of Instruction, Course Content, Interest and Attention, and Instructor. A sixth scale, Total, provides scores for all items combined. Items are rated on a 4-point scale ranging from agree strongly to disagree strongly. The fourth section provides space for 42 optional items if the instructor wishes to include any additional items. These items may either be selected from an item catalog, which is part of the CIEQ system, or written by the instructor. The final section allows for open-ended responses to questions on course content, the instructor, course objectives, papers and homework, examinations, suggested improvements, and an evaluation of the course based upon student satisfaction with the course and student perceptions of its value as an educational experience.

Results. The results of the CIEQ are presented on computer output in four parts. The first part presents course and instructor identification. The second part presents student background information and results for the three general items. Given are the proportion and number responding to each item alternative and the proportion not responding. The mean and the standard deviation are also presented for each of the general items.

The third part lists the responses to the five subscales. Included are the

- percentage responding

- mean response

- standard deviation

- reliability coefficient (based upon an internal consistency calculation)

Also provided are a variety of normative comparisons including

- the rank norm (a comparison of the course with all courses given by instructors at the same rank)

- the level norm (a comparison of the course with all courses at the same course level)

- the institution norm (a comparison of the course with all courses at the university)

- the college norm (a comparison of the course with all other courses in the appropriate college within the university)

- the nationwide norm (a comparison of the course to all the courses throughout the United States which have used the CIEQ)

- the department norm (a comparison of the course with all other courses in a particular department)

The final part lists each of 21 standard items and provides

- the proportion and number responding to each alternative

- the most favorable response

- the mean response

- the standard deviation

- the college-wide norm decile (a comparison of the mean response with those obtained throughout the college or university) for each item

- an optional item listing (if any optional items are used)

Special Features. The optional item catalog (Aleamoni & Carynnk, 1977) contains 350 items divided into 20 categories. The Results Interpretation Manual (Aleamoni & Laham, 1992) provides information on scale development and validation, recommended uses and administrative procedures, description and interpretation of results, and decile norm cutoff scores for seven various subscale databases.

Institutions wishing to use the CIEQ may select one of two options:

- OPTION 1: CIEQ forms may be purchased individually from Comprehensive Data Evaluation Services, Inc. (CODES) and returned for processing.

- OPTION 2: An institution may choose to purchase the computer analysis program and rights to print and use the CIEQ under a royalty arrangement. Institutions purchasing the program receive annual updates of the normative database derived from the hundreds of institutions that have used and/or are currently using the CIEQ. The computer program is written for the Apple Macintosh computer and is designed to be used as a simple, desktop system.

Development and Validation. The CIEQ was developed in 1975 through an analysis of the earlier versions of the Illinois Course Evaluation Questionnaire (CEQ). The original CEQ was based on an initial pool of over 1,000 items collected in the early 1960s, reduced and refined by a variety of techniques, including factor analysis, to a form containing 50 items (Aleamoni & Spencer, 1973). The current version (Form 76) uses normative data from approximately 10,000 course sections at the University of Arizona and the University of Illinois at Urbana-Champaign and 150,000 course sections from other US institutions gathered from 1972 through 1999. Internal consistency reliability coefficients for the five subscales range from .88 to .98 (Aleamoni & Laham, 1992). Test–retest reliability ranges from .92 to .98 for the subscales and the total and from .81 to .94 for individual items (Gillmore, 1973). Aleamoni (1978) reviews several studies of the CEQ that he claims are generalizable to the CIEQ. He reports that the CIEQ is not affected by gender, term, curriculum, class size, instructor rank, required/elective, major/minor, student status, pass/fail, expected grade, and final grade. In addition, the ratings of colleagues and trained judges appear to correlate with CIEQ student ratings (Aleamoni, 1978).

Research on the CIEQ has shown it to be a valid, reliable measure of student reactions to the course and instructor. The CIEQ provides meaningful informa-tion that may be successfully used in a program of instructional improvement or as part of a comprehensive faculty evaluation system designed to provide data for faculty personnel decisions. Figure 15.1 shows a copy of the CIEQ form (front side) and Figure 15.1 (continued) shows the back side that contains the free-response section. Figure 15.2 presents an example of the analysis printout for the CIEQ followed by a copy of the interpretation guide provided each faculty member.

Sample Form and Report. The following pages contain a sample of the CIEQ form (front and back) as well as an example of a faculty report and interpretation guide.

Figure 15.1 CIEQ Form (front side)

ALEAMONI COURSE/INSTRUCTOR EVALUATION QUESTIONNAIRE (CIEQ) (FORM 76)
COMPREHENSIVE DATA EVALUATION SERVICES, INC. © LAWRENCE M. ALEAMONI, 1975

MARKING INSTRUCTIONS

MARK:
AS — IF YOU AGREE STRONGLY WITH THE ITEM
A — IF YOU AGREE MODERATELY WITH THE ITEM
D — IF YOU DISAGREE MODERATELY WITH THE ITEM
DS — IF YOU DISAGREE STRONGLY WITH THE ITEM

MARK ONLY ONE RESPONSE PER ITEM USING PENCIL ONLY
ERASE CHANGED ANSWERS CLEANLY AND COMPLETELY.

STANDARD ITEM SECTION

1. It was a very worthwhile course.
2. I would take another course that was taught this way.
3. The instructor seemed to be interested in students as individuals.
4. The course material was too difficult.
5. It was easy to remain attentive.
6. NOT much was gained by taking this course.
7. I would have preferred another method of teaching in this course.
8. The course material seemed worthwhile.
9. The instructor did NOT synthesize, integrate or summarize effectively.
10. The course was quite interesting.
11. The instructor encouraged development of new viewpoints and appreciations.
12. I learn more when other teaching methods are used.
13. Some things were NOT explained very well.
14. The instructor demonstrated a thorough knowledge of the subject matter.
15. This was one of my poorest courses.
16. The course content was excellent.
17. Some days I was NOT very interested in this course.
18. I think that the course was taught quite well.
19. The course was quite boring.
20. The instructor seemed to consider teaching as a chore or routine activity.
21. Overall, the course was good.

PLEASE FILL OUT THE OTHER SIDE

Arreola, R. A. (2000). Developing *a Comprehensive Faculty Evaluation System 2/e.* Bolton, MA: Anker Publishing Co., Inc.

Figure 15.1 (continued)   CIEQ Form (back side)

C I E Q

PLEASE USE THIS SIDE OF THE FORM FOR YOUR PERSONAL COMMENTS ON TEACHER EFFECTIVENESS AND GENERAL COURSE VALUE. YOUR INSTRUCTOR WILL NOT SEE YOUR COMPLETED EVALUATION UNTIL AFTER FINAL GRADES ARE IN FOR YOUR COURSE.

COURSE CONTENT
PLEASE GIVE YOUR COMMENTS ON THE COURSE CONTENT, SUBJECT MATTER AND ANY PARTICULAR RELEVANCE THIS COURSE HAS HAD TO YOUR AREA OF STUDY.

INSTRUCTORS
WRITE THE NAME OF YOUR PRINCIPAL INSTRUCTOR _____ T.A. _____
WHAT ARE YOUR GENERAL COMMENTS ABOUT THE INSTRUCTOR(S) IN THIS COURSE?

COURSE/INSTRUCTIONAL OBJECTIVES
WERE THE OBJECTIVES CLEARLY STATED FOR THIS COURSE?   YES _____ NO _____   COMMENT:

PAPERS AND HOMEWORK
COMMENT ON THE VALUE OF BOOKS, HOMEWORK AND PAPERS (IF ANY) IN THIS COURSE.

EXAMINATIONS
COMMENT ON THE EXAMINATIONS AS TO DIFFICULTY, FAIRNESS, ETC.

GENERAL
1. WHAT IMPROVEMENTS WOULD YOU SUGGEST FOR THIS COURSE?

2. WHAT IS YOUR EVALUATION OF THIS COURSE BASED UPON (A) YOUR SATISFACTION WITH WHAT YOU GOT OUT OF THIS COURSE AND (B) WHETHER IT WAS A VALUABLE EDUCATIONAL EXPERIENCE OR A DISAPPOINTMENT? PLEASE COMMENT.

PLEASE FILL OUT THE OTHER SIDE

Arreola, R. A. (2000). Developing *a Comprehensive Faculty Evaluation System 2/e*. Bolton, MA: Anker Publishing Co., Inc.

Figure 15.2 Example of CIEQ Analysis Printout

CIEQ Analysis Fall 1999

ALEAMONI COURSE/INSTRUCTOR EVALUATION QUESTIONNAIRE

Instructor: ALEAMONI **Class: EDP 646** **Sample size: 10**
Process Date: 12/7/99 **College Code: 78933**

Class Description Results

Class Information

	Fr	So	Jr	Sr	Grad	Oth	OMIT
%	0.00	0.30	0.10	0.40	0.20	0.00	0.00
#	0	3	1	4	2	0	0

Gender

	M	F	OMIT
%	0.20	0.80	0.00
#	2	8	0

Course Option

	Req	Elec	OMIT
%	0.70	0.30	0.00
#	7	3	0

Pass-Fail Option

	Yes	No	OMIT
%	0.10	0.90	0.00
#	1	9	0

Major-Minor

	Maj	Min	Oth	OMIT
%	0.90	0.10	1.00	0.00
#	9	1	0	0

Expected Grade

	A	B	C	D	E	OMIT
%	0.30	0.30	0.30	0.00	0.00	0.10
#	3	3	3	0	0	1

Content Rating

	V.P.	Poor	Fair	Good	V.G.	Ex	OMIT			
%	0.00	0.10	0.00	0.20	0.20	0.50	0.00	Mean	=	5.00
#	0	1	0	2	2	5	0	S.D.	=	1.33

Instructor Rating

	V.P.	Poor	Fair	Good	V.G.	Ex	OMIT			
%	0.00	0.10	0.10	0.10	0.20	0.50	0.00	Mean	=	4.90
#	0	1	1	1	2	5	0	S.D.	=	1.29

Course Rating

	V.P.	Poor	Fair	Good	V.G.	Ex	OMIT			
%	0.00	0.10	0.10	0.10	0.20	0.50	0.00	Mean	=	4.80
#	0	1	1	1	2	5	0	S.D.	=	1.69

Subscale Results

Subscale	Items	% Res	Mean	S.D.	Rel.	IR	CL	D	C	UA	N
Attitude	4	1.00	3.28	1.06	0.98	4	5	3	4	5	6
Method	4	1.00	3.13	1.09	0.94	6	7	6	6	6	7
Content	4	1.00	3.30	0.91	0.68	8	8	8	8	8	9
Interest	4	1.00	3.08	1.07	0.88	7	7	5	6	7	7
Instructor	5	0.98	3.27	0.93	0.91	4	5	2	4	5	5
Total	21	1.00	3.21	1.01	0.98	6	7	5	6	6	7

IR=Instructor Rank; CL=Class Level; D=Department; C=College; UA=University of Arizona; N=Nationwide. NA in a normative decile category indicates that normative data is not available for this category or that this category is not applicable to the current data.

Arreola, R. A. (2000). Developing *a Comprehensive Faculty Evaluation System 2/e*. Bolton, MA: Anker Publishing Co., Inc.

Figure 15.2 (continued)   Example of CIEQ Analysis Printout

Instructor: ALEAMONI   **Class: EDP 646**   **Sample size: 10**
Process Date: 12/7/99   **College Code: 78933**

Individual Item Results

1. It was a very worthwhile course.

	AS	A	D	DS	OMIT	BEST	MEAN	S.D.	DEC
%	0.70	0.00	0.20	0.10	0.00	AS	3.30	1.16	5
#	7	0	2	1	0				

2. I would take another course that was taught this way.

	AS	A	D	DS	OMIT	BEST	MEAN	S.D.	DEC
%	0.70	0.00	0.20	0.10	0.00	AS	3.00	1.16	7
#	7	0	2	1	0				

3. The instructor seemed to be interested in students as individuals.

	AS	A	D	DS	OMIT	BEST	MEAN	S.D.	DEC
%	0.50	0.20	0.20	0.00	0.10	AS	3.33	0.87	4
#	5	2	2	0	1				

4. The course material was too difficult.

	AS	A	D	DS	OMIT	BEST	MEAN	S.D.	DEC
%	0.00	0.00	0.30	0.70	0.00	DS	3.70	0.48	10
#	0	0	3	7	0				

5. It was easy to remain attentive.

	AS	A	D	DS	OMIT	BEST	MEAN	S.D.	DEC
%	0.50	0.30	0.20	0.00	0.00	AS	3.30	0.82	8
#	5	3	2	0	0				

6. NOT much was gained by taking this course.

	AS	A	D	DS	OMIT	BEST	MEAN	S.D.	DEC
%	0.00	0.30	0.00	0.70	0.00	DS	3.40	0.97	5
#	0	3	0	7	0				

7. I would have preferred another method of teaching this course.

	AS	A	D	DS	OMIT	BEST	MEAN	S.D.	DEC
%	0.20	0.10	0.20	0.50	0.00	DS	3.00	1.25	6
#	2	1	2	5	0				

8. The course material seemed worthwhile.

	AS	A	D	DS	OMIT	BEST	MEAN	S.D.	DEC
%	0.50	0.30	0.20	0.00	0.00	AS	3.30	0.82	6
#	5	3	2	0	0				

9. The instructor did NOT synthesize, integrate or summarize effectively.

	AS	A	D	DS	OMIT	BEST	MEAN	S.D.	DEC
%	0.00	0.10	0.30	0.60	0.00	DS	3.50	0.71	8
#	0	1	3	6	0				

10. The course was quite interesting.

	AS	A	D	DS	OMIT	BEST	MEAN	S.D.	DEC
%	0.50	0.20	0.20	0.10	0.00	AS	3.10	1.10	5
#	5	2	2	1	0				

Arreola, R. A. (2000). Developing *a Comprehensive Faculty Evaluation System 2/e.* Bolton, MA: Anker Publishing Co., Inc.

Figure 15.2 (continued)   Example of CIEQ Analysis Printout

11. The instructor encouraged development of new viewpoints and appreciations.

	AS	A	D	DS	OMIT	BEST	MEAN	S.D.	DEC
%	0.50	0.10	0.30	0.10	0.00	AS	3.00	1.15	4
#	5	1	3	1	0				

12. I learn more when other teaching methods are used.

	AS	A	D	DS	OMIT	BEST	MEAN	S.D.	DEC
%	0.00	0.20	0.40	0.40	0.00	DS	3.20	0.79	9
#	0	2	4	4	0				

13. Some things were not explained very well.

	AS	A	D	DS	OMIT	BEST	MEAN	S.D.	DEC
%	0.10	0.00	0.60	0.30	0.00	DS	3.10	0.88	8
#	1	0	6	3	0				

14. The instructor demonstrated a thorough knowledge of the subject matter.

	AS	A	D	DS	OMIT	BEST	MEAN	S.D.	DEC
%	0.60	0.30	0.10	0.00	0.00	AS	3.50	0.71	4
#	6	3	1	0	0				

15. This was one of my poorest courses.

	AS	A	D	DS	OMIT	BEST	MEAN	S.D.	DEC
%	0.10	0.20	0.10	0.60	0.00	DS	3.20	1.14	3
#	1	2	1	6	0				

16. The course content was excellent.

	AS	A	D	DS	OMIT	BEST	MEAN	S.D.	DEC
%	0.60	0.10	0.10	0.20	0.00	AS	3.10	1.29	6
#	6	1	1	2	0				

17. Some days I was NOT very interested in this course.

	AS	A	D	DS	OMIT	BEST	MEAN	S.D.	DEC
%	0.40	0.10	0.20	0.30	0.00	DS	2.40	1.35	5
#	4	1	2	3	0				

18. I think that the course was taught quite well.

	AS	A	D	DS	OMIT	BEST	MEAN	S.D.	DEC
%	0.50	0.20	0.10	0.20	0.00	AS	3.00	1.25	4
#	5	2	1	2	0				

19. The course was quite boring.

	AS	A	D	DS	OMIT	BEST	MEAN	S.D.	DEC
%	0.00	0.10	0.30	0.60	0.00	DS	3.50	0.71	8
#	0	1	3	6	0				

20. The instructor seemed to consider teaching as a chore or routine activity.

	AS	A	D	DS	OMIT	BEST	MEAN	S.D.	DEC
%	0.20	0.00	0.40	0.40	0.00	DS	3.00	1.15	2
#	2	0	4	4	0				

21. Overall, the course was good.

	AS	A	D	DS	OMIT	BEST	MEAN	S.D.	DEC
%	0.60	0.10	0.20	0.10	0.00	AS	3.20	1.14	4
#	6	1	2	1	0				

Arreola, R. A. (2000). Developing *a Comprehensive Faculty Evaluation System 2/e.* Bolton, MA: Anker Publishing Co., Inc.

A Brief CIEQ Interpretation Guide

The following outline is provided as an aid to the rapid interpretation of CIEQ results. This guide can be used as a checklist when examining the computerized analysis output of the CIEQ. CIEQ interpretation is discussed in complete detail in the *Manual*.

STEP 1. ADEQUACY OF RESULTS

A. Refer to the top of the first page of the CIEQ output. Check the SAMPLE SIZE. If it or number of the students responding is less than one-half of the course enrollment, results may be biased and should be interpreted with caution.

B. At the bottom of the first page is the section entitled SUBSCALE RESULTS that contains a column of figures labeled REL. This column contains the obtained reliabilities for the six subscales of the CIEQ. Any subscale with a REL below .65 should be interpreted with caution. Consult the *Manual* for further details.

STEP 2. COMPARATIVE INFORMATION

A. In all cases, comparative information is provided by decile rank (DEC). The decile rank describes the current course MEAN in relation to other courses that have administered the CIEQ. Decile ranks are always interpreted as follows:

1–3	Substantial improvement needed
4–7	Some improvement needed
8–10	No improvement needed

Differences between adjacent pairs of decile ranks within each interval (e.g., 1 vs. 2, or 4 vs. 5) are not considered to be significantly different.

B. First refer to the SUBSCALE listing at the bottom of output on page 1. Each subscale represents a different aspect of the course as indicated by its title. Decile ranks for the current course/instructor are listed for each subscale in comparison to six normative groups:

1. IR all instructors of the same faculty rank

2. CL all courses at the same grade level (e.g., freshman, sophomore, etc.)

3. D all courses within the same department

4. C all courses within the same college

5. UA all courses at the University of Arizona

6. N all courses that have used the CIEQ in the United States

C. On the following two pages under INDIVIDUAL ITEM RESULTS are listed each of the 21 individual items of the CIEQ along with the proportion (%), frequency (#), mean, and standard deviation (SD) of responses to each individual item of the CIEQ. Also listed are the text of each item and the most favorable response or BEST answer for each item. All means have been scaled such that 4.00 is the most favorable response and 1.00 is the least favorable response, regardless of the initial wording of the item. To the far right of each individual item are listed decile ranks that compare each item mean to the item means obtained in all courses within the same college.

D. In interpreting results, refer first to the decile ranks for subscales. Low deciles for a subscale identify potential problem areas. Individual items can then be examined for more specific information. The subscales are composed of the following individual items:

Attitude	items 1, 6, 15, 21
Method	items 2, 7, 12, 18
Content	items 4, 8, 13, 16
Interest	items 5, 10, 17, 19
Instructor	items 3, 9, 11, 14, 20
Total	items 1–21

STEP 3. DESCRIPTIVE INFORMATION

A. Refer to the top of the first page of CIEQ output. Following the initial titles, information is listed on the composition of the responding sample under the heading Class Description Results. Both the proportion and frequency of responses are listed for each alternative of the following items: Class Information, Gender, Course Option, Pass–Fail Option, Major–Minor, and Expected Grade.

B. The next portion of the output lists the proportion (%), frequency (#), mean, and standard deviation (SD) of responses to three global ratings: Course Content, Instructor Rating, and the Course Rating. A mean value of 6.00 is the most favorable rating. **These three items have NOT been validated and should therefore be used only for the purpose of feedback to the instructor.**

IDEA—Student Ratings of Instruction

Contact: Bill Pallett
   IDEA Center
   Kansas State University
   1627 Anderson Avenue
   Box 3000
   Manhattan, KS 66502
   PH: (800) 255-2757 (532-5970)
   FAX: (785) 532-5637
   Email: idea@ksu.edu
   URL: www.idea.ksu.edu

Format. The IDEA system requires instructors to describe their course objectives prior to administering the rating form. The instructor is asked to rate the importance, on a 3-point scale (essential, important, or minor importance), of each of 12 IDEA objectives. The importance the instructor assigns to each objective is taken into account in tabulating results. The optically scanned rating form is divided into seven parts.

The first section consists of 20 items, which deal with five dimensions of instruction: student–faculty contact; involving students; establishing expectations; clarity of communication; and assessment/feedback. Items are scored on a 5-point scale ranging from hardly ever to almost always. The second section deals with the students' evaluation of their progress on 12 course objectives, including gaining factual knowledge, acquiring "team" skills, developing creative capacities, and clarifying/developing personal values. Students are asked to compare the progress made on each objective with the progress made in other courses. Each item is scored on a 5-point scale ranging from low (lowest 10% of courses taken) to high (highest 10% of courses taken). The third section deals with three course characteristics: amount of reading, amount of work in other assignments, and difficulty of subject matter. Ratings are compared to other courses on a 5-point scale ranging from much less than most courses to much more than most. The next section includes a self-rating of student attitudes and behaviors in the course. Each item is scored on a 5-point scale from definitely false to definitely true. The fifth section consists of five

"experimental questions" which the IDEA Center is studying for possible inclusion in future revisions of the form. The sixth section is for optional instructor-designed multiple-choice questions. Finally, the form provides a space for students to make open-ended comments. A "short form" version, appropriate for "summative" but not "formative" evaluation, is also available. It employs only Sections 2, 4, and 6 of the standard form.

Results. The IDEA report consists of seven parts plus identifying information (faculty and course name, number of students enrolled, percent providing ratings). The first two parts summarize evaluation results for overall measures (Part I) and for specific objectives (Part II). Both "unadjusted" and "adjusted" averages are compared with results in a very large national database. "Adjusted" results take into account factors which influence ratings but which are beyond the control of the instructor (class size; "course-related" student motivation; academic habits/effort; etc.). The overall evaluation measures, presented both numerically and graphically, include progress on instructor-chosen objectives, improved student attitude, overall excellence of the teacher, and overall excellence of the course. Part II provides similar information for the specific objectives selected as "important" or "essential" by the instructor. Part III (Methods) summarizes responses to the 20 items dealing with teaching procedures found on Section 1 of the standard form (but not included on the "short form"). Averages are reported graphically for each item and for scales designed to measure five instructional dimensions. Items are labeled as "strengths," "weaknesses," or "in-between" depending on how their averages differ from classes of similar size and student motivation level. A second section of Part III is intended to facilitate improvement efforts by identifying "strengths" and "weaknesses" which research by the Center has shown to be most relevant to specific teaching objectives. Part IV summarizes student descriptions of course characteristics, and also reports a course description provided by the instructor (including principal instructional methods; intended audience; special circumstances; and the amount of emphasis given to such matters as writing, computer applications, and quantitative skills). Section V provides statistical detail: frequencies, averages, and standard deviations for all items (including optional instructor-designed items).

Special Features. The IDEA system is a commercial rating package. Charges for forms and processing vary depending upon the number of forms ordered and classes processed. Forms must be ordered from the Center and returned to them for processing. Institutions receive three copies of the IDEA computer report; interpretation aids are incorporated in the report. For an additional fee, participating institutions may receive "Group Summary Reports" (which combine results for all classes or for selected subgroups) and "Faculty Summary Reports" (which summarize all reports for a given faculty member over a specified period of time). The Center publishes *Exchange*, an occasional newsletter, and a series of technical and nontechnical publications on topics in faculty evaluation and development. National workshops on selected topics are offered annually, and consultative services can also be arranged.

Development and Validation. The development and initial validation of the IDEA system is described by Hoyt (1973) and Hoyt and Cashin (1977). Items on instructor objectives were originally formed from earlier taxonomic classifications, factor analytic work, and input from award-winning teachers, faculty–student committees, and users of IDEA. The 1998 revision employed the advice of users in eliminating three of these and adding five that reflect higher education's contemporary emphases on team skills, values, lifelong learning, and critical thinking. The 20 teaching method items (10 of which are new) were written to reflect Chickering and Gamson's (1987) seven principles and were selected on the basis of their unique contribution to the prediction of outcomes. Items on course management and student characteristics were included primarily to adjust outcome measures by taking into account factors that were beyond the control of the instructor. The reliability of the five scales of teaching methods ranged from .76 to .91, averaging .86 for classes of 15 to 34 students. For individual items, reliabilities in similar classes ranged from .71 to .91, averaging .83. A principal indicator of validity was the finding that student ratings of progress on objectives were positively related to instructor ratings of importance of objectives. Also, relationships between teaching methods and progress on objectives were consistent with theoretical expectations. Multiple regression analyses showed that each of the 20 teaching methods made an independent contribution to the prediction of at least one progress rating, and that the relevance of specific instructor behaviors varied with class size. Factors which were used to adjust outcome measures included class size, student desire to take the course regardless of who taught it, the portion of "difficulty" ratings and of "effort" ratings which could not be attributed to the instructor, and a measure of "other student motivation." More recent technical reports (e.g., Cashin & Perrin, 1978; Sixbury & Cashin, 1995a & 1995b; Hoyt et al., 1998) provide additional data on reliability and validity as well as a description of the computational procedures and comparative databases used in producing reports for the latest version of IDEA.

Sample Form and Report. The following pages contain a sample of the IDEA student rating form (front and back) as well as an example of a faculty report. The IDEA system also provides institutional summary reports.

Figure 15.3   IDEA Survey Form—Student Reactions to Instruction and Courses (front side)

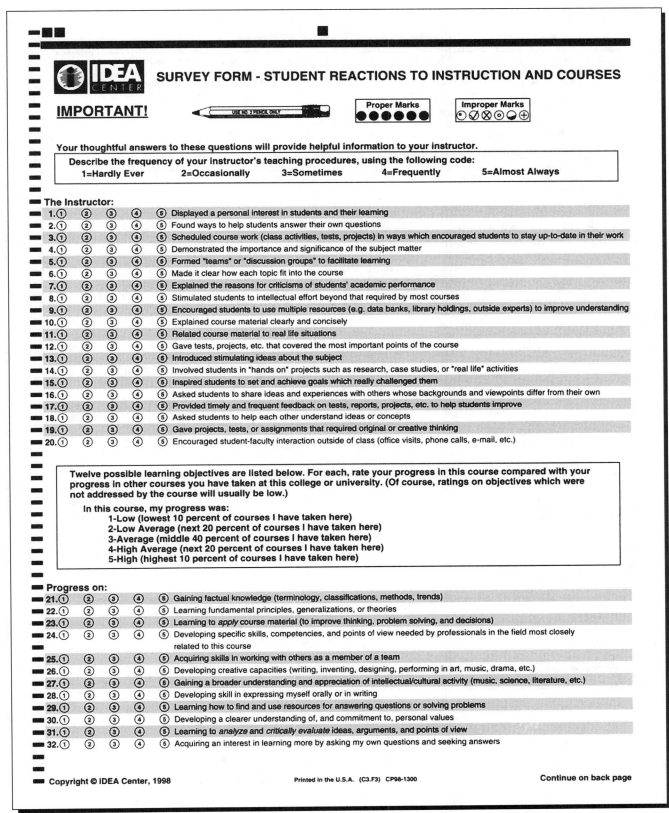

Arreola, R. A. (2000). Developing *a Comprehensive Faculty Evaluation System 2/e*. Bolton, MA: Anker Publishing Co., Inc.

On the next three items, compare this course with others you have taken at this institution, using the following code:

| 1=Much Less than Most Courses | 2=Less than Most Courses | 3=About Average | 4=More than Most Courses | 5=Much More than Most Courses |

The Course:

33. ① ② ③ ④ ⑤ Amount of reading
34. ① ② ③ ④ ⑤ Amount of work in other (non-reading) assignments
35. ① ② ③ ④ ⑤ Difficulty of subject matter

Describe your attitudes and behavior in this course, using the following code:

| 1=Definitely False | 2=More False Than True | 3=In Between | 4=More True Than False | 5=Definitely True |

Self Rating:

36. ① ② ③ ④ ⑤ I had a strong desire to take this course.
37. ① ② ③ ④ ⑤ I worked harder on this course than on most courses I have taken.
38. ① ② ③ ④ ⑤ I really wanted to take a course from this instructor.
39. ① ② ③ ④ ⑤ I really wanted to take this course regardless of who taught it.
40. ① ② ③ ④ ⑤ As a result of taking this course, I have more positive feelings toward this field of study.
41. ① ② ③ ④ ⑤ Overall, I rate this instructor an excellent teacher.
42. ① ② ③ ④ ⑤ Overall, I rate this course as excellent.

For the following items, blacken the space which best corresponds to your judgment:

| 1=Definitely False | 2=More False Than True | 3=In Between | 4=More True Than False | 5=Definitely True |

43. ① ② ③ ④ ⑤ As a rule, I put forth more effort than other students on academic work.
44. ① ② ③ ④ ⑤ The instructor used a variety of methods--not only tests--to evaluate student progress on course objectives.
45. ① ② ③ ④ ⑤ The instructor expected students to take their share of responsibility for learning.
46. ① ② ③ ④ ⑤ The instructor had high achievement standards in this class.
47. ① ② ③ ④ ⑤ The instructor used educational technology (e.g., Internet, e-mail, computer exercises, multi-media presentations, etc.) to promote learning.

EXTRA QUESTIONS
If your instructor has extra questions, answer them in the space designated below (questions 48-66):

48. ① ② ③ ④ ⑤   58. ① ② ③ ④ ⑤
49. ① ② ③ ④ ⑤   59. ① ② ③ ④ ⑤
50. ① ② ③ ④ ⑤   60. ① ② ③ ④ ⑤
51. ① ② ③ ④ ⑤   61. ① ② ③ ④ ⑤
52. ① ② ③ ④ ⑤   62. ① ② ③ ④ ⑤
53. ① ② ③ ④ ⑤   63. ① ② ③ ④ ⑤
54. ① ② ③ ④ ⑤   64. ① ② ③ ④ ⑤
55. ① ② ③ ④ ⑤   65. ① ② ③ ④ ⑤
56. ① ② ③ ④ ⑤   66. ① ② ③ ④ ⑤
57. ① ② ③ ④ ⑤

Your comments are invited on how the instructor might improve this course or teaching procedures. Use the space below for comments (unless otherwise directed). *Note: Your written comments may be returned to the instructor. You may want to PRINT to protect your anonymity.*

Institution: _____   Instructor: _____

Course Number: _____   Time and Days Class Meets: _____

Comments: _____
_____
_____
_____
_____
_____
_____

Arreola, R. A. (2000). Developing *a Comprehensive Faculty Evaluation System 2/e.* Bolton, MA: Anker Publishing Co., Inc.

Figure 15.4   Sample IDEA Report

The IDEA Report
Communications 0000 (MWF 11:30)
IDEA Center
www.idea.ksu.edu

Faculty Name: SAMPLE, AX   Number Enrolled: 18   Term: Fall   1998-1999
Institution: ALPHA UNIVERSITY   Number Responding: 15   % Responding: 83.3

Your results are considered fairly reliable; it is unlikely that re-rating by the same students would produce more than a moderate change in your report. The percentage of enrollees who provided ratings is high; results can be considered representative of the class as a whole.

Sections and Purposes of the Report

Page	Section	Purpose
2	I. Overall Measures of Teaching Effectiveness	Primarily for **administrative use** in helping to make personnel recommendations. *Only this page and Page 6 are essential if this is the only use you plan to make of the report.*
3	II. Student Ratings of Progress on Specific Objectives	Primarily to identify the **teaching objectives** where improvement is most needed
4-5	III. Teaching Methods or Style Related to Student Ratings of Progress	Primarily to help develop a **strategy for improving teaching** methods
6	IV. Course Description/Context	Primarily to **assist in interpreting** the results by considering the context in which the course was taught
7-8	V. Statistical Detail	Primarily to provide details which may help you or your consultants to **understand or interpret** the report accurately
8	VI. Processing Error Messages	Identifies errors resulting from incomplete information provided on the Faculty Information Form

Definitions
Raw Score: Results obtained by using students' numerical ratings, all of which are based on a scale of 1 (low) to 5 (high).
Adjusted Score: Ratings which have been statistically adjusted to take into account factors which affect ratings but which are beyond the instructor's control (size of class; student desire to take course regardless of who taught it; course difficulty not attributable to instructor; student effort not attributable to instructor; and other student motivational influences)
T Score: A statistically derived score which makes it easy to compare various measures. Unlike raw scores which have different averages and standard deviations (variabilities), T Scores all have an <u>average of 50</u> and a <u>standard deviation of 10</u>. This means that 40% of all T Scores will be in the range of 45-55, while less than 2% will be below 30 or above 70.
Similar Classes: On Page 4, ratings of specific teaching methods are compared with national averages for classes of "similar size and level of student motivation." Your ratings are compared with those from one of 20 groups defined by considering both class size (less than 15; 15-34; 35-99; or 100 or more) and average student response to "I had a strong desire to take this course" (under 3.0; 3.0-3.4; 3.5-3.9; 4.0-4.4; or 4.5 or above).

Understanding the Graphs
Most results are presented on graphs. Unadjusted T Scores are shown by the symbol ✕; adjusted T Scores are shown by the symbol ◆. In most cases, we use a line on both sides of a symbol to indicate that ratings have a "margin of error"; the line represents ± one standard error of measurement, a statistical indication of the reliability of the measure.

A Few Words of Caution
1. New items on the IDEA form are marked by an asterisk (*) because they have been tested on only 3,668 classes. Comparisons with the national database on these items will be less stable than for the items retained from the original IDEA form which are based on over 35,000 classes rated during the 1993-94 and 1994-95 academic years.

2. Student ratings can make a useful contribution to the appraisal of teaching effectiveness and to the development of improvement strategies. However, they have distinct limitations which need to be acknowledged before appropriate use can be made of them. Please read the enclosed *Overview of Student Ratings: Value and Limitations.*

Arreola, R. A. (2000). Developing *a Comprehensive Faculty Evaluation System 2/e.* Bolton, MA: Anker Publishing Co., Inc.

Figure 15.4 (continued)   Sample IDEA Report

Section II Overall Measures of Teaching Effectiveness

This section compares your results with those for other instructors and courses in the national database on four OVERALL MEASURES OF TEACHING EFFECTIVENESS. **The primary value of this information is to aid in making administrative recommendations; if this is the only use you will make of the report, you need to consult only these results and the context provided by Part IV, page 6.** Please remember that most of the classes included in the database have been taught in a reasonably successful manner; therefore, a rating which is "below average" does not necessarily mean that the quality of instruction was unacceptable.

Overall Measures of Effectiveness	T-Score Unadj. Adj.	2% of all classes	28% of all classes	40% of all classes (Avg. range)	28% of all classes	2% of all classes	Your Average (5-Point Scale) Raw	Adjusted
1. Progress on Relevant (Essential and Important) Objectives	58 / 55						NA₁	NA₁
2. Improved Student Attitude	50 / 46						3.9	3.6
3. Overall Excellence of Teacher	51 / 52						4.2	4.3
4. Overall Excellence of Course	51 / 44						3.9	3.5

20   30   40   50   55   60   70   80
T Score--Comparison with all Classes in National Database

⊢×⊣ Unadjusted T Score ± one standard error of measurement
⊢◆⊣ Adjusted T Score ± one standard error of measurement (adjusted for class size; student desire to take course regardless of who taught it; course difficulty not attributable to instructor; student effort not attributable to instructor; and other student motivational influences)

You may wish to assign these ratings to categories like those which have been used historically with the IDEA system. Simply assign T Scores to categories as follows: **Low** (lowest 10%)=T Score below 37; **Low Average** (next 20%)=T Score 37-44; **Average** (middle 40%)=T Score 45-55; **High Average** (next 20%)=T Score 56-63; and **High** (highest 10%)=T Score above 63.

1. Progress on Relevant (Essential and Important) Objectives. Because student learning is the central purpose of teaching, and because you chose the objectives considered by this measure, this is probably the most vital measure of effectiveness. A double weight is given to student ratings of progress on objectives you chose as *Essential*, and a single weight to those chosen as *Important*; objectives identified as being of *Minor or No Importance* were ignored in developing this measure.

2. Improved Student Attitude. The graph shows the average response of students to item 40, "As a result of taking this course, I have more positive feelings toward this field of study." This rating is most meaningful for courses which are taken by many non-majors. Most teachers hope that such students will develop a respect and appreciation for the discipline even if they choose to take no additional courses in it.

3. Overall Excellence of Teacher. This shows the average response to item 41, "Overall, I rate this instructor an excellent teacher." Overall impressions of a teacher affect student attitudes, effort, and learning.

4. Overall Excellence of Course. This shows the average response to item 42, "Overall, I rate this course as excellent." This evaluation is likely determined by a number of factors (e.g., teaching style, student satisfaction with course outcomes, and characteristics such as organization, selection of readings and^or other influences).

NA₁: Based on a combination of ratings where an average on a 5-point scale is not comparable.

Arreola, R. A. (2000). Developing *a Comprehensive Faculty Evaluation System 2/e.* Bolton, MA: Anker Publishing Co., Inc.

Figure 15.4 (continued)   Sample IDEA Report

Section II. Student Ratings of Progress on Specific Objectives

This graph shows student progress ratings on the objectives you chose as *Essential* (Part A) and those you chose as *Important* (Part B). To the degree that students make progress on the objectives you stress, your teaching has been effective.

Part A. Essential Objectives	T-Score Unadj. Adj.	2% of all classes	28% of all classes	40% of all classes (Avg. range)	28% of all classes	2% of all classes	Your Average (5-Point Scale) Raw	Adjusted
24. Professional skills, viewpoints	52 / 45						4.1	3.7
28. Oral and written communication skills	61 / 61						4.5	4.6

Part B. Important Objectives								
26. Creative capacities	61 / 56						4.5	4.3
*31. Analysis and critical evaluation of ideas	62 / 61						4.1	4.1

```
        20      30      40  45  50  55   60      70      80
    T Score--Comparison with all Classes in National Database where the
           Objective was Selected as "Essential" or "Important"
```

⊢×⊣ Unadjusted T Score ± one standard error of measurement
⊢◆⊣ Adjusted T Score ± one standard error of measurement (adjusted for class size; student desire to take course regardless of who taught it; course difficulty not attributable to instructor; student effort not attributable to instructor; and other student motivational influences)

Similar to Section I, you may wish to assign ratings to categories. Simply assign T Scores to categories as follows: **Low** (lowest 10%)=T Score below 37; **Low Average** (next 20%)=T Score 37-44; **Average** (middle 40%)=T Score 45-55; **High Average** (next 20%)=T Score 56-63; and **High** (highest 10%)=T Score above 63.

It is recommended that priority attention be given to *Essential* objectives with progress ratings which are *below average*. The second priority might be directed to *Important* objectives for which progress ratings are *below average*. A third priority might be *Essential* or *Important* objectives for which progress ratings are in the *average* range. If all progress ratings are *above the average* range, it is suggested that your present methods of teaching are effective and changes in your teaching style or approaches do not appear to be needed in order to ensure that your teaching promotes student learning. If improvement is needed, strategies can be formulated by examining "Strengths" and "Weaknesses" associated with progress ratings on the objectives chosen for priority attention. These are identified in **Section III** of this report.

Note: Students in your class also rated their progress on the objectives which you classified as being of *Minor or No Importance*. These ratings are considered irrelevant in judging your teaching effectiveness. However, a review of student ratings on these objectives, found in **Section V** (Statistical Detail), may provide you with insights about some "unintended" or "additional" effects of your instruction.

*New Item

Arreola, R. A. (2000). Developing *a Comprehensive Faculty Evaluation System 2/e.* Bolton, MA: Anker Publishing Co., Inc.

Figure 15.4 (continued)   Sample IDEA Report

Faculty Name: SAMPLE, AX   Term: Fall   1998-1999
Course: Communications 0000   Page 4

Section III. Teaching Methods or Style Related to Student Ratings of Progress

This section focuses on specific teaching methods. Results are given in two parts. **Part One** graphically compares ratings of your teaching methods with those of others who teach classes similar to this one in terms of size and level of student motivation. **Part Two** identifies the teaching methods most closely related to attaining your *Important* and *Essential* objectives, providing a basis for developing improvement strategies. **Part Three** highlights potential areas to emphasize for improvement efforts and teaching strengths that should be retained.

Part One: The graphs below classify methods as "strengths" if your rating was at least 0.3 above average for classes of similar size and level of student motivation and as "weaknesses" if your rating was at least 0.3 below the average for such classes. Although effectiveness generally improves when weaknesses are overcome while maintaining strengths, not all teaching methods promote progress on every teaching objective. The methods which are especially relevant to each of your *Essential* and *Important* objectives are identified in **Part Two** (page 5).

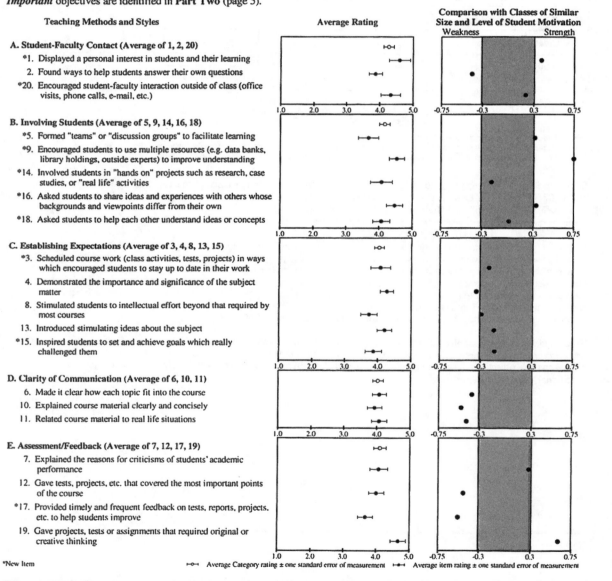

Teaching Methods and Styles

A. Student-Faculty Contact (Average of 1, 2, 20)
 *1. Displayed a personal interest in students and their learning
  2. Found ways to help students answer their own questions
 *20. Encouraged student-faculty interaction outside of class (office visits, phone calls, e-mail, etc.)

B. Involving Students (Average of 5, 9, 14, 16, 18)
 *5. Formed "teams" or "discussion groups" to facilitate learning
 *9. Encouraged students to use multiple resources (e.g. data banks, library holdings, outside experts) to improve understanding
 *14. Involved students in "hands on" projects such as research, case studies, or "real life" activities
 *16. Asked students to share ideas and experiences with others whose backgrounds and viewpoints differ from their own
 *18. Asked students to help each other understand ideas or concepts

C. Establishing Expectations (Average of 3, 4, 8, 13, 15)
 *3. Scheduled course work (class activities, tests, projects) in ways which encouraged students to stay up to date in their work
  4. Demonstrated the importance and significance of the subject matter
  8. Stimulated students to intellectual effort beyond that required by most courses
 13. Introduced stimulating ideas about the subject
 *15. Inspired students to set and achieve goals which really challenged them

D. Clarity of Communication (Average of 6, 10, 11)
  6. Made it clear how each topic fit into the course
 10. Explained course material clearly and concisely
 11. Related course material to real life situations

E. Assessment/Feedback (Average of 7, 12, 17, 19)
  7. Explained the reasons for criticisms of students' academic performance
 12. Gave tests, projects, etc. that covered the most important points of the course
 *17. Provided timely and frequent feedback on tests, reports, projects, etc. to help students improve
 19. Gave projects, tests or assignments that required original or creative thinking

Average Rating

Comparison with Classes of Similar Size and Level of Student Motivation
Weakness   Strength

*New Item   ⊢O⊣ Average Category rating ± one standard error of measurement   ⊢●⊣ Average item rating ± one standard error of measurement

Arreola, R. A. (2000). Developing *a Comprehensive Faculty Evaluation System 2/e*. Bolton, MA: Anker Publishing Co., Inc.

Figure 15.4 (continued)   Sample IDEA Report

Section III. Teaching Methods or Style Related to Student Ratings of Progress (continued)

Part Two: Column 1 below again lists those objectives you listed as *Essential* or *Important*. Column 2 lists those teaching methods which in combination are most closely related to progress ratings on your chosen objectives. Column 3 separates out those teaching methods rated as "strengths" and those rated as "weaknesses" in comparison to the national average. (The numbers in Columns 2 and 3 refer to the teaching methods numbered 1-20 on the graphical presentations in **Part One, page 4**.)

Column 1	Column 2	Column 3	
Chosen Objectives	Most Relevant Teaching Methods	Most Relevant Strengths/Weaknesses	
		Strengths	Weaknesses
Essential Objectives			
24. Professional skills, viewpoints	3,4,6,7,8,11,12,14,18		4,6,11,12
28. Oral and written communication skills	1,3,5,7,8,9,10,19	1,5,9,19	10
Important Objectives			
26. Creative capacities	1,5,6,7,13,19,20	1,5,19	6
*31. Analysis and critical evaluation of ideas	3,5,8,13,18,19,20	5,19	

Part Three: This section summarizes teaching methods to consider for improvement strategies and methods which are effective and should be retained.

Potential Areas for Improvement Efforts

Generally, improvement efforts are most successful if they focus on no more than three teaching strategies at a time. These results suggest that your improvement strategies might best be chosen from the following teaching methods:

      6. Made it clear how each topic fit into the course

      4. Demonstrated the importance and significance of the subject matter

   10. Explained course material clearly and concisely

   11. Related course material to real life situations

   12. Gave tests, projects, etc. that covered the most important points of the course

Strengths to Retain

In doing so, you should take care to retain the methods which are currently effective, including:

    *5. Formed "teams" or "discussion groups" to facilitate learning

   19. Gave projects, tests or assignments that required original or creative thinking

    *1. Displayed a personal interest in students and their learning

    *9. Encouraged students to use multiple resources (e.g. data banks, library holdings, outside experts) to improve understanding

*New Item

Arreola, R. A. (2000). Developing *a Comprehensive Faculty Evaluation System 2/e*. Bolton, MA: Anker Publishing Co., Inc.

Figure 15.4 (continued)   Sample IDEA Report

Section IV. Course Description/Context

This section describes several aspects of your course. Some of the description summarizes information you supplied when you administered the IDEA form, and some of the information comes from student responses. Information on this page provides the context in which the class was taught and in which interpretation of the ratings should be made. The IDEA Center will conduct additional research on these data to determine more precisely how they can improve interpretation of the report.

Course Description:

Primary Instructional Type:	*Discussion/recitation*	Team Taught:	*Not reported*
Secondary Instructional Type:	*Other/Not Indicated*	Distance Learning:	*Not reported*
Principal Type of Student:	*Underclassmen, general*		

Instructor's Ratings of Special Circumstances:

Positive Impact on Learning	Neither Positive nor Negative Impact	Negative Impact on Learning
Previous experience teaching course	*Physical facilities and/or equipment*	*Adequacy of students' background/preparation*
Desire to teach course	*Changes in teaching approach*	
	Control over course management decisions	
	Student enthusiasm	
	Student effort	
	Technical/instructional support	

Instructor's Ratings of Course Requirements:

Much Required	Some Required	None (or little) Required
Writing		*Computer applications*
Oral communication		*Group work*
Critical thinking		*Mathematical/quantitative work*
Creative/artistic/design endeavor		

Student Ratings of the Course:

	Number of Students Saying:*					Average	T Score
	1	2	3	4	5		
33. Amount of reading	2	3	7	1	0	2.5	43
34. Amount of work in other (non-reading) assignments	0	1	3	7	2	3.8	57
35. Difficulty of subject matter	0	0	7	4	2	3.6	56

*1 = Much less than most courses   2 = Less than most courses   3 = About average   4 = More than most courses   5 = Much more than most courses

Similar to Sections I and II, you may wish to assign ratings to categories. Simply assign T Scores to categories as follows: **Low** (lowest 10%)=T Score below 37; **Low Average** (next 20%)=T Score 37-44; **Average** (middle 40%)=T Score 45-55; **High Average** (next 20%)=T Score 56-63; and **High** (highest 10%)=T Score above 63.

Arreola, R. A. (2000). Developing *a Comprehensive Faculty Evaluation System 2/e*. Bolton, MA: Anker Publishing Co., Inc.

Figure 15.4 (continued)   Sample IDEA Report

Section V. Statistical Detail: Item Frequencies, Averages, and Standard Deviations

Items 1-20: Teaching Methods

Key: 1=Hardly Ever   2=Occasionally   3=Sometimes
     4=Frequently   5=Almost Always

	1	2	3	4	5	Omit	Avg.	s.d.
1.	0	0	0	6	9	0	4.6	0.5
2.	0	1	5	4	5	0	3.9	1.0
3.	0	1	3	5	6	0	4.1	1.0
4.	0	1	2	4	8	0	4.3	1.0
5.	2	0	5	2	6	0	3.7	1.4
6.	0	1	4	3	7	0	4.1	1.0
7.	1	1	1	4	7	1	4.1	1.3
8.	0	2	5	3	5	0	3.7	1.1
9.	0	0	1	5	9	0	4.5	0.6
10.	0	1	5	3	6	0	3.9	1.0
11.	1	1	1	5	7	0	4.1	1.2
12.	0	2	2	5	6	0	4.0	1.1
13.	0	0	4	4	7	0	4.2	0.9
14.	0	2	4	0	9	0	4.1	1.2
15.	0	1	5	4	5	0	3.9	1.0
16.	0	0	3	2	10	0	4.5	0.8
17.	1	2	4	2	6	0	3.7	1.3
18.	0	3	1	3	8	0	4.1	1.2
19.	0	0	0	5	10	0	4.7	0.5
20.	0	0	4	2	9	0	4.3	0.9

Items 21-32: Progress on Objectives

Key: 1=Low   2=Low Average   3=Average
     4=High Average 5=High

	1	2	3	4	5	Omit	Avg.	s.d.
21.	0	1	2	4	8	0	4.3	1.0
22.	1	2	1	5	6	0	3.9	1.3
23.	1	0	4	3	7	0	4.0	1.2
24.	**0**	**2**	**2**	**4**	**7**	**0**	**4.1**	**1.1**
25.	1	0	3	5	6	0	4.0	1.1
26.	**0**	**1**	**1**	**2**	**11**	**0**	**4.5**	**0.9**
27.	2	0	3	3	7	0	3.9	1.4
28.	**0**	**0**	**2**	**3**	**10**	**0**	**4.5**	**0.7**
29.	0	0	3	4	8	0	4.3	0.8
30.	2	1	3	4	5	0	3.6	1.4
31.	**0**	**0**	**5**	**3**	**7**	**0**	**4.1**	**0.9**
32.	0	1	5	2	7	0	4.0	1.1

Bold items were selected as *Essential* or *Important*.

Items 33-35: The Course

Key: 1=Much Less than Most Courses   2=Less than Most Courses
     3=About Average   4=More than Most Courses
     5=Much More than Most Courses

	1	2	3	4	5	Omit	Avg.	s.d.
33.	2	3	7	1	0	2	2.5	0.9
34.	0	1	3	7	2	2	3.8	0.8
35.	0	0	7	4	2	2	3.6	0.8

Items 43-47: Experimental

Key: 1=Definitely False   2=More False Than True
     3=In Between   4=More True Than False
     5=Definitely True

	1	2	3	4	5	Omit	Avg.	s.d.
43.	1	4	1	5	3	1	3.4	1.3
44.	0	2	2	6	4	1	3.9	1.0
45.	0	0	1	9	4	1	4.2	0.6
46.	0	1	2	7	4	1	4.0	0.9
47.	1	1	6	5	1	1	3.3	1.0

Items 36-42: Self-Ratings

Key: 1=Definitely False   2=More False Than True
     3=In Between   4=More True Than False
     5=Definitely True

	1	2	3	4	5	Omit	Avg.	s.d.
36.	1	0	1	1	11	1	4.5	1.2
37.	0	2	4	6	2	1	3.6	0.9
38.	1	2	6	0	5	1	3.4	1.3
39.	1	0	3	4	6	1	4.0	1.2
40.	2	1	0	4	7	1	3.9	1.5
41.	0	1	2	4	7	1	4.2	1.0
42.	0	1	4	4	5	1	3.9	1.0

Arreola, R. A. (2000). Developing *a Comprehensive Faculty Evaluation System 2/e.* Bolton, MA: Anker Publishing Co., Inc.

Figure 15.4 (continued)   Sample IDEA Report

Faculty Name: SAMPLE, AX
Course: Communications 0000

Term: Fall   1998-1999
Page 8

Section V. Statistical Detail: Continued

Items 48-66: Extra Questions

	1	2	3	4	5	Omit	Avg.	s.d.
48.	0	0	4	18	6	0	4.1	0.6
49.	1	3	11	13	0	0	3.3	0.8
50.	3	7	14	4	0	0	2.7	0.9
51.	0	11	7	10	0	0	3.0	0.9
52.	23	0	2	0	3	0	1.6	1.3
53.	4	12	10	2	0	0	2.4	0.8
54.	5	4	9	6	4	0	3.0	1.3
55.	0	0	0	0	0	28	N/A	N/A
56.	0	0	0	0	0	28	N/A	N/A
57.	0	0	0	0	0	28	N/A	N/A

	1	2	3	4	5	Omit	Avg.	s.d.
58.	0	0	0	0	0	28	N/A	N/A
59.	0	0	0	0	0	28	N/A	N/A
60.	0	0	0	0	0	28	N/A	N/A
61.	0	0	0	0	0	28	N/A	N/A
62.	0	0	0	0	0	28	N/A	N/A
63.	0	0	0	0	0	28	N/A	N/A
64.	0	0	0	0	0	28	N/A	N/A
65.	0	0	0	0	0	28	N/A	N/A
66.	0	0	0	0	0	28	N/A	N/A

Section VI. Processing Error Messages

Arreola, R. A. (2000). Developing *a Comprehensive Faculty Evaluation System 2/e*. Bolton, MA: Anker Publishing Co., Inc.

Student Instructional Report II (SIR II)

Contact: Bruce Paternoster
           Student Instructional Report II
           Educational Testing Service
           Mail Stop 55-L, Rosedale Road
           Princeton, NJ 08541-0001
           PH: (609) 683-2247
           FAX: (609) 683-2270
           Email: bpaternoster@ets.org
           URL: www.ets.org/hea

Format. The SIR II rating form consists of 45 core items that are divided into 10 sections with space for up to 10 instructor-prepared supplementary questions. The form is printed on both sides of a scannable answer sheet. The first five sections focus on instructor characteristics, including Course Organization and Planning, Communication, Faculty/Student Interaction, Assignments, Exams and Grading, and Supplementary Instructional Methods. Each of these sections contains five or six questions. Items are scored on a 5-point scale plus the option

of "Not Applicable." The 5-point scale is (5) Very Effective, (4) Effective, (3) Moderately Effective, (2) Somewhat Ineffective, and (1) Ineffective. Questions in these first five sections include such teaching and learning factors as instructor's use of class time, ability to make clear presentations, responsiveness to students, comments on assignments and exams, and the use of practices and tools such as journals, portfolios, computers, case studies, and team learning. The sixth and seventh sections of the SIR II provide the student with a different 5-point scale, asking them to rate the relationship between the course and their self-assessment of their contributions. The choices are (5) Much More than most courses, (4) More Than most courses, (3) About the Same as others, (2) Less Than most courses, and (1) Much Less than most courses. In the Course Outcomes section, the questions are about a student's increase in interest in the subject, progress toward achieving course objectives, and involvement in learning. In the Student Effort and Involvement section, the questions ask for how much effort was put into the course, degree of preparation through homework, and how challenged the student felt. The eighth section asks three questions about Course Difficulty, Work Load, and Pace. The ninth section contains one question asking for an overall evaluation of the quality of instruction using the same 5-point scale as the first five sections. The final section of the SIR II questionnaire asks for student information such as class level, reason for taking the course, English language proficiency, gender, and expected grade. After space for up to 10 instructor-supplied questions, a final paragraph suggests that students make additional comments in writing on a separate sheet of paper.

Results. Three copies of a two-page report are provided for each class evaluated. For each of the questions, the percentages of the total number of completed questionnaires for each of the five ratings is displayed together with the mean score. An overall mean for each section is also printed, and for most of the sections, a comparative mean from either two-year or four-year institutions is also displayed. These means are based on a comparison of the instructor's average score on each item with means from a wide variety of two-year, technical, and four-year institutions that use the SIR II. Item means are flagged with a "+" if they are reliably at or above the 90th percentile of comparative data and with a "−" if they are reliably at or below the 10th percentile of comparative data. When class size is small and/or the percentage of students responding is low, responses may be flagged or not tabulated, reducing the probability of interpreting unreliable data. Separate Comparative Data Guides for two-year and four-year institutions are provided with each set of reports. Each guide contains data analyzed for specific institution types, class size, class level, class type, and subject area. In addition to class reports, institutions may request a Summary Report and/or special Combined Reports.

Special Features. SIR II is a commercial rating system; the questionnaire must be purchased from Educational Testing Service. Sales of questionnaires are separate from processing charges, providing institutions the option of processing the questionnaires themselves. Costs vary with quantity ordered.

Development and Validation. The SIR II is a 1995 revision of the original 1972 SIR (Student Instructional Report). Two new forms were developed and pretested in spring 1994. These forms included five of the scales from the original SIR with questions added or deleted. Three new scales or dimensions were added. These new scales reflected recent emphases on measuring learning outcomes, promoting students' time on task, and effort in their learning. Each of the two pretested forms included a different response format to the same set of items and scales. By having random halves of students in 50 classes respond to the two forms, it was possible to determine which response format was better. Pretesting was carried out at 10 two- and four-year colleges. Traditional item and scale analyses of the two forms included computing means, standard deviations, coefficient alphas, item-to-scale correlations, and factor analyses. A Rasch analysis also compared the response categories for the two forms to determine which provided better variation in student responses. Pilot testing of the final form occurred at a variety of colleges from spring 1995 through spring 1996. Course means and standard deviations were computed for each item and scale. A sample of the data from the pilot testing was used to determine the reliability and construct validity of SIR II. The three kinds of reliability computed established the internal consistency of the items within the scales (coefficient alpha), the number of students needed for consistency of course results (intraclass correlations), and the stability of responses over brief periods of time (test-retest). The factor analysis indicated that the resulting factors matched perfectly with the expected or a priori scales for SIR II.

Research Reports of the SIR also support the SIR II, given their similar research basis. John Centra, professor of education at Syracuse University, performed many studies of the SIR and was also instrumental in developing the SIR II (Centra, 1972a, 1972b, 1973, 1976, 1998; Centra & Gaubatz, 1999). He continues to write research reports from SIR II data. Six research reports based on SIR data covering such topics as comparisons with alumni data, research productivity and teaching effectiveness, relationships with the use of portfolio evaluation, and comparisons with self-ratings are available from Educational Testing Service.

Sample Form and Report. The following is a sample of the SIR II form as well as an example of the faculty report provided.

Figure 15.5   Student Instructional Report II Form (front side)

SIR II Report Number

STUDENT INSTRUCTIONAL REPORT II (SIR II)

This questionnaire gives you the chance to comment anonymously about this course and the way it was taught. Using the rating scale below, mark the one response for each statement that is closest to your view. Fill in the appropriate circle to the right of the statement.

(5)   Very Effective
(4)   Effective
(3)   Moderately Effective
(2)   Somewhat Ineffective
(1)   Ineffective
(0)   Not applicable, not used in the course, or you don't know. In short, the statement does not apply to the course or instructor.

As you respond to each statement, think about each practice as it contributed to your learning in this course.

A. Course Organization and Planning

1. The instructor's explanation of course requirements
2. The instructor's preparation for each class period
3. The instructor's command of the subject matter
4. The instructor's use of class time
5. The instructor's way of summarizing or emphasizing important points in class

B. Communication

6. The instuctor's ability to make clear and understandable presentations
7. The instructor's command of spoken English (or the language used in the course)
8. The instructor's use of examples or illustrations to clarify course material
9. The instructor's use of challenging questions or problems
10. The instructor's enthusiasm for the course material

C. Faculty/Student Interaction

11. The instructor's helpfulness and responsiveness to students
12. The instructor's respect for students
13. The instructor's concern for student progress
14. The availability of extra help for this class (taking into account the size of the class)
15. The instructor's willingness to listen to student questions and opinions

D. Assignments, Exams, and Grading

16. The information given to students about how they would be graded
17. The clarity of exam questions
18. The exams' coverage of important aspects of the course
19. The instructor's comments on assignments and exams
20. The overall quality of the textbook(s)
21. The helpfulness of assignments in understanding course material

E. Supplementary Instructional Methods

Many different teaching practices can be used during a course. In this section (E), rate only those practices that the instructor included as part of this course.

Rate the effectiveness of each practice used as it contributed to your learning.

22. Problems or questions presented by the instructor for small group discussions
23. Term paper(s) or project(s)
24. Laboratory exercises for understanding important course concepts
25. Assigned projects in which students worked together
26. Case studies, simulations, or role playing
27. Course journals or logs required of students
28. Instructor's use of computers as aids in instruction

Questionnaire continued on the other side. ➡

Arreola, R. A. (2000). Developing *a Comprehensive Faculty Evaluation System 2/e.* Bolton, MA: Anker Publishing Co., Inc.

Figure 15.5 (continued)   Student Instructional Report II Form (back side)

For the next **two** sections (F and G), use the rating scale below. Mark the one response for each statement that is closest to your view. Fill in the appropriate circle to the right of each statement.

(5)   **Much More** than most courses
(4)   **More Than** most courses
(3)   About the **Same** as others
(2)   **Less** than most courses
(1)   **Much Less** than most courses
(0)   **Not Applicable**, not used in the course, or you don't know. In short, the statement does not apply to the course or instructor.

Much More than most courses · More Than most courses · About the Same as others · Less than most courses · Much Less than most courses · Not Applicable

F. Course Outcomes

29. My learning increased in this course ....   ⑤ ... ④ ... ③ ... ② ... ① ..... ⓪
30. I made progress toward achieving course objectives ....   ⑤ ... ④ ... ③ ... ② ... ① ..... ⓪
31. My interest in the subject area has increased ....   ⑤ ... ④ ... ③ ... ② ... ① ..... ⓪
32. This course helped me to think independently about the subject matter ......   ⑤ ... ④ ... ③ ... ② ... ① ..... ⓪
33. This course actively involved me in what I was learning .....   ⑤ ... ④ ... ③ ... ② ... ① ..... ⓪

G. Student Effort and Involvement

34. I studied and put effort into the course ....   ⑤ ... ④ ... ③ ... ② ... ① ..... ⓪
35. I was prepared for each class [writing and reading assignments] ......   ⑤ ... ④ ... ③ ... ② ... ① ..... ⓪
36. I was challenged by this course ....   ⑤ ... ④ ... ③ ... ② ... ① ..... ⓪

H. Course Difficulty, Work Load, and Pace

37. For my preparation and ability, the level of difficulty of this course was:
⑤ Very difficult   ④ Somewhat difficult   ③ About right   ② Somewhat elementary   ① Very elementary

38. The work load for this course in relation to other courses of equal credit was:
⑤ Much heavier   ④ Heavier   ③ About the same   ② Lighter   ① Much lighter

39. For me, the pace at which the instructor covered the material during the term was:
⑤ Very fast   ④ Somewhat fast   ③ Just about right   ② Somewhat slow   ① Very slow

I. Overall Evaluation

40. Rate the quality of instruction in this course as it contributed to your learning (try to set aside your feelings about the course content):
⑤ Very effective   ④ Effective   ③ Moderately effective   ② Somewhat Ineffective   ① Ineffective

J. Student Information

41. Which one of the following best describes this course for you?
① A major/minor requirement   ② A college requirement   ③ An elective   ④ Other

42. What is your class level?
① Freshman/1st year   ② Sophomore/2nd year   ③ Junior/3rd year   ④ Senior/4th year   ⑤ Graduate   ⑥ Other

43. Do you communicate better in English or in another language?
① Better in English   ② Better in another language   ③ Equally well in English and another language

44. Sex   ① Female   ② Male

45. What grade do you expect to receive in this course?
① A   ② A-   ③ B+   ④ B   ⑤ B-   ⑥ C   ⑦ Below C

K. Supplementary Questions   If the instructor provided supplementary questions and response options, mark your answers in this section. Mark only one response for each question.

46. ⑤④③②① NA   48. ⑤④③②① NA   50. ⑤④③②① NA   52. ⑤④③②① NA   54. ⑤④③②① NA
47. ⑤④③②① NA   49. ⑤④③②① NA   51. ⑤④③②① NA   53. ⑤④③②① NA   55. ⑤④③②① NA

L. Student Comments   If you would like to make additional comments about the course or instruction, use a separate sheet of paper. You might elaborate on the particular aspects you liked most as well as those you liked least. Also, how can the course or the way it was taught be improved? An additional form may be provided for your comments. **Please give these comments to the instructor.**

If you have any comments about this questionnaire, please send them to:
Student Instructional Report II, Educational Testing Service, Princeton, NJ 08541-0001.

Arreola, R. A. (2000). Developing *a Comprehensive Faculty Evaluation System 2/e.* Bolton, MA: Anker Publishing Co., Inc.

Figure 15.6   SIR II Sample Class Report

STUDENT INSTRUCTIONAL REPORT II

Enrollment	Admin. Date	Report No.	Batch No.
33	00/00	00000	0000

CLASS REPORT

SAMPLE

Assessing Courses and Instruction

PERCENTAGES reported below are based on the total number responding, which is: 33

A. Course Organization and Planning *Think about each practice as it contributed to your learning in this course. . .*	Omit	Not Applicable	5 Very Effective	4 Effective	3 Moderately Effective	2 Somewhat Ineffective	1 Ineffective	Mean
1. The instructor's explanation of course requirements . . .			39	42	18			4.21
2. The instructor's preparation for each class period . . .			42	42	9	6		4.21
3. The instructor's command of the subject matter . . .			39	42	12	6		4.15
4. The instructor's use of class time . . .			42	30	18	6	3	4.03
5. The instructor's way of summarizing or emphasizing important points in class . . .			27	45	6	18	3	3.76

Overall mean for COURSE ORGANIZATION AND PLANNING is: 4.07   The comparative mean for X-year institutions is: x.xx.

B. Communication *Think about each practice as it contributed to your learning in this course.*	Omit	Not Applicable	5 Very Effective	4 Effective	3 Moderately Effective	2 Somewhat Ineffective	1 Ineffective	Mean
6. The instructor's ability to make clear and understandable presentations . . .			30	36	27	6		3.91
7. The instructor's command of spoken English (or the language used in the course) . . .			61	36	3			4.58
8. The instructor's use of examples or illustrations to clarify course material . . .			33	33	30	3		3.97
9. The instructor's use of challenging questions or problems . . .			30	39	27	3		3.97
10. The instructor's enthusiasm for the course material . . .			21	45	30	3		3.85

Overall mean for COMMUNICATION is: 4.06   The comparative mean for X-year institutions is: x.xx.

C. Faculty/Student Interaction *Think about each practice as it contributed to your learning in this course.*	Omit	Not Applicable	5 Very Effective	4 Effective	3 Moderately Effective	2 Somewhat Ineffective	1 Ineffective	Mean
11. The instructor's helpfulness and responsiveness to students . . .			39	33	15	12		4.00
12. The instructor's respect for students . . .			45	24	18	9	3	4.00
13. The instructor's concern for student progress . . .			36	33	15	15		3.91
14. The availability of extra help for this class (taking into account the size of the class) . . .			36	33	21	9		3.97
15. The instructor's willingness to listen to student questions and opinions . . .			39	36	12	6	6	3.97

Overall mean for FACULTY/STUDENT INTERACTION is: 3.97   The comparative mean for X-year institutions is: x.xx.

+ This mean is higher than the comparative mean. See page 4.

– This mean is lower than the comparative mean. See page 4.

For explanation of flagging (*), see "Number of Students Responding," page 4.

Arreola, R. A. (2000). Developing *a Comprehensive Faculty Evaluation System 2/e.* Bolton, MA: Anker Publishing Co., Inc.

Figure 15.6 (continued)   SIR II Sample Class Report

STUDENT INSTRUCTIONAL REPORT II

D. Assignments, Exams, and Grading *Think about each practice as it contributed to your learning in this course*	Omit	Not Applicable	5 Very Effective	4 Effective	3 Moderately Effective	2 Somewhat Ineffective	1 Ineffective	Mean
16. The information given to students about how they would be graded . . .			45	39	15			4.30
17. The clarity of exam questions . . .			36	33	21	9		3.97
18. The exams' coverage of important aspects of the course . . .			33	42	18	6		4.03
19. The instructor's comments on assignments and exams . . .			27	39	21	12		3.82
20. The overall quality of the textbook(s) . . .		6	12	45	15	15	6	3.45
21. The helpfulness of assignments in understanding course material . . .			27	48	21	3		4.00

Overall mean for ASSIGNMENTS, EXAMS, AND GRADING is: 3.93   The comparative mean for X-year institutions is: x.xx.

E. Supplementary Instructional Methods *Rate the effectiveness of each practice used as it contributed to your learning*	Omit	Not Used	5 Very Effective	4 Effective	3 Moderately Effective	2 Somewhat Ineffective	1 Ineffective	Mean
22. Problems or questions presented by the instructor for small group discussions . . .	3	3	21	64	9			***
23. Term paper(s) or project(s) . . .			30	58	12			***
24. Laboratory exercises for understanding important course concepts . . .	12	52	18	9	9			***
25. Assigned projects in which students worked together . . .			33	48	12		6	***
26. Case studies, simulations, or role playing . . .			33	55	12			***
27. Course journals or logs required of students . . .	9	64	9	9	6	3		***
28. Instructor's use of computers as aids in instruction . .	9	70	9	12				***

Means are not reported (***) for SUPPLEMENTARY INSTRUCTIONAL METHODS.

F. Course Outcomes *Mark the response that is closest to your view*	Omit	Not Applicable	5 Much More Than Most Courses	4 More Than Most Courses	3 About the Same as Others	2 Less Than Most Courses	1 Much Less Than Most Courses	Mean
29. My learning increased in this course . . .	3		15	33	33	12	3	3.47
30. I made progress toward achieving course objectives . . .	3		18	30	45	3		3.66
31. My interest in the subject area has increased . . .	3		15	24	33	15	9	3.22
32. This course helped me to think independently about the subject matter . . .	3		24	18	45	9		3.59
33. This course actively involved me in what I was learning . . .	3		27	33	30	6		3.84

Overall mean for COURSE OUTCOMES is: 3.56   The comparative mean for X-year institutions is: x.xx.

G. Student Effort and Involvement *Mark the response that is closest to your view.*	Omit	Not Applicable	5 Much More Than Most Courses	4 More Than Most Courses	3 About the Same as Others	2 Less Than Most Courses	1 Much Less Than Most Courses	Mean
34. I studied and put effort into this course . . .	3		45	12	36	3		4.03
35. I was prepared for each class (writing and reading assignments) . . .	3		33	27	30	3	3	3.88
36. I was challenged by this course . . .	3		33	12	36	9	6	3.59

Overall mean for STUDENT EFFORT AND INVOLVEMENT is: 3.83   The comparative mean for X-year institutions is: x.xx.

+ This mean is higher than the comparative mean. See page 4.

− This mean is lower than the comparative mean. See page 4.   For explanation of flagging (*), see "Number of Students Responding," page 4.

Arreola, R. A. (2000). Developing *a Comprehensive Faculty Evaluation System 2/e.* Bolton, MA: Anker Publishing Co., Inc.

Figure 15.6 (continued)   SIR II Sample Class Report

ASSESSING COURSES and INSTRUCTION

H. Course Difficulty, Workload, and Pace
Mark the response that is closest to your view.

	Omit	Very Difficult	Somewhat Difficult	About Right	Somewhat Elementary	Very Elementary
37. For my preparation and ability, the level of difficulty of this course was . . .	3	6	42	42	3	3

	Omit	Much Heavier	Heavier	About the Same	Lighter	Much Lighter
38. The work load for this course in relation to other courses of equal credit was . . .	3	55	24	15	3	

	Omit	Very Fast	Somewhat Fast	Just About Right	Somewhat Slow	Very Slow
39. For me, the pace at which the instructor covered the material during the term was . . .	3	6	33	55	3	

Means are not appropriate for COURSE DIFFICULTY, WORKLOAD, and PACE.   Review the distribution of students' responses.

I. Overall Evaluation

	Omit	5 Very Effective	4 Effective	3 Moderately Effective	2 Somewhat Ineffective	1 Ineffective	Mean
40. Rate the quality of instruction in this course as it contributed to your learning. (Try to set aside your feelings about the course content.)	3	18	52	21	6		3.84

OVERALL EVALUATION mean is: 3.84

J. Student Information

	Omit	Requirement in Major	College Requirement	Elective	Other
41. Which one of the following best describes this course for you?	3	76	18	3	

42. What is your class level?	Omit	Freshman/ 1st Year	Sophomore/ 2nd Year	Junior/ 3rd Year	Senior/ 4th Year	Graduate	Other
	3			3	85	6	3

43. Do you communicate better in English or in another language?	Omit	Better in English		Better in Another Language	Equally well in English and Another Language	
	3	91		3	3	

44. Sex	Omit	Female	Male
	3	52	45

45. What grade do you expect to receive in this course?	Omit	A	A-	B+	B	B-	C	Below C
	100							

K. Supplementary Questions

	Omit	NA	5	4	3	2	1
46.							
47.							
48.							
49.							
50.							
51.							
52.							
53.							
54.							
55.							

+ This mean is higher than the comparative mean. See page 4.

– This mean is lower than the comparative mean. See page 4.   For explanation of flagging (*), see "Number of Students Responding," page 4.

Arreola, R. A. (2000). Developing *a Comprehensive Faculty Evaluation System 2/e.* Bolton, MA: Anker Publishing Co., Inc.

Figure 15.6 (continued)   SIR II Sample Class Report

INTERPRETING SIR II

The SIR II is designed to:

- Identify areas of strength and/or areas for improvement.
- Provide information on new teaching methods or techniques used in class.
- Provide feedback from students about their courses.

NUMBER OF STUDENTS RESPONDING

The number of students responding can affect the results when the class is very small (fewer than 10 students are enrolled), or when fewer than two-thirds of the students enrolled in the class actually respond. For this reason, a Class Report **will not be produced** when fewer than five students responded, that is, fewer than five completed answer sheets were received for a class.

The degree of accuracy for each item mean increases as the number of students responding increases. For example, the estimated reliability for the Overall Evaluation item is .78 if 10 students respond; .88 if 20 students respond; and .90 if 25 students respond. (A full discussion of the reliability of student evaluation items can be found in *SIR Report No. 3*.) To call attention to possible reliability concerns, a report will be flagged (*) for one or more of the following.

* The number responding **will be flagged** when: 10 or fewer students responded or less than 60 percent of the class responded (this calculation is based on information from the *Instructor's Cover Sheet*).

* An item mean **will not be reported** when: 50 percent or more of the students did not respond, or marked an item "Not Applicable," or fewer than five students responded to an item.

* An overall mean **is not reported** when one or more item means are not reported.

COMPARATIVE DATA (NOT AVAILABLE FOR SIR II PILOT)

The comparative means used throughout this report are based on user data from a sample of two and four year colleges and universities. An institution is identified by type — two-year or four-year — on the Processing Request Form that is returned with the questionnaires for scoring. Either two-year or four-year comparative data are used, based on that identification.

These data are **comparative** rather than normative. That is, they are prepared by combining class reports from institutions at which the questionnaire was administered. The data are updated periodically and are developed and published separately for two-year and for four-year institutions in the *Comparative Data Guides*.

The *Comparative Data Guides* for both two- and four-year colleges contain data analyzed for: size of class, level of class (freshman/sophomore and junior/senior), type of class (lecture, discussion, lab), and several different subject areas. A copy of the appropriate *Guide* is sent to Institutional Coordinators with the SIR II reports.

Local Comparative Data: Equally important and useful are an institution's own comparative data. Such local comparative data — e.g., an Institutional Summary, departmental summaries, program summaries — are available to any user institution. Forms for ordering these reports are included in the *Institutional Coordinator's Manual*.

Understanding Mean Ratings

Ratings can vary by class size and discipline. The *Comparative Data Guides* provide data by various categories to assist users in interpreting the SIR II reports. Please refer to the *Guide* and to the SIR II Guidelines for further information. Since student ratings typically tend to be favorable, it is important to have comparative data to interpret a report fully. For example, while a 3.6 is numerically above average on a 5-point scale, it may be average or even slightly below average in comparison to other means for items in SIR II.

What Makes a Score Difference Significant?

The mean scores on all of the items and scales in this report have been compared against the scores obtained by all of the classes in one of the appropriate comparative data groups (two-year or four-year institutions). Specifically, the scores have been compared against the score values corresponding to the 10th percentile and 90th percentile in the comparative group. If the results indicate a score is sufficiently reliable and is below the 10th percentile or above the 90th percentile, it will be flagged in the report as follows:

   + This class mean is reliably at or above the 90th percentile.

   − This class mean is reliably at or below the 10th percentile.

Scores above the 90th percentile or below the 10th percentile are flagged when there is appropriate statistical confidence that the "true scores" (i.e., the scores that would be obtained if there were no measurement error) fall within these ranges. If a score is flagged with a +, there is less than one chance in 20 that the "true score" is below the 90th percentile; if a score is flagged with a −, there is less than one chance in 20 that the "true score" is above the 10th percentile. (One chance in 20 is the commonly accepted measurement standard for a 95% confidence level.)

Because measurement error varies from class to class, instructors with identical means on the SIR II items may not have the same items flagged. In particular, measurement error tends to be larger when the number of respondents is low and when disagreement among the respondents is high. For example, instructors in small classes are likely to have fewer items flagged than those in large classes because there is less confidence of the reliability of means in small classes.

Arreola, R. A. (2000). Developing *a Comprehensive Faculty Evaluation System 2/e.* Bolton, MA: Anker Publishing Co., Inc.

Chapter References

Aleamoni, L. M. (1978). Development and factorial validation of the Arizona course/instructor evaluation questionnaire. *Educational and Psychological Measurement, 38,* 1063-1067.

Aleamoni, L. M., & Carynnk, D. B. (1977). Optional item catalog (revised), *Information Memorandum No. 6.* Tucson, AZ: University of Arizona, Office of Instructional Research and Development.

Aleamoni, L. M. & Laham, D. (1992). *Arizona course/instructor evaluation questionnaire: Results interpretation manual.* Tucson, AZ: University of Arizona, Office of Instructional Research and Development.

Aleamoni, L. M., & Spencer, R. E. (1973). The Illinois course evaluation questionnaire: A description of its development and a report of some of its results. *Educational and Psychological Measurement, 33,* 669-684.

Cashin, W. E., & Perrin, B. M. (1978, December). *Description of the IDEA system data base—1978-79 (IDEA Technical Report No. 4).* Manhattan, KS: Kansas State University, Center for Faculty Evaluation and Development.

Centra, J. A. (1972a). *The student instructional report: Its development and uses (SIR Report No. 1).* Princeton, NJ: Educational Testing Service.

Centra, J. A. (1972b). *Two studies on the utility of student ratings for instructional improvement. I. The effectiveness of student feedback in modifying college instruction. II. Self-ratings of college teachers: A comparison with student ratings (SIR Report No. 2).* Princeton, NJ: Educational Testing Service.

Centra, J. A. (1973). *Comparisons with alumni ratings, reliability of items, and factor structure (SIR Report No. 3).* Princeton, NJ: Educational Testing Service.

Centra, J. A. (1976). *Two studies on the validity of the student instructional report: I. Student ratings of instruction and their relationship to student learning. II. The relationship between student, teacher, and course characteristics and student ratings of teacher effectiveness (SIR Report No. 4).* Princeton, NJ: Educational Testing Service.

Centra, J. A. (1998). *The development of the student instructional report II.* Princeton, NJ: Educational Testing Service.

Centra, J. A., and Gaubatz, N. B. (1999). *Is there gender bias in student evaluations of teaching?* Princeton, NJ: Educational Testing Service.

Chickering, A., & Gamson, Z. (1987, March). Seven principles of good practice in undergraduate education. *AAHE Bulletin.*

Gillmore, G. M. (1973). *Estimates of reliability coefficients for items and subscales of the Illinois course evaluation questionnaire (Research Report No. 341).* Urbana, IL: University of Illinois, Office of Instructional Resources, Measurement and Research Division.

Hoyt, D. P. (1973). Measurement of instructional effectiveness. *Research in Higher Education, 1,* 367-378.

Hoyt, D. P., & Cashin, W. E. (1977, March). *Development of the IDEA system (IDEA Technical Report No. 1).* Manhattan, KS: Kansas State University, Center for Faculty Evaluation and Development.

Hoyt, D. P., Chen, Y., Pallett, W. H., & Gross, A. B. (1998, November). *Revising the IDEA system for obtaining student ratings of instructors and courses (IDEA Technical Report No. 11).* Manhattan, KS: Kansas State University, the IDEA Center.

Mitchell, J. V. (Ed.). (1983). *Tests in Print.* Lincoln, NE: University of Nebraska, Buros Institute of Mental Measurements.

Mitchell, J. V. (Ed.). (1985). *Mental Measurements Yearbook.* Lincoln, NE: University of Nebraska, Buros Institute of Mental Measurements.

Sixbury, G. R., & Cashin, W. E. (1995a, January). *Description of database for the IDEA diagnostic form (IDEA Technical Report No. 9).* Manhattan, KS: Kansas State University, Center for Faculty Evaluation and Development.

Sixbury, G. R., & Cashin, W. E. (1995b, January). *Comparative data by academic field (IDEA Technical Report No. 10).* Manhattan, KS: Kansas State University, Center for Faculty Evaluation and Development.

16

Case Study and Sample
Faculty Evaluation Procedures

A number of colleges and universities have developed comprehensive faculty evaluation systems employing the eight-step process described in this book. This chapter presents the results of two of these institutions. The eight-step process described in Chapters 1 through 8 contains a number of decision points that can lead in different directions in the development of a comprehensive faculty evaluation system. Thus, no two institutions using this approach will develop precisely the same system.

The first section of this chapter contains the case study of Frostburg State University in constructing its faculty evaluation system using the principles outlined in this book. This section was prepared by Thomas F. Hawk, Ph.D., professor of management at Frostburg State University, specifically for this chapter. Dr. Hawk offers important insights and details concerning the practical and political aspects of developing a comprehensive faculty evaluation system using the steps described in Chapters 1 through 8.

Following the Frostburg State University case study is an excerpt from the *Georgia Perimeter College Faculty Evaluation, Promotion and Tenure Handbook* (1998–99). Although not presented as a case study, the Georgia Perimeter College faculty evaluation manual demonstrates another variation of system developed by the application of the procedures described in this book. In both cases a coordinating task force or committee was appointed and charged with the task of guiding the institution through the eight steps described in Chapters 1 through 8.

The materials shown in this chapter represent separate expressions of the concepts of defining the faculty role model, identifying sources, defining roles, and weighting role and source impact in designing a comprehensive faculty evaluation system. These materials are not presented as idealized models but simply two institutions' interpretation of how to use the process described in this book to design and develop a faculty evaluation system that works for them. The system your institution develops may differ considerably. However, the faculty evaluation systems shown in this chapter contain various forms and procedures that may be of interest as you develop your own faculty evaluation system.

FROSTBURG STATE UNIVERSITY CASE STUDY

Developing a Managed Subjectivity Process of Faculty Evaluation at Frostburg State University
Thomas F. Hawk, Ph.D.

In May 1998, the 25 members of the Frostburg State University Faculty Senate passed the fourth faculty evaluation process in the history of the university, with passage of the first three occurring in 1973, 1981, and 1989. The passage of the new evaluation process was a culmination of four years of subcommittee and committee work triggered by dissatisfaction with the existing departmentally based evaluation process initiated in 1989. The managed subjectivity model for faculty evaluation developed by Raoul A. Arreola was the basis for the 1998 evaluation process.

This case study describes the context for faculty evaluation at Frostburg State University as well as the three years of work of the Faculty Evaluation Subcommittee and the subsequent one year of work of the Faculty Concerns Committee, both operating under the umbrella of the university's Faculty Senate. It highlights the characteristics of the development process, including the major milestones, difficulties, and political considerations.

The Context

Frostburg State University (FSU) is one of the constituent institutions of the University System of Maryland, a system of two research units and 11 universities and colleges operated under a System Board of Regents appointed by the governor. The USM Regents have published an Appointment, Retention, and Tenure Policy and a Post-Tenure Review Policy that specify the general guidelines under which the constituent institutions must design and operate their respective faculty evaluation systems.

FSU enrolls approximately 4,400 undergraduate and 850 graduate students. There are four schools (Arts and Humanities, Business Administration, Education, and Natural and Social Sciences), each with its own dean, under the supervision of the provost/academic vice president. The 23 academic departments have 230 full-time, tenure track faculty, of whom 70% are tenured.

The university's initial faculty evaluation process based on Richard. I. Miller's (1972) seminal work, *Evaluating*

Faculty Performance, was passed in 1973. It was standard across all departments and divided evaluation into five categories, one each for Teaching, Professional Development and Service, Professional Characteristics, Department Service, and College Service. Department heads held primary responsibility for evaluation of each faculty member in all five categories. The Teaching component was based in part upon a single summative rating item at the end of a common 23-item student questionnaire. There was no merit pay attached to the evaluation. Table 16.1 summarizes the 1973 evaluation system.

The 1981 evaluation process, also standard across all departments, combined the five 1973 categories into three general categories of Teaching, Professional Development and Service, and College/Department Service, with evaluation done by either the department chair or a Departmental Evaluation Committee. Teaching carried 60% of the overall evaluation weight, with the other two carrying 20% each. Student ratings constituted 50% of the Teaching category weight. The student rating form was a common questionnaire of seven questions, of which four gave a pedagogical rating and three a rapport rating. High merit pay was at the recommendation of the department chair

Table 16.1   1973 Frostburg State College Faculty Evaluation System (Based in part on the 1972 work of Richard I. Miller)

Historical Overview of Faculty Evaluation Systems at Frostburg State University

Evaluation Category	Category Weight	Evidence	Sub-Weight
1. Teaching	50%–80%	a. Merit based on a single global item embedded in a 33-item student evaluation questionnaire	"Meaningful Part"
		b. Course Materials	As Determined
		c. Optional Classroom Visitations	By Departments
		d. Optional Self-Statement	
2. Professional Development and Service	5%–35%	Ten-item rating scale including evaluation of research and publications	100%
3. Professional Characteristics	5%–35%	Five-item rating scale	100%
4. Department Service	5%–35%	Seven-item rating scale	100%
5. College Service	5%–35%	Six-item rating scale	100%

but limited to only 20% of each department's full-time tenure track faculty. The merit pay amount was determined by the academic administrators. Table 16.2 summarizes the 1981 evaluation system.

The 1989 evaluation process allowed each department to construct its own process within a general framework of the three evaluation categories of Teaching, Professional Development, and Service. Departments were encouraged to use a Departmental Evaluation Committee but could choose to use the department chair if that was the wish of the departmental faculty. The Department Evaluation Committee or the chair was the sole rater in the Professional Development and Service categories and shared that task with students for the Teaching category. The faculty handbook stipulated that each department was to create its own student rating questionnaire to address criteria under the Teaching category. It also specified examples of performance that met the criteria for a rating of Outstanding, Meets Expectations, or Needs Improvement in each of the three major categories. One merit pay unit was available for achieving Meets Expectations in Teaching, Professional Development, and Service. An additional merit pay unit was available for achieving Outstanding in Teaching and an additional half unit was granted for Outstanding performance in each of the Professional Development and Service categories. In effect, the Teaching category received a 50% weight and the other two categories a weight of 25% each. Each school received a merit pay pool equivalent to its percentage of full-time, tenure track faculty at the university. The value of a merit pay unit was determined by dividing the school's merit pay pool by the number of merit units awarded to its faculty. Table 16.3 summarizes the 1989 evaluation system.

Beginning the Process

In the fall of 1994, the Faculty Senate established a Faculty Evaluation Subcommittee under the Faculty Concerns Committee to address a number of faculty evaluation issues. The primary issues were 1) the absence of an articulated evaluation process and evaluation criteria in

Table 16.2 1981 Frostburg State College Faculty Evaluation System

Evaluation Category	Category Weight	Evidence	Sub-Weight
1. Teaching	60%	a. Four pedagogical skills items embedded in a seven-item questionnaire	50%
		b. Course Organization Rating (7 items)	Average of
		c. Teaching Materials (2 items)	b, c, d, e
		d. Optional, evidence of Student Achievement (3 items)	equals 50%
		e. Optional, Classroom Visit	of Weight
2. College/Department Service	20%	Seven-item checklist based upon personal data sheet submitted by faculty member (Basic Service)	60%
		Seven-item checklist (Additional Service)	40%
3. Professional Development and Service	20%	Four-item checklist (Basic Development and Service)	60%
		Seven-item checklist (Additional Development and Service)	40%

An optional self-statement allowed the faculty member to present contextual information.

Table 16.3 1989 Frostburg State University Faculty Evaluation System

Three levels of evaluation: (1) Below Expectations, (2) Meets Expectations, and (3) Outstanding. No specific weights are assigned but merit units are as follows:

1. **Below Expectations**

   Fails to meet in a substantive way any of the criteria for "meets expectations" (0 merit unit).

2. **Meets Expectations**

   Meets basic expectations in the following seven areas of performance (1 merit unit). Examples of performance which meet criteria are included.

   a. Course Syllabus

   b. Teaching Materials

   c. Faculty Teaching Performance

   d. Feedback to Students

   e. Faculty Development

   f. Departmental Contributions

   g. School-Wide and University-Wide Contributions

3. **Outstanding**

   a. Outstanding in Professional Development or Achievement (0.5 merit unit). Must demonstrate levels of achievement substantially beyond "meets expectations" criteria. Examples of such achievements are given.

   b. Outstanding in University, School, and/or Department Service (0.5 merit unit). Five examples of outstanding service are listed.

   c. Outstanding in Teaching (1.0 merit unit). Must ensure "continued development of instructional activities" and demonstrate attitudes, personal characteristics, and behavior indicative of an outstanding teacher. Examples are given.

some departments, 2) the wide range of quality of processes, criteria, and student rating forms in departments that did have an articulated process and criteria, 3) the near total reliance on the student ratings for the Teaching category evaluation in most of the departments, and 4) the difficulty of comparing ratings across departments. The Faculty Concerns Committee of the University's Faculty Senate had been unable to address these issues due to the large number and wide range of issues that came before it for consideration. Therefore, the Committee requested that the Senate establish a Faculty Evaluation Subcommittee to address the faculty evaluation portion of its work.

Since November did not coincide with the normal timing for faculty governance elections, the chair of the Faculty Senate asked for two faculty volunteers from each of the university's four schools, preferably one male and one female faculty from different departments. The resulting volunteers were one male and one female from the School of Business and the School of Arts and Humanities, two males from the School of Natural and Social Sciences, and one male from the School of Education.

At the first meeting, the members elected me as chair after I stipulated that, if elected, we would have as our primary agenda item the overhaul of the existing faculty evaluation system. I then suggested that this effort should be a partnership between the appointed members of the subcommittee and the four school deans. The members of the subcommittee agreed.

We were fortunate in that, at a department chairs retreat in the summer of 1993, the Provost had invited Raoul Arreola to present a half-day seminar on the managed subjectivity evaluation model that he had developed. The chairs received it very positively (I had attended that retreat as chair of the MBA Department). Subsequent to that retreat, the provost sent one chair from the School of Natural and Social Sciences, one faculty member from the School of Education, the dean of Natural and Social Sciences, and the associate provost (all four were tenured faculty members) to the two-day seminar on the Arreola model in Florida. The subcommittee members agreed that we should invite the four to give a presentation on the model.

At the next meeting, the four made their presentation and answered the questions we posed. After a lengthy discussion that explored what we had learned about the model as well as what other possible models we might use, we asked the associate provost if he would ask the provost to purchase copies of the Arreola workbook for the members of the subcommittee if we decided to use the model. He said that was an appropriate suggestion and indicated that he could make the necessary arrangements. After further discussion, we decided to tentatively adopt the model, pending a more thorough understanding of the model after receiving the workbooks. We also agreed that the four who had attended the two-day seminar should become invited working members of the subcommittee. This provided a representative from the provost's office, a second representative from the School of Education, a third representative from the School of Natural and Social Sciences, and the dean of Natural and Social Sciences who was already an invited member. Our subcommittee then consisted of the members listed in Table 16.4.

The Work of the Subcommittee

After the initial organizing meetings in November and December of 1994 and the arrival of the workbooks in January 1995, the subcommittee began its work in earnest at the start of the spring 1995 semester in early February. The subcommittee met on a regular monthly schedule until April 1997 when it passed its completed document to the Faculty Concerns Committee for its consideration before presentation to the Senate.

At my suggestion, the members of the committee agreed that I should take a facilitative approach to the process, that is, refrain as much as possible from taking advocacy positions on agenda content. I then invited the committee members to help me maintain that facilitative approach. There were times when it was difficult to do, but I believe that, for the most part, I succeeded in doing so. Facilitating the process also meant publishing an agenda for each meeting and arranging for a location to accommodate a physically limited member, who served as our secretary.

Throughout the 27-month period, the character of our work went from the general to the specific, with the more global characteristics of the new faculty evaluation process emerging first and leading to consideration of more specific detail in different segments of the system. There was a clear iterative character to the work; however, we struggled with trying to understand the concerns of each other and develop the detail needed to provide an effective and usable system. Preliminary resolution of the detail in one area frequently generated more questions in other areas as well as the more global characteristics and

Table 16.4 Composition of Faculty Evaluation Subcommittee, 1995

Appointed Member	—	Associate Professor of Management (Dept. Chair)*
Appointed Member	—	Associate Professor of Economics (Dept. Chair)
Appointed Member	—	Professor of English
Appointed Member	—	Associate Professor of Communication
Appointed Member	—	Professor of Mathematics
Appointed Member	—	Associate Professor of Chemistry
Appointed Member	—	Associate Professor of Physical Education
Invited Member	—	Associate Professor of Education
Invited Member	—	Professor of Biology (Dept. Chair)
Invited Member	—	Associate Provost (Professor of English)
Invited Member	—	Dean, School of Natural and Social Sciences
Ex Officio	—	Dean, School of Arts and Humanities
Ex Officio	—	Dean, School of Education
Ex Officio	—	Dean, School of Business

* Subcommittee Chair

frequently led to a reexamination of the global framework and/or the detail of an area agreed upon earlier.

The first struggle for the members was to develop a strong working understanding of the managed subjectivity model. Almost every one was diligent in studying the workbook, although we had to do a lot a verbal reinforcement and explanation of concepts in the workbook to get everyone at a relatively equal level of comprehension of the model. This took several months as we attempted to define the main categories and their weight ranges as well as the elements of each category.

During that process, we confronted what we believed to be a major issue: To what degree were we going to depart from the explicit category definitions of Teaching, Professional Achievement and Development, and Service of the 1989 system that were published in the faculty handbook? After considerable discussion it was noted that the committee was going to be asking the faculty to accept a large number of changes in the faculty evaluation system. These changes included 1) negotiating individual role percentages; 2) keeping negotiated weights within established weight ranges; 3) accepting fixed role component weights; 4) accepting the use of data from multiple sources; 5) weighting data from different sources in different amounts; and 6) facing the likely change in the way merit pay was calculated. The committee agreed to attempt to maintain as much of the existing category descriptions as possible in order to give the faculty familiar ground on which to overlay the new process. In the final analysis, however, during the open comment period the faculty indicated that they were more open to changes in the category and element descriptions than we had assumed.

Throughout all of 1995, we made slow but deliberate progress, surviving the departure of one Natural and Social Sciences and one Arts and Humanities faculty appointees and bringing their replacements up to speed with the work. By the end of 1995, however, we were having difficulty dealing with several complex issues, such as the new student rating form and the need for a new merit pay concept. The associate provost was observant enough to recognize the need for some all-day sessions and actively pushed for them during the intersession period of January 1996. Those sessions proved to be crucial in getting us over the hump in developing the basic elements of our new process.

In April 1995, the chair of the Faculty Senate had asked me to make a short status presentation to the Faculty Senate. At that meeting, I had informed the senators that we would not send any proposal to the Faculty Con-

cerns Committee without first holding an open comment and feedback period for all of the academic departments and individual faculty. Therefore, late in the spring 1996 semester, we sent out the preliminary proposal and gave all departments until the end of September to respond.

We continued to meet through the summer and fall of 1996 as we worked with the feedback we were receiving. Critical feedback focused on 1) improving the category definitions, with a lot of encouragement to depart from the existing category definitions in the faculty handbook; 2) incorporating into the Teaching category ways to encourage experimentation and innovation in teaching; 3) improving the student rating form; 4) finding ways to reduce the paperwork required by the process without sacrificing the documentation of performance; and 5) giving the deans oversight and appeal responsibility but keeping primary control of the evaluation process with the Departmental Evaluation Committees, the department chair, and the Faculty Concerns Committee.

By the middle of the spring 1997 semester, we had finished revising our spring 1996 proposal. The timing of completing the revision was fortunate as it was becoming obvious that most of the members of the subcommittee were experiencing burnout with the process. As a result, we formally submitted the revised faculty evaluation process to the Faculty Concerns Committee, stating that we felt we had taken it as far we could. Any further changes would have to originate with the Faculty Concerns Committee. As chair of the Faculty Evaluation Subcommittee, I would function in an advisory role to Faculty Concerns. Additionally, a major overhaul of the faculty governance structure that had passed that spring had resulted in the dissolution of the subcommittee once it finished its work on the evaluation process. All of us on the subcommittee opposed that dissolution due to our expectation of a continued high level of activity for the Faculty Concerns Committee on faculty evaluation issues.

The Work of the Faculty Concerns Committee

During the 1997–1998 academic year, the members of the Faculty Concerns Committee worked with the Department Chairs Council and through the members of the Senate to further improve the proposal. Their efforts did not alter the basic structure of the process. Rather, there was an easing of the stringency of the Professional Achievement and Development Category, the addition of standards in a number of elements where none had existed, and clarification of several administrative provisions, particularly in the area of moving evaluation weights to accommodate assigned time activities in service or professional development activities that substituted for some teaching responsibilities. During that year I worked with the Office of Institutional Research to develop a software program that would automate most of the calculations and provide a standard printout format for student rating results and evaluation results for all faculty and department chairs.

In March 1998, the Faculty Concerns Committee distributed the final version of the evaluation process to the members of the Senate and to the entire university faculty. The Senate gave its first reading at the April meeting and passed it with one dissenting vote at the May meeting, stipulating that implementation would begin with the spring 1999 semester. It also asked the Faculty Concerns Committee to look for ways to bring greater clarity to the process.

Summary of Changes

In the final analysis, the members of the Faculty Evaluation Subcommittee felt that five characteristics of the new system were major improvements in the process of faculty evaluation at Frostburg State University (see Table 16.5 for a summary. The first was the incorpora-

tion of a negotiated range for each of the three evaluation categories, allowing faculty members to address workload and personal preferences in their yearly category weights. The second was the specification of the appropriate sources of rating and rating weights for each element of each major evaluation category. This change was particularly welcomed where students were the appropriate rating source. The third was the combination of the symmetrical rating scale of 1 to 5 and the stepped merit pay scale beginning at the midpoint of 3.0 (see Table 16.6). The fourth was the inclusion of a specific element within the teaching category to encourage innovation, experimentation, and creative instructional development. And the fifth was the documentation of justifications for the ratings in each element of all categories so that there would be an annual check on the progress toward tenure for all untenured faculty. This justification includes a statement assessing the professional behavior of the untenured faculty member for the year.

As a postscript, the Faculty Concerns Committee has continued to work with the new evaluation process during the fall 1998 semester, finding several additional improvements and clarifications to make. And, at the request of the Faculty Concerns Committee, the Senate has

Table 16.5   1998 Frostburg State University Faculty Evaluation System Evaluation Category/Category Weight

Evaluation Category	Category Weight	Evidence	Sub-Weight	Sources (Weight)
1. Teaching	50%–80%	Course materials and course syllabus ratings	25%	Chair Rating (.30) DEC Rating (.70)
		Teaching performance and feedback to students ratings	50%	Student Rating (.65) Chair Rating (.20) DEC Rating (.15)
		Instructional development ratings	25%	Chair Rating (.70) DEC Rating (.30)
2. Professional Development and Achievement	10%–30%	Examples of performance to be rated 3.0, 4.0, and 5.0 on a scale of 1.0 to 5.0 are given.	100%	Chair Rating (.25) DEC Rating (.75)
3. Service	5%–25%	Examples of performance to be rated 3.0, 4.0, and 5.0 on a scale of 1.0 to 5.0 are given.	100%	Chair Rating (.75) DEC Rating (.25)

established an Ad Hoc Task Force on Faculty Evaluation to coordinate the new evaluation process and relieve the Faculty Concerns Committee of the detail work on the process.

Note: I would like to express my appreciation to Dr. Kenneth Stewart, dean of the School of Natural and Social Sciences, for sharing his knowledge of the 1973 and 1981 faculty evaluation processes and for his constructive comments on earlier drafts of this chapter.

Table 16.6 Faculty Merit Pay Calculation

The merit pay system is a stepped system in increments of 0.1, with merit pay awarded for those faculty who achieve an overall rating of at least 2.95. The rating scale is a 5-point scale, where

5.0 = Outstanding Performance

4.0 = Above Expectations

3.0 = Meets Expectations

2.0 = Below Expectations

1.0 = Unacceptable Performance

To calculate the merit unit level for each faculty member, round the overall rating to the nearest tenth (e.g., under the convention that 1 to 4 rounds down and 5 to 9 rounds up, a rating between 3.05 to 3.14 would be rounded to 3.1) and subtract 2.9 from the overall rating (merit pay begins at the 3.0 level).

To calculate the merit unit amount (the dollar value associated with each full merit unit), divide the total merit pay pool by the total number of merit units awarded across the university. For example, assume that the total merit pay pool is $120,000 and the total number of merit unit levels awarded across the university is 220. The merit unit amount would be $545.45 ($120,000/220).

To calculate the merit pay amount for any faculty member, multiply the merit unit amount by the merit unit level for the faculty member. For example, assume that there are seven faculty in a department who end up with the overall ratings as shown below. The merit pay amount for each of the seven faculty members would be as follows:

OVERALL

Faculty	Rating	Merit Unit Level	Merit Pay Amount
Dr. Alfred	3.09	3.1 − 2.9 = 0.2	0.2 × $545.45 = $109.09
Dr. Bowens	3.48	3.5 − 2.9 = 0.6	0.6 × $545.45 = $327.27
Dr. Hiller	3.92	3.9 − 2.9 = 1.0	1.0 × $545.45 = $545.45
Dr. James	4.09	4.1 − 2.9 = 1.2	1.2 × $545.45 = $654.54
Dr. Malloy	4.33	4.3 − 2.9 = 1.4	1.4 × $545.45 = $763.63
Dr. Peters	4.47	4.5 − 2.9 = 1.6	1.6 × $545.45 = $872.72
Dr. Thomas	4.70	4.7 − 2.9 = 1.8	1.8 × $545.45 = $981.81

The same process would be used to calculate the merit pay amount for each of the remaining faculty members at the university. The total merit pay awarded would equal $120,000.

FROSTBURG STATE UNIVERSITY FACULTY EVALUATION SYSTEM

Passed by Faculty Senate, May 1998

Introduction

Academic departments carry out faculty evaluation for four purposes:

1. To inform faculty members regarding the degree to which their performance matches Department/School/University expectations;

2. To supply information and guidance to faculty with respect to professional improvement and development;

3. To establish a base of information for future personnel decisions including contact renewal, tenure, and promotions and;

4. To determine annual merit pay increases.

Components of the System

The faculty evaluation system follows a comprehensive approach to reviewing and evaluating the activities of faculty members within their three major roles. The evaluation process allows faculty members the opportunity to place greater emphasis on one or another of the three major roles in a given year:

- *Teaching*

- *Professional Development and Achievement*

- *Service*

While it is not possible or desirable to identify and review all the roles of a faculty member for evaluation purposes, the roles incorporated within this system for Frostburg State University include those identified as being the most important to all faculty and those that could be reviewed efficiently and effectively. For each major role there are institutional minimum and maximum values (weights) that are derived from the faculty workload guidelines established by the University System of Maryland, giving faculty the opportunity to negotiate a weight for each role. These weights reflect the philosophy and mission of Frostburg State University as to the importance of each role within the faculty member's total set of professional responsibilities.

Data gathered for review and evaluation come from students and from the faculty member. Each rating source—department peers, department chair, and students, as appropriate—has a pre-established weight to reflect the impact each source has on the evaluation of each faculty role. Each faculty member will enter into an evaluation agreement for category weights with the department chair by December 1 for the subsequent year. Those faculty who choose to enter the evaluation process every three years need to negotiate weights yearly, and those weights will be applied at each three-year evaluation.

The minimum and maximum weights allowed in the evaluation system are as follows:

Minimum		Maximum
50%	*Teaching*	80%
10%	*Professional Development & Achievement*	30%
5%	*Service*	25%

A. Procedures

The evaluation process is standard across all of the university's academic departments, including the use of the same student rating form in all courses, except Internships. The process results in a score, or Overall Rating, which summarizes the faculty member's performance.

B. Evaluation Cycle

Yearly evaluation will occur for all untenured, tenure-track faculty; all tenured faculty evaluated in the previous year below a 3.0 rating in any category; and all tenured faculty seeking ratings above 3.0.

Tenured faculty have the option to be evaluated once every three years. When evaluated in the third year, the faculty member must provide information for the current year and for each of the previous two years; however, only the current year's Overall Rating will be calculated for the merit pool. In addition, tenured faculty should request a complete evaluation in the two years preceding a request for a sabbatical or a request for a promotion. Departments employing contractual (full-time and part-time) faculty may design particular evaluation procedures depending on the faculty member's responsibilities in the department and the terms of the contract.

C. Negotiated Category Weights

Faculty negotiate with department chairs differences in individual annual category weights, within the allowable ranges, to reflect differences in faculty interests and workload. The negotiations with the department chair for a given evaluation cycle must take place prior to December 1 in the semester before the evaluated year. In the event of substantive changes in the actual workload, a faculty member may renegotiate the distribution of category weights with the department chair. Faculty with non-standard assignments (reassigned times for department chair, departmental projects, research, etc.) will adjust category rates in the following manner: for each course of reassigned time, the weight typically assigned to teaching will be reduced by 1/4, which will then be added to the appropriate category (Service or Professional Development and Achievement). In such cases, sources, source weights, and elements may also change to reflect the altered Faculty Role.

While tenured faculty are not required to submit an evaluation package every year, they are required to set weights for each evaluation cycle. If a faculty member fails to formally negotiate weights with the chair, default weights will be applied at midpoints: 65% Teaching, 20% Professional Development and Achievement; and 15% Service.

D. Element Ratings

Faculty receive Ratings from each Rating Source within each element based on the following five level scale.

5.0 = Outstanding Performances
4.0 = Above Expectations
3.0 = Meets Expectations
2.0 = Below Expectations
1.0 = Unacceptable Performance

Element Ratings are derived by multiplying each source rating of an element by its assigned source weight and adding the weighted source scores totaling the weighted Element Rating.

E. Category Ratings

The Category Rating is derived by multiplying the Element Rating by the element weight to get the Weighted Element Rating and adding all of the Weighted Element Ratings for the Category.

F. Overall Rating

The Overall Rating is the result of multiplying each Category Rating by the category weight chosen by the faculty member for that year and adding the three weighted Category Ratings.

G. Merit Pay Scale.

The Merit Pay scale is a twenty-one step scale in increments of 0.1, from 3.0 to 5.0. Merit Pay begins at the 3.0 level and increases as a faculty member's Overall Rating rises to 5.0. There is no Merit Pay Increase for an Overall Rating below 3.0. Faculty members must score 3.0 or above to be eligible for merit increases;

Responsibilities of the Evaluators

A. Responsibilities of the Department Evaluation Committee

Each Department may establish a Department Evaluation Committee of three to five individuals on which all faculty will eventually serve through rotation if the Department is large enough; otherwise, the faculty may establish a standing committee or invite faculty from other departments to serve on the committee. The Chair may not serve both as a member of the Department Evaluation Committee and as an independent evaluator. In rare circumstances a department may elect to have the chair as sole evaluator in a given cycle. When necessary to do so, the Faculty Concerns committee must approve the chair as sole evaluator each year.

When the chair is evaluated (separate from the department evaluation of chair's duties) the department will appoint an alternative faculty member to perform the chair's function as evaluator.

The specific duties of the Department Evaluation Committee include:

1. Review the faculty member's self-statement and materials submitted for the three elements of the Teaching category, including student free responses, the Professional Development and Achievement category, and the Service category, rating the faculty member on the numerical scale of 1–5 in the elements of each category;

2. Prepare a brief written justification supporting each element rating for the faculty member.

3. Prepare a written assessment of the professional behavior of the faculty member for the year (praiseworthy collegial conduct should be noted as well as problematic professional conduct); and

4. Forward the completed Department Evaluation Committee Faculty Evaluation Report to the Department Chair.

5. Review the faculty member's self-statement and materials submitted for the three elements of the Teaching category, including student free responses, the Professional Development and Achievement category, and the Service category, rating the faculty member on the numerical scale of 1-5 in the elements of each category;

6. Prepare a brief written justification supporting each element rating for the faculty member.

7. Prepare a written assessment of the professional behavior of the faculty member for the year (praiseworthy collegial conduct should be noted as well as problematic professional conduct); and

8. Forward the completed Department Evaluation Committee Faculty Evaluation Report to the Department Chair.

B. Responsibilities of Faculty Concerns Committee

The Faculty Concerns Committee will have the responsibility for the Faculty Evaluation Procedures. It will annually review and recommend to the Faculty Senate needed changes in the Faculty Evaluation Procedures. In addition, Faculty Concerns will review and approve exceptions and amendments to University Evaluation procedures.

C. Responsibilities of Individual Faculty

Faculty are responsible for providing the information and materials needed for the Department Evaluation Committee and the Chair to carry out their respective rating responsibilities. Faculty are also responsible for writing self-statements to address, as appropriate, the following issues:

1. Express concern over difficulties in planning assignments and activities for courses;

2. Briefly describe how readings, conferences attended, etc., enhanced his/her instructional development;

3. Respond to student perceptions of course content and/or faculty performance in those courses, based, in part, on the Common Student Rating form and free responses; and

4. Send letters of rebuttal to the appropriate School Dean and to the Provost if she/he does not agree with the Chair and/or DEC evaluations/recommendation.

D. Responsibilities of Students

Students will rate faculty using the Common Student Rating Form. Departments may add questions to the student rating form for use by the department evaluation committee and the chair within the department. Those questions, however, will not count in the student rating component of the Performance/Feedback Element. Students will be encouraged to provide Free Responses when they complete the Rating Form.

E. Responsibilities of the Department Chair

1. Insure that the administration of the student ratings during the last two weeks of class includes standard instructions to be given to students prior to each rating;

2. Meet with the Department Evaluations Committee before the evaluation period to establish and articulate a common set of criteria to be used for evaluating department members;

3. Review the faculty member's self-statement and materials submitted for the three elements of the Teaching category, the Professional Development and Achievement category, and the Service category and give the faculty member a numerical rating on a scale of 1-5 in the element of each category;

4. Prepare a brief written justification supporting each element rating for each faculty member;

5. Prepare a written assessment of the professional behavior of the faculty member for the year (praiseworthy collegial conduct should be noted as well as problematic professional conduct);

6. Complete the Department Chair Faculty Evaluation Report;

7. Forward the Department Faculty Evaluation Summary, the DEC Faculty Evaluation Report, and the Department Chair Faculty Evaluation Report for each faculty member to the Dean, with a copy to the faculty member;

8. Communicate the results of the departmental evaluation process to each faculty member, preferably in a face-to-face interview and assist the faculty member in development in needed areas; and

9. Maintain permanent departmental files, including student rating results, student comments, the faculty member's self-statement, the Department Evaluation Committee Faculty Evaluation Report, the departmental merit pay recommendation, and the final contract letter for each full-time faculty member of the department.

F. **Responsibilities of the Dean**

1. Share responsibility with the Department Chair for establishing and maintaining appropriate professional standards for faculty evaluation, including the option of establishing school-wide standards in one or more categories when appropriate; 3

2. Be responsible for reviewing the Overall Element Ratings, the Category Rating, the Overall Rating, and the rating justifications for each full-time faculty member;

3. Forward his/her endorsement of the departmental recommendation for merit level on each faculty member to the Provost; or

4. Should the Dean not concur with the departmental recommendation for merit level, or should a faculty member challenge the evaluation of the Departmental Evaluation Committee and/or the Chair, or if the Dean's overall rating is different from the departmental rating, the Dean will forward his/her rating recommendation and the departmental rating recommendation to the Provost.

G. **Responsibilities of the Provost**

1. Receive and review the recommendations from the Department and the Dean;

2. Be responsible for preparing faculty merit pay recommendations, which he/she will forward to the President.

3. Report a summary of faculty merit pay recommendations to the Faculty Concerns Committee for publication to the faculty. The summary should include; the distribution of faculty Overall Ratings by department and school as well as for the entire university; the average Overall Rating for each department, each school, and the university; and the number of recommendations, by

school, that differed from those provided by the Department.

Description of the Faculty Role Model

Each of the three Categories below contains the descriptions of activities (Elements) that constitute expectations of all faculty members. Similarly, each Element contains specific dimensions that describe the expected activities of all faculty members.

Evaluators will judge the faculty member's performance on using the previously defined five-point scale within each of the Elements as described below. An element rating of 3.0 will be appropriate to performance that does not have any substantive areas of weakness and meets the minimal requirements of the Element. To qualify for a 5.0 rating (Outstanding), the faculty member must demonstrate achievement substantially beyond what is expected for Meets Expectations. In all three categories the Department Evaluation Committee may justify as equivalent other faculty achievement activities.

A. **Teaching Category**
   (Minimum = 50%; Maximum = 80%)

1. *Course Materials and Course Syllabus* (Weight = 25%). Course Syllabus should conform to requirements described on page A-8 of the Faculty Handbook. Course materials should be appropriate, current, and supportive of course goals and objectives. These materials may include

   a) examinations, quizzes, assignments allowing students to demonstrate achievement of course objectives,

   b) appropriate texts, audio-visual aids, handouts, and other significant materials or equipment used reflect current technology; and

   c) evidence that the course content is current and appropriate for the classes.

2. *Teaching Performance and Feedback to Students* (Weight = 50%).

   a) Those rated at the 3.0 level (Meets Expectations) should meet the following minimal requirements:

   • Specified course objectives and provided a reasonable opportunity for students' achievement of those objectives.

- Demonstrated evidence of planning and ability to carry through.

- Demonstrated knowledge of and respect for the subject matter.

- Presented course assignments and materials clearly.

- Encouraged students' questions and expressions of ideas.

- Demonstrated respect for the student as an individual.

- Reasonably adhered to the syllabus or to a change in the syllabus that was provided in a timely manner.

- Posted and maintained those office hours which are expected of all faculty members, or if office hours were pre-empted, provided adequate notice.

- Demonstrated evidence of accurate and timely advising to assigned advisees.

b) Faculty should provide timely and sufficient feedback to the student concerning performance in the class. Examples of feedback, which meet minimum expectations, include:

- returning tests and papers in a reasonable amount of time;

- providing students with periodic summaries of performance;

- issuing mid-semester warnings to students performing at the D or F quality level;

- providing evaluation remarks on the content, logic, organization, clarity, and grammatical correctness of all written papers, such as essays, research papers, projects, and case analyses.

c) Faculty rated at the 4.0 or 5.0 levels demonstrate characteristics, attitude, and behavior in those categories substantially beyond what is expected of 3.0 rating in Teaching Performance and Feedback to students. Such a faculty member:

- Is self-critical; for example, asks for and values the opinions of peers regarding teaching methods;

- Recognizes that classes represent a learning experience for both students and faculty;

- Demonstrates enthusiasm toward students, the profession, and the subject matter;

- Sets a high standard for other faculty, for example by setting high standards for students in courses;

- Provides students with a high quality of constructive comments on papers and other written work;

- Is a motivator of students, resulting in students pursuing study beyond normal course expectations;

- Has classes which are rated as challenging by students, in which grades are awarded competitively, but which continue to be sought out by students;

- Mentors students through activities that facilitate individual student's academic and professional development by providing out-of-class time to students above and beyond what is expected (e.g. study sessions, review session, extracurricular field trips, work with student groups, etc.).

d) In addition, those rated at the 4.0 or 5.0 levels are consistently recognized for providing additional time and commentary to students, for example, in conferences, through extensive commentary, or other appropriate and effective means.

3. *Instructional Development* (Weight = 25%). The Departmental Evaluation Committee may add and/or substitute Professional activities that are not applied to Professional Development and Achievement Category and that are appropriate to the advancement of instruction within its discipline. Examples of Instructional Development activities rated as 3.0 (meets expectations) include:

a) Presenting evidence of experimentation in instructional methods that enhance student learning;

b) Presenting evidence that scholarly activities in the discipline have led to integration of new materials into a course or courses taught by the faculty member,

c) Presenting evidences those scholarly activities (e.g. attending workshops, seminars, and the like) in pedagogy have led to the enhancement of teaching methods by the faculty member.

Faculty rated at the 4.0 or 5.0 levels demonstrate achievement in one or more of these categories substantially beyond what is expected for 3.0 (meets expectations). *Note: Internship instruction will be evaluated according to approved departmental guidelines and evaluation mechanisms.*

B. **Professional Development and Achievement Category** (Minimum = 10%, Maximum = 30%)
Below are examples of performance in the areas of professional development and achievement. Some examples of activities that rate 3.0 (meets expectation) are:

1. Proof of active membership in professional organization (e.g. conference attendance, etc.)

2. Serving in capacities, such as adjudicator, review, or session moderator, to a local professional organization.

3. Participating in a publisher's text review.

4. Sharing expertise within the discipline (locally or regionally).

5. Acting as a journal reviewer

6. Reading in field and presenting evidence of ongoing scholarship in preparation for professional presentation (e.g. workshop, conference paper, and the like).

7. Continuing certification in discipline.

8. Contributing to the development of instructional materials for K-16 programs.

9. Managing a web page; acting as a newsgroup facilitator

The Department Evaluation Committee may add and/or substitute professional activities appropriate to the advancement of the discipline or the development of the faculty member. A faculty member may receive a 4.0 rating for accomplishing more than three of the above activities. Examples of individual activities that rate a 4.0 (above expectations):

10. Regional conference leadership role (e.g. paper presentation, discussant, panel organizer, session chair, etc.)

11. Published book review.

12. Poster presentations at major conferences.

Some examples of activities that rate a 5.0:

13. Production of a publication, performance, workshop, or artistic creation that has received some form of favorable peer review and has received at least regional recognition.

14. Organization of a major regional or national conference.

15. Significant participation in a national or international conference (e.g. paper presentation, workshop).

C. **Service Category**
(Minimum = 5%, maximum = 25%)
Minimum service occurs at department and school level, earning the faculty member a rating of 3.0. Standard service includes:

1. Regular attendance at, and participation in department and school meetings;

2. Fulfillment of normal committee assignment

3. Participation in regular departmental and school activities, as deemed appropriate.

Additional service (beyond regular department duties) may earn faculty a 4.0 or 5.0 rating depending on level of contribution to department/school/university/ community. Some examples include:

4. Service on Faculty Senate, ad hoc committees or task forces.

5. Involvement in major governance activities.

6. Steering major curricular initiatives.

Developing a Comprehensive Faculty Evaluation System

7. Making a substantive contribution to the community in a manner that clearly impacts positively on the community, in a role that requires a high level of involvement and time, and in a manner that is clearly related to the faculty member's professional role.

Department Chairs, Program Coordinators and other reassigned time assignments appropriate to service are automatically rated a 4.0 with a possibility of a 5.0 rating with demonstration of outstanding performance in that activity.

Summary of the Process

The faculty member is responsible for maintaining records of his/her performance, achievements, etc. for each evaluation period (currently, the calendar year). At the end of each year in which the faculty member is to be evaluated he/she must develop an Evaluation Packet which presents evidence of his/her performance, achievements, etc., in each of the three categories (teaching, professional development and achievement, and service) as well as professional behavior. The university will provide the faculty member with the numerical results from the Common Student Rating Form for his or her courses. In addition to the numerical score generated by the rating form, the faculty member is encouraged to use information from student free responses in developing his/her Evaluation Packet.

The numerical score for the faculty member on the Common Student Rating Form will be generated by the University and provided to the faculty member and the department chair. The faculty member will submit his/her evaluation packet to both the Department Evaluation Committee (DEC) and his/her department chair.

The DEC will review the faculty member's evaluation packet, complete the Department Evaluation Committee Faculty Evaluation Report, which includes a rating of the faculty member's performance in each category (including each element within the teaching category) and a justification for each rating, and submit the Report to the chair.

The Chair will review the faculty member's evaluation packet and complete the Department Chair Faculty Evaluation Report, which includes a rating of the faculty member's performance in each category (including each element within the teaching category) and a justification for each rating. The chair, based on his/her rating of the faculty member's evaluation packet and the rating awarded by the DEC, will complete the Department Faculty Evaluation Summary.

The chair will forward the Department Faculty Evaluation Summary Form, the DEC Faculty Evaluation Report, and the Department Chair Faculty Evaluation Report for each faculty member to the school dean, with a copy to the faculty member.

The dean will review the ratings made by the department chair and the DEC and forward the departmental rating recommendation to the provost. If the dean does not concur with the departmental recommendation for merit level or the faculty member challenges the DEC's or the chair's rating, the dean will forward his/her own rating recommendation and the departmental rating recommendation to the provost.

The provost will review the recommendations from the dean and the department and forward faculty merit pay recommendations to the president.

FROSTBURG STATE UNIVERSITY
DEPARTMENT FACULTY EVALUATION SUMMARY FORM

Faculty Member_____ Department_____ Evaluation Period_____

Faculty Member Status (check one)
___ untenured/tenure track faculty
___ tenured faculty, required three-year evaluation
___ tenured faculty, preceding evaluation was below expectations
___ tenured faculty, requesting merit evaluation for year
___ full-time contractual

	Rating	Dept. Avg.
A. Teaching (Negotiated Weight = _____%)		
1. Course Materials and Course Syllabus		
DEC ___ (.70) + Chair ___ (.30) = ____(.25) =	_____	_____
2. Teaching Perform and Feedback to Students		
DEC ___ (.15) + Chair ___ (.20) + Students (.65) = ____(.50) =	_____	_____
3. Instructional Development		
DEC ___ (.30) + Chair ___ (.70) = ____(.25) =	_____	_____
Teaching Category Rating	_____	_____
B. Prof. Development and Achievement (Negotiated Weight = ____%)		
DEC ___ (.75) + Chair ___ (.25) = ____(1.0) =	_____	_____
Development and Achievement Category Rating	_____	_____
C. Service (Negotiated Weight = _____%)		
DEC ___ (.25) + Chair ___ (.75) = ____(1.0) =	_____	_____
Service Category Rating	_____	_____

	Rating	×	Weight		Rating	Dept. Avg.
Teaching Category	_____	×	_____	=	_____	_____
Prof. Achievement Category	_____	×	_____	=	_____	_____
Service Category	_____	×	_____	=	_____	_____
Overall Rating					_____	_____

Rating Source and Faculty Signatures

Dept. Chair _____ Date_____ DEC Chair _____ Date_____

I have read and discussed with my department chair my faculty evaluation for the evaluation year.

Signature _____ Date_____

Developing a Comprehensive Faculty Evaluation System

Georgia Perimeter College Faculty Evaluation Procedure

The following is not a case study but, rather, a presentation of the final faculty evaluation procedure developed by Georgia Perimeter College following the process described in this book. This section has been excerpted, with permission, from the *Georgia Perimeter College Faculty Evaluation, Promotion, and Tenure Handbook* (1998–99). The development of the Georgia Perimeter College system was accomplished by the Process Renewal Team on Faculty Evaluation chaired by professors Margo L. Eden-Camann and Virginia Parks. The manual refers to the Board of Regents' Policy on Faculty Evaluation which is found as an addendum at the end of this chapter.

Georgia Perimeter College's Policy on Faculty Evaluation

In keeping with Board of Regents' Policy, Georgia Perimeter College has adopted the Annual Performance Review of Faculty described herein. The primary purpose of faculty evaluation at Georgia Perimeter College is to promote individual and institutional self-improvement. To ensure that faculty are aware of the expectations of their supervisor and are informed of their progress as members of Georgia Perimeter College faculty, evaluations are completed on an annual basis. This evaluation, which serves as an evaluation of progress and a discussion of expectations for the future, focuses on the objectives and goals of the individual and of the college. Because the results of this evaluation will be the sole determiner of the annual merit pay award made to each faculty member as well as the bases for promotion, tenure, pre-tenure, and post-tenure decisions made by the institution, the college recognizes the need for a consistent system for evaluating its faculty. *(Any academic year in which a leave is taken cannot count as a year's service for purposes of promotion and/or tenure. Merit pay will not be awarded for time on leave.)* However, the college also recognizes the diversity among its faculty and has, therefore, adopted a system of evaluation that values that diversity, asserts that progress may occur in many directions, and recognizes that many types of activities make valuable contributions to the college's success and growth.

All faculty members with teaching responsibilities will be evaluated annually on three components of their performance: teaching effectiveness, service, and professional activities. Faculty members at different points in their academic careers often find that they want or need to direct more effort to one component or another of their responsibilities. The Annual Performance Review allows each faculty member to determine the emphasis that he or she will place on each component of the evaluation and to select, within prescribed ranges, the weight of each component in the overall evaluation.

Because of the great diversity in possible approaches to the act of teaching, the Annual Performance Review, while maintaining a consistent process of evaluation, allows some flexibility to the faculty member. The process supports a multi-source faculty evaluation system which includes self-evaluation, peer evaluation, student evaluation, and department chair evaluation. The system allows the faculty member to determine, within established ranges, the weights of these evaluations in determining the faculty member's teaching effectiveness rating.

This need for flexibility is also reflected in the Evaluation of Service and the Evaluation of Professional Activities. Faculty members may select from a wide range of activities in which to participate each year.

The department chair is responsible for assembling the various parts of the evaluation system and calculating the Faculty Member's Performance Review Summary. The evaluation should be submitted to the dean of academic services and then to the provost on the appropriate campus.

Faculty Evaluation Committee

Purpose. The Faculty Evaluation Committee reviews and revises the evaluation system and promotion and tenure system and recommends improvements, in both content and procedure. The committee's recommendations are submitted by the vice president for academic affairs to the Academic Affairs Policy Council, which advises and makes recommendations for changes to the College Advisory Board, which advises and makes recommendations to the president. The president may accept or reject the recommendations and must approve all changes.

Memberships. Membership consists of faculty from each campus and is representative of the various disciplines. The members are appointed to three-year terms on a rotating basis by the vice president for academic affairs. At least one-third of the membership changes each year.

Meetings. Meetings may be held at any time during the year as need arises as determined by the chairperson.

Chairperson. The chairperson is appointed by the vice president for academic affairs.

A. Faculty Portfolio for Annual Evaluation

The Faculty Portfolio for Annual Evaluation requires each faculty member to provide documentation for the Annual Performance Review in the areas of Teaching Effectiveness, Service, and Professional Activities. It also allows the faculty member to select the weights of the three components of the overall evaluation as well as the weights of the sources in the Evaluation of Teaching Effectiveness. In addition, the guidelines define and limit the types and quantities of information that should be submitted by the faculty member. (The Faculty Portfolio should include the items listed below. Detailed instructions and forms for submission of these items appear on pages 174–199.)

Declaration of Weights. In the spring term of each academic year, each faculty member must submit to his/her department chair the Declaration of Weights Part I: Overall Evaluation (page 176). In conference with the department chair, each faculty member will choose the percentage that he/she wants each area to weigh in the overall evaluation, thereby determining how the evaluation in each area will affect his/her merit pay award for the evaluation period (each selected percentage must be a multiple of ten, and no area may have a weight of zero percent). The Declaration of Weights form will be provided by the department chair. The faculty member should return both copies to the department chair by the announced deadline. The department chair will sign the form, keep the original, and return the copy to the faculty member.

As part of the Faculty Portfolio submitted in the fall term each year, each faculty member must include the Declaration of Weights Part II: Evaluation of Teaching Effectiveness (page 177). Each faculty member will choose the percentage that he/she wants each source to weigh in the evaluation of teaching effectiveness (each selected percentage must be a multiple of ten, and no area may have a weight of zero percent). The faculty member should include the original form in the Faculty Portfolio and keep a copy for his/her records.

Faculty Members Report on Teaching Effectiveness: A Focused Narrative. The Focused Narrative should present evidence of successful practices the faculty member has used *during this evaluation period,* which characterize his/her teaching effectiveness. This narrative should include a discussion of the faculty member's knowledge, course organ-

ization and planning, communication and delivery, and policy/procedure practices. The guidelines for this report appear on page 175.

Only if it is essential that the evaluator see the materials described, faculty members may choose to attach an Addendum to the Focused Narrative including labeled materials to which they have made direct reference in the narrative. The purpose of the addendum is to provide documentation for the narrative. It is separate from the Course Materials Review and will not be reviewed by the Peer Review Panel.

Faculty Members Course Materials. The Course Materials Packet should include materials used by the faculty member during the evaluation period. These materials may have been created by the faculty member, selected from other sources, or created in collaboration with others, but materials not developed by an instructor should acknowledge the original source or the collaborator. The guidelines for submission of the packet and the criteria for its evaluation appear on pages 180–181. While these instructions require all faculty members to submit course syllabi (which adhere to the guidelines in the Faculty Syllabus Checklist page 184) and assessment tools, they also allow instructors to choose to submit materials that best reflect their teaching ability from the following areas: innovative instruction, writing activities, revision of course materials, grading/feedback to students, instructional support materials, and instructional technology. These materials will be reviewed by both the department chair and the Peer Review Panel, a panel of peers elected from the faculty member's department.

Service Report. In the Service Report, faculty will list their activities completed during the evaluation period in the following areas: service to the campus, discipline, and department and service to the college and community. The guidelines for this report appear on page 182. Faculty members should list their activities under the appropriate item in each category. If a service activity does not fit one of the items listed, it may be listed under Other Activities. The department chair will award points for each activity using the Evaluation of Service form on page 192. The Service Rating will be determined using the point scale at the end of that document.

Professional Activities Report. In the Professional Activities Report, faculty will list their activities completed during the evaluation period in the following areas: professional organizations; further education and degrees; scholarly and/or creative activities; awards, grants, artistic commissions, and/or fellowships. The guidelines for this report appear on page 183. Faculty members should list their activities under the appropriate item in each category. If a professional activity does not fit one of the items listed, it may be listed under Other Activities. The department chair will award points for each activity using the Evaluation of Professional Activities form on pages 194–196. The Professional Activities Rating will be determined using the point scale at the end of that document.

Goals. Each faculty member should submit a Review of Goals from the Previous Year using the form on page 177 and establish Goals for the Coming Year using the form on page 177. All faculty must indicate a plan in the area of Teaching Effectiveness and in at least one of the other areas.

Self-Evaluation. In keeping with the Board of Regents policy that requires that evaluation provide an opportunity to assess strengths and weaknesses of faculty performance, the self-evaluation offers the opportunity for personal assessment of one's own teaching effectiveness. Based on the information provided in the Focused Narrative, each faculty member must use the form on pages 178–179 to rate his or her own performance in the area of teaching and provide justification when required.

B. Peer Review of Course Materials

The Board of Regents requires that a faculty member's teaching performance be evaluated by his or her peers. Each faculty member has submitted, as part of the Faculty Portfolio for Annual Evaluation, a packet of course materials used during the evaluation period. The instructions for the submission of this packet appear on page180. These materials will be reviewed and evaluated by a panel of faculty peers elected according to the following procedures:

Course Materials Review Panel. The Course Materials Review Panels will be composed of three department members, elected annually, who

have, at the time of the election, at least one complete year of teaching experience at Georgia Perimeter College. No faculty member serving on a Promotion and Tenure Panel will be eligible for membership The election of the faculty to these panels will be carried out by the appropriate department chair mid-spring term, by secret ballot, from a list of *all* faculty members in the department with at least one year of teaching experience at Georgia Perimeter College. Each faculty member will vote for three candidates. The department chair will vote, but his or her name will not appear on the ballot. The three faculty members with the highest vote totals within the department will be elected. Each department will create at least one panel. Departments with more than twenty faculty members may create two panels using the same process.

Following discussion of each packet, each panel member will complete an individual review of the course materials of every department member. Course materials review for a faculty member serving on a panel will be done by the other two panel members. Each panel member will forward the completed Peer Review of Course Materials forms to the department chair. The department chair will tabulate the rating from each panel member for every department member. The department chair will then calculate the appropriate mean rating for each faculty member's course materials and report it on the Peer Course Materials Evaluation Summary. The mean will be used for annual evaluation

The course materials review for a department chair will be completed by the panel in his/her department. The dean of academic services will calculate the appropriate mean rating for each department chair's course materials and report it on the Peer Course Materials Evaluation Summary.

• Chairperson

1) The chairperson will be elected from the faculty membership of the panel

2) Duties of the chairperson

   a) To ensure that all reviews are conducted within the time frame outlined in the Implementation Timetables

b) To ensure the integrity and confidentiality of the process

c) To ensure the security of the Course Materials Review files at all times

d) To submit the documents to the department chair

e) To serve as the representative of the panel if a faculty member requests further information about the ratings

Course Materials Packet. The following is a list of items to be included in the Course Materials Packet. These materials will be reviewed by the department chair and the Peer Review Panel. Categories one and two **must** be included in your packet.

1) Syllabus for at least one (1) and not more than three (3) courses. (Refer to the Faculty Syllabus Checklist for a description of required and suggested components for all Georgia Perimeter College syllabi.)

2) At least one (1) and not more than three (3) samples of materials demonstrating how you assess student achievement on expected learning outcomes identified in the common course outline. (These materials may include tests but are not limited to tests.)

Choose exactly **three** categories from the list below, and submit no more than three items for each selected category:

3) Sample of materials demonstrating innovative instruction

4) Sample of materials demonstrating the use of writing in a course

5) Sample of materials demonstrating a revision of course materials

6) Sample of materials demonstrating grading techniques and comments to students

7) Sample of instructional support material designed to help students master concepts and content (i.e., study guides, original problem solving sets, concept maps, annotated bibliographies, etc.)

8) Sample of materials demonstrating efforts to incorporate technology into course content

C. Faculty Rating by Students

Beginning in Fall 1997, the Student Instructional Report II (SIR II), published by Educational Testing Service, will be used to elicit student input concerning each faculty member's teaching performance. The report requires students to rate instructors on items organized into ten areas. Six of these areas—Course Organization and Planning; Communication; Faculty/Student Interaction; Assignments, Exams, and Grading; Course Outcomes; and Overall Evaluation—will provide mean ratings used to calculate the Composite Student Rating, a part of the overall evaluation. The other areas—Supplementary Instructional Methods; Student Effort and Involvement, Course Difficulty, Workload and Pace, and Student Information—will provide information to instructors which may help them to improve their teaching effectiveness. The SIR II will be administered annually in the fall term. In some unique circumstances, a spring administration may be necessary. Both the faculty member and the department chair will receive a copy of the results of this evaluation.

D. Department Chairs Evaluation of Faculty Performance

Each year, the department chair will evaluate each faculty member in his/her department in three areas of performance: teaching effectiveness, service, and professional activities. Using the information provided in the Faculty Portfolio for Annual Evaluation, the Peer Evaluation of Course Materials Summary, the Faculty Rating by Students, and other pertinent information, the department chair will evaluate the faculty members teaching effectiveness. Using the information provided in the Service Report and the Professional Activities Report, the department chair will assign points as indicated in the Evaluation of Service and Evaluation of Professional Activities instruments.

E. Faculty Member Performance Review Summary

To complete the Faculty Member Performance Review Summary (pp. 198–199), the department chair will calculate the Overall Teaching Effectiveness Rating of each faculty member using the Declaration of

Weights and the ratings of teaching effectiveness from the Self-Evaluation, Student Rating Summary, Peer Review of Course Materials, and Department Chair's Evaluation of Faculty Performance. After including the Service Rating of Faculty Member and the Professional Activities Rating of Faculty Member, the department chair will calculate the Overall Faculty Evaluation Rating. The department chair will hold a conference with each faculty member to discuss the evaluation. The faculty member will be asked to sign the summary.

F. Evaluation of First-Year Faculty

Because the Faculty Portfolio is submitted in the fall term, reporting activities completed during the previous academic year, faculty joining the institution that fall will not have worked during that evaluation period and, therefore, will have no report. However, the department chair must evaluate the performance of new faculty to support a recommendation for contract renewal. New faculty will be required to turn in a portfolio of activities completed during fall term. The First Term Progress Report will provide evaluative information for the department chair. Additionally, new faculty should submit, at the beginning of the fall term, a set of goals that should guide their professional growth during the first year of employment. These goals should be submitted on the Goals for the Coming Year form from the Faculty Portfolio.

G. Rebuttal of Annual Performance Review of Faculty

The only component of the Annual Performance Review that may be rebutted is the Department Chair's Evaluation of Faculty Performance, including the evaluation of teaching effectiveness, service, and professional activities.

Faculty evaluations by department chairs must be signed and dated by the faculty member and the department chair at the time of evaluation. The faculty member's signature indicates review of the evaluation only (failure to sign the evaluation by the faculty member could become grounds for disciplinary action). A faculty member who wishes to rebut an evaluation by a department chair should follow the procedure outlined below:

1. The faculty member should review and discuss the evaluation with the department chair before the evaluation is placed in the personnel file.

2. If the faculty member disagrees with the evaluation, the faculty member may write a memorandum of rebuttal or explanation of any parts of the evaluation with which there is disagreement. Within *five working days* of the evaluation conference, he/she should send the memorandum to the department chair with copies to the dean of academic services and the campus provost.

3. Upon receipt of a memorandum of rebuttal from a faculty member, the department chair will acknowledge receipt in writing.

4. Any changes in the annual evaluation made as a result of either the conference or the faculty member's written rebuttal must be noted in writing by the department chair. This written acknowledgment of change will be appended to the original evaluation and all copies become a part of the evaluation record along with the memorandum of rebuttal.

5. If the faculty member is dissatisfied with the outcome of the rebuttal, then the faculty member may discuss the evaluation, the memorandum of rebuttal, and any changes which have been noted with the dean of academic services.

6. The evaluation, the memorandum of rebuttal, the department chair's response, and a summary of the conference with the dean of academic services, if any, and any changes to the evaluation which have been noted will become a part of the faculty members permanent file.

7. In addition to signing and dating the evaluation form, the faculty member is required to sign and date any attachments and return the signed evaluation and any attachments to the department chair.

8. The department chair will provide the faculty member with a copy of the evaluation including any changes which have been noted. The department chair will keep a copy of the evaluation and submit the original files through the dean of academic services to the campus provost.

9. The campus provost will submit all completed annual evaluations of faculty to the human resources department, where they will become a part of the faculty member's permanent file.

Faculty Portfolio For Evaluation

Evaluation Period: July 1, _____ – June 30, _____

_____   _____
Faculty Member   Department Chair

_____
Department Campus

Table of Contents

To the best of my knowledge, the information included in my Faculty Portfolio is accurate.
(See Board of Regents' Policy 803.9P6 on page 80.)

_____   _____
Faculty Member's Signature   Date

FACULTY MEMBER'S REPORT ON TEACHING EFFECTIVENESS:

A Focused Narrative

In no more than two typewritten pages, present evidence of successful practices you have used <u>in this evaluation period</u> which characterize your teaching effectiveness in the areas below. Under each area are criteria to consider. These are not necessarily equal components of teaching effectiveness.

1. Knowledge

Faculty member demonstrates knowledge of discipline

Faculty member demonstrates competence with course content that is relevant and thorough

Faculty member increases knowledge of discipline and/or pedagogy

2. Course organization and planning

Faculty member prepares assignments, handouts, exams, and/or activities to promote student interest and enhance learning

Faculty member demonstrates evidence of attention to active learning, writing, and critical thinking skills as appropriate

Faculty member implements course objectives appropriately

3. Communication and delivery

Faculty member uses class time effectively

Faculty member uses effective instructional techniques and tools (including lecture, discussion, audio/visuals, group activities, or technology)

Faculty member demonstrates efforts to stimulate student interest and achievement

4. Policy/procedure practices

Faculty member adheres to established college, discipline, and department policies and procedures

Faculty member performs assigned duties for the conduct of business of the department

Faculty member is available to students outside class

Addendum to the Faculty Member's Report

Attach and label materials to which you make direct reference in your report on teaching effectiveness

DECLARATION OF WEIGHTS TO BE USED IN FACULTY EVALUATION

Evaluation Period: July 1, _____ – June 30, _____

Part I - Overall Evaluation

Instructions: Complete Part I during April 1–May 1 of the academic year prior to the evaluation period. The faculty member should return both copies to the department chair by the announced deadline. The department chair will sign the form, keep the original, and return the copy to the faculty member. The department chair should include this document in the annual evaluation of the faculty member All selected percentages should be within the indicated ranges, in multiples of 10 (i.e., 10%, 20%, 30%, etc.), and must total 100%.

TEACHING EFFECTIVENESS   _____ %
(Choose from 50% – 70%)

SERVICE   _____ %
(Choose from 10% – 30%)

PROFESSIONAL ACTIVITIES   _____ %
(Choose from 10% – 30%)

SIGNATURES:

_____   _____
Faculty Member   Date

_____   _____
Department Chair   Date

Developing a Comprehensive Faculty Evaluation System

Part II - Evaluation of Teaching Effectiveness

Instructions: Complete Part II and submit with the Faculty Portfolio. All selected percentages should be within the indicated ranges, in multiples of 10 (i.e., 10%, 20%, 30%, etc.), and must total 100%.

SELF	(Choose from 10% – 20%)	_____%
PEER	(Choose from 10% – 20%)	_____%
STUDENTS	(Choose from 10% – 20%)	_____%
DEPARTMENT CHAIR	(Choose from 40% – 60%)	_____%
	TOTAL	_____%
		100%

Review of Goals From The Previous Year

Report on your efforts to meet the goals you submitted last year. Please check those areas for which you are supplying a review, and attach a copy of your goals from last year.

___X___ TEACHING EFFECTIVENESS

_____ SERVICE

_____ PROFESSIONAL ACTIVITIES

Goals For The Coming Year

Describe your goals for the coming year. In each area describe the goal you plan to attain, the activities that you will undertake to achieve that goal, the methods you will use to evaluate your efforts, and the resources that you require to achieve the goal. Check the areas for which you are providing a plan. All faculty must indicate a plan in the area of TEACHING EFFECTIVENESS and in at least one of the other areas. Your declaration of weights for faculty evaluation may reflect the goals for the evaluation period.

___X___ TEACHING EFFECTIVENESS

_____ SERVICE

_____ PROFESSIONAL ACTIVITIES

Faculty Member's Self-Evaluation
of Teaching Effectiveness

Rating Scale:

EP — **Exemplary Professional Performance**
Consistently exceeds accepted standards of professional performance
(JUSTIFICATION MUST BE INCLUDED)

HP — **High Professional Performance**
Frequently exceeds accepted standards of professional performance

SP — **Standard Professional Performance**
Consistently meets accepted standards of professional performance

MP — **Minimal Performance**
Does not consistently meet accepted standards of professional performance
(JUSTIFICATION MUST BE INCLUDED)

UP — **Unsatisfactory Performance**
Does not meet minimal standards of professional performance
(JUSTIFICATION MUST BE INCLUDED)

Justification from the Faculty Member's Report on Teaching Effectiveness (for ratings of **EP**, **MP**, or **UP**) must be included on the following page.

1. **Knowledge**   RATING:_____

2. **Course organization and planning**   RATING:_____

3. **Communication and delivery**   RATING:_____

4. **Policy/procedure practices**   RATING:_____

To compute your Teaching Effectiveness Self-Rating, assign the following values:

$$EP = 5 \quad HP = 4 \quad SP = 3 \quad MP = 2 \quad UP = 1$$

Directions: Add the four values assigned to the ratings, and divide by four to calculate the Teaching Effectiveness Rating by the faculty member. Do not round.

TEACHING EFFECTIVENESS SELF-RATING: _____

Faculty Member's Self-Evaluation of Teaching Effectiveness

(continued)

Justification of ratings of EP, MP, **or** UP from the previous page should follow. Ratings of HP or SP require no response.

1. Knowledge:

2. Course Organization and Planning:

3. Communication and Delivery:

4. Policy/Procedure Practices:

COURSE MATERIALS DESCRIPTION

The following is a list of categories of course materials that may be included in your packet. Keep in mind that these materials will be reviewed by your department chair and Peer Review Panel. To facilitate their review, clearly identify each component of your materials packet. The faculty evaluation system recognizes that instructors select course materials from a variety of sources; however, materials not developed by an instructor should acknowledge the original source.

Categories one and two **must** be included in your packet:

1. Syllabus for at least one (1) and not more than three (3) courses (Refer to the Faculty Syllabus Checklist for a description of required and suggested components for all Georgia Perimeter College syllabi.)

2. At least one (1) and not more than three (3) samples of materials demonstrating how you assess student achievement on expected learning outcomes identified in the common course outlines (These materials may include tests but are not limited to tests.)

Choose exactly **three** categories from the list below, and submit no more than three items for each selected category:

3. Sample of materials demonstrating innovative instruction

4. Sample of materials demonstrating the use of writing in a course

5. Sample demonstrating a revision of course materials

6. Sample of materials demonstrating grading techniques and comments to students

7. Sample of instructional support materials from one course designed to help students master concepts and content (i.e., study guides, original problem-solving sets, concept maps, annotated bibliographies, etc.)

8. Sample of materials demonstrating efforts to incorporate technology into course content

COURSE MATERIALS EVALUATION CRITERIA

1. **Syllabus**

   Syllabus follows guidelines identified in the Georgia Perimeter College Faculty Syllabus Checklist.

   Syllabus clearly explains instructor's expectations (i.e., grading attendance, assignments, deadlines, projects).

   Syllabus identifies learning resources for the course and their locations.

   Syllabus is free of grammatical errors and communicates in simple, clear, positive language.

2. **Assessment of Achievement of Expected Learning Outcomes**

   Assignments, projects, and exams are related to the outcome(s) identified for the course.

3. **Innovative Instruction**

   Instructional activity is clearly related to the outcome(s) identified for the course.

   Instructional activity is appropriate for the target student population.

   Instructional activity promotes mastery of concept(s) or content of the course.

   Instructional activity involves students' participation.

4. **Writing Activity**

   Writing activity is clearly related to the outcome(s) identified for the course.

   Writing activity is appropriate for the target population.

   Writing activity promotes mastery of concept(s) or content of the course.

5. **Revision of Course Materials**

   Revision of course materials is clearly related to course outcome(s).

   Revision of course materials is appropriate to target student population.

   Revision of course materials promotes mastery of concept(s) and content of course.

6. **Grading/Feedback to Students**

   Grading policy agrees with Georgia Perimeter College policy.

   Grading techniques are fair and appropriate for course.

   Written feedback to students offers constructive criticism and suggestions for improvement.

7. **Instructional Support Materials**

   Instructional support materials are clearly related to the outcome(s) identified for the course.

   Instructional support materials are appropriate for the target student population.

   Instructional support materials promote mastery of concept(s) or content of the course.

   Instructional support materials are free of grammatical errors and are written in simple, clear, positive language.

8. **Instructional Technology**

   Instructional technology use is clearly related to the outcome(s) identified for the course.

   Instructional technology use is appropriate for the target student population.

   Instructional technology use promotes mastery of concept(s) or content of the course.

SERVICE REPORT

Instructions: Under the appropriate items below, list all service activities completed during the period under evaluation.

A. **Service to the Campus, Discipline, and Department**

- Membership on campus, discipline, or department committee

- Chair of campus, discipline, or department committee

- Leader of campus, discipline, or department workshop or presentation

- Mentor of new faculty member

- Mentor of part-time faculty

B. **Service to College and Community**

- Membership on college-wide councils or committees

- Chair of college-wide council or committee

- Leader of college-wide or community workshops, courses, or presentations

- Organizer of lecture series

- Advisor to student organization recognized by SGA

- Advisor/editor of college publication

- Application of your recognized area of expertise in the community without pay

- Participation in college-sponsored outreach activities

C. **Other activities:**

List those activities, other than the ones noted above, which directly contributed to either the academic or administrative functioning of the college.

Professional Activities Report

Instructions: Under the appropriate items below, list all professional activities completed during the period under evaluation.

A. Professional Organizations
- Held current membership in professional organization
- Served on a committee of a professional organization
- Held an elective or appointed office or chaired a committee of a state or local professional organization
- Held an elective or appointed office or chaired a committee of a regional or national professional organization

B. Further Education and Degrees
- Received credit for a graduate course (other than dissertation or thesis hours)
- Participated in scholarly, pedagogical, or technological workshops or presentations at Georgia Perimeter College (excluding those that were required)
- Participated in workshops, summer institutes, short courses, audited a graduate level course, etc. (excluding Georgia Perimeter College Activities)
- Completed a graduate degree from an accredited institution

C. Scholarly and/or Creative Activities
- Attended a professional conference
- Gave a presentation at a professional conference (indicate national/regional or state/local conference)
- Served on a discussion roundtable/panel
- Published an article, short story, or poem in a scholarly publication
- Published a book
- Published a new edition of a book
- Published a book review in an appropriate scholarly publication
- Served as an editor of a scholarly publication
- Served as a referee for a scholarly publication
- Reviewed a manuscript for publication
- Published a comment, note, or letter to the editor in a scholarly publication
- Published an article, short story, or poem in a non-scholarly publication

D. Awards, Grants, Artistic Commissions, and/or Fellowships
- Received an award, grant, artistic commission, or fellowship (excluding tuition grants for graduate study)
- Served on a grant review panel

E. Other activities:
- List those activities, other than the ones noted above, which directly contributed to either the academic or administrative functioning of the college.

F. Fine Arts and Humanities Faculty only
- Performed in a musical, dramatic, or media production
- Created a musical, dramatic, or media work which was performed, published, exhibited, and/or broadcast
- Directed or produced a musical, dramatic, or media event/performance/broadcast recording/exhibition
- Designed and/or implemented the technical work (scene, costume, lighting, sound, etc.) for a musical, dramatic, or media production

FACULTY SYLLABUS CHECKLIST

This checklist includes required and suggested components of syllabi at Georgia Perimeter College as indicated in the *Georgia Perimeter College Policy Manual*. It may be used by faculty at the college as a convenience in composing syllabi.

REQUIRED COMPONENTS:

Information about the Instructor

_____Name   _____Office number   _____Office hours

_____Times when students may contact you   _____Office phone number

Course Information

_____ Heading (college name)   _____ Course ID (e.g., PADL 101 400)

_____ Course title and location   _____ Required textsñtitles, authors, editions

_____ Course description   _____ Course objectives reflecting Expected Educational Results

_____ Attendance Policy

Schedule Information

_____ Dates of major assignments, papers, field trips, projects, etc.

_____ Dates of midterm and/or other important tests

_____ Disclaimer stating dates may change

_____ Date and time of final exam

Grading Information

_____ Course requirements: exams, quizzes, classroom participation, projects, and papers including the percentage each counts toward the final grade

_____ Policies on missed exams and late work

_____ Grading scale and standards

Other Statements*

_____ *Americans with Disabilities Act*   _____ *Academic Honesty*

_____ *Equal Opportunity*   _____ *Affirmative Action*

* This information may be included in departmental handouts distributed with the syllabus.

SUGGESTED COMPONENTS:

_____ Recommended supplemental course materials

_____ Schedule of class meetings, including subject matter and topics to be covered as well as pre-class readings and other assignments

_____ Unique class procedure/structures, such as cooperative learning, peer review, panel presentations, portfolios, case studies, journals or learning logs, and others

_____ Special components: science and computer labs, tutorials, computer classroom, Instructional Support Services Lab, and others

Developing a Comprehensive Faculty Evaluation System

Peer Evaluation of Course Materials

_____ **Evaluation Period: July 1, _____ – June 30, _____**
Faculty Member

For the purposes of peer evaluation of course materials, professional performance is defined as the faculty member's ability to select, create, and use course materials.

Rating Scale:

EP — **Exemplary Professional Performance**
Consistently exceeds accepted standards of professional performance
(JUSTIFICATION MUST BE INCLUDED)

HP — **High Professional Performance**
Frequently exceeds accepted standards of professional performance

SP — **Standard Professional Performance**
Consistently meets accepted standards of professional performance

MP — **Minimal Performance**
Does not consistently meet accepted standards of professional performance
(JUSTIFICATION MUST BE INCLUDED)

UP — **Unsatisfactory Performance**
Does not meet minimal standards of professional performance
(JUSTIFICATION MUST BE INCLUDED)

Directions: Using the criteria identified for each category as a guideline, assign a rating to each applicable category using the rating scale above.

I. **Faculty member was required to include items from categories one and two below. Rate both categories.**

   1. Syllabus   RATING:_____

   2. Assessment of Achievement of Learning Outcomes   RATING:_____

II. **Faculty member selected three of the following categories. For those categories not chosen, write "NS" (*not selected*) in the rating blank. Rate the other categories.**

   3. Innovative Instruction   RATING:_____

   4. Writing Activity   RATING:_____

   5. Revision of Course Materials   RATING:_____

   6. Grading/Feedback   RATING:_____

   7. Instructional Support Materials   RATING:_____

   8. Instructional Technology   RATING:_____

To compute your Teaching Effectiveness Self-Rating, assign the following values:

$$EP = 5 \quad HP = 4 \quad SP = 3 \quad MP = 2 \quad UP = 1$$

Directions: Add the five values assigned to the ratings, and divide by five to calculate the Course Materials Rating by the faculty member. Do not round.

Course Materials Rating: _____

_____   _____
Peer Reviewer Signature   **Date**

PEER EVALUATION OF COURSE MATERIALS SUMMARY

Record the course materials rating from each of the Peer Evaluation of Course Materials for the indicated faculty member.

Faculty Member:_____   Date: _____

   1. Peer Reviewer #1   Rating: _____

   2. Peer Reviewer #2   Rating: _____

   3. Peer Reviewer #3   Rating: _____

For faculty members who are not members of the Course Materials Review Panel, compute the Peer Rating of Course Materials as follows: add the ratings and divide by three. Round to two decimals.

Faculty members who are members of the Course Materials Review Panel will not rate their own materials. To compute the Peer Rating of Course Materials for members of the Course Materials Peer Review Panel, add the ratings and divide by two. Round to two decimals.

Peer Rating of Course Materials:_____

GEORGIA PERIMETER COLLEGE

Annual Performance Review Of Faculty Member

Evaluation Period: July 1, _____ – June 30, _____

_____   _____
Faculty Member   Department Chair

_____   _____
Department   Campus

Table of Contents

I. **Evaluation/Rating Forms**

    A. Student Rating Summary

    B. Faculty Members Self-Evaluation of Teaching Effectiveness (from the Faculty Portfolio for Evaluation)

    C. Peer Evaluation of Course Materials Summary

    D. Department Chair Evaluation/Rating

        1. Evaluation of Teaching Effectiveness of Faculty Member by Department Chair

        2. Evaluation of Service

        3. Evaluation of Professional Activities

II. **Performance Review Summary and Support Documents**

    A. Summary of Weights to Be Used in Faculty Evaluation

    B. Faculty Member Performance Review Summary

Faculty Member's Acknowledgment: I have reviewed the attached evaluations with my department chair. If I wish to submit a written response, I will do so within five working days of the evaluation conference. The response must be signed, dated, attached to the original evaluation form, and submitted to the campus academic dean.

SIGNATURES:

_____   _____
Faculty Member's Signature   Date

_____   _____
Department Chair   Date

_____   _____
Campus Academic Dean   Date

STUDENT RATING SUMMARY

1. Identify each class by name and section number, e.g., ECON2OI-140.

   Class 1 _____   Class 2 _____

   Class 3 _____   Class 4 _____

   Class 5 _____   Class 6 _____

   Class 7 _____   Class 8 _____

2. For areas A, B, C, D, F, and I, record the mean from the STUDENT INSTRUCTOR RATING II (SIR II) report for each class. Calculate a mean for each area by adding the means for each class in that area and dividing by the number of classes reported. Round to two decimals.

   A. Course Organization and Planning

   Class 1 _____   Class 2 _____   Class 3 _____   Class 4 _____

   Class 5 _____   Class 6 _____   Class 7 _____   Class 8 _____   **Area Mean** _____

   B. Communication

   Class 1 _____   Class 2 _____   Class 3 _____   Class 4 _____

   Class 5 _____   Class 6 _____   Class 7 _____   Class 8 _____   **Area Mean** _____

   C. Faculty/Student Interaction

   Class 1 _____   Class 2 _____   Class 3 _____   Class 4 _____

   Class 5 _____   Class 6 _____   Class 7 _____   Class 8 _____   **Area Mean** _____

   D. Assignments, Exams, and Grading

   Class 1 _____   Class 2 _____   Class 3 _____   Class 4 _____

   Class 5 _____   Class 6 _____   Class 7 _____   Class 8 _____   **Area Mean** _____

   F. Course Outcomes

   Class 1 _____   Class 2 _____   Class 3 _____   Class 4 _____

   Class 5 _____   Class 6 _____   Class 7 _____   Class 8 _____   **Area Mean** _____

   I. Overall Evaluation

   Class 1 _____   Class 2 _____   Class 3 _____   Class 4 _____

   Class 5 _____   Class 6 _____   Class 7 _____   Class 8 _____   **Area Mean** _____

3. To calculate the Composite Student Rating, add the area means for A, B, C, D, F, and I; and divide by six. Round to two decimals.

COMPOSITE STUDENT RATING _____

Evaluation of Teaching Effectiveness
of Faculty Member
by Department Chair

Under each area are criteria to consider. These are not necessarily equal components of teaching effectiveness.

1. **Knowledge**

   Faculty member demonstrates knowledge of discipline.

   Faculty member demonstrates competence with course content that is relevant and thorough.

2. **Course organization and planning**

   Faculty member prepares assignments, handouts, exams, and/or activities to promote student interest and enhance learning.

   Faculty member demonstrates evidence of attention to active learning, writing, and critical thinking skills as appropriate.

   Faculty member implements course objectives appropriately.

3. **Communication and delivery**

   Faculty member uses class time effectively.

   Faculty member uses effective instructional techniques and tools (including lecture, discussion, audio/visuals, group activities, or technology).

   Faculty member demonstrates efforts to stimulate student interest and achievement.

4. **Policy/procedure practices**

   Faculty member adheres to established college, discipline, and department policies and procedures.

   Faculty member performs assigned duties for the conduct of business of the department.

   Faculty member is available to students outside class.

Evaluation of Teaching Effectiveness
of Faculty Member
by Department Chair

Rating Scale:

EP — **Exemplary Professional Performance**
Consistently exceeds accepted standards of professional performance
(JUSTIFICATION MUST BE INCLUDED)

HP — **High Professional Performance**
Frequently exceeds accepted standards of professional performance

SP — **Standard Professional Performance**
Consistently meets accepted standards of professional performance

MP — **Minimal Performance**
Does not consistently meet accepted standards of professional performance
(JUSTIFICATION MUST BE INCLUDED)

UP — **Unsatisfactory Performance**
Does not meet minimal standards of professional performance
(JUSTIFICATION MUST BE INCLUDED)

Justification for ratings of EP, MP, or UP must be included on the following page.

1. Knowledge   RATING:_____

2. Course organization and planning   RATING:_____

3. Communication and delivery   RATING:_____

4. Policy/procedure practices   RATING:_____

To compute your Teaching Effectiveness Self-Rating, assign the following values:

$$EP = 5 \quad HP = 4 \quad SP = 3 \quad MP = 2 \quad UP = 1$$

Directions: Add the four values assigned to the ratings, and divide by four to calculate the Teaching Effectiveness Rating of the faculty member. Do not round.

**TEACHING EFFECTIVENESS RATING
OF FACULTY MEMBER BY DEPARTMENT CHAIR:** _____

Evaluation of Teaching Effectiveness of Faculty Member
by Department Chair
(Continued)

Justification of ratings of EP, MP, or UP from the previous page should follow. Ratings of HP or SP require no response.

1. Knowledge _____

_____

_____

2. Course organization and planning _____

_____

_____

3. Communication and delivery _____

_____

_____

4. Policy/procedure practices _____

_____

_____

EVALUATION OF SERVICE

Instructions: After reviewing the Service Report in the Faculty Portfolio for Annual Evaluation, determine points for each of the appropriate items below.

A. Service to the Campus, Discipline, and Department

_____ Membership on campus, discipline, or department committee
(4 points per committee, maximum 12 points)

_____ Chair of campus, discipline, or department committee
(2 points in addition to membership points, maximum 4 points)

_____ Leader of campus, discipline, or department workshop or presentation
(2 – 4 points each, maximum of 8 points)
(4 points for the preparation and original offering of the presentation,
2 points for repeating a previous presentation)

_____ Mentor of new faculty member (4 points)

_____ Mentor of part-time faculty (2 points)

B. Service to College and Community

_____ Membership on college-wide councils or committees
(6 points per committee or council, maximum 12 points)

_____ Chair of college-wide council or committee
(4 points in addition to membership points)

_____ Leader of college-wide or community workshops, courses, or presentations
(2 – 4 points each, maximum 8 points)(4 points for the preparation and original
offering of the presentation, 2 points for repeating a previous presentation)

_____ Organizer of lecture series
(2 points, maximum of 2 points)

_____ Advisor to student organization recognized by SGA
(4 points, maximum 4 points)

_____ Advisor/editor of college publication
(4 points)

_____ Application of recognized area of expertise in the community without pay
(2 points per activity, maximum 4 points)

_____ Participation in college-sponsored outreach activities
(2 points, maximum 2 points)

Evaluation of Service (continued)

C.   Other activities: Those activities, other than the ones noted above, which directly contributed to either the academic or administrative functioning of the college

_____ (1 – 8 points; points should be assigned based upon the significance of the activity and the amount of effort involved and should be in line with other listed activities of comparable scope)

Total Service Points

Service Points	Rating Scale
27 and above	Exemplary Performance
18–26	High Performance
9–17	Standard Performance
5–8	Minimal Performance
0–4	Unsatisfactory Performance

To assign the Service Rating of Faculty Member, use the following values:

EP = 5   HP = 4   SP = 3   MP = 2   UP = 1

Service Rating of Faculty Member: _____

EVALUATION OF PROFESSIONAL ACTIVITIES

Instructions: After reviewing the Professional Activities Report in the Faculty Portfolio for Annual Evaluation, determine points for each of the appropriate items below.

A. Professional Organizations

_____ Held current membership in professional organization
(2 points each, maximum of 6 points)

_____ Served on a committee of a professional organization
(2 points each, maximum of 4 points)

_____ Held an elective or appointed office or chaired a committee of a state or local
professional organization (4 points each, maximum of 8 points)

_____ Held an elective or appointed office or chaired a committee of a regional or national
professional organization (6 points each, maximum of 12 points)

B. Further Education and Degrees

_____ Received credit for a graduate course (other than dissertation or thesis hours)
(4 points per course, maximum of 8 points)

_____ Participated in scholarly, pedagogical, or technological workshops or presentations at
Georgia Perimeter College (excluding those that were required)
(2 points each, maximum 4 points)

_____ Participated in workshops, summer institutes, short courses, audited a graduate level course, etc.
(excluding Georgia Perimeter College activities) (2 points each, maximum of 4 points)

_____ Completed a graduate degree from an accredited institution
(6 points each)

C. Scholarly and/or Creative Activities

_____ Attended a professional conference
(2 points each, maximum of 6 points)

_____ Gave a presentation at a professional conference
(4 points per presentation at a state or local conference, 6 points per presentation
at a regional or national conference, maximum of 10 points)

_____ Served on a discussion roundtable/panel
(2 points each, maximum of 4 points)

_____ Published an article, short story, or poem in a scholarly publication
(6 points each, maximum of 12 points)

_____ Published a new edition of a book
(4 points each, maximum of 8 points)

C. Scholarly and/or Creative Activities (continued)

_____ Published a book review in an appropriate scholarly publication
(4 points per review, maximum of 8 points)

_____ Served as an editor of a scholarly publication
(4 points each, maximum of 8 points)

_____ Served as a referee for a scholarly publication
(1 point per submission refereed, maximum 2 points)

_____ Reviewed a manuscript for publication
(1 point per manuscript, maximum 2 points)

_____ Published a comment, note, or letter to the editor in a scholarly publication
(1 point each, maximum of 2 points)

_____ Published an article, short story, or poem in a nonscholarly publication
(2 points each, maximum of 4 points)

D. Awards, Grants, Artistic Commissions, and/or Fellowships

_____ Received an award, grant, artistic commission, or fellowship
(excluding tuition grants for graduate study)
(2 points for a local award, grant, commission, or fellowship)
(4 points for a statewide award, grant, commission, or fellowship)
(6 points for a regional award, grant, commission, or fellowship)
(8 points for a national or international award, grant, commission, or fellowship)

_____ Served on a grant review panel (2 points, maximum of 2 points)

E. Other activities: Those activities, other than the ones noted above, which directly contributed to either the academic or administrative functioning of the college

_____ (1–8 points; points should be assigned based upon the significance of the
accomplishment and the amount of effort involved and should be in line with
other listed activities of comparable scope)

F. Fine Arts and Humanities Faculty only

_____ Performed in a musical, dramatic, or media production (6 points each, maximum of 12 points)

_____ Created a musical, dramatic, or media work which was performed, published, exhibited, and/or broadcast (8 points each, maximum of 12 points)

_____ Directed or produced a musical, dramatic, or media event, performance, broadcast, recording, exhibition (6 points each, maximum of 12 points)

_____ Designed and/or implemented the technical work (scenery, costume, lighting, sound, etc.) for a musical, dramatic, or media production (4 points each, maximum of 8 points)

Total Professional Activities Points_____

Professional Activities Points	Rating Scale
27 and above	Exemplary Performance
18–26	High Performance
9–17	Standard Performance
5–8	Minimal Performance
0–4	Unsatisfactory Performance

To assign the Service Rating of Faculty Member, use the following values:

$$EP = 5 \quad HP = 4 \quad SP = 3 \quad MP = 2 \quad UP = 1$$

Professional Activities Rating of Faculty Member: _____

Report the Professional Activities Rating on Faculty Members Performance Review Summary.

SUMMARY OF WEIGHTS TO BE USED IN FACULTY EVALUATION

(From the Faculty Portfolio)

Evaluation Period: July 1, _____ – June 30, _____

Part I— Overall Evaluation

Instructions: Part I was completed at the end of the academic year prior to the evaluation period. The faculty member should have a copy, and the department chair should include the document in the annual evaluation of the faculty member. All selected percentages should be within the indicated ranges, in multiples of 10 (i.e., 10%, 20%, 30%, etc.), and must total 100%.

TEACHING EFFECTIVENESS   _____ %
(Choose from 50% – 70%)

SERVICE   _____ %
(Choose from 10% – 30%)

PROFESSIONAL ACTIVITIES   _____ %
(Choose from 10% – 30%)

Part II

Instructions: Report weights submitted with the Faculty Portfolio.

TEACHING EFFECTIVENESS

SELF	(Choose from 10% – 20%)	_____%
PEER	(Choose from 10% – 20%)	_____%
STUDENTS	(Choose from 10% – 20%)	_____%
DEPARTMENT CHAIR	(Choose from 40% – 60%)	_____%
	TOTAL	_____%
		100%

FACULTY MEMBER PERFORMANCE REVIEW SUMMARY

INSTRUCTIONS

Step 1. Calculate the Overall Teaching Effectiveness Rating, using the Declaration of Weights and the ratings of Teaching Effectiveness from the Self-Evaluation, Student Rating Summary, and Evaluation of Teaching Effectiveness of Faculty Member by Department Chair.

Example:

1. Suppose the percentages from a faculty member's declaration of weights were as follows:

TEACHING EFFECTIVENESS

SELF (Choose from 10% – 20%)	20%
PEER (Choose from 10% – 20%)	20%
STUDENTS (Choose from 10%-20%)	10%
DEPARTMENT CHAIR (Choose from 40% -60%)	50%
Total	100%

2. Suppose the faculty members' ratings were as follows:

TEACHING EFFECTIVENESS

SELF-RATING	4.25
PEER RATING OF COURSE MATERIALS	3.75
STUDENT RATING	4.00
DEPARTMENT CHAIR RATING	3.75

Calculate the Overall Teaching Effectiveness Rating using the following formula:

.2(Self Rating) + .2(Peer Rating) + .1(Student Rating) + .5(Department Chair Rating)

.2(4.25) + .2(3.75) + .1(4.00) + .5(3.75) = 3.875

The faculty member's overall Teaching Effectiveness rating is 3.875.

Step 2. Report the Service Rating of Faculty Member

Step 3. Report the Professional Activities Rating of Faculty Member

Step 4. Calculate the Overall Faculty Evaluation Rating, using the Declaration of Weights and ratings for Teaching Effectiveness (50% – 70%), Service (10% – 30%), and Professional Activities (10% – 30%).

FACULTY MEMBER PERFORMANCE REVIEW SUMMARY

_____ _____
Faculty Member   Department Chair

_____ _____
Department   Campus

Calculation of the Teaching Effectiveness Rating

Declared Weights:

SELF   (10% – 20%)   _____

PEER   (10% – 20%)   _____

STUDENTS   (10% – 20%)   _____

DEPARTMENT CHAIR   (40% – 60%)   _____

(Self %)(Self Rating) + (Peer %)(Peer Rating) + (Student %)(Student Rating)+ (DC %)(DC Rating)

(   )(   ) + (   )(   ) + (   )(   ) + (   )(   )

Round to two decimals.

1. **TEACHING EFFECTIVENESS RATING**   _____

2. **SERVICE RATING**   _____

3. **PROFESSIONAL ACTIVITIES RATING**   _____

4. **Calculation of the Overall Faculty Evaluation Rating**

   Declared Weights:

   Teaching Effectiveness   (From 50% – 70%)   _____

   Service   (From 10% – 30%)   _____

   Professional Activities   (From 10% – 30%)   _____

   (Teaching Effectiveness %)(Teaching Effectiveness Rating) + (Service %)(Service Rating) +
   (Professional Activities %)(Professional Activities Rating)

   (   )(   ) + (   )(   ) + (   )(   )

Round to two decimals.

Overall Faculty Evaluation Rating: _____

ADDENDUM

Georgia Perimeter College Faculty Evaluation Handbook

Board of Regents' Policy on Faculty Evaluation (Policy 803.07)

In 1996, the Board of Regents of the University System of Georgia accepted the report of the Task Force on Faculty and Staff Development and adopted many of that group's recommendations. Included in those adopted measures are policies concerning faculty evaluation.

Purpose

The purpose of faculty evaluation is to provide regular feedback to faculty members regarding their performance so that they can provide high quality service to institutions in the University System of Georgia. Regular evaluations can provide an opportunity to assess strengths and weaknesses of faculty performance. Faculty evaluation should encourage and reward superior performance and offer the opportunity for career development when the process identifies ways to improve the performance. Each institution must establish procedures for evaluation of faculty. These procedures must include the following:

Annual Evaluation of Faculty

1. Evaluation of faculty members must take place each year.

2. Each institution must establish the criteria for evaluation consistent with Board of Regents' policy and the statutes and mission of the institution.

3. Each institution must specify who is responsible for the annual evaluation of faculty members and provide appropriate training for those who undertake this responsibility.

4. Faculty members with teaching responsibilities must be evaluated on the criterion of teaching effectiveness.

As defined by the institution, the measures of teaching effectiveness must include at a minimum a combination of written student evaluations and peer evaluations. The procedures for conducting these evaluations must be specified in writing by the institution.

5. Each institution must require that the faculty member's participation in faculty development during the current year and the faculty member's plans for the coming year be included in the annual evaluation. The person responsible for the annual evaluation should participate as appropriate in evaluating past and planned faculty development activities.

6. Faculty members must receive a written report of the evaluation. The faculty member, if he or she desires, shall have the opportunity to add a written response to the written report of the evaluation. The person responsible for the annual evaluation may then comment on this response if he or she desires. At that point, the written evaluation, together with any written response to it by the evaluated faculty member and any comment upon that response by the person responsible for preparing it should be sent to the administrative office at least one level above the faculty member's administrative unit, as specified by the institution. *(Changing the Results of Higher Education — Faculty and Staff Development 1996, pp. 41-42).*

Chapter References

Faculty evaluation, promotion, and tenure handbook. (1998-98). DeKalb, GA: Georgia Perimeter College.

Miller, R. I. (1972). *Evaluating faculty performance.* San Francisco, CA: Jossey-Bass.

17

Bibliography

These selected resources represent several aspects of the field of faculty evaluation. Many of these resources have been cited as references for various sections of this handbook. This listing is intended to serve only as an entry resource for those wishing to pursue a review of the literature as they develop their own comprehensive faculty evaluation system. It is not intended to represent an exhaustive listing of all references in the field of faculty evaluation.

AAUP. (1998). *Post-tenure review: An AAUP response.* Washington, DC: American Association of University Professors.

Abbott, R. D., Wulff, D. H., Nyquist, J. D., Ropp, V. A., & Hess, C. W. (1990). Satisfaction with processes of collecting student opinions about instruction: The student perspective. *Journal of Educational Psychology, 82*(2), 201-206.

Abpianalp, P. H., & Baldwin, W. R. (1983). Good teaching—a rewardable feat. *Journal of Optometric Education, 8*(3), 19-22.

Abrami, P. C. (1989). How should we use student ratings to evaluate teaching? *Research in Higher Education, 30*(2), 221-227.

Abrami, P. C. (1980). Using student rating norm groups for summative evaluations. *Proceedings, 6,* 124 -32. (Sixth International Conference on Improving University Teaching).

Abrami, P. C. (1985). Dimensions of effective college instruction. *Review of Higher Education, 8,* 211-28.

Abrami, P. C., Cohen, P. A., & d'Apollonia, S. (1988). Implementation problems in meta-analysis. *Review of Educational Research, 58*(2), 151-179.

Abrami, P. C., & d'Apollonia, S. (1991). Multidimensional students' evaluations of teaching effectiveness—generalizability of "N = 1" research: Comment on Marsh (1991). *Journal of Educational Psychology, 83*(3), 411-415.

Abrami, P. C., & Mizener, D. A. (1982). *Student/instructor attitude similarity, course ratings and student achievement.* Paper presented at the annual meeting of the American Psychological Association, Washington, DC. (ERIC ED 233 144).

Abrami, P. C., & Mizener, D. A. (1983). Does the attitude similarity of college professors and their students produce "bias" in course evaluations? *American Educational Research Journal, 20*(1), 123-36.

Abrami, P. C., & Mizener, D. A. (1985). Student/instructor attitude similarity, student ratings, and course performance. *Journal of Educational Psychology, 77,* 693-702.

Abrami, P. C., & Murphy, V. (1980). *A catalogue of systems for student evaluation of instruction.* Montreal, Canada: McGill University, Centre for Teaching and Learning.

Abrami, P. C., d'Apollonia, S., & Cohen, P. A. (1990). Validity of student ratings of instruction: What we know and what we do not know. *Journal of Educational Psychology, 82*(2), 219-231.

Abrami, P. C., Dickens, W. J., Perry, R. P., & Leventhal, L. (1980). Do teacher standards for assigning grades affect student evaluations of instruction? *Journal of Educational Psychology, 72,* 107-118.

Abrami, P. C., Leventhal, L., & Perry, R. P. (1982). Educational seduction. *Review of Educational Research, 52,* 446-464.

Aiken, Lewis R. (1983). Number of response categories and statistics on a teacher rating scale. *Educational and Psychological Measurement, 43*(2), 397-401.

Aleamoni, L. M. (1976). Evaluation of instruction via student ratings. *Note to the Faculty, No. 3*. Tucson, AZ: University of Arizona, Office of Instructional Research and Development.

Aleamoni, L. M. (1984, October). Peer evaluation. *Note to the Faculty, No. 15*. Tucson, AZ: The University of Arizona.

Aleamoni, L. M. (1999). Student rating myths versus research facts: An update. *Journal of Personnel Evaluation in Education, 13*(2), 153-166.

Aleamoni, L. M. (1972). A review of recent reliability and validity studies on the Illinois Course Evaluation Questionnaire (CEQ), *Research Memorandum No. 127*. Urbana, IL: University of Illinois, Measurement and Research Division.

Aleamoni, L. M. (1972). Response to Professor W. Edwards Deming's "memorandum on teaching." *The American Statistician, 26*(4), 54.

Aleamoni, L. M. (1973). Course evaluation questionnaire at the University of Illinois. *Evaluation, 1*(2), 73-74.

Aleamoni, L. M. (1973). Teaching—its place in the college or university reward system. In *Midwest association for physical education of college women annual report and conference proceedings* (pp. 26-32). Ypsilanti, MI: Eastern Michigan University, University Printing.

Aleamoni, L. M. (1973). The usefulness of student evaluations in improving college teaching. In A. L. Sockloff (Ed.), *Proceedings: The first invitational conference on faculty effectiveness as evaluated by students* (pp. 42-58). Philadelphia, PA: Temple University, Measurement and Research Center.

Aleamoni, L. M. (1976). On the invalidity of student ratings for administrative personnel decisions. *Journal of Higher Education, 47*(5), 607-610.

Aleamoni, L. M. (1976). Proposed system for rewarding and improving instructional effectiveness. *College University, 51*(3), 330-338.

Aleamoni, L. M. (1976). Typical faculty concerns about student evaluation of instruction. *National Association of Colleges and Teachers of Agriculture Journal, 20*(1), 16-21.

Aleamoni, L. M. (1977). Concepts and principles in the evaluation of instruction (courses and instructors). In the *1977 north central regional symposium on the improvement of instruction proceedings: Quality of instruction in agriculture and the renewable resources* (pp. 32-36). Madison, WI: University of Wisconsin.

Aleamoni, L. M. (1977). How can an institution improve and reward instructional effectiveness? *Faculty Development and Evaluation in Higher Education, 3*(4), 4-9.

Aleamoni, L. M. (1977). Indicators of the quality of instruction. In the *1977 North Central Regional Symposium on the Improvement of Instruction Proceedings: Quality of Instruction in Agriculture and the Renewable Resources* (pp. 16-18). Madison, WI: University of Wisconsin.

Aleamoni, L. M. (1977). Student evaluations of instruction proven useful and reliable. *Evaluation, 4*, 58.

Aleamoni, L. M. (1978). Development and factorial validation of Arizona course/instructor evaluation questionnaire. *Educational and Psychological Measurement, 38*, 1063-1067.

Aleamoni, L. M. (1978). The usefulness of student evaluations in improving college teaching. *Instructional Science, 7*, 95-105.

Aleamoni, L. M. (1979). Improvement of instruction should be the primary focus of instructional evaluation. *Note to the Faculty, No. 8*. Tucson, AZ: University of Arizona, Office of Instructional Research and Development.

Aleamoni, L. M. (1979). *Arizona course/instructor evaluation questionnaire*. Tucson, AZ: University of Arizona, Office of Instructional Research and Development.

Aleamoni, L. M. (1980). Evaluation as an integral part of instructional and faculty development. In L. P. Grayson & J. M. Biedenbach (Eds.), *Proceedings: 1980 college industry education conference* (pp. 120-123). Columbia, SC: American Society for Engineering Education.

Aleamoni, L. M. (1980). The use of student evaluations in the improvement of instruction. *National Association of Colleges and Teachers of Agriculture, 24*(3), 18-21.

Aleamoni, L. M. (1980). Are there differences in perceived teaching effectiveness between males and females in anthropology? *Resources in Education*. (ERIC ED 176 706).

Aleamoni, L. M. (1980). Students can evaluate teaching effectiveness. *National Forum, 60*(4), 41.

Aleamoni, L. M. (1981). Student ratings of instructor and instruction. In J. Milman (Ed.), *Handbook on teacher evaluation*. Beverly Hills, CA: Sage.

Aleamoni, L. M. (1981). Systematizing student ratings of instruction. In T. L. Sherman & M. Hassett (Eds.), *Evaluation of introductory college mathematics programs*. Tempe, AZ: Rocky Mountain Mathematics Consortium.

Aleamoni, L. M. (1982). Components of the instructional setting. *Instructional Evaluation, 7*(1), 11-16.

Aleamoni, L. M. (1982). Instructional improvement in the college classroom. In G. W. Bell (Ed.), *Professional preparation in athletic training*. Champaign, IL: Human Kinetics Publishers.

Aleamoni, L. M. (1984). The dynamics of faculty evaluation. In P. Seldin (Ed.), *Changing practices in faculty evaluation*. San Francisco, CA: Jossey-Bass.

Aleamoni, L. M. (1984). Developing a comprehensive system to improve and reward instructional effectiveness. *Resources in Education*. (ERIC ED 245 765).

Aleamoni, L. M. (1987). Evaluating instructional effectiveness can be a rewarding experience. *Journal of Plant Disease, 71*(4), 377-379.

Aleamoni, L. M. (1987). Some practical approaches for faculty and administrators. In L. M. Aleamoni (Ed.), *Techniques for instructional improvement and evaluation*. San Francisco, CA: Jossey-Bass.

Aleamoni, L. M. (1987). Student rating myths versus research facts. *Journal of Personnel Evaluation in Education, 1*, 111-119.

Aleamoni, L. M. (1987). Typical faculty concerns about student evaluation of teaching. In L. M. Aleamoni (Ed.), *Techniques for instructional improvement and evaluation*. San Francisco, CA: Jossey-Bass, Inc.

Aleamoni, L. M. (1988). Evaluation as reflection. In L. M. Aleamoni & D. Kishore (Eds.), *Evaluation and testing in instructional systems* (p. 258). Hyderabad, India: National Academy of Agricultural Research Management.

Aleamoni, L. M. (1988). Instructional process. In L. M. Aleamoni & D. Kishore (Eds.), *Evaluation and testing in instructional systems* (p. 4). Hyderabad, India: National Academy of Agricultural Research Management.

Aleamoni, L. M. (1990). Faculty development research in colleges, universities, and professional schools: The challenge. *Journal of Personnel Evaluation in Education, 3*, 193-195.

Aleamoni, L. M., & Carynnk, D. B. (1977). *Optional item catalog (revised), Information Memorandum No. 6*. Tucson, AZ: University of Arizona, Office of Instructional Research and Development.

Aleamoni, L. M., & Everly, J. C. (1971). Illinois course evaluation questionnaire useful in collecting student opinion. *National Association of Colleges and Teachers of Agriculture Journal, 15*(4), 99-100.

Aleamoni, L. M., & Graham, M. H. (1974). The relationship between CEQ ratings and instructor's rank, class size, and course level. *Journal of Educational Measurement, 11*, 189-202.

Aleamoni, L. M., & Hexner, P. Z. (1980). A review of the research on student evaluation and report on the effect of different sets on instructions on student course and instructor evaluation. *Instructional Science, 9*, 67-84.

Aleamoni, L. M., & Laham. (1992). *Arizona course/instructor evaluation questionnaire: Results interpretation manual*. Tucson, AZ: University of Arizona, Office of Instructional Research and Development.

Aleamoni, L. M., & Spencer, R. E. (1973). The Illinois course evaluation questionnaire: A description of its development and a report of some of its results. *Educational and Psychological Measurement, 33*, 669-684.

Aleamoni, L. M., & Stevens, J. (1984). The effectiveness of consultation in support of student evaluation feedback: A ten year follow-up. *The Pen, 7*.

Aleamoni, L. M., & Stevens, J. J. (1984). Peer evaluation. *Note to the Faculty, No. 15*. Tucson, AZ: University of Arizona.

Aleamoni, L. M., & Stevens, J. J. (1986). *Arizona course/instructor evaluation questionnaire (CIEQ): Results interpretation manual*. Tucson, AZ: University of Arizona, Office of Instructional Research and Development.

Aleamoni, L. M., & Thomas, G. S. (1980). Differential relationships of student, instruction, and course characteristics to general and specific items on course evaluation questionnaire. *Teaching of Psychology, 7*(4), 233-235.

Aleamoni, L. M., & Yimer, M. (1973). An investigation of the relationship between colleague rating, student rating, research productivity, and academic rank in rating instructional effectiveness. *Journal of Educational Psychology, 64*(3), 274-277.

Aleamoni, L. M., & Yimer, M. (1974). *Graduating Senior Ratings Relationship to Colleague Rating, Student Rating, Research Productivity, and Academic Rank in Rating Instructional Effectiveness (Research Report No. 352)*. Urbana, IL: University of Illinois, Office of Instructional Resources, Measurement and Research Division.

Aleamoni, L. M., Yimer, M., & Mahan, J. M. (1972). Teacher folklore and sensitivity of a course evaluation questionnaire. *Psychological Reports, 31*, 607-614.

Amin, M. E. (1993). Correlates of course evaluation at the faculty of letters and social sciences of the University of Yaounde. *Assessment and Evaluation in Higher Education, 18*(2), 135-141.

Andreson, L. W., et al. (1987). Competent teaching and its appraisal. *Assessment and Evaluation in Higher Education, 12*(1), 66-72.

Andrews, H. A. (1985). *Evaluating for excellence.* Stillwater, OK: New Forums Press.

Anikeef, A. M. (1953). Factors affecting student evaluation of college faculty members. *Journal of Applied Psychology, 37,* 458-460.

Arreola, R. A., & Aleamoni, L. M. (1990, Fall). Practical issues in designing and operating a faculty evaluation system (pp. 37-55). In M. Theall & J. Franklin, (Eds.), *Student ratings of instruction: Issues for improving practice.* New Directions for Teaching and Learning, No. 43. San Francisco, CA: Jossey-Bass.

Arreola, R. A. (1979, December). Strategy for developing a comprehensive faculty evaluation system. *Engineering Education,* 239-244.

Arreola, R. A. (1983). Establishing successful faculty evaluation and development programs (pp. 83-93). In A. Smith (Ed.), *Evaluating faculty and staff.* New Directions for Community Colleges, No. 41. San Francisco, CA: Jossey-Bass.

Arreola, R. A. (1983). Students can distinguish between personality and content/organization in rating teachers. *Phi Delta Kappan, 65*(3), 222-223.

Arreola, R. A. (1984). Evaluation of faculty performance: Key issues. In P. Seldin (Ed.), *Changing practices in faculty evaluation* (pp. 79-85). San Francisco, CA: Jossey-Bass.

Arreola, R. A. (1987, August/September). A faculty evaluation model for community and junior colleges (pp. 65-74). In L. Aleamoni (Ed.), *Techniques for evaluating and improving instruction.* New Directions for Teaching and Learning, No. 31. San Francisco, CA: Jossey-Bass.

Arreola, R. A. (1987, Fall). The role of student government in faculty evaluation (pp. 39-46). In L. Aleamoni (Ed.), *Techniques for evaluating and improving instruction.* New Directions for Teaching and Learning, No. 31. San Francisco, CA: Jossey-Bass.

Arreola, R. A. (1989, Spring). Defining and evaluating the elements of teaching (pp. 3-12). In W. Cashin (Ed.), *Proceedings of the sixth annual academic chairperson's conference.* Manhattan, KS: Kansas State University, Center for Faculty Evaluation and Development.

Arreola, R. A. (1983, July). What do student ratings measure? *The Articulating Paper, 4*(5). The College of Dentistry, The University of Tennessee, Memphis.

Arreola, R. A. (1986). Evaluating the dimensions of teaching. *Instructional Evaluation, 8*(2), 4-14.

Arubayi, E. (1986). Students' evaluation of instruction in higher education: A review. *Assessment and Evaluation in Higher Education, 11*(1), 1-10.

Avi-Itzhak, T., & Kremer, L. (1983). The effects of organizational factors on student ratings and perceived instructions. *Higher Education, 12*(4), 411-418.

Avi-Itzhak, T., & Kremer, L. (1985). An investigation into the relationship between university faculty attitudes toward student rating and organizational and background factors. *Educational Research Quarterly, 10*(2), 31-38.

Baird, J. S., Jr. (1987). Perceived learning in relation to student evaluation of university instruction. *Journal of Educational Psychology, 79*(1), 90-91.

Baker, A. M. (1986). Validity of Palestinian University students' responses in evaluating their instructors. *Assessment and Evaluation in Higher Education, 11*(1), 70-75.

Ballard, M. J., Reardon, J., & Nelson, L. (1976). Student and peer rating of faculty. *Teaching of Psychology, 3,* 115-119.

Banks, R. F. (1997). *Post-tenure review: A summary of other comparable university policies.* East Lansing, MI: Michigan State University.

Bannister, B. D., Kinicki, A. J., & Denisi, A. J. (1987). A new method for the statistical control of rating error in performance ratings. *Educational and Psychological Measurement, 47*(3), 583-596.

Banz, M. L., & Rodgers, J. L. (1985). Dimensions underlying student ratings of instruction: A multidimensional scaling analysis. *American Educational Research Journal, 22*(2), 267-272.

Barke, C. R., Tollefson, N., & Tracy, D. B. (1983). Relationship between course entry attitudes and end-of-course ratings. *Journal of Educational Psychology, 75*(1), 75-85.

Barnes, L. L. B., & Barnes, M. W. (1993). Academic discipline and generalizability of student evaluations of instruction. *Research in Higher Education, 34*(2), 135-149.

Basow, S. A., & Distenfeld, M. S. (1985). Teacher expressiveness: More important for male teachers than female teachers? *Journal of Educational Psychology, 77,* 45-52.

Basow, S. A., & K. G. Howe. (1987). Evaluations of college professors: Effects of professors' sex-type and sex and students' sex. *Psychological Reports, 60,* 671-678.

Basow, S. A., & Silberg, N. T. (1987). Student evaluations of college professors: Are female and male professors rated differently? *Journal of Educational Psychology, 79*(3), 308-314.

Batista, E. E. (1976). The place of colleague evaluation in the appraisal of college teaching: A review of the literature. *Research in Higher Education, 4*(3), 257-271.

Bednash, G. (1991). Tenure review: Process and outcomes. *Review of Higher Education, 15*(1), 47-63.

Behrendt, R. L., & Parsons, M. H. (1983). Evaluation of part-time faculty (pp. 33-43). In A. Smith (Ed.), *Evaluating faculty and staff.* New Directions for Community Colleges, Vol. 11, No. 1. San Francisco, CA: Jossey-Bass.

Bejar, I. I. (1975). A survey of selected administrative practices supporting student evaluation of instructional programs. *Research in Higher Education, 3,* 77-86.

Bell, M. E. (1977). Peer evaluation as a method of faculty development. *Journal of the College and University Personnel Association, 28*(4), 15-17.

Bendig, A. W. (1952). A preliminary study of the effect of academic level, sex, and course variables on student rating of psychology instructors. *Journal of Psychology, 34,* 21-26.

Bendig, A. W. (1953). Relation of level of course achievement of students, instructor, and course ratings in introductory psychology. *Educational and Psychological Measurement, 13,* 437-488.

Bennett, J. B. (1985). Periodic evaluation of tenured faculty performance (pp. 65-73). New Directions for Higher Education, Vol. 13, No. 1. San Francisco, CA: Jossey-Bass.

Bennett, S. K. (1982). Student perceptions of and expectations for male and female instructors: Evidence relating to the question of gender bias in teaching. *Journal of Educational Psychology, 74,* 170-179.

Benton, S. E. (1982). Rating college teaching: Criterion validity studies of student evaluation-of-instruction instruments. *AAHE-ERIC/ Higher Education Report No. 1.* Washington, DC: American Association for Higher Education. (ERIC ED 221 147).

Bergman, J. (1980). Peer evaluation of university faculty: A monograph. *College Student Journal, 14*(3, Pt. 2), 1-21.

Bingham, R. D., et al. (1982). The personal assessment feedback program for prospective teachers. *Action in Teacher Education, 4*(4), 55-57.

Blackburn, R. T., & Clark, M. J. (1975). An assessment of faculty performance: Some correlates between administrators, colleague, student and self-ratings. *Sociology of Education, 48,* 242-256.

Blai, B. J. (1982). *Faculty perceptions of "effective" teachers: A parallel-perceptions inquiry.* (ERIC ED 219 029).

Bogue, E. G. (1967). Student appraisal of teaching effectiveness in higher education: Summary of the literature. *Education Quest, 11,* 6-10.

Boice, R. (1984). Reexamination of traditional emphases in faculty development. *Research in Higher Education, 21*(2), 195-209.

Bonge, D. (1982). Using TA ratings to validate student evaluations: A reply to Lamberth and Kosteski. *Teaching of Psychology, 9*(2), 102.

Borgatta, E. F. (1970). Student ratings of faculty. *American Association of University Professors Bulletin, 56,* 6-7.

Bowen, H. R., & Schuster, J. H. (1986). *American professors: A national resource imperiled.* New York, NY: Oxford University Press.

Boyer, E. L. (1990*). Scholarship reconsidered: Priorities of the professoriate.* Princeton, NJ: Carnegie Foundation for the Advancement of Teaching.

Brandenburg, D. C., & Aleamoni, L. M. (1976). *Illinois course evaluation questionnaire: Results interpretation manual, Form 73.* Urbana, IL: University of Illinois, Office of Instructional Resources, Measurement and Research Division.

Brandwein, A. C., & DiVittis, A. (1985). The evaluation of peer tutoring program: A quantitative approach. *Educational and Psychological Measurement, 45*(1), 15-27.

Braskamp, L. A. & Ory, J. C. (1999). *Assessing faculty work.* San Francisco, CA: Jossey-Bass.

Braskamp, L. A. (1982). Evaluation systems are more than information systems (pp. 55-66). New Directions for Higher Education, No. 10. San Francisco, CA: Jossey-Bass.

Braskamp, L. A., Brandenburg, D. C., & Ory, J. C. (1984). *Evaluating teaching effectiveness: A practical guide.* Beverly Hills, CA: Sage.

Braskamp, L. A., et al. (1982). Faculty uses of evaluative information. (ERIC ED 218 308).

Braskamp, L. A., Ory, J. C., & Pieper, D. M. (1980). Written student comments: Dimensions of instructional quality. *Journal of Educational Psychology, 73,* 65-70.

Braunstein, D. N., Klein, G. A., & Pachla, M. (1973). Feedback, expectancy, and shifts in student ratings of college faculty. *Journal of Applied Psychology, 58,* 254-258.

Braxton, J. M., Bayer, A. F., & Finkelstein, M. J. (1992). Teaching performance norms in academia. *Research in Higher Education, 33*(5), 533-569.

Brown, D. L. (1976). Faculty ratings and student grades: A university-wide multiple regression analysis. *Journal of Educational Psychology, 68,* 573-578.

Bruton, B. T., & Crull, S. R. (1981). Causes and consequences of student evaluation of instruction. *Research in Higher Education, 17*(3), 195-206.

Bryant, J., Comisky, P. W., Crane, J. S., & Zillman, D. (1980). Relationship between college teachers' use of humor in the classroom and students' evaluations of their teachers. *Journal of Educational Psychology, 72*, 511-519.

Burdsal, C. A., & Bardo, J. W. (1986). Measuring students' perceptions of teaching: Dimensions of evaluation. *Educational and Psychological Measurement, 46*, 63-79.

Cadwell, J., & Jenkins, J. (1985). Effects of the semantic similarity of items on student ratings of instructors. *Journal of Educational Psychology, 77*, 383-393.

Cahn, D. D. (1983). Relative importance of perceived understanding in initial interaction and development of interpersonal relationships. *Psychological Reports, 52*, 923-929.

Cahn, D. D. (1983). Relative importance of perceived understanding in students' evaluation of teachers. *Perceptual and Motor Skills, 59*, 610.

Camp, R. C., Gibbs, M. C., Jr., & Masters II, R. J. (1988). The finite increment faculty merit pay allocation model. *Journal of Higher Education, 59*(6), 652-667.

Carr, J. W., & Padgett, T. C. (1992). Legal liability when designing or adopting student rating forms. In R. A. Arreola (Ed.), *Proceedings of the first annual CEDA conference on practical issues in faculty evaluation* (pp. 68-76). Memphis, TN: Center for Educational Development and Assessment.

Cashin, W. E. (1983). Concerns about using student ratings in community colleges (pp. 57-65). In A. Smith (Ed.), *Evaluating faculty and staff.* New Directions for Community Colleges, No. 41. San Francisco, CA: Jossey-Bass.

Cashin, W. E. (1995). *Student ratings of teaching: The research revisited. Idea paper, No. 32.* Manhattan, KS: Kansas State University, Center for Faculty Evaluation and Faculty Development.

Cashin, W. E., & Bruce, B. M. (1983). Do college teachers who voluntarily have their courses evaluated receive higher student ratings? *Journal of Educational Psychology, 75*(4), 595-602.

Cashin, W. E., & Downey, R. G. (1992). Using global student rating items for summative evaluation. *Journal of Educational Psychology, 84*(4), 563-572.

Cashin, W. E., & Perrin, B. M. (1978, December). *Description of the IDEA system data base—1978-79 (IDEA Technical Report No. 4).* Manhattan, KS: Kansas State University, Center for Faculty Evaluation and Development.

Centra, J. A. (1972a). *The student instructional report: Its development and uses (SIR Report No. 1).* Princeton, NJ: Educational Testing Service.

Centra, J. A. (1973). *Comparisons with alumni ratings, reliability of items, and factor structure (SIR Report No. 3).* Princeton, NJ: Educational Testing Service.

Centra, J. A. (1976). *Two studies on the validity of the student instructional report: I. Student ratings of instruction and their relationship to student learning. II. The relationship between student, teacher, and course characteristics and student ratings of teacher effectiveness (SIR Report No. 4).* Princeton, NJ: Educational Testing Service.

Centra, J. A. (1972b). *Two studies on the utility of student ratings for instructional improvement. I. The effectiveness of student feedback in modifying college instruction. II. Self-ratings of college teachers: A comparison with student ratings (SIR Report No. 2).* Princeton, NJ: Educational Testing Service.

Centra, J. A. (1973). Effectiveness of student feedback in modifying college instruction. *Journal of Educational Psychology, 65*, 395-401.

Centra, J. A. (1973). The student as godfather? The impact of student ratings on academia. In A. L. Sockloff (Ed.), *Proceedings of the first invitational conference on faculty effectiveness as evaluated by students.* Philadelphia, PA: Temple University, Measurement and Research Center.

Centra, J. A. (1975). Colleagues as raters of classroom instruction. *Journal of Higher Education, 46*, 327-338.

Centra, J. A. (1979). *Determining faculty effectiveness.* San Francisco, CA: Jossey-Bass.

Centra, J. A. (1981). Research productivity and teaching effectiveness. *Educational Testing Service Research Reports* (81-11). Princeton, NJ: Educational Testing Service.

Centra, J. A. (1983). Research productivity and teaching effectiveness. *Research in Higher Education, 18*(4), 379-389.

Centra, J. A. (1998*). The Development of the Student Instructional Report II.* Princeton, NJ: Educational Testing Service.

Centra, J. A. (1999). *Reflective faculty evaluation: Enhancing teaching and determining faculty effectiveness.* San Francisco, CA: Jossey-Bass.

Centra, J. A., & Bonesteel, P. (1990, Fall). College teaching: An art or a science? (pp. 37-55). In M. Theall & J. Franklin (Eds.), *Student ratings of instruction: Issues for improving practice*. New Directions for Teaching and Learning, No. 43. San Francisco, CA:

Centra, J. A., Gaubatz, N. B. (1999). *Is there gender bias in student evaluations of teaching?* Princeton, NJ: Educational Testing Service,

Champion, C. H., Green, S. B., & Sauser, W. I. (1988). Development and evaluation of shortcut-derived behaviorally anchored rating scales. *Educational and Psychological Measurement, 48*(1), 29-41.

Charkins, R. J., O'Toole, D. M., & Wetzel, J. N. (1985). Linking teacher and student learning styles with student achievement and attitudes. *Journal of Economic Education, 16*(2), 111-120.

Chism, N. (1999). *Peer review of teaching: A sourcebook*. Bolton, MA: Anker Publishing.

Chiu, C., & Alliger, G. M. (1990). A proposed method to combine ranking and graphic rating in performance appraisal: The quantitative ranking scale. *Educational and Psychological Measurement, 50*(3), 493-503.

Ciscell, R. E. (1987). Student ratings of instruction: Change the timetable to improve instruction. *Community College Review, 15*(1), 34-38.

Clark, B. L. (1984). Responding to students: Ughs, awks, and ahas. *Improving College and University Teaching, 32*(4), 169-172.

Clark, K. E., & Keller, R. J. (1954). Student ratings of college teaching. In R. A. Eckert (Ed.), *A university looks at its program*. Minneapolis, MN: University of Minnesota Press.

Clift, J., et al. (1989). Establishing the validity of a set of summative teaching performance scales. *Assessment and Evaluation in Higher Education, 14*(3), 193-206.

Cohen, P. A. (1980). Effectiveness of student-rating feedback for improving college instruction: A meta-analysis of findings. *Research in Higher Education, 13,* 321-341.

Cohen, P. A. (1980). *A meta-analysis of the relationship between student ratings of instruction and student achievement*. Ann Arbor, MI: The University of Michigan. (Doctoral Dissertation).

Cohen, P. A. (1981). Student ratings of instruction and student achievement: A meta-analysis of multi-section validity studies. *Review of Educational Research, 51,* 281-309.

Cohen, P. A. (1982). Validity of student ratings in psychology courses: A research synthesis. *Teaching of Psychology, 9*(2) 78-82.

Cohen, P. A. (1990, Fall). Bringing research into practice (pp. 37-55). In M. Theall & J. Franklin (Eds.), *Student ratings of instruction: Issues for improving practice*. New Directions for Teaching and Learning, No. 43. San Francisco, CA: Jossey-Bass.

Cohen, P. A., & Herr, G. A. (1979). A procedure for diagnostic instructional feedback: The formative assessment of college teaching (FACT). *Educational Technology, 19,* 18-23.

Cohen, P., & McKeachie, W. J. (1980). The role of colleagues in the evaluation of college teaching. *Improving College and University Teaching, 28*(4), 147-154.

Coleman, J., & McKeachie, W. J. (1980). Effects of instructor/course evaluations on student course selections. *Journal of Educational Psychology, 73,* 224-226.

Comer, J. C. (1980). The influence of mood on student evaluations of teaching. *Journal of Educational Research, 73,* 229-232.

Conway, R., et al. (1993). Peer assessment of an individual's contribution to a group project. *Assessment and Evaluation in Higher Education, 18*(1), 45-56.

Cook, S. S. (1989). Improving the quality of student ratings of instruction: A look at two strategies. *Research in Higher Education, 30*(1), 31-45.

Cooper, C. R. (1982). Getting inside the instructional process: A collaborative diagnostic process for improving college teaching. *Journal of Instructional Development, 3,* 2-10.

Cooper, P. J., Stewart, L. P., & Gudykunst, W. B. (1982). Relationship with instructor and other variables influencing student evaluations of instruction. *Communication Quarterly, 30*(4), 308-315.

Costin, F., Greenough, W. T., & Menges, R. J. (1971). Student ratings of college teaching: Reliability, validity, and usefulness. *Review of Educational Research, 41,* 511-535.

Cowen, D. L. (1976). Peer review in medical education. *Journal of Medical Education, 51*(2), 130-131.

Cranton, P. A., & Smith, R. A. (1986). A new look at the effect of course characteristics on student ratings of instruction. *American Educational Research Journal, 23,* 117-128.

Cranton, P., & Smith, R. A. (1990). Reconsidering the unit of analysis: A model of student ratings of instruction. *Journal of Educational Psychology, 82*(2), 207-212. Special section with title "Instruction in Higher Education."

Crook, J., et al. (1982). A question of timing: When is the best time to survey graduates to obtain feedback about an educational program? *Assessment and Evaluation in Higher Education, 7*(2), 152-158.

Cundy, D. T. (1982). Teacher effectiveness and course popularity: Patterns in student evaluations. *Teaching Political Science, 9*(4), 164-173.

Darling-Hammond, L., Wise, A. E., & Pease, S. R. (1983). Teacher evaluation in the organizational context: A review of the literature. *Review of Educational Research, 53*(3), 285-328.

DeCette, J., & Kenney, J. (1982). Do grading standards affect student evaluations of teaching? Some new evidence on an old question. *Journal of Educational Psychology, 74*, 308-314.

DeJung, J. E. (1964). Effects of rater frames of reference on peer ratings. *Journal of Experimental Education, 33*(2), 121-131.

Deming, W. E. (1972). Memorandum on teaching. *The American Statistician, 26*, 47.

DeNeve, H. M. F., & Janssen, P. J. (1982). Validity of student evaluation of instruction. *Higher Education, 11*(5), 543-552.

Derry, J. O. (1977). *The cafeteria system: A new approach to course and instructor evaluation.* West Lafayette, IN: Purdue University.

Dick, R. C. (1983). Paper giving, play directing, and paid consulting: A position paper on faculty evaluation. *Association for Communication Administration Bulletin, 44*, 5-8.

Dick, W. (1982). Evaluation in diverse educational settings. *Viewpoints in Teaching and Learning, 58*(3), 84-89.

Dienst, E. R. (1981). *Evaluation of colleagues.* Paper presented at the 65th annual meeting of the American Educational Research Association, April 13-17, Los Angeles, CA. (ERIC ED 209 341).

Donald, J. (1982). A critical appraisal of the state of evaluation in higher education in Canada. *Assessment and Evaluation in Higher Education, 7*(2), 108-126.

Donald, J. (1984). Quality indices for faculty evaluation. *Assessment and Evaluation in Higher Education, 9*(1), 41-52.

Donald, J. (1985). The state of research on university teaching effectiveness (pp. 7-20). In J. Donald & A. M. Sullivan (Eds.), *Using research to improve teaching.* New Directions for Teaching and Learning, No. 23. San Francisco, CA: Jossey-Bass.

Dowell, D. A., & Neal, J. A. (1982). A selective review of the validity of student ratings of teaching. *Journal of Higher Education, 53*(1), 51-62.

Downie, N. W. (1952). Student evaluation of faculty. *Journal of Higher Education, 23*, 495-496, 503.

Doyle, K. O. (1975). *Student evaluation of instruction.* Lexington, MA: Lexington Books.

Doyle, K. O. (1983). *Evaluating teaching.* Lexington, MA: Lexington Books.

Doyle, K. O., & Crichton, L. I. (1978). Student, peer, and self evaluations of college instructors. *Journal of Educational Psychology, 70*(5), 815-826.

Doyle, K. O., & Whitely, S. E. (1974). Student ratings as criteria for effective teaching. *American Educational Research Journal, 11*, 259-274.

Dressel, P. L. (1982). Values (virtues and vices) in decision making (pp. 31-43). New Directions for Higher Education, Vol. 10, No. 1. San Francisco, CA: Jossey-Bass.

Drucker, A. J., & Remers, H. H. (1951). Do alumni and students differ in their attitudes toward instructors? *Journal of Educational Psychology, 42*, 129-143.

Earl, S. E. (1986). Staff and peer assessment—measuring an individual's contribution to group performance. *Assessment and Evaluation in Higher Education, 11*(1), 60-69.

Easton, J. Q. (1985). National study of effective community college teachers. *Community & Junior College Quarterly of Research and Practice, 9*(2), 153-163.

Ebel, K. E. (1972). *Professors as teachers.* San Francisco, CA: Jossey-Bass.

Elton, L. (1984). Evaluating teaching and assessing teachers in universities. *Assessment and Evaluation in Higher Education, 9*(2), 97-115.

Erdle, S., & Murray, H. G. (1986). Interfaculty differences in classroom teaching behaviors and their relationship to student instructional ratings. *Research in Higher Education, 24*, 115-127.

Erdle, S., Murray, H. G., & Rushton, J. P. (1985). Personality, classroom behavior, and student ratings of college teaching effectiveness: A path analysis. *Journal of Educational Psychology, 77*(4), 394-407.

Everly, J. C., & Aleamoni, L. M. (1972). The rise and fall of the advisor … Students attempt to evaluate their instructors. *Journal of the National Association of Colleges and Teachers of Agriculture, 16*(2), 43-45.

Feldman, K. A. (1988). Effective college teaching from the students' and faculty's view: Matched or mismatched priorities? *Research in Higher Education, 28*(4), 291-344.

Feldman, K. A. (1989). Instructional effectiveness of college teachers as judged by teachers themselves, current and former students, colleagues, administrators, and external (neutral) observers. *Research in Higher Education, 30*(2), 137-194.

Feldman, K. A. (1990). An afterword for the association between student ratings of specific instructional dimensions and student achievement: Refining and extending the synthesis of data from multisection validity studies. *Research in Higher Education, 31*(4), 315-318.

Feldman, K. A. (1993). College students' views of male and female college teachers: Part II—Evidence from students' evaluations of their classroom teachers. *Research in Higher Education, 34*(2), 151-211.

Feldman, K. A. (1976). Grades and college students' evaluations of their courses and teachers. *Research in Higher Education, 4,* 69-111.

Feldman, K. A. (1978). Course characteristics and college students' rating of their teachers: What we know and what we don't. *Research in Higher Education, 9,* 199-242.

Feldman, K. A. (1983). Seniority and instructional experience of college teachers as related to evaluations they receive from their students. *Research in Higher Education, 18(*1), 3-124.

Feldman, K. A. (1984). Class size and college students' evaluations of teachers and courses: A closer look. *Research in Higher Education, 21*(1), 45-116.

Feldman, K. A. (1986). The perceived instructional effectiveness of college teachers as related to their personality and attitudinal characteristics: A review and synthesis. *Research in Higher Education, 24,* 139-213.

Feldman, K. A. (1987). Research productivity and scholarly accomplishment of college teachers as related to their instructional effectiveness. *Research in Higher Education, 26,* 227-298.

Feldman, K. A. (1992). College students' views of male and female college teachers: Part I—Evidence from the social laboratory and experiments. *Research in Higher Education, 33* (3), 317-375.

Feldman, R. S., Saletsky, R. D., Sullivan, J., & Theiss, A. (1983). Student locus of control and response to expectations about self and teacher. *Journal of Educational Psychology, 75*(1), 27-32.

Ferber, M. A., & Huber, J. A. (1975). Sex of student and instructor: A study of student bias. *American Journal of Sociology, 80,* 949-963.

Fink, L. D. (1984). The situational factors affecting teaching (pp. 37-60). In J. Donald & A. M. Sullivan (Eds.), *The first year of college teaching.* New Directions for Teaching and Learning, No. 17. San Francisco, CA: Jossey-Bass.

Fitzgerald, M. J., & Grafton, C. L. (1981). Comparisons and implications of peer and student evaluation for a community college faculty. *Community & Junior College Research Quarterly, 5*(4), 331-337.

Frankhouser, W. M., Jr. (1984). The effects of different oral directions as to disposition of results on student ratings of college instruction. *Research in Higher Education, 20*(3), 367-374.

Freilich, M. B. (1983). A student evaluation of teaching techniques. *Journal of Chemical Education, 60*(3), 218-221.

French-Lazovik, G. (Ed.). (1982). *Practices that improve teaching evaluation.* New Directions for Teaching and Learning, No. 11. San Francisco, CA: Jossey-Bass.

Frey, P. W. (1976). Validity of student instructional ratings: Does timing matter? *Journal of Higher Education, 47,* 327-336.

Frey, P. W. (1973). Student ratings of teaching: Validity of several rating factors. *Science, 182,* 83-85.

Frey, P. W. (1978). A two-dimensional analysis of student ratings of instruction. *Research in Higher Education, 9,* 69-91.

Frey, P. W., Leonard, D. W., & Beatty, W. W. (1975). Student ratings of instruction: validation research. *American Educational Research Journal, 12,* 435-447.

Fry, S. A. (1990). Implementation and evaluation of peer marking in higher education. *Assessment and Evaluation in Higher Education, 15*(3), 177-189.

Gage, N. L. (1961). The appraisal of college teaching. *Journal of Higher Education, 32,* 17-22.

Gessner, P. K. (1973). Evaluation of instruction. *Science, 180,* 566-569.

Gibbs G., et al. (1985). Son of teaching tips, or 106 interesting ways to teach. *Journal of Geography in Higher Education, 9*(1), 55-68.

Gibbs, G., Habeshaw, S., & Habeshaw, T. (1984). *53 interesting things to do in your lectures.* Bristol, England: Technical and Educational Services, Ltd.

Gibson, K. (1992). Communicating with faculty using a diagnostic performance appraisal process. *Resources in Education.* (ERIC ED 354 053).

Gigliotti, R. J. (1987). Expectations, observations, and violations: Comparing their effects on course ratings. *Research in Higher Education, 26*(4), 401-415.

Gigliotti, R. J., & Buchtel, F. S. (1990, June). Attributional bias and course evaluations. *Journal of Educational Psychology, 82*(2), 341-351.

Gillmore, G. M. (1973). *Estimates of reliability coefficients for items and subscales of the Illinois course evaluation questionnaire (Research Report No. 341).* Urbana, IL: University of Illinois, Office of Instructional Resources, Measurement and Research Division.

Gillmore, G. M. (1984). Student ratings as a factor in faculty employment decisions and periodic review. *Journal of College and University Law, 10*(4), 557-576.

Gillmore, G. M., & Brandenburg, D. C. (1974). *Would the proportion of students taking a class as a requirement affect the student rating of the course? (Research Report No. 347)*. Urbana, IL: University of Illinois, Office of Instructional Resources, Measurement and Research Division.

Gillmore, G. M., Kane, M. T., & Smith, P. L. (1983). The dependability of student evaluations of teaching effectiveness: Matching the conclusions to the design. *Educational and Psychological Measurement, 43*(4), 1015-1018.

Goldfinch, J., & Raeside, R. (1990). Development of a peer assessment technique for obtaining individual marks on a group project. *Assessment and Evaluation in Higher Education, 15*(3), 210-231.

Goodhartz, A. S. (1948). Student attitudes and opinions relating to teaching at Brooklyn College. *School and Society, 68*, 345-349.

Goodman, M. J. (1990). The review of tenured faculty: A collegial model. *Journal of Higher Education, 61*(4), 408-424.

Goodwin, L. D., & Stevens, E. A. (1993). The influence of gender on university faculty members' perceptions of "good" teaching. *Journal of Higher Education, 64*(2), 166-185.

Grasha, A. F. (1977). *Assessing and developing faculty performance*. Cincinnati, OH: Communication and Education Associates.

Gray, D. M., & Brandenburg, D. C. (1985). Following student ratings over time with a catalog-based system. *Research in Higher Education, 22*(2), 155-168.

Greene, M. M. (1982). The use of microcomputers in educational evaluation. *The computer: Extension of the human mind.* (Proceedings of the 3rd Annual Summer Conference). Eugene, OR: University of Oregon, College of Education. (ERIC ED 219 870).

Greenwood, G. E., & Ramagli, H. J. (1980). Alternatives to student ratings of college teaching. *Journal of Higher Education, 51*(6), 673-684.

Grush, J. E., & Costin, F. (1975). The student as consumer of the teaching process. *American Educational Research Journal, 12*, 55-66.

Gutherie, E. R. (1949). The evaluation of teaching. *Educational Record, 30*, 109-115.

Guthrie, E. R. (1954). *The evaluation of teaching: A progress report.* Seattle, WA: University of Washington.

Hammons, J. (1983). Faculty development: A necessary corollary to faculty evaluation (pp. 75-82). In A. Smith (Ed.), *Evaluating faculty and staff.* New Directions for Community Colleges, Vol. 11, No. 1. San Francisco, CA: Jossey-Bass.

Hanna, G. S., Hoyt, D. P., & Aubrecht, J. D. (1983). Identifying and adjusting for biases in student evaluations of instruction: Implications for validity. *Educational and Psychological Measurement, 43*(4), 1175-1185.

Harris, E. L. (1982). Student ratings of faculty performance: Should departmental committees construct the instruments. *Journal of Educational Research, 76*(2), 100-106.

Hativa, N., & Raviv, A. (1993). Using a single score for summative evaluation by students. *Research in Higher Education, 34*(5), 625-646.

Haugen, R. E. (1984). Educationists and academics: Ratings of community college instructors. *Community & Junior College Quarterly of Research and Practice, 8*(1-4), 103-113.

Hausknecht, M. (1982). Bromides and ideology. *Academe, 68*(6), 24-28.

Hayes, J. R. (1971). Research, teaching, and faculty fate. *Science, 172*, 227-230.

Healy, P. (1999, March 26). Massachusetts governor seeks to free some colleges from tenure and most regulations. *The Chronicle of Higher Education*, p. A43.

Hebron, C. d. W. (1984). An aid for evaluating teaching in higher education. *Assessment and Evaluation in Higher Education, 9*(2), 145-163.

Heilman, J. D., & Armentrout, W. D. (1936). The rating of college teachers on ten traits by their students. *Journal of Educational Psychology, 27*, 197-216.

Helmstadter, G. C., & Krus, D. J. (1982). The factorial validity of student ratings in faculty promotions. *Educational and Psychological Measurement, 42*(4), 1135-1139.

Hildebrand, M., Wilson, R. C., & Dienst, E. R. (1971). *Evaluating University Teaching.* Berkeley, CA: University of California, Center for Research and Development in Higher Education.

Hogan, T. P. (1973). Similarity of student ratings across instructors, courses, and time. *Research in Higher Education, 1*, 149-154.

Hollander, E. P. (1956). The friendship factor in peer nomination. *Personnel Psychology,* (9), 435-447.

Howard, G. S., & Maxwell, S. E. (1980). Correlation between student satisfaction and grades: A case of mistaken causation? *Journal of Educational Psychology, 72*, 810-820.

Howard, G. S., Conway, C. G., & Maxwell, S. E. (1985). Construct validity of measures of college teaching effectiveness. *Journal of Educational Psychology, 77*(2), 187-196.

Hoyt, D. P. (1973). Measurement of instructional effectiveness. *Research in Higher Education, 1*, 367-378.

Hoyt, D. P., & Cashin, W. E. (1977, March). *Development of the IDEA system (IDEA Technical Report No. 1)*. Manhattan, KS: Kansas State University, Center for Faculty Evaluation and Development.

Hoyt, D. P., Chen, Y., Pallett, W. H., & Gross, A. B. (1998, November). *Revising the IDEA system for obtaining student ratings of instructors and courses (IDEA Technical Report No. 11)*. Manhattan, KS: Kansas State University, the IDEA Center.

Hunnicutt, G. G., Lesher-Taylor, R. L., & Keeffe, M. J. (1991). An exploratory examination of faculty evaluation and merit compensation systems in Texas colleges and universities. *CUPA Journal, 42*(1), 13-21.

Husbands, C. T., & Fosh, P. (1993). Students' evaluation of teaching in higher education: Experiences from four European countries and some implications of the practice. *Assessment and Evaluation in Higher Education, 18*(2), 95-114.

Hutton, J. (1979). *Evaludent: A manual of course and instructor evaluation*. Morgantown, WV: West Virginia University, School of Dentistry.

Isaacs, G. (1989). Changes in ratings for staff who evaluated their teaching more than once. *Assessment and Evaluation in Higher Education, 14*(1), 1-10.

Isaacson, R. L., McKeachie, W. J., Milholland, J. E., Lin, Y. G., Hofeller, M., Baerwaldt, J. W., & Zinn, K. L. (1964). Dimensions of student evaluations of teaching. *Journal of Educational Psychology, 55*, 344-351.

Iyaser, M. M. (1984). Responding to colleagues: Setting standards in multiple-section courses. *Improving College and University Teaching, 32*(4), 173-179.

Jacobson, C. R. (1983). Outstanding teachers: How do UND students describe them. *Instructional Development Report*. Grand Forks, ND: University of North Dakota, Office of Instructional Development, Box 8161, University Station. (ERIC ED 224 427).

Jensen, M. D. (1987, April). *Ethics, grades, and grade inflation: Student evaluations as a factor in multi-sectioned courses*. Paper presented at the Joint Meeting of the Central States Speech Association and the Southern Speech Communication Association, St. Louis, MO. (ERIC ED 281 259).

Jolly, B., & Macdonald, M. M. (1987). More effective evaluation of clinical teaching. *Assessment and Evaluation in Higher Education, 12*(3), 175-190. Jossey-Bass.

Kagan, D. M. (1990). Ways of evaluating teacher cognition: Inferences concerning the Goldilocks principle. *Review of Educational Research, 60*(3), 419-469.

Kane, M. T., Gillmore, G. M., & Crooks, T. J. (1976). Student evaluations of teaching: The generalizability of class means. *Journal of Educational Measurement, 13*, 171-184.

Kaplan, W. A. (1978). *The law of higher education: A comprehensive guide to legal implications of administrative decision making*. San Francisco, CA: Jossey-Bass.

Kappelman, M. M. (1983). The impact of external examinations on medical education programs and students. *Journal of Medical Education, 58*(4), 300-308.

Kaschark, E. (1978). Sex bias in student evaluations of college professors. *Psychology of women quarterly, 2*, 235-243.

Kierstead, D., D'Agostino, P., & Dill, H. (1988). Sex role stereotyping of college professors: Bias in students' ratings of instructors. *Journal of Educational Psychology, 80*(3), 342-344.

Kimlicka, T. M. (1982). Student evaluation of course content, teaching effectiveness and personal growth in an experimental course. *College Student Journal, 16*(2), 198-200.

Kingsbury, M. (1982). How library schools evaluate faculty performance. *Journal of Education for Librarianship, 22*(4), 219-238.

Kinney, D. P., & Smith, S. P. (1992). Age and teaching performance. *Journal of Higher Education, 63*(3), 282-302.

Kirkpatrick, J. S., & Aleamoni, L. M. (1983). *Experimental research in counseling*. Springfield, IL: Charles C. Thomas.

Kloeden, P. E., & McDonald, R. J. (1981). Student feedback in teaching and improving an external mathematics course. *Distance Education, 2*(1), 54-63.

Koehler, W. F. (1986). From evaluations to an equitable selection of merit-pay recipients and increments. *Research in Higher Education, 25*(3), 253-263.

Kohlan, R. G. (1973). A comparison of faculty evaluations early and late in the course. *Journal of Higher Education, 44*, 587-595.

Kratochwill, T. R. (1978). *Single subject research: Strategies for evaluating change*. New York, NY: Academic Press.

Kremer, J. (1991). Identifying faculty types using peer ratings of teaching, research, and service. *Research in Higher Education, 32*(4), 351-361.

Kremer, J. F. (1990). Construct validity of multiple measures in teaching, research, and service and reliability of peer ratings. *Journal of Educational Psychology, 82*(2), 213-218. Special section with title "Instruction in Higher Education."

Kulik, J. A., & Kulik, C. L. C. (1974). Student ratings of instruction. *Teaching of Psychology, 1,* 51-57.

Kulik, J. A., & McKeachie, W. J. (1975). The evaluation of teachers in higher education. *Review of Research in Education, 3,* 210-240.

Kurz, R. S., Meuller, J. J., Gibbons, J. L., & DiCataldo, F. (1989). Faculty performance: Suggestions for the refinement of the concept and its measurement. *Journal of Higher Education, 60*(1), 43-58.

L'Hommedieu, R., Menges, R. J., & Brinko, K. T. (1990). Methodological explanations for the modest effects of feedback from student ratings. *Journal of Educational Psychology, 82*(2), 232-241. Special section with title "Instruction in Higher Education."

Lacefield, W. E. (1986). Faculty enrichment and the assessment of teaching. *Review of Higher Education, 9*(4), 361-379.

Land, M. L., & Smith, L. R. (1980). Student perception of teacher clarity in mathematics. *Journal for Research in Mathematics Education, 11,* 137-146.

Land, M. L., & Smith, L. R. (1980). Student ratings and teacher behavior: An experimental study. *Research Report:* Missouri Southern State College.

Larson, R. (1984). Teacher performance evaluation—what are the key elements? *NASSP Bulletin, 68*(469), 13-18.

Leatherman, C. (1999, April 9). Growth in positions off the tenure track is a trend that's here to stay, study finds. *The Chronicle of Higher Education,* p. A14.

Lee, B. A. (1985). Federal court involvement in academic personnel decisions: Impact on peer review. *Journal of Higher Education, 56*(1), 38-54.

Lee, B. A. (1983). Balancing confidentiality and disclosure in faculty peer review. Impact of Title VII legislation. *Journal of College and University Law, 9*(3), 279-314.

Lester, D. (1982). Students evaluation of teaching and course performance. *Psychological Reports, 50,* 1126.

Leventhal, L., Perry, R. P., & Abrami, P. C. (1977). Effects of lecturer quality and student perception of lecturer's experience on teacher ratings and student achievement. *Journal of Educational Psychology, 69,* 360-374.

Leventhal, L., Turcotte, S. J. C., Abrami, P. C., & Perry, R. P. (1983). Primacy/recency effects in student ratings of instruction: A reinterpretation of gain-loss effects. *Journal of Educational Psychology, 75*(5), 692-704.

Levinson-Rose, J., & Menges, R. J. (1981). Improving college teaching: A critical review of research. *Review of Educational Research, 51*(3), 403-434.

Licata, C. M. (1985). An investigation of the status of post-tenure faculty evaluation in selected community colleges. *ASHE 1985 Annual Meeting Paper.* Paper presented at the Annual Meeting of the Association for the Student of Higher Education, Chicago, IL. (ERIC ED 259 635).

Lichty, R. W., & Peterson, J. M. (1979). *Peer evaluations: A necessary part of evaluating teaching effectiveness.* Duluth, MN: University of Minnesota. [NSD 52721] (ERIC ED 175352).

Lin, Y. (1984). The use of student ratings in promotion decision. *Journal of Higher Education, 55*(5), 583-589.

Linsky, A. S., & Straus, M. A. (1973). Student evaluation of teaching. *Teaching Sociology, 1*(1), 103-118.

Linsky, A. S., & Straus, M. A. (1975). Student evaluations, research productivity, and eminence of college faculty. *Journal of Higher Education, 46,* 89-102.

Lovell, G. D., & Haner, C. F. (1955). Forced-choice applied to college faculty rating. *Educational and Psychological Measurement, 15,* 291-304.

Magnusen, K. O. (1987). Faculty evaluation, performance, and pay: Application and issues. *Journal of Higher Education, 58*(5), 516-529.

Mahmoud, M. M. (1991). Descriptive models of student decision behaviour in evaluation of higher education. *Assessment and Evaluation in Higher Education, 16*(2), 133-148.

Marchant, G. J., & Newman, I. (1991). *Faculty evaluation and reward procedures: Views from education administrators.* Paper presented at the Annual Meeting of the American Educational Research Association, Chicago, IL. (ERIC ED 331 377).

Marlin, J. W., Jr. (1987). Student perception of end-of-course evaluations. *Journal of Higher Education, 58*(6), 704-716.

Marques, T. E., Lane, D. M., & Dorfman, P. W. (1979). Toward the development of a system for instructional evaluation: Is there consensus regarding what constitutes effective teaching? *Journal of Educational Psychology, 71,* 840-849.

Marsh, H. W. (1983). Multitrait-multimethod analysis: Distinguishing between items and traits. *Educational and Psychological Measurement, 43*(2), 351-358.

Marsh, H. W. (1986). Applicability paradigm: Students' evaluations of teaching effectiveness in different countries. *Journal of Educational Psychology, 78*(6), 465-473.

Marsh, H. W. (1991). Multidimensional students' evaluations of teaching effectiveness: A test of alternative higher-order structures. *Journal of Educational Psychology, 83*(2), 285-296.

Marsh, H. W. (1991, September). A multidimensional perspective on students' evaluations of teaching effectiveness: Reply to Abrami and d'Apollonia. *Journal of Educational Psychology, 83*(3), 416-421.

Marsh, H. W. (1977). The validity of students' evaluations: Classroom evaluations of instructors independently nominated as best and worst teachers by graduating seniors. *American Educational Research Journal, 14,* 441-447.

Marsh, H. W. (1980). Research on students' evaluations of teaching effectiveness: A reply to Vecchio. *Instructional Evaluation, 4,* 5-13.

Marsh, H. W. (1980). The influence of student, course, and instructor characteristics on evaluations of university teaching. *American Educational Research Journal, 17,* 219-237.

Marsh, H. W. (1982). Factors affecting students' evaluations of the same course by the same instructor on different occasions. *American Educational Research Journal, 19*(4), 485-497.

Marsh, H. W. (1982). Validity of students' evaluations of college teaching: A multitrait-multimethod analysis. *Journal of Educational Psychology, 74*(2), 264-279.

Marsh, H. W. (1983). Multidimensional ratings of teacher effectiveness by students from different academic settings and their relation to student/course/instructor characteristics. *Journal of Educational Psychology, 75*(1), 150-166.

Marsh, H. W. (1984). Students' evaluations of university teaching: Dimensionality, reliability, validity, potential biases, and utility. *Journal of Educational Psychology, 76,* 707-754.

Marsh, H. W. (1993). The use of students' evaluation and an individually structured intervention to enhance university teaching effectiveness. *American Educational Research Journal, 30*(1), 217-251.

Marsh, H. W., & Bailey, M. (1993). Multidimensional students' evaluations of teaching effectiveness. *Journal of Higher Education, 64*(1), 1-18.

Marsh, H. W., & Cooper, T. L. (1981). Prior subject interest, students' evaluations and instructional effectiveness. *Multivariate Behavioral Research, 16,* 81-104.

Marsh, H. W., & Hocevar, D. (1984). The factorial invariance of student evaluations of college teaching. *American Educational Research Journal, 21*(2), 341-366.

Marsh, H. W., & Overall, J. U. (1979). Long-term stability of students' evaluations: A note on Feldman's "Consistency and variability among college students in rating their teachers and courses." *Research in Higher Education, 10,* 139-47.

Marsh, H. W., & Overall, J. U. (1980). Validity of students' evaluations of teaching effectiveness: Cognitive and affective criteria. *Journal of Educational Psychology, 72,* 468-475.

Marsh, H. W., & Overall, J. U. (1981). The relative influence of course level, course type, and instructor on students' evaluations of college teaching. *American Educational Research Journal, 18,* 103-112.

Marsh, H. W., & Ware, J. E. (1982). Effects of expressiveness, content coverage, and incentive on multidimensional student rating scales: New interpretations of the Dr. Fox effect. *Journal of Educational Psychology, 74*(1), 126-134.

Marsh, H. W., Fleiner, H., & Thomas, C. S. (1975). Validity and usefulness of student evaluations of instructional quality. *Journal of Educational Psychology, 67,* 833-839.

Marsh, H. W., Overall, J. U., & Kesler, S. P. (1979). Class size, students' evaluations, and instructional effectiveness. *American Educational Research Journal, 16,* 57-70.

Marsh, H. W., Overall, J. U., & Kesler, S. P. (1979). Validity of student evaluations of instructional effectiveness: A comparison of faculty self-evaluations and evaluations by their students. *Journal of Educational Psychology, 71,* 149-160.

Martin, R. E., et al. (1983). A planned program for evaluation and development of clinical pharmacy faculty. *American Journal of Pharmaceutical Education, 47*(2), 102-107.

Maslow, A. H., & Zimmerman, W. (1956). College teaching ability, scholarly activity, and personality. *Journal of Educational Psychology, 47,* 185-189.

Mathias, H. (1984). The evaluation of university teaching: Context, values, and innovation. *Assessment and Evaluation in Higher Education, 9*(2), 79-96.

Mathias, H., & Rutherford, D. (1981). Course evaluation at Birmingham: Some implications for the assessment and improvement of university teaching. *Studies in Educational Evaluation, 7*(3), 263-266.

Mathias, H., & Rutherford, D. (1982). Lecturers as evaluators: The Birmingham experience. *Studies in Higher Education, 7*(1), 47-56.

Matthews, J. R. (1982). Evaluation: A major challenge for the 1980s. *Teaching of Psychology, 9*(1), 49-52.

McBean, E. A., & Al-Nassri, S. (1982). Questionnaire design for student measurement of teaching effectiveness. *Higher Education, 11*(3), 273-288.

McBean, E. A., & Lennox, W. C. (1982). Issues of teaching effectiveness as observed via course critiques. *Higher Education, 11*(6), 645-655.

McBean, E. A., & Lennox, W. C. (1985). Effect of survey size on student ratings of teaching. *Higher Education, 14*(2), 117-25.

McCabe, M. V. (1982). Faculty attitudes toward evaluation at southern universities. *Phi Delta Kappan, 63*(6), 419.

McCallum, L. W. (1984). A meta-analysis of course evaluation data and its use in the tenure decision. *Research in Higher Education, 21*(2), 150-158.

McCarthy, P. R., & Shmeck, R. R. (1982). Effects of teacher self-disclosure on student learning and perceptions of teacher. *College Student Journal, 16*(1), 45-49.

McConnell, D., & Hodgson, V. (1985). The development of student constructed lecture feedback questionnaires. *Assessment and Evaluation in Higher Education, 9*(3), 2-27.

McDaniel, E. D., & Feldhusen, J. F. (1970). Relationships between faculty ratings and indexes of service and scholarship (pp. 619-620). *Proceedings of the 78th annual convention of the American Psychological Association, 5.*

McGrath, E. J. (1962). Characteristics of outstanding college teachers. *Journal of Higher Education, 33,* 148.

McIntyre, C. J. (1978). *Peer evaluation of teaching.* Paper presented at the American Educational Research Association convention, Toronto, Canada, August 31–September 1. (ERIC ED 180295).

McKeachie, W. J. (1990). Research on college teaching: The historical background. *Journal of Educational Psychology, 82*(2), 189-200. Special section with title "Instruction in Higher Education."

McKeachie, W. J. (1979). Student ratings of faculty: A reprise. *Academe, 65,* 384-397.

McKeachie, W. J. (1983). The role of faculty evaluation in enhancing college teaching. *National Forum: Phi Kappa Phi Journal, 63*(2), 37-39.

McKeachie, W. J. (1986). *Teaching tips: A guidebook for the beginning college teacher.* Lexington, MA: D. C. Heath.

McKeachie, W. J. (1997). Student ratings—the validity of use. *American Psychologist, 52,* 1218-1225.

McKeachie, W. J., & Lin, Y. G. (1979). A note on validity of student ratings of teaching. *Educational Research Quarterly, 4*(3), 45-47.

McKeachie, W. J., Lin, Y. G., & Mendelson, C. N. (1978). A small study to assess teacher effectiveness: Does learning last? *Contemporary Educational Psychology, 3,* 352-357.

McKeachie, W. J., Lin, Y. G., Daugherty, M., Moffett, M. M., Neigler, C., Nork, J., Walz, M., & Baldwin, R. (1980). Using student ratings and consultation to improve instruction. *British Journal of Educational Psychology, 50,* 168-174.

Meier, R. S., & Feldhusen, J. F. (1979). Another look at Dr. Fox: Effect of stated purpose for evaluation, lecturer expressiveness, and density of lecture content on student ratings. *Journal of Educational Psychology, 71,* 339-345.

Menges, R. J. (1973). The new reporters: Students rate instruction (pp. 59-75). In C. R. Pace (Ed.), *Evaluating learning and teaching.* New Directions in Higher Education, No. 4. San Francisco, CA: Jossey-Bass.

Menges, R. J. (1979). Evaluating teaching effectiveness: What is the proper role for students? *Liberal Education, 65,* 356-370.

Menges, R. J. (1988). Research on teaching and learning: The relevant and the redundant. *Review of Higher Education, 11*(3), 259-268.

Meredith, G. M. (1979). Brief scale for teaching appraisal in engineering courses. *Perceptual and Motor Skills, 45,* 817-818.

Meredith, G. M. (1979). Factored items for appraising classroom effectiveness of teaching assistants. *Psychological Reprints, 45,* 229-230.

Meredith, G. M. (1979). Summative evaluation of teaching effectiveness in legal education. *Perceptual and Motor Skills, 49,* 765-766.

Meredith, G. M. (1980). Brief scale for measuring the impact of a textbook. *Perceptual and Motor Skills, 51,* 370.

Meredith, G. M. (1980). Impact of lecture size on student-based ratings of instruction. *Psychological Reports, 46,* 21-22.

Meredith, G. M. (1980). Marker items for evaluating graduate-level teaching assistants. *Psychological Reprints, 46.*

Meredith, G. M. (1982). Grade-related attitude correlates of instructor/course satisfaction among college students. *Psychological Reports, 50,* 1142.

Meredith, G. M. (1982). Marker items for a single-factor scale for appraisal of teaching in architecture courses. *Perceptual and Motor Skills, 55*(2), 678.

Meredith, G. M. (1983). Factor-specific items for appraisal of laboratory and seminar/discussion group experiences among college students. *Perceptual and Motor Skills, 56*(1), 133-134.

Meredith, G. M., & Ogasawara, T. H. (1981). Lecture size and students' ratings of instructional effectiveness. *Perceptual and Motor Skills, 52*, 353-354.

Mikula, A. R. (1979). *Using peers in instructional development.* Paper presented at the conference on Faculty Development and Evaluation in Higher Education, Orlando, FL (ERIC ED 172 599).

Miller, A. H. (1988). Student assessment of teaching in higher education. *Higher Education, 17*, 3-15.

Miller, M. D. (1982). Factorial validity of a clinical teaching scale. *Educational and Psychological Measurement, 42*(4), 1141-1147.

Miller, M. T. (1971). Instructor attitudes toward, and their use of, student ratings of teachers. *Journal of Educational Psychology, 62*, 235-239.

Miller, R. I. (1972). *Evaluating faculty performance.* San Francisco, CA: Jossey-Bass.

Miller, R. I. (1987). *Evaluating faculty for promotion and tenure.* San Francisco, CA: Jossey-Bass.

Miller, S. (1984). Student rating scales for tenure and promotion. *Improving College University Teaching, 32*(2), 87-90.

Millis, B. J. (1992). Conducting effective peer classroom observations (pp. 189-201). In D. Wulff & J. Nyquist (Eds.), *To Improve the Academy, 11.* Stillwater, OK: New Forums Press.

Milman, J. (Ed.) (1981). *Handbook of teacher evaluation.* Beverly Hills, CA: Sage Publications.

Milton, O., & Shoben, E. J., Jr. (1968). *Learning and the professor.* Athens, OH: Ohio University Press.

Mintzes, J. J. (1982). Relationship between student perceptions of teaching behavior and learning outcomes in college biology. *Journal of Research in Science Teaching, 19*(9), 789-794.

Mitchell, J. V. (Ed.). (1983). *Tests in print.* Lincoln, NE: University of Nebraska, Buros Institute of Mental Measurements.

Mitchell, J. V. (Ed.). (1985). *Mental measurements yearbook.* Lincoln, NE: University of Nebraska, Buros Institute of Mental Measurements.

Moore, D., Schurr, K. T., & Henriksen, I. W. (1991). Correlations of national teacher examination core battery scores and college grade point average with teaching effectiveness of first-year teachers. *Educational and Psychological Measurement, 51*(4), 1023-1028.

Moses, I. (1986) Student evaluation of teaching in an Australian University—Staff perceptions and reactions. *Assessment and Evaluation in Higher Education, 11*(2), 117-129.

Moses, I. (1986). Self and student evaluation of academic staff. *Assessment and Evaluation in Higher Education, 11*(1), 76-86.

Moses, I. (1989). Role and problems of heads of departments in performance appraisal. *Assessment and Evaluation in Higher Education, 14*(2), 95-105.

Murphy, K. R., Balzer, W. K., Kellam, K. L., & Armstrong, J. G. (1984). Effects of the purpose of rating on accuracy in observing teacher behavior and evaluating teacher performance. *Journal of Educational Psychology, 76*, 45-54.

Murray, H. G. (1982). *Use of student instructional ratings in administrative personnel decisions at the University of Western Ontario.* Paper presented at the annual meeting the American Psychological Association, Washington, DC. (ERIC ED 223 162).

Murray, H. G. (1975). Predicting student ratings of college teaching from peer ratings of personality types. *Teaching of Psychology, 2*(2), 66-69.

Murray, H. G. (1979). Evaluation of university teaching: A selective bibliography. E. Roe (Ed.), *Labyrinth 5: Clearinghouse bulletin for higher education research and development units in Australia and New Zealand.* Brisbane, Australia: University of Queensland, Tertiary Education Institute. (Reprinted in Ontario Universities Program for Instructional Development Newsletter, February/March 1980).

Murray, H. G. (1979). Student evaluation of teaching and its use for decisions regarding tenure and promotion at the University of Western Ontario. *Tertiary Education Institute Newsletter*, University of Queensland, Australia.

Murray, H. G. (1979). *Student evaluation of university teaching: Uses and abuses (Report # 5).* Vancouver, Canada: University of British Columbia, Centre for the Improvement of Teaching.

Murray, H. G. (1980). *Evaluating university teaching: A review of research.* Toronto, Canada: Ontario Confederation of University Faculty Associations.

Murray, H. G. (1983). Low-inference classroom teaching behaviors and student ratings of college teaching effectiveness. *Journal of Educational Psychology, 75*(1), 138-149.

Murray, H. G. (1984). The impact of formative and summative evaluation of teaching in North American universities. *Assessment and Evaluation in Higher Education, 9*(2), 117-132.

Murray, H. G. (1985). Classroom teaching behaviors related to college teaching effectiveness (pp. 21-34). In J. Donald & A. M. Sullivan (Eds.), *Using research to improve teaching*. New Directions for Teaching and Learning, No. 23. San Francisco, CA: Jossey-Bass.

Murray, H. G., & Newby, W. G. (1982). Faculty attitudes toward evaluation of teaching at the University of Western Ontario. *Assessment and Evaluation in Higher Education, 7*(2), 144-151.

Murray, H. G., Rushton, J. P., & Paunonen, S. V. (1990). Teacher personality traits and student instructional ratings in six types of university courses. *Journal of Educational Psychology, 82*(2), 250-261.

Myers, C. J., Rubeck, R. F., & Meredith, K. (1983). An investigation of non-response bias in medical student assessment of instruction. *Research in Higher Education, 19*(4), 461-467.

Needham, D. (1982). Improving faculty evaluation and reward systems. *Journal of Economic Education, 13*(1), 6-18.

Nespoli, L. A., & Radcliffe, S. K. (1983). *Student evaluation of college services (Research Report No. 29)*. Columbia, MD: Howard Community College. (ERIC ED 224 541).

Newell, S., & Price, J. H. (1983). Promotion, merit, and tenure decisions for college health education faculty. *Health Education, 14*(3), 12-15.

Newstead, S. E., & Arnold, J. (1989). The effect of response format on ratings of teaching. *Educational and Psychological Measurement, 49*(1), 33-43.

Newton, R. R. (1982). Performance evaluation in education. *Journal of the College and University Personnel Association, 33*(2), 39-43.

Nimmer, J. G., & Stone, E. F. (1991). Effects of grading practices and time of rating on student ratings of faculty performance and student learning. *Research in Higher Education, 32*(2), 195-215.

Null, E. J., & Nicholson, E. W. (1972). Personal variables of students and their perception of university instructors. *College Student Journal, 6*, 6-9.

O'Connell, W. R., & Smartt, S. H. (1979). *Improving faculty evaluation: A trial strategy, a report of the SREB faculty evaluation project*. Atlanta, GA: Southern Regional Education Board.

O'Hanlon, J. O., & Mortensen, L. (1980). Making teacher evaluation work. *Journal of Higher Education, 51*, 664-672.

Ohara, T., & Purcell, D. T. (1981). Factors affecting student reported achievement: Necessary information to determine effective instructional strategies (pp. 658-664). *Proceedings of the seventh international conference on improving university teaching*.

O'Hear, M. F., & Poherson, V. E. (1982). Computer-generated evaluation in developmental programs. *Journal of Developmental and Remedial Education, 6*(1), 20-23.

Orpen, C. (1980). Student evaluation of lecturers as an indicator of instructional quality: A validity study. *Journal of Educational Research, 74*, 5-7.

Ory, J. C. (1980). Evaluative criteria: How important and to whom? *Center on Evaluation Development and Research Quarterly, 13*, 14-16.

Ory, J. C. (1982). Item placement and wording effects on overall ratings. *Educational and Psychological Measurement, 42*(3), 767-775.

Ory, J. C., & Braskamp, L. A. (1981). Faculty perceptions of the quality and usefulness of three types of evaluative information. *Research in Higher Education, 15*, 271-282.

Ory, J. C., & Parker, S. A. (1989). Assessment activities at large, research universities. *Research in Higher Education, 30*(4), 375-385.

Ory, J. C., Brandenburg, D. C., & Pieper, D. M. (1980). Selection of course evaluation items by and low rated faculty. *Research in Higher Education, 12*, 245-253.

Ory, J. C., Braskamp, L. A., & Pieper, D. M. (1980). The congruency of student evaluation information collected by three methods. *Journal of Educational Psychology, 72*, 181-185.

Overall, J. U., & Marsh, H. W. (1979). Midterm feedback from students: Its relationship to instructional improvement and students' cognitive and affective outcomes. *Journal of Educational Psychology, 71*, 856-865.

Overall, J. U., & Marsh, H. W. (1980). Students' evaluations of instruction: A longitudinal study of their stability. *Journal of Educational Psychology, 72*, 321-325.

Overall, J. U., & Marsh, H. W. (1982). Students' evaluations of teaching: An update. *AAHE Bulletin, 35*(4), 9-13.

Pace, R. C. (Ed.). (1973). *Evaluating learning and teaching*. New Directions for Higher Education, No. 1, Vol. 4. San Francisco, CA: Jossey-Bass.

Palmer, J. (1983). Sources and information: Faculty and administrator evaluation (pp. 109-118). In A. Smith (Ed.), *Evaluating faculty and staff*. New Directions for Community Colleges, No. 11, Vol. 1. San Francisco, CA: Jossey-Bass.

Pasen, R. M. (1977, June). *The differential effect of grade, sex, and discipline on two global factors: A within-class analysis of student ratings of instruction.* Evanston, IL: Northwestern University. (Ph.D. Dissertation).

Pasen, R. M., Frey, P. W., Menges, R. J., & Rath, G. J. (1978). Different administrative directions and student ratings on instruction: Cognitive versus affective states. *Research in Higher Education, 9,* 161-168.

Payne, B. D. (1984). Interrelationships among college supervisor, supervising teacher, and elementary pupil ratings of student teaching. *Educational and Psychological Measurement, 44*(4), 1037-1043.

Pearson, P., & Tiefel, V. (1982). Evaluating undergraduate library instruction at the Ohio State University. *Journal of Academic Librarianship, 7*(6), 351-357.

Perkins, D., & Abbott, R. (1982). Validity of student ratings for two affective outcomes of introductory psychology. *Educational and Psychological Measurement, 42*(1), 317-323.

Perry, R. P. (1985). Instructor expressiveness: Implications for improving teaching (pp. 35-49). In J. Donald & A. M. Sullivan (Eds.), *Using research to improve teaching.* New Directions for Teaching and Learning, No. 23. San Francisco, CA: Jossey-Bass.

Perry, R. P., Abrami, P. C., & Leventhal, L. (1979). Educational seduction: The effect of instructor expressiveness and lecture content on students ratings and achievement. *Journal of Educational Psychology, 71,* 107-116.

Peterson, C., & Cooper, S. (1980). Teacher evaluation by graded and ungraded students. *Journal of Educational Psychology, 72,* 682-685.

Peterson, K., Gunne, G. M., Miller, P., & Rivera, O. (1984). Multiple audience rating form strategies for student evaluation of college teaching. *Research in Higher Education, 20*(3), 309-321.

Peterson, M. W., & White, T. H. (1992). Faculty and administrator perceptions of their environments: Different views or different models of organization? *Research in Higher Education, 33*(2), 177-204.

Petrie, H. G. (1982). Program evaluation as an adaptive system (pp. 17-29). New Directions for Higher Education, No. 10. San Francisco, CA: Jossey-Bass.

Pfister, F. C., & Chrisman, L. G. (1983). The evaluation of professional training for librarianship. *Catholic Library World, 54*(10), 399-405.

Pinkney, J., & Williams, V. (1982). Taking your programs to court: Evaluating a new evaluation strategy. *Journal of College Student Personnel, 23*(3), 209-216.

Pittman, R. B. (1985). Perceived instructional effectiveness and associated teaching dimensions. *Journal of Experimental Education, 54*(1), 34-39.

Pohlmann, J. T. (1975). A multivariate analysis of selected class characteristics and student ratings of instruction. *Multivariate Behavioral Research, 10*(1), 81-91.

Poole, L. H., & Dellow, D. A. (1983). Evaluation of full-time faculty (pp. 19-31). In A. Smith (Ed.), *Evaluating faculty and staff.* New Directions for Community Colleges, Vol. 11, No. 1. San Francisco, CA: Jossey-Bass.

Pugach, M. C., & Rahs, J. D. (1983). Testing teachers: Analysis and recommendations. *Journal of Teacher Education, 34*(1), 37-43.

Quay, R. H. (1982). *On programs and principles in the evaluation of higher education: A bibliography of Paul L. Dressel.* Monticello, IL: Vance Bibliographies. (Public Administration Series Bibliography, P-900).

Rayder, N. F. (1968). College student ratings of instructors. *Journal of Experimental Education, 37,* 76-81.

Razor, J. E. (1979). *The evaluation of administrators and faculty members—or evaluating the "boss" and each other.* Paper presented at the Midwest Association for Health, Physical Education, and Recreation, Madison, WI. (ERIC ED 180 355).

Renner, R. R., & Greenwood, G. E. (1985). Professor "X": How experts rated his student ratings. *Assessment and Evaluation in Higher Education, 10*(3), 203-212.

Renner, R. R., et al. (1986). Responsible behaviour as effective teaching: A new look at student rating of professors. *Assessment and Evaluation in Higher Education, 11*(2), 138-145.

Renz, F. J. (1984). Study examining the issues of faculty evaluation. *Resources in Education.* (ERIC ED 243 559).

Reynolds, A. (1992). What is competent beginning teaching? A review of the literature. *Review of Educational Research, 62*(1), 1-35.

Rhodes, F. H. T. (1990). *The new American university.* Chicago, IL: David Dodds Henry Series, University of Illinois.

Rice, R. E., (1991). Toward a broader conception of scholarship: The American context. In I. T. G. Whitson & R. C. Geiger (Eds.), *Research and higher education: The United Kingdom and the United States.* Bristol, PA: Society for Research into Higher Education and Open University Press.

Rich, H. E. (1976). Attitudes of college and university faculty toward the use of student evaluation. *Educational Research Quarterly, 1*(3), 17-28.

Riley, J. W., Ryan, B. F., & Lipschitz, M. (1950). *The student looks at his teacher.* New Brunswick, NJ: Rutgers University Press.

Rodin, M. J. (1982). By a faculty member's yard-stick, student evaluations don't measure up. *Teaching Political Science, 9*(4), 174-176.

Rodin, M., & Rodin, B. (1972). Student evaluations of teachers. *Science, 177,* 1164-1166.

Rodin, M., Frey, P. W., & Gessner, P. K. (1975). Student evaluation. *Science, 187,* 555-559.

Rogerts, T. H., & Gamson, Z. F. (1982). Evaluation as a developmental process: The case of liberal education. *Review of Higher Education, 5*(4), 225-238.

Root, L. S. (1987). Faculty evaluation: Reliability of peer assessments of research, teaching, and service. *Research in Higher Education, 26*(1), 71-84.

Roskens, R. W. (1983). Implications of Biglan model research for the process of faculty advancement. *Research in Higher Education, 18*(3), 285-297.

Rotem, A., & Glasman, N. S. (1977). Evaluation of university instructors in the United States: The context. *Higher Education, 6,* 75-92.

Rotem, A., & Glasman, N. S. (1979). On the effectiveness of student evaluation feedback to university instructors. *Review of Educational Research, 49,* 497-511.

Rubin, D. L. (1992). Nonlanguage factors affecting undergraduates' judgments of nonnative English-speaking teaching assistants. *Research in Higher Education, 33*(4), 511-531.

Rushinek, A., Rushinek, S. F., & Stutz, J. (1981). The effects of computer assisted instruction upon computer facility and instructor ratings. *Journal of Computer-Based Instruction, 8*(2), 43-44.

Rushinek, A., Rushinek, S. F., & Stutz, J. (1982). Improving instructor evaluations by the use of computer-assisted instruction in business data processing. *AEDS Journal, 15*(3), 151-163.

Saaty, T. L., & Ramanujam, V. (1983). An objective approach to faculty promotion and tenure by the analytical hierarchy process. *Research in Higher Education, 18*(3), 311-331.

Sacken, D. M. (1990). Taking teaching seriously: Institutional and individual dilemmas. *Journal of Higher Education, 61*(5), 548-564.

Sagen, H. B. (1974). Student, faculty, and department chairmen ratings of instructors: Who agrees with whom? *Research in Higher Education, 2,* 265-272.

Salomone, R. E., & Vorhies, A. L. (1985). Just rewards: Ensuring equitable salary reviews. *Educational Record, 66*(3), 44-47.

Salsberg, H. E., & Schiller, B. (1982). A decade of student evaluations. *College Student Journal, 16*(1), 84-88.

Sauter, R. C., & Walker, J. K. (1976). A theoretical model for faculty "peer" evaluation. *American Journal of Pharmaceutical Education, 40*(2), 165-166.

Schein, M. W. (1985). Student achievement as a measure of teaching effectiveness. *Journal of College Science Teaching, 14*(6), 471-474.

Scheurich, V., Graham, B., & Drolette, M. (1983). Expected grades versus specific evaluations of the teacher as predictors of students' overall evaluation of the teacher. *Research in Higher Education, 19*(2), 159-173.

Schneider, L. S. (1975). *Faculty opinion of the spring 1974 peer evaluation.* (ERIC ED 104 493).

Scott, O. (1978). Anomalies in the construction and suggested uses of inventories of students' appraisals of college instruction. *Psychological Reports, 43,* 563-566.

Scott, O., & Harrison, P. L. (1978). *A comparison of alternate forms of a global item for appraising teaching effectiveness.* Paper presented at the meeting of the Georgia Educational Research Association, West Georgia College, Carrollton, GA.

Scott, O., & Hsu, Y. (1982). Effect of item context on students' global appraisals of instruction. *Perceptual and Motor Skills, 54*(3), Part 2, 1191-1194.

Scott, O., Perrodin, A. F., & Schnittjer, C. (1978). The stability of students' appraisal of college instruction: A further look. *College Student Journal, 12,* 338-342.

Scriven, M. (1980). The evaluation of college teaching. *National Council Professional Inservice Education News, 1.*

Scwier, R. A. (1982). Design and use of student evaluation instruments in instructional development. *Journal of Instructional Development, 5*(4), 28-34.

Seldin, P. (1980). *Successful faculty evaluation programs.* Crugers, NY: Coventry Press.

Seldin, P. (1982). Improving faculty evaluation systems. *Peabody Journal of Education, 59*(2), 93-99.

Seldin, P. (1982). Self-assessment of college teaching. *Improving College and University Teaching, 30*(2), 70-74.

Seldin, P. (1984). *Changing practices in faculty evaluation.* San Francisco, CA: Jossey-Bass.

Seldin, P. (1988). *Evaluating and developing administrative performance.* San Francisco, CA: Jossey-Bass.

Seldin, P. (1991). *The teaching portfolio: A practical guide to improved performance and promotion/tenure decisions (1st edition)*. Bolton, MA: Anker.

Seldin, P. (1993). *Successful use of teaching portfolios*. Bolton, MA: Anker.

Seldin, P. (1993, October). How colleges evaluate professors 1983 v. 1993. *AAHE Bulletin*, 6-12.

Seldin, P. (1997). *The teaching portfolio: A practical guide to improved performance and promotion/tenure decisions (2nd edition)*. Bolton, MA: Anker.

Selmes, C. (1989). Evaluation of teaching. *Assessment and Evaluation in Higher Education, 14*(3), 167-178.

Shapiro, E. G. (1990). Effect of instructor and class characteristics on students' class evaluations. *Research in Higher Education, 31*(2), 135-148.

Sherman, T. M. (1978). The effects of student formative evaluation of instruction on teacher behavior. *Journal of Educational Technology Systems, 6*, 209-217.

Silvernail, D. L., & Johnson, J. L. (1992). The impact of interactive televised instruction on student evaluations of their instructors. *Educational Technology, 32*(6) 47-50.

Singhal, S. (1968). *Illinois course evaluation questionnaire items by rank of instructor, sex of the instructor, and sex of the student (Research Report No. 282)*. Urbana, IL: University of Illinois, Office of Instructional Resources, Measurement and Research Division.

Singhal, S., & Stallings, W. M. (1967). *A study of the relationships between course evaluations by students and severity of grading by instructors in freshman rhetoric at the University of Illinois (Research Report No. 252)*. Urbana, IL: University of Illinois, Measurement and Research Division.

Sixbury, G. R. & Cashin, W. E. (1995a, January). *Description of database for the IDEA diagnostic form (IDEA Technical Report No. 9)*. Manhattan, KS: Kansas State University, Center for Faculty Evaluation and Development.

Sixbury, G. R. & Cashin, W. E. (1995b, January*). Comparative data by academic field (IDEA Technical Report No. 10)*. Manhattan, KS: Kansas State University, Center for Faculty Evaluation and Development.

Skoog, G. (1980). Improving college teaching through peer observation. *Journal of Teacher Education, 31*(2), 23-25.

Small, A. C., Hollenbeck, A. R., & Haley, R. L. (1982). The effect of emotional state on student ratings of instructors. *Teaching of Psychology, 9*(4), 205-208.

Smith, A. (1983). A conceptual framework for staff evaluation (pp. 3-18). In A. Smith (Ed.), *Evaluating faculty and staff*. New Directions for Community Colleges, Vol. 11, No. 1. San Francisco, CA: Jossey-Bass.

Smith, A. (1983). Concluding comments (pp. 105-107). In A. Smith (Ed.), *Evaluating faculty and staff*. New Directions for Community Colleges, Vol. 11, No. 1. San Francisco, CA: Jossey-Bass.

Smith, L. R. (1982). A review of two low-inference teacher behaviors related to performance of college students. *Review of Higher Education, 5*(3), 159-167.

Smith, M. (1982). Protecting confidentiality of faculty peer review records: Department of Labor vs. the University of California. *Journal of College and University Law, 8*(1), 20-53.

Smith, P. L. (1979). The generalizability of student ratings of courses: Asking the right questions. *Journal of Educational Measurement, 16*, 77-87.

Smith, Ronald A., & Cranton, Patricia A. (1992). Students' perceptions of teaching skills and overall effectiveness across instructional settings. *Research in Higher Education, 33*(6), 747-764.

Smock, H. R. (1982). Planning for an evaluation of network and institutionalization (pp. 67-73). New Directions for Higher Education, Vol. 10, No. 1. San Francisco, CA: Jossey-Bass.

Sorcinelli, M. D. (1984). An approach to colleague evaluation of classroom instruction. *Journal of Instructional Development, 7*(4), 11-17.

Spencer, R. E. (1965). *Course evaluation questionnaire anonymous vs. identified student response (Research Report No. 202)*. Urbana, IL: University of Illinois, Measurement and Research Division.

Spencer, R. E., & Aleamoni, L. M. (1970). A student course evaluation questionnaire. *Journal of Educational Measurement, 7*(3), 209-210.

Stallings, W. M., & Singhal, S. (1968). *Some observations on the relationships between productivity and student evaluations of courses and teaching (Research Report No. 274)*. Urbana, IL: University of Illinois, Office of Instructional Resources, Measurement and Research Division.

Stedman, C. H. (1983). The reliability of a teaching effectiveness rating scale for assessing faculty performance. *Tennessee Education, 12*(3), 25-32.

Stevens, J. J., & Aleamoni, L. M. (1984). A preliminary study of methods for the evaluation of televised instruction (pp. 386-394). In L. P. Grayson & J. M. Biedenbach (Eds.), *Engineering education: Preparation for life*. 92nd annual ASEE conference proceedings. Washington, DC: American Society for Engineering Education.

Stevens, J. J., & Aleamoni, L. M. (1985). Issues in the development of peer evaluation systems. *Instructional Evaluation, 8* (1), 4-9.

Stevens, J. J., & Aleamoni, L. M. (1985). The use of evaluative feedback for instructional improvement: A longitudinal perspective (pp. 285-304). *Instructional Science, 13.*

Stier, W. F., Jr. (1982). *Faculty evaluation: A positive approach.* (ERIC ED 223 119).

Stumpf, S. A. (1979). Assessing academic program and department effectiveness using student evaluation data. *Research in Higher Education, 11,* 353-364.

Stumpf, S. A., & Freedman, R. D. (1979). Expected grade co-variation with student ratings of instruction: Individual versus class effects (pp. 293-302). *Journal of Educational Psychology, 71.*

Stumpf, S. A., Freedman, R. D., & Aguanno, J. (1979). Validity of the course-faculty instrument (CFI): Intrinsic and extrinsic variables. *Educational and Psychological Measurement, 39,* 153-158.

Stumpf, S. A., Freedman, R. D., & Aguanno, J. A. (1979). A path analysis of extrinsic factors related to student ratings of teaching effectiveness. *Research in Higher Education, 11,* 111-123.

Stumpf, S. A., Freedman, R. D., & Krieger, K. M. (1979). Validity extension of the Course Faculty Instrument (CFI). *Research in Higher Education, 11,* 13-22.

Sullivan, A. M. (1985). The role of two types of research on the evaluation and improvement of university teaching (pp. 71-82). In J. Donald & A. M. Sullivan, *Using research to improve teaching.* New Directions for Teaching and Learning, No. 23. San Francisco, CA: Jossey-Bass.

Sullivan, A. M., & Skanes, G. R. (1974). Validity of student evaluation of teaching and the characteristics of successful instructors. *Journal of Educational Psychology, 66,* 584-590.

Swanson, R. A., & Sisson, D. J. (1971). The development, evaluation, and utilization of a departmental faculty appraisal system. *Journal of Industrial Teacher Education, 9*(1), 64-79.

Theall, M., & Franklin, J. (1990). Student ratings in the context of complex evaluation systems (pp. 37-55). In M. Theall & J. Franklin (Eds.), *Student ratings of instruction: Issues for improving practice.* New Directions for Teaching and Learning, No. 43. San Francisco, CA: Jossey-Bass.

Thomas, A. (1989). Further education staff appraisal: What teachers think. *Assessment and Evaluation in Higher Education, 14*(3), 149-157.

Thomas, D., et al. (1982). The relationship between psychological identification with instructors and student ratings of college courses. *Instructional Science, 11*(2), 139-154.

Thompson, G. E. (1988). Difficulties in interpreting course evaluations: Some Bayesian insights. *Research in Higher Education, 28*(3), 217-222.

Thorman, J. H. (1982). Criterion referenced evaluation and its effect on achievement and attitude. *Performance and Instruction, 21*(10), 15-18.

Tiberius, R. G., Sackin, H. D., Slingerland, J. M., Jubas, K., Bell, M., & Matlow, A. (1989). The influence of student evaluative feedback on the improvement of clinical teaching. *Journal of Higher Education, 60*(6), 665-681.

Todd-Mancillas, W. R., & Essig, T. (1982). Alternative approaches to evaluating communication instruction. *Association for Communication Administration Bulletin, 42,* 56-61.

Tollefson, H., & Hracy, D. B. (1983). Comparison of self-reported teaching behaviors of award-winning and non-award winning university faculty. *Perceptual and Motor Skills, 56*(1), 39-44.

Tollefson, N. (1983). Course ratings as measures of instructional effectiveness. *Instructional Science, 12*(4), 389-395.

Tollefson, N., Chen, J. S., & Kleinsasser, A. (1989). The relationship of students' attitudes about effective teaching to students' ratings of effective teaching. *Educational and Psychological Measurement, 49*(3), 529-536.

Turcotte, S. J. C., & Leventhal, L. (1984). Gain-loss versus reinforcement-affect ordering of student rating of teaching: Effect of rating instructions. *Journal of Educational Psychology, 76*(5), 782-791.

Uguroglu, M. E., & Dwyer, M. M. (1981). Staff review system. *Improving College and University Teaching, 29*(3), 121-24.

Ulricht, K. (1982). Summative evaluation of a course of study in computer science. *Higher Education, 1*(6), 713-724.

Van Allen, G. H. (1982). Students rate community college faculty as slightly above average. *Community College Review, 10*(1), 41-43.

Vasta, R., & Sarmiento, R. F. (1979). Liberal grading improves evaluations but not performance. *Journal of Educational Research, 71,* 207-211.

Voeks, V. W. (1962). Publications and teaching effectiveness. *Journal of Higher Education, 33,* 212.

Walker, B. D. (1969). An investigation of selected variables relative to the manner in which a population of junior college students evaluate their teachers. *Dissertation Abstracts, 29*(9-B), 3474.

Walker, C. J. (1982). Study efficiency: Where teaching effectiveness and learning effectiveness meet. *Teaching of Psychology, 9*(2), 92-95.

Ward, M. D., et al. (1981). *The observer effect in classroom visitation.* Paper presented at the 65th annual meeting of the American Educational Research Association, Los Angeles, CA. (ERIC ED 20444384).

Ware, J. E., & Williams, R. G. (1975). The Dr. Fox effect: A study of lecturer effectiveness and ratings of instruction. *Journal of Medical Education, 50,* 149-156.

Ware, J. E., & Williams, R. G. (1977). Discriminate analysis of student ratings as a means of identifying lecturers who differ in enthusiasm or information giving. *Educational and Psychological Measurement, 37,* 627-639.

Waters, L. K., Reardon, M., & Edwards, J. E. (1983). Multitrait-multimethod analysis of three rating formats. *Perceptual and Motor Skills, 55*(3, Pt. 1), 927-933.

Watkins, D. (1990). Student ratings of tertiary courses for "alternative calendar" purposes. *Assessment and Evaluation in Higher Education, 15*(1) 12-21.

Watkins, D., & Thomas, B. (1991). Assessing teaching effectiveness: An Indian perspective. *Assessment and Evaluation in Higher Education, 16*(3), 185-198.

Weaver, C. H. (1960). Instructor rating by college students. *Journal of Educational Psychology, 51,* 21-25.

Webb, W. B. (1955). The problem of obtaining negative nominations in peer ratings. *Personnel Psychology, 8,* 61-63.

Weber, L. J., & Frary, R. B. (1982). Profile uniqueness in student ratings of instruction. *Journal of Experimental Education, 51*(1), 42-45.

Webster, D. S. (1985). Institutional effectiveness using scholarly peer assessments as major criteria. *Review of Higher Education, 9*(1) 67-82.

Weeks, K. M. (1990). The peer review process: Confidentiality and disclosure. *Journal of Higher Education. 61*(2), 198-219.

Wherry, R. J., & Fryer, D. H. (1945). Buddy ratings: popularity contest or leadership criteria? *Personnel Psychology, 2,* 147-159.

Whitely, S. E., & Doyle, K. O. (1979). Validity and generalizability of student ratings from between-classes and within-class data. *Journal of Educational Psychology, 71,*117-124.

Whitley, J. S. (1984). Are student evaluations constructive criticism? *Community and Junior College Journal, 54* (7), 41-42.

Whitman, N., & Weiss, E. (1982). Faculty evaluation: The use of explicit criteria for promotion, retention, and tenure. *AAHE-ERIC/Higher Education Research Report, No. 2.* Washington, DC: American Association for Higher Education. (ERIC ED 221-148).

Whitmore, J., & Gillespie, P. P. (1983). Resolved: That directing plays and readers theater productions should be evaluated more as a part of teaching than as research and creative work. *Association for Communication Administration Bulletin, 44,* 21-24.

Widmeyer, W. N., & Loy, J. W. (1988). When you're hot, you're hot: Warm-cold effects in first impressions of persons and teaching effectiveness. *Journal of Educational Psychology, 80*(1), 118-121.

Wigington, H., Tollefson, N., & Rodriquiez, E. (1989). Students' ratings of instructors revisited: Interactions among class and instructor variables. *Research in Higher Education, 30*(3), 331-344.

Williams, E. (1992). Student attitudes towards approaches to learning and assessment. *Assessment and Evaluation in Higher Education, 17*(1) 45-58.

Williams, E. D. (1982). *Teacher and course evaluations that really discriminate.* Paper presented at the annual meeting of the Rocky Mountain Psychological Association, April 28–May 1. (ERIC ED 223 135).

Williams, R. G., & Ware, J. E. (1976). Validity of student ratings of instruction under different incentive conditions: A further study of the Dr. Fox effect. *Journal of Educational Psychology, 68,* 48-56.

Wilson, R. C. (1990). Commentary: The education of a faculty developer. *Journal of Educational Psychology, 82*(2) 272-724. Special section with title "Instruction in Higher Education."

Wilson, R. C. (1986). Improving faculty teaching: Effective use of student evaluations and consultants. *Journal of Higher Education, 57,* 196-211.

Wilson, T. C. (1988). Student evaluation-of-teaching forms: A critical perspective. *Review of Higher Education, 12*(1), 79-95.

Wilson, T., & Stearns, J. (1985). Improving the working relationship between professor and TA (pp. 35-45). In J. D. W. Andrews (Ed.), *Strengthening the teaching assistant faculty.* New Directions for Teaching and Learning, No. 22. San Francisco, CA: Jossey-Bass.

Wilson, W. R. (1999, September/October). Student rating teachers. *Journal of Higher Education, 70*(5). Copyright 1932, 1999 by The Ohio State University.

Wood, K., Linsky, A. S., & Straus, M. A. (1974). Class size and student evaluations of faculty. *Journal of Higher Education, 45,* 524-534.

Wood, P. H. (1977). *The description and evaluation of a college department's faculty rating system.* Paper presented at the annual meeting of the American Educational Research Association, New York, NY. (ERIC ED 142 128).

Wood, P. H. (1978*). Student and peer ratings of college teaching and peer ratings of research and service: Four years of departmental evaluation.* Paper presented at the 62nd annual meeting of the American Educational Research Association, Toronto, Canada. (ERIC ED 155 218).

Wotruba, T. R., & Wright, P. L. (1975). How to develop a teacher-rating instrument: A research approach. *Journal of Higher Education, 46,* 653-663.

Wulff, D. H., et al. (1985). The student perspective on evaluating teaching effectiveness. *ACA Bulletin, 53,* 39-47.

Yongkittikul, C., Gillmore, G. M., & Brandenburg, D. C. (1974). *Does the time of course meeting affect course rating by students? (Research Report No. 346).* Urbana, IL: University of Illinois, Office of Instructional Resources, Measurement and Research Division.

Young, R. J., & Gwalamubisi, Y. (1986). Perceptions about current and ideal methods and purposes of faculty evaluation. *Community College Review, 13*(4), 27-33.

Index

The following typographical conventions used in this index are: *f* and *t* identify figures and tables, respectively.